PROGRAMMING THE IBM 1130

**Prentice-Hall
Series in Automatic Computation**

George Forsythe, editor

MARTIN, *Man-Computer Dialogue*

MARTIN, *Programming Real-Time Computing Systems*

MARTIN, *Systems Analysis for Data Transmission*

MARTIN, *Telecommunications and the Computer*

MARTIN, *Teleprocessing Network Organization*

MARTIN AND NORMAN, *The Computerized Society*

MATHISON AND WALKER, *Computers and Telecommunications: Issues in Public Policy*

MCKEEMAN, et al., *A Compiler Generator*

MINSKY, *Computation: Finite and Infinite Machines*

MOORE, *Interval Analysis*

PLANE AND MCMILLAN, *Discrete Optimization: Integer Programming and Network Analysis for Management Decisions*

PRITSKER AND KIVIAT, *Simulation with GASP II: a FORTRAN-Based Simulation Language*

PYLYSHYN, editor, *Perspectives on the Computer Revolution*

RICH, *Internal Sorting Methods: Illustrated with PL/1 Program*

RUSTIN, editor, *Computer Networks*

RUSTIN, editor, *Debugging Techniques in Large Systems*

RUSTIN, editor, *Formal Semantics of Programming Languages*

SACKMAN AND CITRENBAUM, editors, *On-Line Planning: Towards Creative Problem-Solving*

SALTON, editor, *The SMART Retrieval System: Experiments in Automatic Document Processing*

SAMMET, *Programming Languages: History and Fundamentals*

SCHULTZ, *Digital Processing: A System Orientation*

SCHWARZ, et al., *Numerical Analysis of Symmetric Matrices*

SHERMAN, *Techniques in Computer Programming*

SIMON AND SIKLÓSSY, editors, *Representation and Meaning: Experiments with Information Processing Systems*

SNYDER, *Chebyshev Methods in Numerical Approximation*

STERLING AND POLLACK, *Introduction to Statistical Data Processing*

STOUTMEYER, *PL/1 Programming for Engineering and Science*

STROUD, *Approximate Calculation of Multiple Integrals*

STROUD AND SECREST, *Gaussian Quadrature Formulas*

TAVISS, editor, *The Computer Impact*

TRAUB, *Iterative Methods for the Solution of Polynomial Equations*

VAN TASSEL, *Computer Security Management*

VARGA, *Matrix Iterative Analysis*

VAZSONYI, *Problem Solving by Digital Computers with PL/1 Programming*

WAITE, *Implementing Software for Non-Numeric Application*

WILKINSON, *Rounding Errors in Algebraic Processes*

ZIEGLER, *Time-Sharing Data Processing Systems*

PROGRAMMING THE IBM 1130

Second Edition

ROBERT K. LOUDEN

General Manager of Programming Development
Memorex Corporation

GEORGE LEDIN, Jr.

Institute of Chemical Biology
University of San Francisco

PRENTICE-HALL, INC.

Englewood Cliffs, New Jersey

© 1972, 1967
by Prentice-Hall, Inc.
Englewood Cliffs, N.J.

ISBN: 0-13-730275-4

Library of Congress Catalog Card No.: 73-180224

10 9 8 7 6 5 4 3 2 1

Printed in the United States of America

PRENTICE-HALL INTERNATIONAL, INC., *London*
PRENTICE-HALL OF AUSTRALIA, PTY. LTD., *Sydney*
PRENTICE-HALL OF CANADA, LTD., *Toronto*
PRENTICE-HALL OF INDIA PRIVATE LIMITED, *New Delhi*
PRENTICE-HALL OF JAPAN, INC., *Tokyo*

PREFACE

1649993

     This book is a programming textbook, an introduction to programming techniques for the IBM 1130 data processing system. Sufficient material has been included to satisfy the requirements of a one-semester course at the first-year or second-year college level. Many examples and problems have been included to clarify the material and to facilitate its use as a textbook, and examples of engineering, logical, commercial and real-time programs are provided.

     Programming techniques are emphasized, and explanations of the computing equipment and how the equipment operates are held to a minimum. The various reference manuals published by IBM should be used for additional background on the details of the operations of these systems.

     The organization of this book differs from many previous texts on programming in that FORTRAN and RPG are presented as the primary programming languages for the 1130. The increased flexibility of the FORTRAN language as used on the 1130 and the high-speed compilers developed for this system have relegated symbolic and machine language programming to the role of secondary languages, used primarily to handle the small percentage of programs for which FORTRAN and RPG are still not suited.

     After a short exposition of programming concepts and 1130 equipment, the book devotes several chapters to a detailed development of FORTRAN. Additional detail on the equipment is then presented, followed by machine language and assembly language programming. Assembly language programming is thus presented as a language which has capabilities beyond those of FORTRAN, and which can be used to provide special subroutines for use by FORTRAN-oriented program libraries.

     The above organization permits the student to write meaningful programs as early as Chapter 3. More important, it allows him to concentrate first on such fundamentals as program strategy and the use of disk storage memory rather than on the arbitrary details of 1130 machine codes. Finally, it reflects the manner in which most 1130 systems are programmed in working installations. The book can also be used to implement a "machine language first" progression by skipping the FORTRAN chapters until after machine language has been covered.

     At the end of the book are two chapters on RPG programming. 1130 users will find these chapters useful as an introduction to an interesting and very powerful programming technique. It is hoped that a combination of FORTRAN and RPG in a single book will provide a broad background in programming for the user of either language.

The 1130 family of computers is capable of sampling the whole spectrum of digital programming techniques and applications. The ultimate purpose of this book is to use the 1130 as an entry point to the big new world of programming. In a few years the details of operations of the 1130 may be of little interest, but the programming techniques described here should still be very much alive.

Many people have contributed valuable comments and suggestions during the development of this book. We are also deeply indebted to the International Business Machines Corporation for their cooperation in furnishing most of the illustrations.

Robert K. Louden
George Ledin

CONTENTS

PROGRAMMING THE IBM 1130

CHAPTER 1: PROGRAMMING CONCEPTS

1-1   Digital Computer Programming

During the last few years we have learned of many new applications for digital computers, including space navigation, the checking of income tax returns, and the selection of compatible blind dates. Behind each of these applications stand the programmers who told the computer how to do the job. The computers which we use for so many purposes today can solve a problem with superhuman speed and get the right answer every time, but only if the method of solution is made known to the computer in great detail. The programmer must know how to solve the problem and also how to describe the method of solution in terms of instructions which the computer can execute. The programmer is primarily concerned with organizing a problem into a sequence of operations which can be performed on a digital computer and then translating the problem into a set of commands which can be read and performed by the computer so as to solve the problem.

Programming usually consists of the following four parts:

1)   *Analyzing* or organizing the problem into a logical sequence of steps or tasks

2)   *Coding* the problem into a sequence of computer instructions which can be read and acted upon by the computer

3)   *Debugging* the coded computer instructions by testing the instructions on the computer and recoding the problem until correct answers are obtained

4)   *Documenting* the analysis, coding, input and answers to the problem so that the work may be understood by other programmers who may need to modify it in the future

Although this book will emphasize coding, debugging and documenting, analysis is usually the most difficult part of any programming problem. Examples of complete programs including analysis are found in Chapters 8 and 9.

1-2   Programmable Problems

The first electronic digital computers were developed in the 1940's to solve problems in differential equations and various scientific applications, including astronomy and ballistics. The few computers available in the 1940's were slow, expensive and hard to program. Now, however, low cost and relative ease of programming have enabled thousands of engineering, business, educational and

1

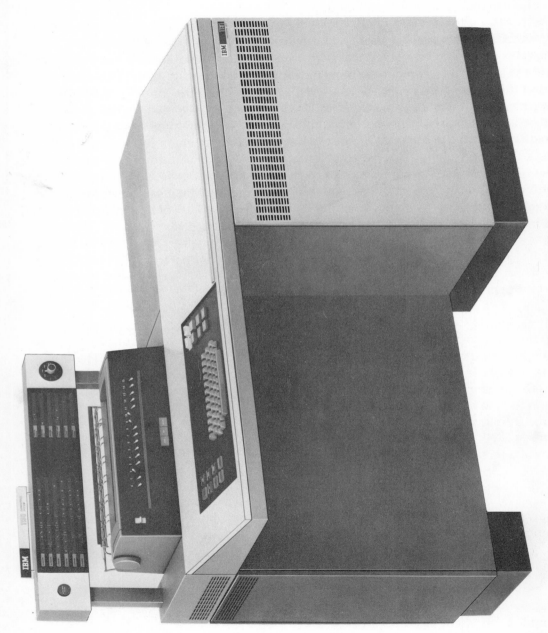

Figure 1-1   IBM 1130 Computing System

research organizations to acquire digital computers such as the IBM 1130 Computing System shown in Figure 1-1 to solve engineering and scientific problems. Few large engineering projects of any kind are undertaken today without computers.

During the 1950's digital computers became commercially available in quantity throughout the world, and many of these computers were used to solve the problems of commercial data processing such as maintaining inventories, sending out bills to customers and calculating payroll checks. Today many thousands of computers are installed to handle such commercial applications. The bills you receive in the mail and the checks that you write to pay the bills are documents that, through the use of punched hole codes or magnetically encoded ink, will probably be read directly by computers.

In the 1960's real-time applications (where the computer must respond to and perhaps control a continually changing process or problem) *and time-sharing applications* (where the computer is expected to share its time between two or more problems concurrently) *have developed into major markets for computers.* Today many computers are wired directly into real-time industrial processes, reading electrical signals from thermocouples and other instruments, computing the performance of the process, and then sending out computed signals to turn valves, start motors, and thus control the process.

Time-sharing has grown to the point where some operating systems today can provide remote consoles to permit several programmers to work concurrently on a single computer as if each programmer had the computer all to himself. The computer may be hundreds or thousands of miles from the programmer, linked to him by telephone or even microwave radio links. It has become practical to allow several computers to exchange information with each other automatically over long distance lines. Systems can now be set up to allow an 1130 system to receive problems and automatically pass them on to a remotely located larger computer if the problems exceed a certain size.

Some of the most interesting problems for computer programmers are the so-called logical problems. These problems involve logical patterns rather than numerical calculations, and they include language translation, game playing by computers, pattern recognition and learning programs which can enable the computer to modify its answers based upon past results and thus appear to learn by experience.

The digital computer has paid its way in all these application areas because of a combination of speed and reliability. Speed permits up to several hundred thousand arithmetic operations per second in the 1130 system, and reliability permits the execution of many billions of operations without error. As digital computers continue to become larger, faster and less expensive, so the list of programmable problems for which digital computers can be economically justified will continue to grow, until some day we may each have our own personal computer keeping track of bank balances, taxes, phone numbers and appointments.

The 1130 computer is not the fastest or the biggest digital computer currently available. Of all the computers currently manufactured by IBM, the 1130 is among the least expensive. The more powerful IBM computers are members of the System/360 and System/370 families.

1-3   The Stored Program Concept

Digital computers possess four primary functions: input, output, control and memory. For the 1130 input usually consists of information on punched cards and punched paper tape. Output consists of information on punched cards, punched paper tape and printed documents. These devices are discussed in Chapter 2.

The control function consists of circuits which provide decision-making and arithmetic capability and which can transfer information between the memory and the input and output devices. The control function executes the instructions which form the computer program.

The memory function is performed by tens of thousands of doughnut-shaped magnetic cores which store both the data and the instructions to be used by the computer in the execution of programs. *A bit or binary digit in computer memory is represented by a single magnetic core.* Each core can be magnetized in either of two directions, and the direction can be changed under computer control in a fraction of a microsecond. One magnetized direction or "state" is assigned the meaning of "off" or "zero"; the other direction is assigned the meaning of "on" or "one." Note that numbers do not actually exist in the memory of the computer; *the memory consists entirely of patterns of bits which may be combined into codes to represent numbers, letters or logical data.*

The memory of the 1130 comes in sizes of 4096, 8192, 16,384 or 32,768 words. *Each word consists of 16 bits which may represent an instruction or data.* A single instruction (such as add) occupies one or two words; a data variable (such as the number 1596) occupies one or more words, depending upon the number of digits and the format of the data variable. Words in computer memory may be thought of as boxes where instructions or data may be kept.

The concept of storing both data and instructions in the memory of the computer was first presented by John von Neumann and Herman Goldstine in 1945. Before that time computer memories had been used only for data storage, while instructions were wired into plugboards or read and executed one at a time. *Storing the instructions in the core memory of the computer allows the computer to modify*

4

its instructions in the same way that data is modified and thus permits the computer to modify its program while the program is being executed. The tremendous flexibility of digital computers stems primarily from this stored program concept.

The stored program concept also makes it possible to load the memory of a computer with instructions required to solve a problem and then reload the computer memory a few seconds later with instructions for the solution of a different problem. The computer is able to move quickly from one problem to another. It is a general purpose tool rather than a specialized tool.

Core memory is referred to as primary or high speed memory; a word of information can be read out of or written into core memory in from two to four millionths of a second or microseconds, depending upon the model of 1130 employed.

A form of secondary or bulk memory is available for 1130 systems in the form of disk storage. A single two-surface disk resembling a phonograph record is used. Each disk contains 512,000 words of memory, which again may be either instructions or data. The instructions and data on the disk must be read into core memory before the instructions can be executed or the data can be processed, so words in secondary memory cannot be used as rapidly as words in primary memory.

Primary memory can be thought of as information in your head which can be used immediately; secondary memory may be thought of as information in a book which must be looked up. Primary memory is faster, but secondary memory is bigger and cheaper.

1-4 Machine Language Instructions

Consider the equation

$$A = B/(C+D) \tag{1-1}$$

An equation such as (1-1) is given to the computer as a command to evaluate the mathematical expression to the right of the equal sign and then replace the value to the left of the equal sign with the value of the expression. Rather than a statement of equality, the equation is a command to compute a new value for the variable A. Computing this equation upon a digital computer involves the following: take the value assigned to the data variable B, divide the B value by the sum of the values assigned to the data variables C and D, and assign the result to the data variable A. Arithmetic operations such as divide and add are carried out in a special register inside the computer, not part of the computer memory, called the accumulator. If the variables A, B, C and D are specified to be integers (whole numbers), then seven instructions will be necessary to compute equation (1-1). These instructions will

1) load the value of C into the accumulator register

2) add the value of D to the contents of the accumulator

3) store the contents of the accumulator into a temporary memory location

4) load the value of B into the accumulator

5) shift the accumulator to align it properly for division

6) divide the accumulator by the contents of the temporary memory location

7) store the contents of the accumulator into data variable A.

The above instructions are equivalent to the operations which would be performed upon a desk calculator in computing equation (1-1), and the accumulator is used in the same manner as the main register on a desk calculator.

In the 1130 primary memory the instructions would be stored as patterns of bits, 16 bits per word, which might be represented by ones and zeros as follows:

1)	(load)	1100010000000000	0001010110111010
2)	(add)	1000010000000000	0001010101011000
3)	(store)	1101001110000000	
4)	(load)	1100010000000000	0001010111011100
5)	(shift)	0001100010010000	
6)	(divide)	1010101110000000	
7)	(store)	1101010000000000	0001010111101110

Note that some instructions require two words (or 32 bits) while the rest require one word. The same instructions, such as store, may require one or two words depending upon the location in memory to be used. The variables A, B, C and D will be stored in other words in memory. *If A is stored in word number 100, 100 is said to be the address of A.* The instruction to store the accumulator contents in A must include a bit pattern which represents the address of A. The address of a word in memory which is used to store an instruction or data variable is the location or word number of the word just as the address of your house is the location or house number of the house.

Since the bit pattern represents the actual status of magnetic core memory which would be used by the computer in executing the instructions, *the bit patterns*

6

*of instructions are called machine language instructions, and the manual preparation
of these bit patterns is called machine language programming.* Machine language
programming was the usual method of programming until well into the 1950's.

1-5   Symbolic Programming and Assemblers

The early machine language programmers did not usually write programs
by writing a string of zeros and ones, however. Instead they wrote abbreviated
symbolic instructions using letters, such as "LD C" for "load the value of C." Then
they manually translated the abbreviated instructions into bit patterns referring to
specific word locations in computer memory. Each symbolic data variable such as C
had to be assigned the address of the word or words which would contain the value
of the variable.

It soon became apparent that the job of translating abbreviated instructions
into bit patterns, finding available word addresses for data variables and assembling
the whole into a sequence of executable bit patterns could be done by the computer.
In other words, *a computer program could be prepared which would accept as input
the abbreviated symbolic instructions and produce as output the bit patterns of
machine language programming. Such programs are called assemblers. The abbreviated symbolic notation for instructions is called symbolic language or assembly
language.*

An assembly language program to compute equation (1-1) might include
the following symbolic instructions:

1)	(load)	LD	L	C
2)	(add)	A	L	D
3)	(store)	STO	3	−126
4)	(load)	LD	L	B
5)	(shift)	SRT		16
6)	(divide)	D	3	−126
7)	(store)	STO	L	A

Each of the above instructions translates into a specific instruction in machine
language occupying one or two words of computer memory.

Assembly language made it unnecessary to program in the bit patterns of the
computer, but it was still necessary to program using the rudimentary instructions
of the computer such as load and add.

If a computer program could be prepared to translate symbolic instructions and symbolic variables into bit patterns which could be executed as computer instructions, why couldn't a program be prepared to translate algebraic equations into executable bit patterns? Such a program would have to determine which machine language instructions would be required to compute the equation, and the program would also have to assign memory addresses for all data variables encountered in the equation.

The first general programs to translate algebraic equations into machine language appeared in 1956, and the most widely accepted of these early algebraic translators was called FORTRAN, which stands for FORmula TRANslation. *Such programs are called compilers, since they must compile a list of required instructions and then translate the instructions into bit patterns. The FORTRAN language today consists of equations and other statements which can be translated by the FORTRAN compiler.*

The computation of equation (1-1) in FORTRAN might be written as

$$A = B/(C+D)$$

which is exactly the way equation (1-1) first appeared back in Section 1-4.

FORTRAN was originally developed to handle the mathematics of scientific and engineering applications. Since 1956 many new features have been added to FORTRAN to improve its ability to describe alphabetic data and logical problems. Other compilers have been developed, including BASIC, PL/I and COBOL.

1-7   Software as the Programmer's Interface to Hardware

Programming systems such as FORTRAN and assembly language are frequently called software, while computing equipment such as memory units and line printers are frequently called hardware. Today programmers describe their programs in software systems, which then control the hardware in the execution of the programs. The software appears to the programmer like the controls on a modern automobile; the programmer is able to control the hardware through the software without continually keeping track of the details of hardware operation.

All problems, however, cannot easily be written in compiler systems such as FORTRAN and COBOL. New and more general compiler languages such as PL/I are becoming available, and these new languages are expected to handle almost all types of problems. If so, assembly and machine language programming may finally disappear from the repertoire of the average programmer. Until then the FORTRAN programmer will still find it necessary to use assembly language programming for occasional data and hardware operations which cannot be expressed in the FORTRAN language.

The advantages of programming in a compiler language go far beyond the obvious advantage of writing in a more readable language than assembly or machine language. Since the compiler language is more concise, the program as written by the programmer is shorter, with less chance for clerical errors. The program should be easier to debug, and easier to explain to associates who may have to maintain it. Also, the program written in compiler language may be compiled and executed upon other computers than the computer for which the program was originally written, even if the others have different machine languages. The last statement will be true if the same type of compiler exists for other computers. FORTRAN compilers exist today for a majority of the computers on the market.

1-8   Source Language and Object Programs; Compiler Efficiency

A program as it is originally written in FORTRAN or another compiler language is called a source program; it is said to be written in source language. As we have seen, this source program then becomes input data for the compiler program, and the compiler program translates the source program into a set of executable bit patterns or machine language instructions. *Machine language instructions which have been produced by a compiler or assembler are called an object program.* The normal procedure required to execute a program written in source language (such as FORTRAN) is

1)   load the compiler into computer memory

2)   have the compiler read and translate the source program

3)   load the output from the compiler (object program) into computer memory

4)   execute the object (machine language) program.

A frequently asked question is: Can the object program execute as efficiently as a program written directly in assembly or machine language to do the same job? Efficiency in programming is almost always a compromise between speed of execution and minimal use of memory. Consider the problem of writing a program to take the square root of any integer between 1 and 10,000. At one extreme, a trial procedure could be used which would guess at the answer, then square the guess to see if it was correct, and move toward the correct answer for the next guess. Such a procedure would take little memory but might take a long time. At the other extreme, a table of all possible answers (square roots) could be stored in 10,000 memory addresses and the number whose square root was required could be used to calculate the

9

address of the answer. Such a procedure would be very fast but would use up more than 10,000 words of memory.

Compiler generated object programs will almost always require more memory than programs written in machine language, because the compiler will provide for more error checking and more choices of procedure than a single program might require. The execution speed of the object program may be about as fast as a good program written in machine language, or it may run slower (up to several times slower in extreme situations). The speed depends upon whether the program does things which the compiler language handles efficiently (such as arithmetic and reading and writing) or whether the program does things which the compiler language does not handle as efficiently as does machine language (such as the manipulation of letters or bit patterns inside words).

Computers today are much faster and much less expensive than they were only a few years ago, and continued improvements in both speed and cost are antici-pated in the future. Although one can argue that compilers have saved work for programmers while making extra work for computers, the difficulties of machine language and assembly language programming have convinced most computer users that the use of compilers is economically justified. In the case of the 1130 system, where the operating cost of the computer may be comparable to the salary of the programmer, the justification is particularly easy to find.

1-9   Monitor Systems and Batch Processing

The early compiler systems required a complicated procedure before a pro-gram written in source language could be executed to produce useful answers. The compiler had to be loaded into memory, the source program had to be loaded as input (perhaps more than once), the object program had to be punched out, and finally the memory of the computer had to be cleared and the object program loaded into memory so that the object program could be executed. Ideally the programmer should be able to send a source language program to the computer and expect to get answers back immediately and automatically. This automatic operation became feasible in the late 1950's through the use of secondary memory.

If the compiler instructions and the object program instructions could be stored in secondary memory (disk files or magnetic tape), then the computer could proceed automatically to compile the source program, store the object program in secondary memory, reload the object program into core or primary memory, and produce answers. Furthermore, the computer could automatically start reading in the next job or program when the first job was finished.

The idea of automatically shifting from one job to a second job upon com-pletion of the first job became known as automatic batch processing, and the programming systems which facilitated this type of operation became known as monitors. A monitor can read the first few instructions of a new job, determine if that job requires a FORTRAN compilation, pull in the FORTRAN compiler program from secondary memory if required, set up the resulting object program in core memory, allow the object program to execute and produce answers, and then start reading the first few instructions of the next job and proceed accordingly. A monitor can also allow several different programs to share the same data, so that one program can produce answers for use in another program. The 1130, when equipped with disk storage, is capable of fully automatic monitor operation.

1-10   Real-Time Programming

An example of a real-time computing application might be a computer program used to compute the current position of an orbiting space vehicle. (Such a program is presented in Chapter 8.) If the program were being used to determine the point at which the space vehicle would meet another vehicle, obviously the program would be of little use if the time required to compute the position of the vehicle exceeded the time remaining before the vehicles met. Such a program has a very definite real-time requirement: the program must be able to evaluate changes in position in much less time than that required for the vehicle to actually reach a new position.

Real-time computation may be defined as a situation where the input data to the computer is changing with time and the time required to compute answers directly affects the answers. A weekly payroll application is not considered to be a real-time application. Although the payroll must be out on time, the time required to compute the payroll is usually nowhere near a week. If the computing time for the payroll is a week, a faster computer is in order.

More conventional real-time applications include the control and data acquisition applications involving industrial processes such as steel mills, paper mills, petroleum refineries and manufacturing plants. Here the computer may be wired to instruments (thermocouples, pressure sensors, etc.) which allow the computer to measure the performance of the process directly. The computer may also be wired to controllers such as set point stations which can be used to adjust the process automatically. The 1130 is being used in real-time process applications.

Another area of real-time application for computers involves communication systems. A computer may be wired to many terminals and may be required to switch messages coming in from the terminals or to supply data in answer to questions coming from the terminals. Airline reservation systems, which use secondary memory to keep a continuously updated passenger list for each flight and make information from the passenger lists available to hundreds of terminals across the country, are examples of communication systems in real-time.

Real-time applications present new programming challenges: responding to interrupts according to changing priorities and moving many different programs in and out of core storage to handle a changing environment.

1-11   Time-Sharing and Multiprogramming

Real-time applications have produced a need to share the memory of the computer between two or more programs, with each program engaged in handling a separate real-time problem. For instance, one program might respond to traffic from remote communication terminals while another program designs bridges and performs other engineering calculations in the time available between communications from the terminals. Both core storage and use of the accumulator and other registers could be allocated between these programs on a priority basis, with the communication program probably having the higher priority. Only one program is actually computing with the accumulator at any point in time; the other program is waiting for a chance at the accumulator when the active program finishes its problem of the moment or becomes tied up in a lengthy read or write operation. In such a system, control of the computer could be tossed back and forth between these two programs several times in a single second.

Multiprogramming occurs when several programs are able to operate concurrently from core memory, and usually involves the relocation of an incoming program into whatever memory space is currently available. A typical multiprogramming application might involve the use of several consoles by programmers who were sending FORTRAN instructions to the computer, with a different program being developed at each console. The computer would be expected to compile and execute all these programs concurrently.

1-12   Problems

1)   Do you have enough familiarity with the following words to use them in sentences?

    a)   analyzing a problem

    b)   coding a program

    c)   debugging a program

    d)   documenting a program

    e)   computer programming

    f)   real-time applications

    g)   time-sharing

h)   learning programs

i)   input and output functions

j)   punched cards

k)   magnetic core memory

l)   bits and words in memory

m)   instructions and data in memory

n)   primary and secondary memory

o)   the stored program concept

p)   machine language instructions

q)   arithmetic operations and the accumulator

r)   symbolic programming

s)   assemblers and compilers

t)   FORTRAN, COBOL and PL/I

u)   source language and object programs

v)   monitors and batch processing

w)   multiprogramming and multiprocessing

2)   Each bit in memory is a single magnetic core. If the average 1130 system has 8,192 words of 16 bits each, how many magnetic cores are wired into the core memory?

3)   A microsecond is a millionth of a second and a millisecond is a thousandth of a second. If an 1130 computer can add together two 16-bit numbers in 4.25 microseconds, how many additions could be performed in a second? In a millisecond?

4)   A nanosecond is a billionth of a second, and a nanosecond is also approximately equal to the time a ray of light takes to travel one foot. How far could a ray of light travel in 4.25 microseconds?

CHAPTER 2: BITS, CODES AND COMPUTING EQUIPMENT

2-1   Data Words in Memory

In the last chapter we learned that primary memory consists of magnetic cores, that each core represents a bit of information, and that each core can be magnetized in two different directions to represent "on" and "off" or "one" and "zero." The cores are grouped into words of 16 cores or bits each, and the total primary memory of the computer can range from 4,096 words to 32,768 words.

The 1130 system provides 16 bits in each word which may be arranged in patterns to represent numbers, letters, logical conditions such as "yes" and "no," and patterns representing computer instructions such as "add" and "subtract." The 1130 has two parity bits in each word. The 1130 thus has 18 bits in each word, but only 16 of the bits can contain bit patterns representing data or instructions.

It is important to remember that the 1130 does not process numbers and letters directly; instead it processes bit patterns which we define to represent letters and numbers. The bit patterns become symbols for the letters and numbers, and for this reason computers are sometimes called symbol processors. The letters and numbers we send into the computers are encoded into bit patterns and manipulated by the computers to form other bit patterns which are decoded into letters and numbers and printed out as answers. One code that can be used to represent numbers inside computers is the binary number code.

2-2   The Binary Number System

The decimal number system that we use in everyday arithmetic requires ten different digits including zero. The value of a decimal digit depends upon the digit itself and upon the position of the digit in a number; for example, the digit 3 in the number 362 has a value of 3 times 10 to the second power, or 300. If we use the notation * to mean "times" and ** to mean "to the power," then

$$362 \text{ equals } 3*10**2 \text{ plus } 6*10**1 \text{ plus } 2*10**0 \qquad (2\text{-}1)$$

The above notation can be used to express any decimal number as a series of powers of ten. Remember that any number (except zero) to the power of zero equals one.

We probably use a ten-based or decimal number system because we have ten fingers. Our computer has only two directions of magnetization for each bit. The computer is thus able to get only two digits out of each bit (which we call 0 and 1), and after two digits the computer must carry over into the next bit position just as we carry over into the next decimal position when we run out of fingers. *Each bit position in a word of computer memory can correspond to a power of two, just as each position in a decimal number corresponds to a power of ten.*

The preceding technique can also be used to convert binary (base two) numbers into decimal (base ten) numbers. A binary number is written as a bit pattern of zeros and ones, such as 10110. The binary number 10110 can be expressed as a series of powers of two:

10110_2 equals $1*2**4$ plus $0*2**3$ plus $1*2**2$ plus $1*2**1$

plus $0*2**0$

equals 16 plus 0 plus 4 plus 2 plus 0

equals 22_{10}. (2-2)

The subscripts 2 and 10 indicate numbers in binary and decimal notation, respectively. So 10110 in binary notation equals 22 in decimal notation.

In the memory of the 1130 computer the number 22 could be carried in a 16-bit word as 0000000000010110. *The left-hand bit (also called the high-order bit) represents the sign of the number; 0 means plus and 1 means minus. The remaining 15 bits represent the magnitude of the number.* The largest positive number which can be represented in a single 16-bit word is thus $2**14$ plus $2**13$ plus $2**12$ ... plus (finally) $2**0$ which is equal to 32,767 in decimal or 0111111111111111 in binary.

Addition in binary follows rules similar to the rules for addition in decimal; i.e., if the sum at any point exceeds 1 a carry is made into the next position to the left. Consider the following two additions:

22	0000000000010110
19	0000000000010011
41	0000000000101001

(2-3)

The rules for binary addition can be summarized as follows: $0 + 0 = 0$, $0 + 1 = 1$, $1 + 0 = 1$, and $1 + 1 = 0$ with a carry into the next column to the left. In decimal arithmetic the carry is made if the sum exceeds nine; in binary the carry is made if the sum exceeds one.

Negative numbers are carried in the memory of the 1130 in twos complement form. Ordinary binary numbers can be converted to twos complement notation by changing each 0 in the number to a 1 and changing each 1 in the number to a 0 (which is called complementing), and then adding a binary 1 to the result. The number 22, which is 10110 in binary, is 01010 in twos complement form. The number −22 would be carried in memory as 1111111111101010 where the high-order 1 is

15

the sign bit. The largest negative number which can be represented in a single 16-bit word is –32,768 in decimal or 1000000000000000 in twos complement binary notation. *Zero in memory is always simply 0000000000000000.*

Bit patterns from two adjacent words in memory can be used to represent one 32-bit number, and the 1130 has an accumulator register with an extension 32 bits wide to accommodate these larger numbers. The high-order bit of the left-hand word is used to represent the sign of the number, and positive numbers up to 2,147,483,647 in decimal can be represented as the sum of $2^{**}30$ plus $2^{**}29$ plus . . . plus $2^{**}0$. Negative numbers are represented in twos complement notation providing magnitudes up to –2,147,483,648 in decimal, or 10000000000000000000000 0000000000 in twos complement binary.

Techniques have been developed to facilitate the manual conversion of large binary numbers to decimal and vice versa, and to facilitate the multiplication and division of binary numbers using only a pencil and paper. A good discussion of these techniques is presented in the IBM SRL publication number A26-5881, *IBM 1130 Functional Characteristics.* Small numbers may be converted by inspection of the powers of two or ten, however, and larger numbers may be converted through the use of conversion tables and hexadecimal notation as described below.

2-3   Hexadecimal Notation

Writing 16-bit binary numbers like, say, 0100100011101011 is tedious and subject to clerical errors. Various notations have been developed to represent binary numbers and other bit patterns in a more compact notation than the use of a digit for each bit. The hexadecimal notation has become standard for the 1130 system. *Hexadecimal notation is based upon powers of 16, and uses 16 different digits.* The digits have values ranging from 0 to 15, but since 15 requires two digits in decimal it became necessary to create new digits to represent hexadecimal values above the digit 9. *For convenience, the letters A through F are used as digits to represent hexadecimal values from 10 through 15.* A short table of decimal, hexadecimal and binary numbers is shown on the facing page.

One hexadecimal digit can represent all possible combinations of four bits. Four hexadecimal digits can represent all possible combinations of 16 bits by taking the bits four at a time. For example, the word in memory 0110101001111010 can be broken up into the four subpatterns of 0110 1010 0111 1010 which can be represented by the hexadecimal digits 6, A, 7 and A. So the 16-bit pattern 011010100111 1010 can be represented by 6A7A in hexadecimal, and hexadecimal becomes a shorthand notation for binary numbers or bit patterns. Appendix E consists of a conversion table for hexadecimal and decimal numbers, and the conversion between hexadecimal and binary numbers can easily be made by substituting the four-bit pattern represented by each hexadecimal digit.

16

Decimal	Hexadecimal	Binary
0	0	0
1	1	1
2	2	10
3	3	11
4	4	100
5	5	101
6	6	110
7	7	111
8	8	1000
9	9	1001
10	A	1010
11	B	1011
12	C	1100
13	D	1101
14	E	1110
15	F	1111
16	10	10000

$$(2\text{-}4)$$

Manual conversion from hexadecimal notation to decimal notation can always be accomplished by expressing the hexadecimal number as a series of powers of 16. For example, the hexadecimal number 6A7A (equal to 0110101001111010 in binary) can be expressed as

6A7A equals 6*16**3 plus 10*16**2 plus 7*16**1 plus 10*16**0

equals 6*4096 plus 10*256 plus 7*16 plus 10

equals 24,576 plus 2,560 plus 112 plus 10

equals 27,258

$$(2\text{-}5)$$

(Remember that A in hexadecimal notation equals 10 in decimal notation.) One method of converting large binary numbers to decimal consists of writing the binary number in hexadecimal and then converting the hexadecimal number to decimal notation as described above.

Conversion of large negative binary numbers in twos complement notation requires a preliminary conversion to binary by subtracting one and then reversing the 0 and 1 bits (complementing). Consider the twos complement number 1001000101011101. Subtracting one from this number results in 1001000101011100, and reversing the 0 and 1 bits results in 0110111010100011, which can be split into the four subpatterns 0110 1110 1010 0011 and written in hexadecimal as –6EA3, where the minus sign indicates the sign of the original binary number. The hexadecimal number –6EA3 can then be converted to decimal using powers of 16 or the conversion table in Appendix E. Notice that if the memory word containing 1001000101011101 was considered as an arbitrary bit pattern, not a binary number, then the word could be expressed directly in hexadecimal notation as 915D, which would accurately describe the bit pattern but would not utilize the sign bit to indicate a negative number.

The arithmetic rules for the addition, subtraction, multiplication and division of both hexadecimal and binary numbers are similar to the equivalent operations with decimal numbers. As it is seldom necessary to do hexadecimal or binary arithmetic (except binary addition) while writing a computer program, these arithmetic rules are developed through problems at the end of this chapter.

2-4   Real Numbers and Floating-Point Notation

Up to this point we have assumed that the numbers to be represented in computer memory are integers; i.e., whole numbers without fractions. *Most practical problems, particularly in engineering applications, involve fractional or "real" numbers.* Integers such as 27 or 129 might be used to express the number of people in a room or the number of legs on a centipede, but so-called real numbers such as 4.38 or 251.86 would be needed to accurately describe the length of a stick or the volume of a bottle.

A common problem of both hand calculations and programming where real numbers are involved is how to keep track of the decimal point in a series of arithmetic operations. Although it is possible to assume the position of an imaginary decimal (or binary) point and to remember the position of the point in simple calculations, *complex problems involving real numbers of widely differing sizes make it necessary to provide some automatic scheme to insure the proper positioning of the decimal point after each operation. One such scheme is called floating-point notation.*

Any real number can be represented as the product of two other numbers, one of which is a decimal fraction and the other is a power of ten. For example, 36.425 can be represented as .36425 times ten to the second power. If we use the letter E to mean "times ten to the power," then 36.425 can be written as .36425E2. *This method of representing real numbers is called exponential or scientific notation.* The table below shows how several real numbers appear in scientific notation.

Common Notation	Scientific Notation
93,427,104.	.93427104E8
.000934271	.934271E−3
1.9986	.19986E1
−667.0	−.667E3
−.0384	−.384E−1

The examples of scientific notation in the above table indicate that the power of ten or the exponent (the number to the right of E) is simply the number of places that the decimal point must be shifted to convert to common notation. A negative exponent such as E–3 indicates that the decimal point should be shifted three places to the left; a positive exponent such as E8 indicates that the decimal point should be shifted eight places to the right.

Floating-point notation in the 1130 system consists of using two binary numbers to represent the fractional part and the exponent part of numbers originally written in scientific notation. The binary number representing the fractional part of the original number is called the mantissa; the binary number representing the exponent is called the characteristic.

The characteristic of floating-point numbers is an eight-bit pattern formed by adding a constant of 128 to the original binary exponent. Note that the exponent represented in the computer is a binary exponent corresponding to the power of two required to shift the binary point of the original number to convert the original number to a binary fraction. The eight-bit pattern can represent characteristics ranging from 0 to 255, and the addition of 128 to the exponent allows the characteristic to represent binary exponents ranging from –128 to +127. A binary exponent of eight would be represented by a characteristic of 136 or 10001000 in computer memory; an exponent of –3 would be represented by a characteristic of 125 or 01111101 in memory.

Notice that nonnegative exponents will always result in a characteristic which has a 1 in the high-order or left-hand position; negative exponents will result in a characteristic which has a 0 in the high-order position. The characteristic in this notation is always positive so a sign bit is not required. The range of binary exponents from –128 to +127 corresponds to powers of ten ranging from about –38.5 to +38.1, since two to the 127th power is about equal to ten to the 38.1 power. The floating-point characteristics in the 1130 system can thus handle decimal exponents from about E–38 to E38.

The mantissa of floating-point numbers can consist of 23 bits (standard range format) or 31 bits (extended range format). An additional bit is used with each mantissa to represent the sign of the original number; a 0-bit means positive sign and a 1-bit means negative. The 23-bit size of the standard range mantissa can represent decimal fractions of up to about 6.9 digits, since two to the 23rd power is about equal to ten to the 6.9 power. Similarly, the 31-bit size of the extended range mantissa can represent decimal fractions of up to about 9.3 digits, since two to the 31st power is about equal to ten to the 9.3 power. The extended range floating-point format thus provides about 50 percent more precision than does the standard range format, and the extended range format should be used whenever precision in excess of six digits is needed to provide the level of accuracy required by a particular problem or program.

Standard precision floating-point formats occupy two 16-bit words in computer memory for each floating-point number, and extended precision floating-point formats occupy three 16-bit memory words for each floating-point number. The arrangement of the characteristic and mantissa in computer memory is shown below.

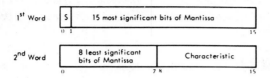

Figure 2-1   Standard Range Floating-Point Format in Memory

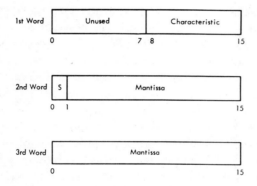

Figure 2-2   Extended Range Floating-Point Format in Memory

Floating-point arithmetic in the 1130 system is done by programming; i.e., programs have been written to add, subtract, multiply and divide numbers represented in the above formats in computer memory. Some computers have special hardware to permit floating-point arithmetic operations to be performed by a single instruction. In the 1130, the floating-point programs or routines contain many instructions to shift the mantissas of arithmetic operands until they have matching characteristics, to perform the required arithmetic operation, and then to shift the resulting mantissa and adjust the resulting characteristic until the high-order bit of the mantissa is a 1-bit. *This last shifting operation is called normalizing.*

It should not be assumed that automatic floating-point operations allow the programmer to ignore completely the magnitudes of the numbers that he is using in a calculation inside the computer. Roundoff and truncation difficulties can occur (by multiplying or dividing very large or very small numbers) which fall outside the allowable range of the computer.

2-5 Alphameric Character Notation (EBCDIC Code)

*Individual characters, including letters, digits and special characters such as $, *, & or @ are normally carried in computer memory in the Extended Binary Coded Decimal Interchange Code (EBCDIC).* EBCDIC is an eight-bit code, permitting two characters to be carried in each 16-bit word in memory. A partial list of all 256 EBCDIC codes is presented in Appendix D. As examples, the EBCDIC code for the letter A is 11000001 in binary or C1 in hexadecimal; the EBCDIC code for the digit 5 is 11110101 in binary or F5 in hexadecimal.

2-6 IBM Card Code and the 1442 Card Read Punch

Punched cards containing 80 columns of up to 12 punches per column are the most common medium for transmitting both instructions and data to and receiving data from the computer. Data in the form of characters are represented by one character per card column. The 12 punches available per column can also represent 12 bits in computer memory, so that the bit patterns of computer memory may be represented by about one and a half card columns per 16-bit word in memory. The characters require one, two or three punches in a column, and the code which represents the characters in memory as they are read from or punched into cards is called the IBM Card Code. As shown in Figure 2-3, the three punches which represent a plus sign are represented in memory by three 1-bits and nine 0-bits in the 12 high-order bits of a single 16-bit word, with the bit pattern corresponding to the pattern of punches in the card column. Card punches are referred to from the top of the card to the bottom as the 12-zone punch, the 11-zone punch and the digit punches zero through nine, as shown in Figure 2-3. The plus sign character is thus represented by a 12-6-8 punch in the card, by a 1000000010100000 in IBM Card Code in computer memory, and perhaps later by a 01001110 in EBCDIC for manipulation as data inside the computer. The code conversion from IBM Card Code to EBCDIC can be performed by a program of instructions that do a table look-up to convert one code into another. A table of IBM card codes can be found in Appendix D.

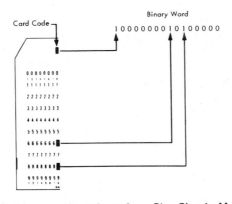

Figure 2-3   IBM Card Code for a Plus Sign in Memory

21

The 1442 Card Read Punch is the most commonly used device for reading and punching cards under computer control in the 1130 system. Two models of the 1442 are used: the Model 6 which reads up to 300 cards per minute and punches up to 80 card columns per second, and the Model 7 which reads up to 400 cards per minute and punches up to 160 card columns per second. A 1442 Model 5 which punches cards at up to 160 card columns per second may be attached to an 1130. The 1442 is a single path machine. All cards pass from a single read hopper through a reading station, followed by a punching station and then into one of two stackers. The choice of which stacker to use is made by instructions in the computer. The path that each card takes in passing through the 1442 is shown in Figure 2-4.

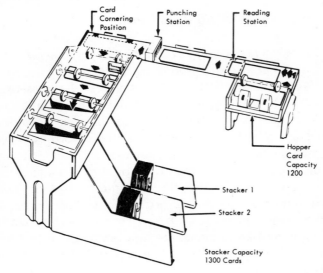

Figure 2-4   Card Path of 1442 Card Read Punch

The 1442 itself is shown in Figure 2-5. From the programmer's point of view, the single card path makes it possible to punch data into a card which has just been read. The programming problems of single path operation are discussed in Section 3-9.

Two faster card readers, the 2501 Card Reader Model A1 and A2, can be attached to an 1130 with a 1442 Model 5 Card Punch instead of the 1442 Models 6 and 7. The 2501 Model A1 reads up to 600 cards per minute while the 2501 Model A2 reads up to 1000 cards per minute.

2-7   Paper Tape Codes, Readers and Punches

Every 1130 system using IBM's FORTRAN compiler or Assembler has either punched card or paper tape facilities. The paper tape is one inch wide and has eight tracks or channels. One channel is used for a stop code to stop the reading of the tape. Another channel is used for a checking bit, leaving six channels for instructions

Figure 2-5 IBM 1442 Card Read Punch

or data. The eight channels are read into and punched from bit positions 0-7 of a word in core memory, as shown in Figure 2-6.

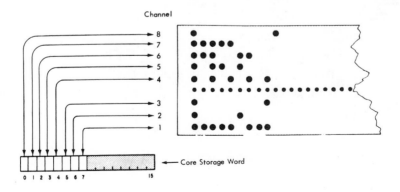

Figure 2-6 Paper Tape Format

23

Channel 5 is the check bit channel. Odd parity is used for checking; i.e., the check bit will be present if the number of punches in the character code is even, thus insuring that the total number of punches in a single character code will always be odd. (Exception: if all eight channels are punched, the character is ignored.) The paper tape codes are usually converted to EBCDIC code or to binary numbers for manipulation inside the computer. Paper tape codes are listed in Appendix D as two hexadecimal characters for each code.

The 1054 Paper Tape Reader and the 1055 Paper Tape Punch both operate at a speed of 14.8 characters per second. The 1134 Paper Tape Reader, which reads 60 characters per second, has replaced the 1054 on many 1130 systems.

Figure 2-7   IBM 1054 Paper Tape Reader

Figure 2-8   IBM 1055 Paper Tape Punch

2-8   Console Keyboard and Console Typewriter Codes

An input keyboard is built into the computer console of the 1130. The code for each character read into the computer from this keyboard is similar to the IBM Card Code used with the 1442 Card Read Punch. The keyboard of the 1130 console is shown in Figure 2-9.

Several of the keys shown in Figure 2-9 serve specific control functions as described below:

      INT REQ — Depressing this key sets an interrupt device to execute a pro-
            gram which will read characters from the keyboard, and terminates
            the program currently executing.

      EOF — This key terminates a message from the keybaord by sending a code
            to the computer which can be used as an end-of-message signal.

      BACKSPACE (left-pointing arrow) — This key generates a code which can
            cause the computer to ignore the previous character.

      ERASE FIELD (reentry) — This key generates a code which can cause the
            computer to ignore the entire message and to consider what follows
            as an entire new transmission.

      ALPHA and NUM — These keys select lower- and uppercase mode on the
            keyboard. Note that the keyboard must be in uppercase (NUM)
            mode to enter characters on the upper part of the keys.

      REST KB (restore) — This key permits the operators to unlock the keys if
            they should become locked.

      KEYBOARD SELECT (PROCEED) LIGHT — This light comes on whenever
            the computer has instructed the keyboard to accept a character.

*Characters cannot be typed into the keyboard unless the SELECT or PRO-
CEED light is on.* The normal sequence of keyboard operations is as follows: the operator enters an INT REQ, the computer responds to the resulting interrupt by turning on the SELECT (PROCEED) light, the operator enters a character which causes another interrupt in the computer, and turns off the SELECT (PROCEED) light, the computer then responds to the interrupt by turning on again the SELECT or PROCEED light, etc. The computer responses are controlled by a program in memory which interprets the incoming characters and controls the keyboard acccord-ingly. After each character is entered, the program must usually convert the character from keyboard code to typewriter code (which, as we will see, is a different code) and then print the character on the typewriter above the keyboard before turning on the SELECT (PROCEED) light to accept the next character from the keyboard. All this may take a noticeable fraction of a second. If the operator attempts to enter a

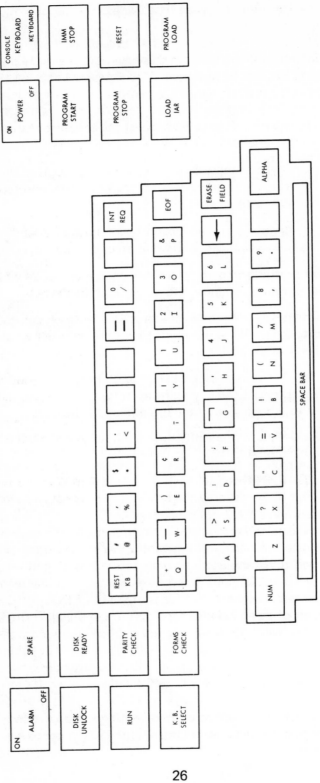

Figure 2-9   Keyboard of 1130 Console

character before the PROCEED light comes on, he will find the keyboard locked so that the character cannot be entered.

The console typewriter on the 1130 system prints at a rate of 14.8 characters per second. This typewriter uses a rotating and tilting spherical printing element, and the code used to drive it from the computer is called a tilt-rotate code. The tilt-rotate code transmitted from the computer to the typewriter is an eight-bit code consisting of six data bits plus a bit to indicate upper or lower case and a bit to indicate whether the data is a character to be printed or a control function such as tab, color-shift, etc. The format of this code in memory is shown in Figure 2-10, and the codes are listed in Appendix D as two hexadecimal characters for each code.

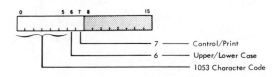

Figure 2-10 Typewriter Code Format in Computer Memory

2-9   Printer Code

Large quantities of printed output are usually printed on line printers which effectively print an entire line at a time rather than a single character as typewriters do. The IBM 1132 Printer, shown in Figure 2-11, can print output from the 1130 system at speeds up to 82 lines per minute of alphameric information (letters and numbers) or up to 110 lines per minute of numeric information. The printed line contains up to 120 characters.

The 1132 Printer contains 120 round print wheels, each with 48 different characters. As the print wheels rotate one revolution for each printed line, a program in the computer sends a 1-bit to each print wheel as the character to be printed rotates to a position opposite the output page or form.

Two faster line printers, the 1403 Printer Model 6 and Model 7, can be attached to an 1130 instead of the 1132 Printer. The 1403 Model 6 prints up to 340 lines per minute and the 1403 Model 7 prints up to 600 lines per minute.

2-10   Plotter Code

Graph plotting is a very useful method of presenting computer output, particularly the output of engineering calculations. The 1130 system can attach the IBM 1627 Plotter shown in Figure 2-12.

Figure 2-11   IBM 1132 Printer

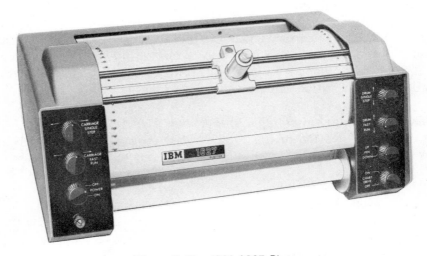

Figure 2-12   IBM 1627 Plotter

The 1627 Plotter comes in two models. Model 1 has a plotting area 11 inches by 120 feet, and Model 2 has a plotting area 29.5 inches by 120 feet. Both models use a pen which moves in increments of 1/100 of an inch. The 1627 Model 1 can move 18,000 increments per minute, while the 1627 Model 2 can move 12,000 increments per minute. The arrangement of the pen and paper spools is shown in Figure 2-13.

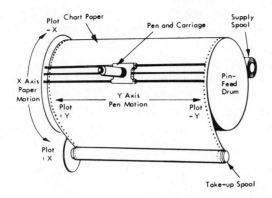

Figure 2-13   1627 Pen and Paper Arrangement

Notice that the pen moves along the Y axis while the paper is fed from a supply spool to a take-up spool and moves along the X axis. Relative to the paper, the pen of the 1627 Plotter can be incremented or moved 1/100 of an inch at a time in any one of eight directions, as shown in Figure 2-14, and the pen can also be raised from and lowered to the paper. A six-bit pattern is transmitted from the computer to the 1627 to produce each of the ten control motions shown in Figure 2-14.

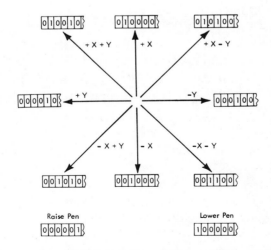

Figure 2-14   1627 Pen and Paper Motion and Control Code

2-11   Summary

This chapter has served to give us a look at the codes used in the 1130 system and a first look at some of the input-output equipment used with this computer. Other equipment such as the disk storage unit will be described in later chapters. A thorough discussion of the controls and indicators associated with all this equipment can be found in the various IBM publications listed in the bibliography. This book is not meant to provide complete detail on the operation of the input-output equipment since the programmer will, in almost every case, use IBM-written programs to control this equipment.

The reader may well be convinced at this point that there are so many codes, notations and bit patterns associated with the 1130 system that he will never remember enough of them to program the computer. As we will see in the next chapter, however, the FORTRAN programmer is not usually concerned with the details of the various codes.

2-12   Problems

1) Using the powers of two notation of Section 2-2, convert the following binary numbers to decimal notation:

   0000000000001010   (answer: 10 in decimal)

   0000000000101100   (answer: 44 in decimal)

   0000000000010011

   0000000000000101

   0000000000101101

2) Perform the indicated binary additions. Remember that the rules for binary addition are 0 + 0 = 0, 0 + 1 = 1, 1 + 0 = 1, and 1 + 1 = 0 with a carry into the next column to the left. Check your answers by converting all numbers to decimal and re-adding in decimal:

1100	101100	10111	10010
+1010	+010110	+10011	+10010

   answer: 10110

3) Subtract in each of the additions indicated in Problem 2, checking the results by conversion to decimal notation. The rules for binary subtraction are 0 – 0 = 0, 1 – 0 = 1, 1 – 1 = 0, and 0 – 1 = 1 with a borrow from the next column to the left.

4)   Express the binary numbers in Problem 1 in twos complement nota-
     tion. (For the first number, the complement is 1111111111110101,
     and adding a binary 1 results in a twos complement of
     1111111111110110.)

5)   The rules for binary multiplication are (using * to indicate "times")
     0 * 0 = 0, 0 * 1 = 0 amd 1 * 1 = 1. Perform binary multiplications
     on the numbers in Problem 2, checking the results by conversion to
     decimal notation.

6)   Separate each of the binary numbers in Problem 1 into four four-bit
     patterns and express the patterns as hexadecimal digits as described
     in Section 2-3. (For the first number, the patterns are 0000 0000
     0000 1010, and the hexadecimal representation is 000A.)

7)   Considering the twos complement notations developed in Problem 4
     as arbitrary bit patterns, express the patterns in hexadecimal notation.
     (For the first number, 1111111111110110 becomes FFF6.)

8)   Using powers of 16 notation from Section 2-3, convert the hexadeci-
     mal numbers developed in Problem 6 to decimal notation. (For the
     first number, 000A = 0*16**3 + 0*16**2 + 0*16**1 + 10*16**0
     which is equal to 10.)

9)   Using the results of the binary multiplications performed in Problem
     5, develop rules for binary long division.

10) What is the largest decimal integer that can be represented in a
     binary number of eight bits? (Answer: 255.) In 10 bits? In 23 bits?
     In 31 bits?

11) Express the following real numbers in the scientific or exponential
     notation of Section 2-4:

     459.73   (answer: .45973E3)

     .006435

     −79112.836

     93000641.

12) For each of the following eight-bit binary exponents, find the
     corresponding eight-bit characteristic:

     00001010   (answer: 10001010)

−00001001

00001111

−00000101

13) If a mantissa of 23 bits can represent a precision of about 6.9 decimal digits, how many decimal digits could be represented by a mantissa of 16 bits? Of 31 bits? Of 55 bits?

14) What would be the bit pattern of a word in memory containing the EBCDIC codes for the letters AZ? (Answer: 1100000111101001.) For the digits 74? For the special characters $*?

15) If the letter A is read into core memory in IBM Card Code, what will be the bit pattern in memory? (Answer: 1001000000000000.) What will be the pattern for Z? For the digit 7? For the special character $?

16) What are the bit patterns representing the characters A, Z, 7 and $ in typewriter code? In paper tape code? In 1403 Printer code?

CHAPTER 3:   FORTRAN

3-1   A Very Small FORTRAN Program

Consider the following, which is a complete FORTRAN program:

```
C-----THIS PROGRAM COMPUTES AREAS OF CIRCLES FROM DIAMETERS.
1        READ (2, 10) DIAM
         AREA = 3.1416 *(DIAM * 0.5) ** 2
         WRITE (1, 11) DIAM, AREA
         GO TO 1
10       FORMAT (F10.3)
11       FORMAT (' FOR A DIAMETER OF', F10.3, ' THE AREA IS', F10.3)
         END
```

Each line of the FORTRAN program is called a statement. The eight statements above can be explained as follows:

C----- An optional comment statement to describe what the program will do next.

1   A READ statement to read the next value of the diameter from input-output unit 2 according to format 10.

An arithmetic statement to compute the area as 3.1416 times half of the diameter to the second power.

A WRITE statement to write the value of the diameter and the value of the area on input-output unit 1 according to format 11.

A control statement to go to statement 1 to get another value of the diameter.

10   A FORMAT statement which specifies that DIAM will be read as a field of ten characters with three characters to the right of the decimal point.

11   A FORMAT statement including words in quotes which will be printed with the current values of DIAM and AREA.

An END statement to indicate the last statement of the source program to the FORTRAN compiler.

If input-output unit 1 refers to the console typewriter, the printed output for a diameter of 2.0 would appear as follows:

FOR A DIAMETER OF   2.000 THE AREA IS   3.141

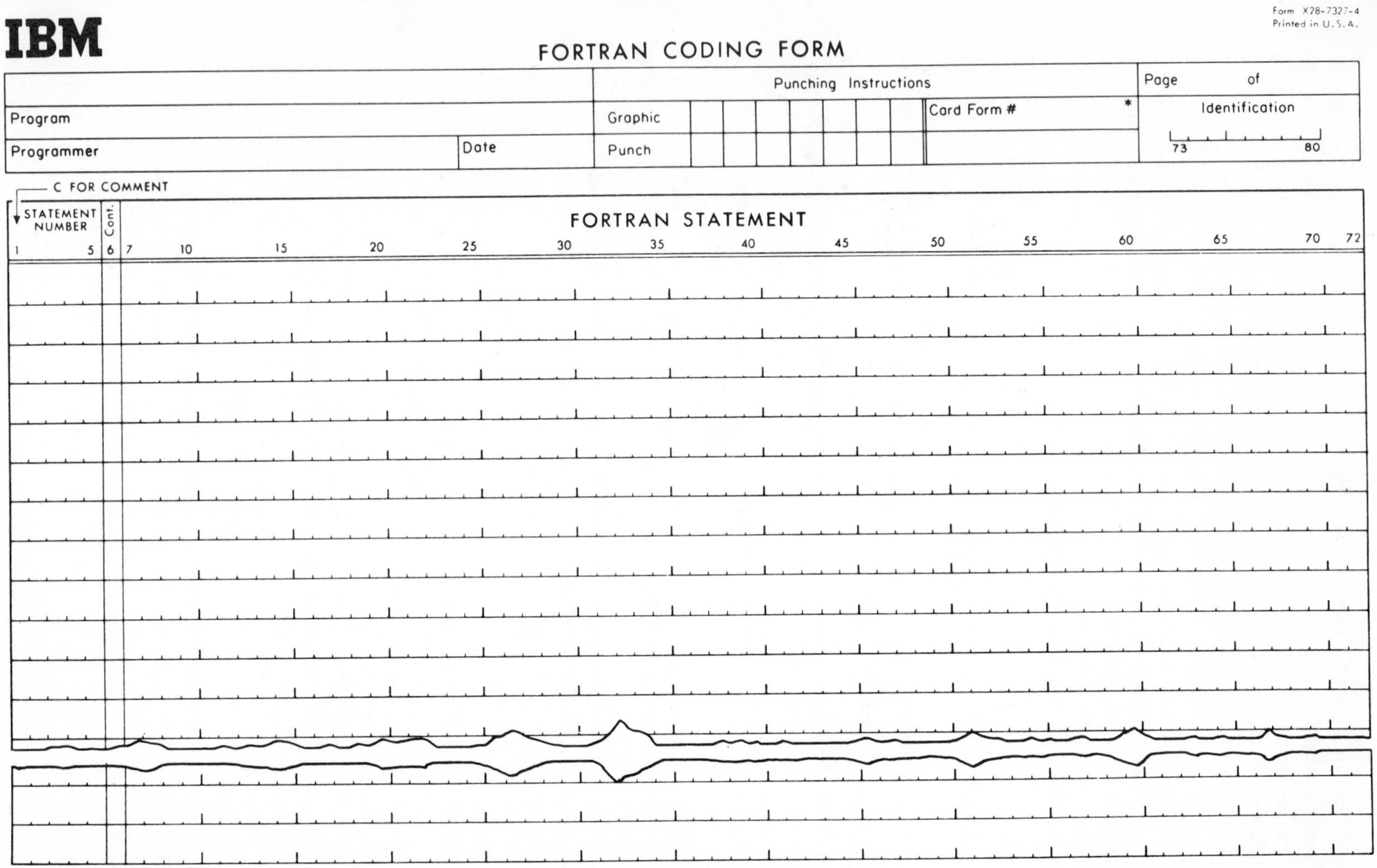

Figure 3-1 FORTRAN Coding Form

* A standard card form, IBM electro 888157, is available for punching source statements from this form.

If input-output unit 2 refers to the 1442 Card Read Punch, the program will read successive cards, each containing a value of the diameter in card columns 1-10, and will print successive lines of output upon the console typewriter until the 1442 runs out of data cards. Each diameter will be read in IBM Card Code (Section 2-6) and converted to floating-point number representation in core memory (Section 2-4).

The area will be calculated using programmed floating-point arithmetic, and the resulting floating-point number will be converted (by a conversion program) into tilt-rotate code and printed (Section 2-9). A few statements in FORTRAN can cause a great deal of data processing to take place inside the computer. Now we will take a close look at the rules for writing these statements.

3-2   FORTRAN Statements

FORTRAN statements are usually written upon a coding form or pad which provides 80 columns of information per line (corresponding to the 80 columns of information in an IBM punched card). A typical FORTRAN coding form is the IBM Form No. X28-7327 shown in Figure 3-1. The characters used in writing FORTRAN statements consist of letters of the alphabet, digits and special characters. Any character which is not a letter or a digit, such as + – * / = , is called a special character. A blank is a special character.

Columns one to five of the form must be used to number those statements which are referred to by other statements. Any integer from 1 to 99999 may be used as a statement number, and the numbers do not have to be in any particular order. Statement numbers may appear anywhere in columns one to five, but must not contain characters other than the digits zero to nine. Embedded blanks in statement numbers are ignored. Statement numbers should be used only on statements which will be referred to by other statements; the presence of unnecessary statement numbers will tend to increase the time required for compilation of the program and waste memory space inside the computer.

Column six is used to indicate that the information in the remainder of the statement is a continuation of the last previous statement. Up to five lines of continuation (up to five lines with a character in column six) may be used to extend the length of a single FORTRAN statement. Any character in column six except a blank or zero will indicate continuation.

Columns 7 to 72 contain the statement itself. Blank spaces may be used almost anywhere to increase readability but blanks should not be placed inside FORTRAN words like READ or inside variable names or constants or inside numeric specifications in FORMAT statements. Columns 73 to 80 are not processed by the FORTRAN compiler, and may contain the name of the program and serialization numbers for the program card deck or be left blank.

35

If column one contains the character C, the whole statement is called a comment statement. Comment statements are used by the programmer to help explain the operation of the program to other programmers and are not processed by the FORTRAN compiler. The comments may appear in columns 2 to 80 and may contain both normal and special characters. However, it is often recommended that columns 73 through 80 of each card be used only for identification and sequencing. Comment statements cannot be continued by means of a character in column six; each line of a comment is a separate statement and must have a C in column one. Blank cards inside a FORTRAN program are printed as blank lines in the program listing but are otherwise ignored by the computer. Thus, comments may be made more prominent in a listing by separating them from other statements with blank cards.

3-3   FORTRAN Constants

Constants such as 3.1416, 015 and 2 in FORTRAN statements may be either real (floating-point) constants or integer (whole number) constants. *Real constants are written in ordinary notation with a decimal point* (such as 3.1416, 0.5, .5, 93041.6 or .00045) *or else real constants are written in the scientific or exponential notation of Section 2-4* (such as .31416E1, .5E0, .930416E5 or .45E–3). Any decimal number may be followed by an exponent of one or two digits, so that the number 1.25 might also be written as .125E1, .125E01, 12.5E–1, 125.E–2 or even .000125E04. *Integer constants* (2, 23616, 54, 102 or 4096) *are written without decimal points.*

Neither real nor integer constants should contain imbedded blanks, commas or other characters (23616 should not be written as 23 616 or 23,616 or 2$3616). Both real and integer constants may be signed with a preceding plus or minus sign (+23616 or –23616). If no sign is furnished, the constant is assumed to be positive.

Integer constants must not exceed 32,767 or be less than –32,768. Positive real constants must not exceed 10^{38} or be less than 10^{-38}. The number of digits (precision) of a real constant cannot be more than 6.9 digits (standard range) or 9.3 digits (extended range) as described in Section 2-4. The 9.3 digit precision must be requested by a control card or record at the beginning of the program and all the floating-point numbers in the program would then be in extended range format.

3-4   FORTRAN Variables and TYPE Statements

Variables such as DIAM and AREA in the program of Section 3-1 are used to represent quantities (or alphanumeric codes) *which may change during the execution of the program. Variable names must consist of one to five letters and numbers* (not special characters), *and the first character in the name should be a letter.* If the variable name starts with one of the letters I, J, K, L, M or N the variable will usually represent an integer number; if the variable name does not start with I, J, K, L, M or N, the variable will usually represent a real (floating-point format) number.

Variable names should be chosen to carry a maximum of meaning to whoever will read the statements in the program. Instead of DIAM and AREA, the variable names X and Y could have been used, but X and Y would have no meaning to the reader. D and A would be better, but DIAM and AREA are better still. Occasionally we might want to call integer variables by names like DIAM and AREA, but we are apparently prevented from doing so by the rule that integer variable names must start with I, J, K, L, M or N. We can circumvent this difficulty in two ways: first, by calling the variables IDIAM and IAREA; second, by the use of a TYPE statement. *The TYPE statement is used to specify that a variable name which would ordinarily be integer type represents a real variable or that a variable name which would ordinarily be real type represents an integer variable.* To specify that DIAM and AREA are to represent integer variables we would use the following TYPE statement:

> INTEGER DIAM, AREA

Similarly, to specify that IDIAM and IAREA are to represent real variables, we would write the TYPE statement

> REAL IDIAM, IAREA

The examples in this book will assume that variable names starting with I, J, K, L, M or N represent integer variables unless there is a statement to the contrary.

REAL and INTEGER statements must be the very first statements in any program in which they are used so that the FORTRAN compiler will be able to tell whether to use floating-point or integer arithmetic operations with each variable name when the variable name first appears in the program.

3-5   Common Errors in Constants and Variables

The following examples illustrate the rules which must be followed in writing FORTRAN constants and variables:

Constant or Variable	Explanation
MOMENT	No good, more than five characters
¢FOOT	No good, contains a special character
6FOOT	No good, does not start with a letter
G7A43	OK, is a variable
X1000	OK, is a variable
6.743	OK, is a real constant
SI,ZE	No good, contains a special character

Constant or Variable	Explanation
67430.E-4	OK, is constant of 6.743
67,430.E-4	No good, contains a comma
-563	OK, is an integer constant
6.79E009	No good, the exponent is more than two digits
99.243E	No good, the exponent is missing
.00498E87	No good, the exponent is out of range
-98.	OK, is a real constant
-98	OK, is an integer constant
PLACE	OK, is a variable
+5793	OK, is an integer constant
+57930	No good, the integer is out of range
894736452.325	OK, but only six leftmost digits are significant
-42719	No good, the integer is out of range
.000000000000968	OK, but .968E-12 is better
7,485	No good, contains a comma
A4	OK, is a variable
WEIGHT	No good, more than five characters
WATE	That's better

3-6 FORTRAN Expressions

*Expressions in FORTRAN are used to specify computations involving constants, variables and arithmetic operators. The arithmetic operators are +, -, *, / and ** which represent addition, subtraction, multiplication, division and exponentiation (to the power), respectively.* If all the constants and variables in an expression are real, the expression is said to be in real mode. If all of the constants and variables in an expression are integers, then the expression is said to be in integer mode. If both real and integer constants and variables are combined in a single expression, the expression is said to be in mixed mode, except that an integer exponent in an otherwise real expression does not alter the real mode of the expression.

The simplest possible expression would be a single constant or variable. *Any expression may be enclosed in parentheses* to denote the sequence in which arithmetic operations are to be performed, just as parentheses are used in algebra. For every left parenthesis there must be a right parenthesis; this is called balancing the parentheses. The sequence of operations is also implied by the operators used. In any expression exponentiation will be performed first, followed by multiplication and division, followed by addition and subtraction, except as indicated otherwise by parentheses.

Nested parentheses can be used to control the sequence of operations in complicated expressions. When multiple pairs of parentheses are present, operations will be performed from inside the innermost parentheses to the outermost parentheses, using the implied sequence of operations within each pair of parentheses.

Two operators may never appear adjacent to each other. The multiplication operator (*) must be used; multiplication cannot be implied simply by writing constants and variables next to each other (e.g., 3M does not mean 3*M).

A special case is represented by the expression A**B**C. In 1130 FORTRAN, A**B**C is taken to mean A**(B**C), which is not at all the same as (A**B)**C. In other words, A**B**C specifies that A will be raised to the power of (B to the power of C).

A word of caution is in order concerning mixed mode expressions. Although 1130 FORTRAN accepts such expressions (many other FORTRAN systems do not), all mixed expressions are evaluated or computed in the real (floating-point) format. This means that all integer constants and variables appearing in mixed mode expressions will be converted or reformatted into floating-point notation each time that the expression is evaluated. Since the conversion can needlessly use up time on the computer, mixed mode expressions should be used sparingly. Instead of X + 1, X + 1. is more efficient.

3-7   Common Errors in Expressions

The most common error in previous FORTRAN systems probably consisted of inadvertently writing in mixed mode. Since mixed mode expressions are permitted in 1130 FORTRAN, we will have to be aware of the less common errors listed below:

Expression	Explanation	Mode Implied
A	OK	Real
(A)	OK	Real
((A))	OK	Real
5.*A	OK, 5. times A	Real
5 *A	OK, 5 times A	Mixed
5*L	OK, 5 times L	Integer
5L	No good, no * operator	Integer
(5*L)	OK, 5 times L	Integer
((5*L)	No good, ( ) don't balance	Integer
ACC*WATE/G	OK, ACC times WATE over G	Real
A + B**I	OK, A plus B to the power of I	Real
A+−B	No good, two adjacent operators	Real
A+(−B)	OK, but A−B is better	Real
A/B + C	OK, (A/B) plus C	Real
A/(B + C)	OK, A/(B + C)	Real
A + B * C	OK, A plus (B*C)	Real

Division in integer mode causes any remainder to be lost: ten divided by four is two in integer arithmetic.

3-8   FORTRAN Arithmetic Statements

The actual computation of answers in FORTRAN programs is specified by arithmetic statements such as

AREA = 3.1416 * (DIAM * .05) ** 2

The statement always consists of a single variable (never a constant) to the left of the equal sign and a valid FORTRAN expression to the right of the equal sign.

The equal sign in an arithmetic statement does not carry the same meaning as does the equal sign in an algebraic equation. In an arithmetic statement the equal sign means "is replaced by" rather than "is equal to." The above arithmetic statement is a command to replace the current value of the variable AREA with the computed value of the expression 3.1416 * (DIAM * 0.5) ** 2. Consider the statement

N = N + 1

In algebra the above statement would be meaningless, but in FORTRAN the meaning is: "The value of N is replaced by the value of N plus one." To execute the statement the computer will load the bit pattern of a word in core memory representing the value of N into the accumulator register, add the bit pattern of a word representing the constant 1, and store the bit pattern representing the sum back into the word which represents the value of N. After the execution of the statement, the variable N will be larger by one than N was before the statement was executed.

The variable on the left of an arithmetic statement and the expression on the right of the equal sign do not have to be in the same mode. For example, the statement

A = J + K

would cause the computer to compute the integer value of J plus K, convert the resulting sum to floating-point format, and store the floating-point value in A (assuming that A is a real variable and that J and K are integers). Similarly, the statement

LENTH = WIDTH

would cause the computer to convert the real variable WIDTH to integer notation and store the integer value in LENTH.

The following is a list of valid FORTRAN arithmetic statements gathered from programs to be developed in later chapters. In reading these statements, try

40

to determine the sequence of arithmetic operations commanded by each statement.

```
RZERO = ALT + RADUS
KSQR = K * K
VCIRC = VESCP/1.414214
PHID = -90.
TIME = 0.
R = RMAX*C3*C3
C1 = ((TIME + TZERO)/C2)**.6666667
TZERO = C2*(ECC*PAR - PAR)
SLOPE = (FX - FLAST)/(X - XLAST)
TRIAL = FACTR*X+(1.-FACTR)*FX
NEXT = 16*(K1-1)+4*(K2-1)+K3
M2 = -1
NEWMV = 100*(L1+1)+10*(L3+1)+L2-4*L3
```

Notice that although spaces must not be written between the characters of a variable name or constant, spaces or blanks may be used between operators, constants and variables to improve the readability of FORTRAN statements.

3-9 Simple READ and WRITE Statements

All the values of the variables used in any FORTRAN program become available for computation in one of two ways: *either the values are read into core memory through the use of READ statements, or else the values appear to the left of an equal sign (=) in an arithmetic statement.* In the small FORTRAN program of Section 3-1, the value of the variable AREA is obtained from an arithmetic statement, while DIAM is read into memory by a READ statement.

The first time variable names such as AREA and DIAM are encountered by the FORTRAN compiler, the names are entered into a dictionary or symbol table which enables the FORTRAN compiler to associate each variable name with the address of a word or words in core memory. If the same variable names are encountered in other statements later in the same program, the FORTRAN compiler will associate the names with the previously assigned addresses in core memory. In this way the compiler is able to keep track of where the value of each variable in the program is actually stored inside the memory of the computer. Constants are handled in the same way.

Every READ statement in 1130 FORTRAN consists of the word READ followed by

1) an integer constant (unsigned) or an integer variable name specifying the unit number of the input device to be used

41

2)   an integer constant specifying the number of a FORMAT
       statement describing the format of the input data

3)   a list of variable names which corresponds to the formats described
       in a FORMAT statement. (If no variable fields are specified in the
       FORMAT statement, the list may be omitted.)

The input device number and FORMAT statement number are always enclosed in
parentheses. The READ statement in Section 3-1,

1   READ (2, 10) DIAM

referred to unit number 2, FORMAT statement number 10, and a list of variables
consisting only of the variable DIAM.

*Data to be read or written are segmented into groups of characters and
numbers called records.* A record on punched cards is a single card, and a record to
be printed is a single line for a line printer. Paper tape and magnetic tape do not have
such an obvious way of fixing the end of each record since a single reel of paper tape
or magnetic tape can hold many thousands of characters. A special code, known as a
record mark or end-of-line code, is used to signify the end of a record of data on paper
tape and magnetic tape. This record mark character is supplied automatically by the
FORTRAN system when data are written upon these devices by a FORTRAN program

Input and output unit numbers are fixed on the 1130 as shown below. The
table also includes the maximum number of characters which can be formatted in a
single record for the different input and output devices.

Unit Number	Unit Description	Maximum Record Size
1	Console Printer	120 (characters)
2	1442 Card Read Punch	80
3	1132 Printer	120 + control
4	1134/1054/1055 paper tape	80 + 80 case shifts
5	1403 Printer	120
6	Console Keyboard	80
7	1627 Plotter	20
8	2501 Card Reader	80
9	1442 Model 5 Punch	80
10	Disk Storage	320

The use of a carriage control character on line printers is discussed in Section 5-6.
Formatted magnetic tape records are held to a maximum of 144 characters per
record.

*Since the 1442 is a single path machine used for both input and output,
care must be taken to avoid punching (writing) into a card intended for reading only.*

42

This problem will arise when both READ and WRITE statements referring to the 1442 are used in a single program. A READ statement to the 1442 will cause a single card to be moved from the read hopper through the read station. A WRITE statement to the 1442 will cause a card to move from the read station through the punch station, or if no card is at the read station, a card will move all the way from the read hopper through the punch station. If a READ statement is followed by a WRITE statement, the WRITE statement will punch into the last card which has been read. This is useful in some programs. When reading and punching of the same card is not desired, an extra READ statement without a list of variable names should be inserted between the last READ statement and the first WRITE statement.

The unit number in a READ or WRITE statement may be specified by the current value of an integer variable. For example,

    NCRDS = 2
    READ (NCRDS, 10) DIAM

would have exactly the same result as

    READ (2,10) DIAM

The ability to use integer variables to designate unit numbers allows the programmer to run a single FORTRAN program on many different types of computers with different input and output unit numbers. Some of the programs in this book were first run on an IBM 7094, a computer very unlike the 1130 system. The usual input unit for data on punched cards on the 7094 is unit number 5. By simply changing the statement

    NCRDS = 2

to a statement

    NCRDS = 5

the program could read punched card input on the 7094. Since there are usually several READ statements in a single program, it is much easier to change the value of the integer variable NCRDS once than to change the unit number in every READ statement in the program.

The FORMAT statement number must be specified by an integer; a variable name cannot be used. FORMAT statements are described in Section 3-10.

The list of variable names may consist of many variables separated by commas. There is no limit on the number of variables which may be read by a single READ statement, and both real and integer variables may appear in the list in any sequence.

43

The *WRITE statement is used to transmit variables from core memory to an output device in the same way that the READ statement is used to transmit variables from an input device to core memory.* The same rules apply to input and output unit numbers, FORMAT statement numbers, and variable lists in both READ and WRITE statements. Other features of READ and WRITE statements, such as the ability to handle arrays of variables and indexed lists, will be described in Chapter 5.

3-10 Simple FORMAT Statements — Numeric Conversion

FORMAT statements describe the format of data on punched cards, paper tape, or paper to be printed. FORMAT statements may appear anywhere in a FORTRAN program before the END. The same FORMAT statement may be referenced by several READ and WRITE statements.

In the past FORMAT statements have been the most common cause of programming errors by beginning FORTRAN programmers. We will cover the basic forms of numeric conversion in this section, basic alphameric conversion in Section 3-11, and multiline formats and arrays in Chapter 5.

Numeric conversion refers to the conversion of real and integer type numbers in core memory to EBCDIC code (Section 2-5) and to the further conversion required to convert EBCDIC code to the code of a particular output device such as the 1442 Card Read Punch (Section 2-6), the 1055 Paper Tape Punch (Section 2-7), the Console Typewriter (Section 2-8) or the 1132 Printer (Section 2-9). This conversion takes place during a WRITE operation from core memory to the output device, and conversion must also take place in the reverse sequence when numeric data is read from any input device and converted to EBCDIC and then to real or integer type format in core memory by a READ operation. The actual code conversions are handled by instructions called into action by the FORTRAN compiler. When programming in the FORTRAN language, it is only necessary to indicate the type of conversion desired and how many card columns, paper tape rows, or typewriter character positions will be affected. *Three kinds of numeric conversion are provided: I (for integer) conversion, F (for fixed decimal point) conversion and E (for exponential notation) conversion.*

I Conversion

The general form used to specify I conversion is Iw, where I indicates I conversion and the w indicates the field width; i.e., the number of digits or the number of columns or characters to be used. (An example is I4, indicating a field width of four digits.) If, during a WRITE operation, the number to be written is larger than the field width (for example, writing 12473 with an I4 specification) a field of asterisks (****) will be written on the output device. Some examples of printed output which might be written using a specification of I4 are shown below:

Value in Core Memory	Printed Output
28493	****
0001	1
-63	-63
-487	-487
1.43	Error, not an integer
58.8	Error, not an integer

Notice that leading zeros are replaced by blank characters. Remember that the largest number that can be represented in core memory in FORTRAN integer format is 32767, which effectively limits the size of numbers which can be read or written using I conversion. The largest negative integer is -32768.

F Conversion

The general form of F conversion is Fw.d, where F indicates F conversion, w indicates the field width, and d indicates the number of digits to the right of the decimal point. An example is F10.3, indicating a field width of ten digits or characters with three digits to the right of the decimal point. The field width must be large enough to contain space for both the decimal point and the sign of the number during WRITE operations. For READ operations the sign and the decimal point may be left out of the data field on punched cards or paper tape; if they are left out, the decimal point will be implied where specified by the F specification. If a decimal point is present in the data field coming into the computer during a READ operation, the decimal point location in the data will override the decimal point location in the F specification. If a number during a WRITE operation is too large for the whole number part of the specified field width, a field of asterisks will be written. Below are examples of printed output which might be written using a specification of F6.2:

Value in Core Memory	Printed Output
3475.38	******
-.4	-.40
93	Error, not floating point
8.3947	8.39
136	Error, not floating point
3.75	3.75

Leading zeros are replaced by blanks. Only real (floating-point) variables can be designated for F conversion; integer variables such as 93 or 136 will not be converted. Remember that the largest floating-point number contains about 9.3 digits in extended range (three-word format) as described in Section 2-4. If the number to be written contains more digits in its decimal fraction than are provided for in the d part of the specification, the extra digits will be truncated or dropped off as shown in the example of 8.3947.

E Conversion

The general form of E conversion is Ew.d, where E indicates E conversion, w indicates the field width, and d indicates the number of digits to the right of the decimal point. (An example is E10.3, indicating a field of ten digits with three digits to the right of the decimal point.) The field width must now be large enough to contain the sign of the number, the decimal point, the letter E and three spaces or digit positions for the exponent. E conversion is exponential notation conversion, which means that E conversion is best suited for real variables with a wide range of magnitudes.

During READ operations it is not necessary to provide space for the sign of the number. The exponent may be signed or unsigned and may consist of one or two digits, but it must not exceed 38 (see Section 2-4). The value of a number in exponential notation is the fractional part of the number times ten to the exponent power. During READ operations the letter E may be left out of the exponent, but if this is done the exponent must start with either a plus sign or a minus sign. During READ operations the exponent may also be left out entirely; this results in F conversion format which is acceptable as input to an E specification. Data in E format is also acceptable as input to an F specification. As in F conversion, the decimal point may be left out of data fields coming into the computer during a READ, causing the decimal point position to be implied by the E specification in the FORMAT statement. Also, a decimal point may be present in the input data in a position other than that specified by the E specification; if the decimal point is present in the data, it will override the decimal point in the E specification. The examples below show printed output which could be written using a specification of E10.3:

Value in Core Memory	Printed Output
49.6378	.496E 02
−839.6	−.839E 03
−.0000456	−.456E−04
.3675	.367E 00
−45	Error, not floating point

As in the case of F conversion, an integer variable presented for E conversion will not be converted.

I, F and E specifications usually require that all data to be read into the computer be right-justified; i.e., that there be no blank columns to the right of the data in the input field. No blank columns may appear between the characters in an input field, but blanks may appear to the right or left of the characters. Blanks, however, are read as zeros, and right-hand blanks will change the value of the data.

In a typical FORMAT statement the above specifications are written as a list separated by commas, with the whole list enclosed in parentheses. The specifications in the list are associated with the variable names in the READ or WRITE statement which referred to the FORMAT statement. As an example, the statements

$$WRITE \ (3,11) \ J, \ A, \ B, \ C$$
11   FORMAT (I4, F10.3, E10.2, F8.4)

would produce the following printed output if J = 438, A = 59.4367, B = .000000497 and C = 1.99684:

438   59.436   .49E–06   1.9968

An unsigned integer in front of the I, F or E specification can cause the specification to be repeated for several variables. For example,

1   FORMAT (3F10.4)

is equivalent to

1   FORMAT (F10.4, F10.4, F10.4)

3-11   Simple FORMAT Statements — Alphameric Conversion

It is necessary to be able to describe input and output formats involving letters and special characters as well as the I, F and E specifications for numeric data conversion described in the previous section. Three specifications are provided for alphameric data: the quote, H and A specifications. The A and H specifications are discussed in Section 5-5.

Quote Conversion

The quote specification allows the programmer simply to place strings of letters and special characters within quote marks in a FORMAT statement so that the characters in the string will be printed or punched out by a WRITE statement. If a string of characters surrounded by quote marks is used in a FORMAT

47

statement referenced by a READ statement, the READ statement will cause the string of characters between the quote marks to be replaced by the same number of characters coming into the computer from the input record (such as a punched card or paper tape) being read. Quote conversion does not require that the programmer count the number of characters in the string; quote conversion is thus less subject to error and should be used whenever possible in preference to A and H conversion. If it is necessary to put the quote character in an output message, a pair of quotes ('') will cause a single ' to be printed.

As an example, consider statement 11 of Section 3-1:

11   FORMAT (' FOR A DIAMETER OF', F10.3, ' THE AREA IS', F10.3)

The WRITE statement in Section 3-1 which referenced statement 11 is

WRITE (1,11) DIAM, AREA

The WRITE statement will cause the characters FOR A DIAMETER OF to be printed on the console typewriter, followed by a ten-character field for the value of DIAM, followed by the characters THE AREA IS, followed finally by a ten-character field for the value of the variable AREA. For a DIAM value of 10. the WRITE statement would produce

FOR A DIAMETER OF   10.000 THE AREA IS   78.540

If FORMAT statement 11 were referenced by a READ statement, 17 characters (the exact number of characters in FOR A DIAMETER OF) would be read into the first pair of quotes in the FORMAT statement, the next ten characters would be converted into a real variable by the F10.3 specification, the next 12 characters (the number of characters in THE AREA IS including blanks) would be read into the second pair of quotes in the FORMAT statement, and the next ten characters would be converted into a real variable by the second F10.3 specification. The characters read in would replace any previous characters in the FORMAT statement. The total number of characters specified in FORMAT statement 11 is $17 + 10 + 12 + 10 = 49$, so card columns 1-49 would be converted if statement 11 were referenced by a READ statement using card input. The card columns after column 49 would not be used.

3-12   GO TO Statements

The statement GO TO 1 in the FORTRAN program of Section 3-1 is used to transfer control of the program unconditionally to statement 1, which will cause statement 1 to be executed immediately after the statement GO TO 1. In this way the program can be made to repeat a sequence of FORTRAN statements. In Section 3-1 the sequence of statements caused the computer repeatedly to read

48

cards containing a diameter, to compute the area of a circle from the diameter and finally to write the diameter and area upon the console typewriter.

The GO TO statement is a control statement which may transfer to any executable statement in the FORTRAN program. An executable statement is a statement which causes the computer to take some specific action each time the statement is encountered as the statements are executed in sequence. READ, WRITE and arithmetic statements are examples of executable statements; FORMAT, TYPE and END statements are not executable. FORMAT statements carry information about input-output formats to be used by READ and WRITE statements; a single FORMAT statement can be referenced by many different READ and WRITE statements. FORMAT statements are used only by the READ and WRITE statements which refer to them and can be located anywhere in the sequence of statements in a FORTRAN program. TYPE and END statements carry information to be used by the FORTRAN compiler in compiling the object program.

3-13   IF Statements

The GO TO statement of Section 3-11 provided an unconditional transfer to another executable statement. GO TO statements cannot handle conditional transfers. Conditional transfers are needed to branch to another part of the program after a group of statements has been executed perhaps ten times or to branch whenever the value of a program variable exceeds the value of a constant or another variable. *Conditional transfers are handled in the FORTRAN language by IF statements and by the computed GO TO statement,* which will be discussed in Chapter 5. The IF statement really means "test and branch."

An example of an IF statement is

IF (B**3 + 8.) 29, 473, 14

where the parentheses may contain any valid FORTRAN expression (which may itself contain parentheses) and the numbers 29, 473 and 14 refer to the three statement numbers to which control will be transferred. If (when the IF statement is executed) the current value of the expression in parentheses is negative, control will go to the first statement (number 29 in the example). If the current value of the expression is zero, control will go to the second statement (number 473 in the example). If the current value of the expression is greater than zero, control will go to the third statement (number 14 in the example).

3-14   Conditional Transfers and Program Loops

As an example of the use of IF statements, consider the problem of computing ten values of AREA from ten values of DIAM in the program of Section 3-1

49

and then transferring control to another part of the program at some new statement number 345. To do this, one must

    a)   set up a new variable to count the AREAs computed

    b)   increment the new variable once for each AREA

    c)   test the new variable to see if ten AREAs have been computed

    d)   transfer to statement 345 or compute the next AREA.

The resulting program might appear as follows:

```
        NUMBR = 1
1       READ (2 10) DIAM
        AREA = 3.1416 * (DIAM * 0.5) ** 2
        WRITE (1,11) DIAM, AREA
        NUMBR = NUMBR + 1
        IF (NUMBR – 10) 1, 1, 345
10      FORMAT (F10.3)
11      FORMAT (' FOR A DIAMETER OF', F10.3, ' THE AREA IS', F10.3)
345     STOP
        END
```

The new variable which will keep track of the number of AREAs is NUMBR. The statement NUMBR = 1 sets up or initializes NUMBR; the statement NUMBR = NUMBR + 1 increments NUMBR by one for each AREA computed; the IF statement tests NUMBR and transfers to statement 345 if NUMBR is greater than ten; otherwise control will go back to statement 1. NUMBR is made an integer variable because integer arithmetic executes faster than floating-point arithmetic and is less subject to roundoff or truncation errors. In general, counting in FORTRAN should be done with integers.

The statements starting with statement 1 and ending with the IF statement constitute a loop of statements which will be executed ten times before control is finally transferred to statement 345. Notice that the statement which initializes NUMBR must be outside the loop. The four requirements of initializing, incrementing, testing and transferring are basic to all repetitive or looping operations in digital computers.

The statement 345 is a STOP statement which serves to stop the computer at the end of a program. The STOP statement is further discussed in Section 5-8 with the END statement which is always the last statement in any FORTRAN program.

3-15   Summary and Further Examples

In this chapter we have presented enough of the 1130 FORTRAN language to permit writing simple but complete programs. Additional FORTRAN capabilities, including more FORMAT options, are developed in succeeding chapters. The problems of Section 3-15 will serve to develop the familiarity with basic FORTRAN which will be needed when we move on to more complex applications.

Consider the area of a triangle, equal to half of the base dimension of the triangle times the height of the triangle. Suppose that we wanted to read pairs of bases and heights and calculate the areas of the resulting triangles, printing the results of the calculation only if the area exceeds ten square inches. Now we must use an IF statement to determine whether or not to print the results. The program is

```
C------ THIS PROGRAM COMPUTES THE AREAS OF TRIANGLES.
C------ ONLY AREAS GREATER THAN 10 SQUARE INCHES WILL BE PRINTED.
       NCRDS = 2
       NWRIT = 1
12     READ (NCRDS, 21) BASE, HITE
       AREA = 0.5 * BASE * HITE
       IF (AREA - 10.) 12, 12, 10
10     WRITE (NWRIT, 20) BASE, HITE, AREA
       GO TO 12
21     FORMAT (2F10.3)
20     FORMAT (' FOR A BASE OF', F10.3, ' AND A HEIGHT OF', F10.3
      X' THE AREA IS', F10.3)
       END
```

Notice that the IF statement makes the decision whether or not to print. FORMAT statement 20 continues on a second card as indicated by the X in column six. Two variables, NCRDS and NWRIT, are used to designate the unit numbers for the card reader and the typewriter. The statements which assign values to NCRDS and NWRIT are located ahead of statement 12 so that they will only be executed once at the beginning of the program. Why is this desirable?

Notice also that we are multiplying by 0.5 rather than dividing by two in the statement which computes the AREA. Multiplication is preferable to division because multiplication can be performed more rapidly than division.

Rather than print out FOR A BASE OF and AND A HEIGHT OF on each line we might prefer to print three column headings at the top of the printed output report and then simply print three columns of numbers for BASE, HITE and AREA. We could set this up by putting the following statements ahead of statement 12:

```
        WRITE (NWRIT, 30)
30      FORMAT (' TRIANGLE AREA REPORT, MAY 15, 1968, FROM JOHN
        XSMITH')
        WRITE (NWRIT, 31)
31      FORMAT (' BASE OF TRIANGLE  HEIGHT OF TRIANGLE   RESULTING
        XAREA')
```

Statement 20 inside the original program would now be changed to read

```
20      FORMAT (F10.3, 2F20.3)
```

The WRITE statements referring to FORMAT statements 30 and 31 will set up the column headings and the F20.3 specification in FORMAT statement 20 will space the calculated results so as to fall under the column headings.

3-16   Problems

1) Find the errors, if any, in each of the following FORTRAN statements:

```
    C = A + 15,600 * B
    LENTH = A - (HITE - 3.) ** 3)
    9PAC = ALPHA/BETA
    14.6 = DOG + CAT
    HEIGHT = 7. * WIDTH
    FORCE = WGT + -POINT
    JTEST - 9 = 47
    JAVA = K + 56900
```

2) What is the implied mode (real or integer) of the arithmetic expression on the right side of the above statements?

3) Find the error in the following FORMAT statements:

```
    1      FORMAT ('THE ANSWERS ARE', 3F5.6)
    2      FORMAT ('TRY THESE', 'E15.4', F15.4)
    3      FORMAT ('THE CHARACTERS ARE', 5I7.3
```

4) If the area of a triangle is half the base of the triangle times the height of the triangle, rewrite the program of Section 3-1 to compute the areas of triangles from cards containing bases and heights.

5) Write a program to calculate the sum of all the integers from 1 to 100.

6) Write a program to read 100 cards, each containing a real number, and save the value of the largest number to be typed out when the last card has been read.

7)   If A = 2., B = 4., C = 2. and D = 4., what value of X will result from execution of each of the following statements?

$$X = A * B / C * D$$
$$X = (A * B) / (C * D)$$
$$X = A * B / C / D$$

8)   Write a program which will, after reading a variable MONEY, determine the number of quarters, dimes, nickels and pennies to make an amount of change equal to MONEY using the minimum number of coins. Assume MONEY to be an integer variable in pennies.

9)   Rewrite the program of Problem 8, using instead of MONEY a real variable VALUE expressed in dollars and decimal fractions of a dollar.

10)   Write a message with the aid of your 1130. Your program, when executed, should print this message. Here is an example:

DON'T BE TOO CONFIDENT. YOU'RE ONLY BEGINNING.

I'VE FINALLY LEARNED HOW TO USE QUOTE CONVERSION.

11)   Write a program which will print geometric figures of your own choosing. The sides of these figures should be printed with suitable characters such as * or letters such as X or digits such as 0. Note that you may write this program in at least two ways: you may use quote conversion in FORMAT statements or you may input the characters, letters or digits as data with a READ statement. The second way will be the easier one after you learn more FORTRAN from Chapter 5. An example of what the output should look like is illustrated here:

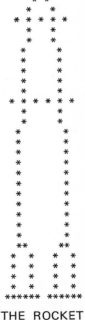

THE ROCKET

53

12) What does the following program accomplish?

```
10  READ (2,11) NUMBR
11  FORMAT (I4)
15  IF (NUMBR-1) 10,20,30
20  GO TO 35
30  IF (NUMBR-3) 40, 50, 60
35  WRITE (3, 36)
36  FORMAT (' THE NUMBER IS 1')
40  WRITE (3, 41) NUMBR
41  FORMAT (' THE NUMBER IS ', I4)
50  WRITE (3, 51) NUMBR
51  FORMAT (' THE NUMBER IS ', I4)
60  GO TO 10
    END
```

Are all the statement numbers necessary? Suppose that your input deck consists of ten cards, containing the following numbers in the first four columns of each card:

```
   2
  10
   4
   3
   1
  76
   0
   2
   1
 985
```

What will the output look like?

13) Write a program which will read ten arbitrary nonzero integers of magnitude greater than 1, and print the reciprocals of these. NOTE: If you print these reciprocals using integer mode, the output will be ten zeros; therefore, first convert the integers read into real numbers and then obtain the reciprocals and output using the F-conversion code.

14) Write a program which will read ten arbitrary real numbers of magnitude less than 1000., and print the square roots of these. Before proceeding to extract the roots note the following: First, an exponent written with an integer numerator/integer denominator fraction is equivalent to a zero exponent if the numerator of the fraction is equal to 1 and the denominator is greater than 1; hence 1/2 = 0 whereas 1./2. = 0.5. Second, the negative numbers read

will have to be screened out before the taking of the square root; you may do this with an IF statement, directing the 1130 to print the message

THE NUMBER IS NEGATIVE. THERE IS NO REAL ROOT.

or some other appropriate explanation for each such case.

15) Enhance the programs written for Problems 13 and 14 by printing table headers of your own choice. Examples:

TABLE OF RECIPROCALS

and

TABLE OF SQUARE ROOTS
NUMBER   SQUARE ROOT

16) The equation used to calculate the uniform payment PAYMT required to pay off a mortgage of amount A, interest rate I and number of payments N is

$$PAYMT = A \frac{I(1 + I)^N}{(1 + I)^N - 1}$$

Write a program to calculate PAYMT after reading A, I and N.

17) Derive the equations required and write a program to calculate and print out a table of the amount of principal and interest in each payment needed to pay off a mortgage and the balance owed after each uniform payment, reading the same input variables as in Problem 10.

18) A prime number is an integer, greater than one, which is only divisible by itself and one. Write a program to examine all the positive integers, starting with one, two, three, etc., and print out those numbers which are prime. When you run this program, stop it after a suitable number of primes have been printed by pushing the STOP button at the computer console. Make use of the fact that integer mode division drops the remainder, so that if a trial number is divided by a smaller number, the product of the smaller number and the quotient will not equal the trial number unless the smaller number is a factor of the trial number.

CHAPTER 4: RUNNING, DEBUGGING AND DOCUMENTING A PROGRAM

4-1 FORTRAN Control Records

After a FORTRAN program is written on coding forms the FORTRAN statements are usually punched into punched cards or paper tape before the statements are read into the computer to be compiled into a FORTRAN object program. Only the object program can be executed to get answers; the FORTRAN statements simply describe to the FORTRAN compiler the calculations that the object program must perform. Other information must also be furnished to the compiler besides the FORTRAN statements themselves. The additional information, known as control records, tells the compiler what to print out during the compilation process, what input and output units will be used by the program, the name of the program, and any other information that the programmer wishes to have printed along with the program.

In this chapter we will consider in detail only those control records required by the 1130 FORTRAN compiler. The disk storage monitor requires additional control records which are discussed in Chapter 7. Also, we will assume that the FORTRAN statements (source program) have been punched on punched cards, as is the case in most 1130 installations. The procedures involved in the use of paper tape are similar, from the standpoint of control records and console operations, to the card version procedures.

The control records are punched with an asterisk in column one. An asterisk in both columns one and two indicates that the record is a comment to be printed at the top of each page during compilation. Any unrecognizable record is ignored by the compiler. A single asterisk followed by NAME and a word of one to five characters provides a method for naming main programs. The name will then be punched starting in column 73 of each card in the object deck, and will also be printed on each page during compilation. Blank columns are ignored in all FORTRAN control records. A list of FORTRAN control records follows:

```
** A COMMENT MESSAGE, CONTAINING NAME, DATE, OR JOB NUMBER
 * NAME AREAS
 * IOCS (CARD, TYPEWRITER, KEYBOARD, 1132 PRINTER, DISK, PAPER TAPE,
        MAGNETIC TAPE, 2501 READER, 1442 PUNCH, 1403 PRINTER, PLOTTER,
        UDISK)
 * LIST SOURCE PROGRAM
 * LIST SUBPROGRAM NAMES
 * LIST SYMBOL TABLE
 * LIST ALL
 * EXTENDED PRECISION
 * ONE WORD INTEGERS
```

```
*  ARITHMETIC TRACE
*  TRANSFER TRACE
*  ORIGIN  xxxxx
```

Punched cards or paper tape records containing the FORTRAN control records are placed ahead of the first FORTRAN statement of the program to be compiled. The control records may be in any sequence.

The * NAME record is used to provide a name by which main programs may be referred to by the Disk Monitor program in later loading and storing operations. The * NAME record is not used with subroutines (Chapter 6) because subroutines are named in either FUNCTION or SUBROUTINE statements. The name of the program in the * NAME record starts with the first nonblank character after the word NAME.

The * IOCS record is used to tell the compiler what input and output units will be used by the program being compiled. The compiler cannot get this information from the READ and WRITE statements in the program because integer variables may be used for input-output unit designations (Section 3-9), so the * IOCS record must be used with every program. The input and output units are specified by a list of words separated by commas and enclosed in parentheses. All allowable units are included in the above list; the units not used should be deleted. KEYBOARD refers to input to the computer through the typewriter keyboard. CARD refers to the 1442 Card Read Punch; CARD cannot be used in combination with 1442 PUNCH, which refers to the punch-only model of the 1442. The * IOCS record is used only for main programs; subroutines (Chapter 6) must use the IOCS units selected by the main program which calls the subroutines. Several * IOCS records may be used if needed.

The * LIST SOURCE PROGRAM record will cause the FORTRAN source statements to be printed during compilation. The * LIST SUBPROGRAM NAMES will produce a listing of all subroutines and subprograms used by the program being compiled, such as input and formatting routines. The * LIST SYMBOL TABLE will cause the absolute or relative location in core memory of each variable, constant, and statement number in the program to be printed during compilation. The * LIST ALL record will list everything described in this paragraph.

The * EXTENDED PRECISION record specifies that each real variable in the program will be assigned to three words of memory (instead of two), and will provide a precision of about 9.3 decimal digits (Section 2-4). All integers will then be assigned to three words of memory, unless * ONE WORD INTEGERS is present. * ONE WORD INTEGERS will cause each integer to be stored in a single word of core memory; otherwise integers will be assigned to the same number of words in memory as real variables, even though the magnitude of the integers must still fall between −32,768 and +32,767. USASI Basic FORTRAN standards, set up to encourage compatibility between FORTRAN systems on different types of computers, require that both real and integer variables and constants normally use the same amount of memory. Since the * ONE WORD INTEGERS specification will usually save a considerable amount of core memory, it should be used with all 1130 programs containing integer variables or constants.

Two trace specifications, * ARITHMETIC TRACE and * TRANSFER TRACE, are available to help in debugging (checking out) FORTRAN programs. * ARITHMETIC TRACE will cause every result which is passed across an equal sign in an arithmetic statement to be printed during execution (not compilation) of the program when Console Entry Switch 15 is up. Integer results are printed in I6 format with a preceding asterisk, and real results are printed in E15.8 or E17.10 format, depending on precision, with a preceding asterisk. In a similar manner the * TRANSFER TRACE will print the expression values of all IF statements with a double asterisk, and also print the index of every COMPUTED GO TO statement (to be covered in Chapter 5) with a triple asterisk during the execution of the program if Console Entry Switch 15 is on.

It is possible to trace only part of a program through the use of special FORTRAN call statements in the program to control the starting and stopping of trace operations. The statement

CALL TSTOP

will stop the tracing operation even if Console Entry Switch 15 is on, and the statement

CALL TSTRT

will restart the tracing operation if it has been previously stopped by the use of CALL TSTOP. Three conditions must be satisfied to permit tracing:

1) The * ARITHMETIC TRACE and/or * TRANSFER TRACE records must be used

2) Console Entry Switch 15 must be on during program execution

3) Either CALL TSTOP has not been executed, or else a CALL TSTRT has been executed since the last CALL TSTOP.

The * ORIGIN xxxxx record causes the compiler to produce absolute object code beginning at the address punched in the record: xxxxx represents either a decimal constant in the range 0-32,767, or a hexadecimal constant, preceded by a '/', in the range 0000-7FFF. This record may be used in 1130 systems operating under the Disk Monitor System, Version 2, Level 4 (DMS V2L4) and higher.

As an example of the use of FORTRAN control records, consider the following listing for the AREAS program of Section 3-13:

```
**   AREAS PROGRAM, WRITTEN BY JOHN DOE, 5/30/68
*   NAME AREAS
*   IOCS (CARD, TYPEWRITER)
*   ONE WORD INTEGERS
*   LIST ALL
C-----THIS PROGRAM COMPUTES THE AREAS OF TEN CIRCLES FROM THEIR
C-----DIAMETERS.
        NUMBR = 1
1       READ (2,10) DIAM
        AREA = 3.1416 * (DIAM * 0.5) ** 2
        WRITE (1,11) DIAM, AREA
        NUMBR = NUMBR + 1
        IF (NUMBR - 10) 1, 1, 345
345     STOP
10      FORMAT (F10.3)
11      FORMAT (' FOR A DIAMETER OF', F10.3, ' THE AREA IS', F10.3)
        END
```

The first record is a comment giving the program name, author, and date for the benefit of the computer operator. The next three control records specify the program name and input-output devices to be used, and ask for a complete listing to accompany the FORTRAN statements printed during the compilation. The FORTRAN statements follow immediately behind the last control record, and the program is terminated by the usual END statement which tells the FORTRAN compiler that the last statement in the source program has been reached and that no more FORTRAN statements should be read. The above listing includes all of the FORTRAN control records and FORTRAN statements necessary to compile the AREAS program.

4-2   FORTRAN Compiler Operation

This section describes the operation of the FORTRAN compiler on 1130 systems with disk storage. Both the compiler and the compiled object program are stored upon the disk when disk storage is used, resulting in much faster compilation and execution than is possible without disk storage. The details of card reader and console operation, and the resulting printed output from the compiler, are similar for both disk and non-disk oriented systems.

To cause the computer to compile and execute a FORTRAN program on a disk-oriented 1130 system it is necessary to

1)   load part of the Disk Monitor program into core memory from disk storage

2)   cause the Disk Monitor program to load the FORTRAN compiler program from disk storage to core memory

3)   compile the source program and store the compiled program on the disk

4)   load the compiled program (object program) back into core memory and execute it to produce answers.

All of the four steps above can be controlled by a deck of control records arranged as follows:

1)   a cold start card to load part of the Disk Monitor program

2)   two monitor control records, // JOB T and // FOR, to cause the loading of the FORTRAN compiler

3)   the source program preceded by FORTRAN control records

4)   another monitor control record, // XEQ, to load and execute the compiled program.

The Disk Monitor program is a large program written by IBM to control the movement of programs and data to and from disk storage under the control of Disk Monitor control records. Chapter 7 is devoted to a discussion of disk storage operation and the various features of the Disk Monitor program.

The cold start card contains many punches per card column; it is a card containing many instructions in machine language to load part of the Disk Monitor program and transfer control of the computer to the Disk Monitor program. The cold start card is not needed if your program follows immediately behind another program which has used the Disk Monitor.

The complete deck to be sent to the computer to compile and execute the AREAS program will thus consist of the following:

```
(the cold start card)
// JOB  T
// FOR
**  AREAS PROGRAM, WRITTEN BY  JOHN  DOE, 5/30/68
*  NAME  AREAS
*  IOCS (CARD, TYPEWRITER)
*  ONE  WORD  INTEGERS
*  LIST  ALL
C-----THIS PROGRAM COMPUTES THE AREAS OF TEN CIRCLES FROM THEIR
C-----DIAMETERS.
       NUMBR = 1
1      READ (2,10) DIAM
       AREA = 3.1416 * (DIAM * 0.5) ** 2
       WRITE (1,11) DIAM, AREA
       NUMBR = NUMBR + 1
```

```
        IF (NUMBR – 10) 1, 1, 345
345     STOP
10      FORMAT (F10.3)
11      FORMAT (' FOR A DIAMETER OF', F10.3, ' THE AREA IS', F10.3)
        END
// XEQ
```
(data cards follow the // XEQ card, ten cards for ten diameters)

When the combined deck of monitor control records, FORTRAN control records and source statements has been prepared, the following console operations should be performed:

1) Push the Non-Process Run Out button on the 1442 and hold it for a couple of seconds. This will flush out any cards which may have been left in the card reader through the carelessness of a previous user.

2) Push the STOP and RESET buttons on the 1130 console.

3) Place the combined card deck in the read hopper of the 1442 (face down, nine-edge first) and push the START button on the 1442. This will cause the first card in the deck to be moved to the read station inside the 1442.

4) Set the 16 console entry switches in the off (down) position, and then push the PROGRAM LOAD button on the 1130 console. From this point on the compilation should proceed under automatic control of the Disk Monitor program.

Even if none of the * LIST control records is used, the compiler will print out the following summary information near the end of the compilation:

```
FEATURES SUPPORTED
 EXTENDED PRECISION
 ONE WORD INTEGERS
 TRANSFER TRACE
 ARITHMETIC TRACE
 IOCS
CORE REQUIREMENTS FOR (name of program)
COMMON nnnnn VARIABLES nnnnn PROGRAM nnnnn
```

where nnnnn stands for the number of words of core memory required for the COMMON area (described in Section 6-7), the program variables and the object program instructions.

If the source program contained errors which were detected by the FORTRAN compiler, the message printed will be of the form

C nn ERROR AT STATEMENT NUMBER aaaaa + bbb

where nn is the error number as listed in Appendix C, aaaaa is the first preceding statement that had a statement number, and bbb is the number of statements from the last numbered preceding statement to the statement containing the error. Specification statements (such as DIMENSION) are not part of the count of statements unless the specification statements contain errors.

The time required for a FORTRAN compilation using a 1442 Model 7 Card Read Punch will depend upon whether or not the * LIST ALL control record is used to obtain a complete program listing. If no listing is requested, the compile time will be about 30 seconds plus half a second for each FORTRAN statement. If a complete program listing is requested on the 1132 Printer, the compile time will be about 30 seconds plus 1.5 seconds for each FORTRAN statement. For very long or very complex programs, the total time may be slightly higher than indicated above.

4-3   FORTRAN Execution Operation

The execution of the compiled program should proceed immediately as requested by the // XEQ control record. The ten data cards may be followed by the // JOB card for another program; if not, then a couple of blank cards should be inserted after the last data card to permit the last data card to be read. The 1442 Card Read Punch is designed to stop on the next to last card in the read hopper to give the operator a chance to refill the hopper if he is processing a large file of cards. If this stop occurs, the last card can be read by simply pushing the START button on the 1442.

4-4   So Your Program Didn't Run

If your program did not produce answers as expected, it stopped in one of the three following situations:

    Case A: the program did not compile (the summary information at the
              end of the compilation was not printed)

    Case B: the program compiled but did not execute (it produced no output)

    Case C: the program executed but produced wrong answers.

Case A: No Compilation

This situation, once the bane of FORTRAN programmers, has now been greatly improved by the approximately five dozen error messages provided by the

1130 compiler to describe different programming mistakes which can be identified by the compiler. These error messages are listed in Appendix C. In the very unlikely event that you get neither compilation nor error messages, try to isolate the trouble by breaking up the program into smaller but still executable segments. Compile each segment separately, carefully inspecting each statement for violation of the rules listed in Chapter 3.

Case B: No Execution

If the program compiles but does not execute, some sort of tracing technique may be in order. The control records for * ARITHMETIC TRACE or * TRANSFER TRACE or both can be used, or, if these traces produce too much output for easy understanding, additional WRITE statements can be added to the program to print out intermediate results. Remember that the trace routines will print only if data switch 15 is up; the data switch allows you to trace parts of the program while running through the rest of the program at full speed. If the trace routines produce no output, the makeup of the FORTRAN execute deck and subroutine library are probably in error. Check to make sure that you are not held up by a last card stop as described in Section 4-3.

Case C: Wrong Answers

If your only trouble is getting wrong answers, you are to be congratulated! At this point you almost have a running program. First look for any strings of asterisks in the printed output. These indicate variables which were too big to fit the FORMAT which you specified for them.

The next step is to add WRITE statements to the program in an attempt to isolate the statements which are causing the errors. Use a couple of simple general purpose FORMAT statements such as

```
1       FORMAT (10I6)
2       FORMAT (5F10.3)
```

and several WRITE statements such as

```
        WRITE (3,1) I, J, K, LAST, KLOG, JNOW, MASS, NUMB
        WRITE (3,2) DOG, CAT, VELOC, ALPHA, BETA, GAMMA
```

in order to dump as many variables as possible for examination. The WRITE statements should be well scattered throughout the program to make sure that no part of the program can deviate very much from what you expected without executing one of the WRITE statements and providing evidence of misbehavior.

Next consider the use of the trace routines. Although many programmers like trace routines, we have always felt that using a trace routine was like shooting ants with a machine gun: strictly a last resort. More meaningful information can usually be obtained by adding WRITE statements to the program so that there are no big blocks of computation without printed output for checking purposes. (The extra WRITE statements can be removed after the program is debugged.) All input data should be printed out shortly after they are read to ensure that the input data are really what you expected.

If the above methods do not produce quick results, it is possible that the program is too large to be easily debugged. Experienced FORTRAN programmers try to avoid debugging more than about 50 statements at a time, and beginning programmers should probably limit the amount of untried code in a single compilation to about ten statements. The mad scientist whose first attempt at programming is a 500 statement masterpiece written as a single program will get much madder when he tries to compile and execute it. Segment the program into small blocks of statements which can be executed separately so as to restrict and isolate any programming difficulties.

A rule which is frequently ignored by beginners is the following: Every variable which is used in a WRITE statement or on the right side of the equal sign in an arithmetic statement must have been previously read by a READ statement or computed on the left side of the equal sign in an arithmetic statement. Another way of putting this is: You can't make use of variables that have not been defined by reading or computing. Check your program to make sure this fundamental rule is observed. If you do use undefined variables, you are using core memory locations which may contain any old bit pattern left over from previous operations in the computer, and as a result, anything can happen.

Another debugging technique which is used on computers with line printers like the 1132 and 1403 is the core dump. Separate utility programs are available to dump every word in core storage on the printer in hexadecimal notation. Although the core dump may seem to be a simple way to find out exactly what went on in the computer, the difficulties of hexadecimal notation combined with relating core storage addresses to program variable names make this another machine gun technique to be used, in our judgment, only as a last resort.

Roundoff and truncation errors can be introduced by various combinations of floating-point arithmetic. Attempts to divide by zero are generally ignored by the computer. Division by numbers near zero may result in floating-point overflow (exponents greater than 38). If it is necessary to divide by a variable which may go to zero, check the variable with an IF statement immediately before the division and select an alternate calculation if the variable is zero.

4-5   Program Documentation

To write and debug a computer program and produce correct answers is usually less than half of the programmer's job. The rest of the job is documenting what he has done so that others will be able to understand the results of the program, run the program on the computer and, if necessary, change the program to produce different results in the future. Program documentation is required for any program that will be run again and the documentation is best developed at the same time as the actual programming for a problem.

Although a big, complex program to be used by many people will require more formal documentation than a small, simple program to be used only by a single programmer, program documentation should always include information in each of the following areas:

1)   An abstract should briefly state the purpose of the program.

2)   A deck key should identify the card decks or paper tapes involved, how these decks or tapes are serialized, and how many cards are in each deck.

3)   A description of the method of solution and its limitations of accuracy, its restrictions of input data ranges, and its pertinent equations should explain the method of attack used in writing the program.

4)   A sample data case with the resulting printed output should illustrate the formats required for input and output.

5)   A complete program listing, such as that provided by the * LIST ALL control specifications on the FORTRAN compiler, should provide detailed programming information, including definitions of all variable names.

6)   Finally, flow diagrams should be included to enable a reader unfamiliar with the program to understand the decisions and resulting transfers in the program without having to struggle to comprehend the structure of the program from the mass of detail found in the listings.

A small program such as the program to compute the areas of circles in Section 3-1 could be adequately documented on a couple of pages. At the other extreme, a program to simulate the response of suspension bridges to high velocity wind forces could require the efforts of a large team of programmers, thousands of FORTRAN statements, and documentation running to hundres of pages. Without documentation the latter program would become worthless in a matter of weeks as the programmers became involved in other assignments and forgot the tricks and strategies which they had used as a team.

4-6   Flow Diagrams

Figure 4-1 is a complete flow diagram for the area program of Section 3-1. The basic operations of the program are enclosed within rectangles (to indicate computation), trapezoids (to indicate input-output operations) and circles (to indicate statement numbers or transfer points). The words START and END may also be enclosed within circles and used to mark the logical starting and ending points of the program. Notice that the area program as shown has a starting point but no ending point; the program always returns to statement 1 to read the next value of the diameter DIAM. The practice of putting program operations in enclosures whose shapes indicate the type of operations involved makes the flow diagram easier to read, since the basic function of any enclosure can be understood at a glance.

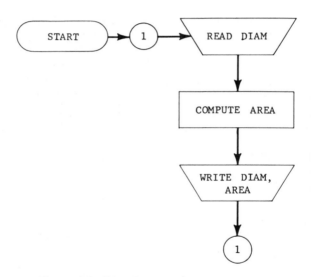

Figure 4-1   Flow Diagram for Area Program

The arrows in the flow diagram indicate the sequence of operations to be performed by the computer. Ordinarily these arrows are drawn from left to right or from top to bottom of the flow diagram. Long arrows can be avoided by terminating a short arrow in a circle containing a statement number. For example, the arrow at the bottom of Figure 4-1 could have been drawn all the way back to the trapezoid containing READ DIAM. Instead the arrow simply terminates in a circle indicating statement 1, the statement number of READ DIAM. The presence of a circle containing "1" immediately before the trapezoid containing READ DIAM indicates that READ DIAM is statement 1.

Figure 4-2 shows a flow diagram which might be used to describe the area program including an IF statement (Section 3-13). The IF statement and other conditional transfers are enclosed in diamond-shaped boxes in the flow diagram. Two or more arrows will come out of a diamond-shaped box, and the arrows should be labeled YES or NO, + or –, etc., to indicate the various alternatives of the conditional transfer.

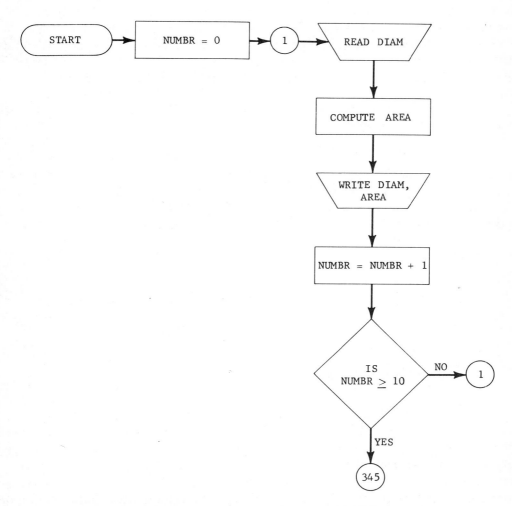

Figure 4-2   Flow Diagram for Area Program with IF Statement

Boxes indicating computation may contain actual FORTRAN statements such as NUMBR = 0, or they may contain simple descriptions such as COMPUTE AREA. Flow diagrams can be written to provide complete logical detail or simply to show the main structures of the program logic. The complexity of the program and the preferences of the programmer will determine the level of detail required.

4-7   Some Programming Hints

It must be emphasized that FORTRAN statements constitute a set of commands which the computer must attempt to execute whether the commands make any sense or not. Most calculations can be programmed in FORTRAN in several different ways, some of which will execute faster or perhaps require less core memory than others. The following hints can result in faster, more efficient programs.

Counting operations should be done with integers; floating-point should be saved for calculations involving fractions or very large numbers (larger than 32,767). Integer arithmetic is much faster in the computer since integer arithmetic is handled directly by single machine language instructions while floating-point arithmetic is performed by subroutines involving dozens of machine language instructions. In general, the 1130 system can execute about 50 integer additions in the time required to execute one floating-point addition.

When possible, multiply instead of dividing. Don't divide by five; multiply by 0.2 instead, because multiplication in both integer and floating-point arithmetic is about twice as fast as division. Take a long look at the /'s in your program and see if they cannot be replaced with an * by the reciprocal of the number you were going to use as a divisor. Subtraction, incidentally, takes exactly as long as does addition.

Don't do any calculation twice. Don't write things like

$$X = Y + A + B$$
$$Z = W + A + B$$

Instead write

$$AB = A + B$$
$$X = Y + AB$$
$$Z = W + AB$$

to avoid calculating A + B a second time. Search your program for arithmetic expressions like A + B which appear more than once and segregate them into separate statements which calculate temporary variables like AB in the example. This idea not only saves time; it saves core memory as well.

Don't READ or WRITE a lot of material which is not essential to the output your program is supposed to produce, because reading and writing usually take far more time than computing. It is good practice to write out the input data used in a calculation to make sure that the computer actually read the numbers you thought it read, but elaborate FORMAT statements which must be read or written many times during the execution of the program may not be worth the time or the memory required to process them.

68

4-8   A Program to Make Change

Consider the problem of writing a program which will read an amount in dollars and cents and then calculate and print the smallest number of dollars, quarters, dimes, nickels and pennies required to equal the original amount. The program might be written as follows:

```
C-----THIS PROGRAM COMPUTES CHANGE FROM DOLLAR AMOUNTS.
C-----READ THE DOLLAR AMOUNT TO BE ANALYZED.
      NREAD = 6
      NWRIT = 1
20    READ (NREAD, 21) AMONT
21    FORMAT (F5.2)
C-----NOW CALCULATE THE REQUIRED CHANGE.
      NCENT = 100. * AMONT + .5
C-----NCENT IS THE NUMBER OF CENTS IN THE AMOUNT.
      NDOLL = NCENT/100
      NCENT = NCENT - 100 * NDOLL
C-----NDOLL IS THE NUMBER OF DOLLARS REQUIRED.
      NQUAR = NCENT/25
      NCENT = NCENT - 25 * NQUAR
C-----NQUAR IS THE NUMBER OF QUARTERS REQUIRED.
      NDIME = NCENT/10
      NCENT = NCENT - 10 * NDIME
C-----NDIME IS THE NUMBER OF DIMES REQUIRED.
      NICKL = NCENT/5
      NCENT = NCENT - 5 * NICKL
C-----NICKL IS THE NUMBER OF NICKELS REQUIRED.
C-----NCENT IS NOW THE NUMBER OF PENNIES REQUIRED.
C-----NOW PRINT THE CHANGE REQUIRED.
      WRITE (NWRIT, 19) AMONT, NDOLL, NQUAR, NDIME, NICKL, NCENT
19    FORMAT (F5.2, ' AMOUNT,', I5, ' DOLLARS,' I5, ' QUARTERS,',
      XI5, ' DIMES,', I5, ' NICKELS,', I5, ' PENNIES.')
C-----GO TO BEGINNING OF PROGRAM TO READ NEXT AMOUNT.
      GO TO 20
      END
```

After reading the amount, the program calculates the number of cents in the amount as the integer variable NCENT. The addition of .5 insures that NCENT will not be one cent off due to rounding (see Section 6-1). Then the program subtracts the number of dollars, quarters, dimes, nickels and pennies which can be divided into NCENT. The variable NCENT is reduced by 25 for each quarter, by ten for each dime, etc. The required change (together with the original amount) is printed, and the next amount is then read. Notice that units 1 and 6 are used for input and output; unit 1 is the console typewriter. In analyzing this program remember that the remainder is dropped in integer division; for example, 90 divided by 25 equals 3.

The variable AMONT is read in floating-point format. An example of AMONT could be 5.93, which would require five dollars, three quarters, one dime, one nickel and three pennies.

4-9   Problems

1) Draw a flow diagram for the program of Section 4-8.

2) Show how the program might be changed to handle half dollars in addition to quarters, dimes, nickels and pennies.

3) Write a program to accept as input a quantity of coins of various denominations (quarters, dimes, nickels and pennies) and calculate the dollar and cents value of the quantity of coins.

4) Draw a flow diagram for the program of Problem 3.

5) The following program is correct. However, using a few elementary programming hints given in this chapter, you may be able to rewrite it to accomplish the same computational tasks.

```
        SUM = 0.
        ADD = 1.
5       SUM = SUM + ADD
        ADD = ADD + 1.
        WRITE (3,10) SUM
10      FORMAT (' ', F5.0)
        IF (SUM – 500.) 5, 5, 15
15      RATIO = SUM/ADD
        SUM = SUM/500.
        ADD = ADD/32.
        WRITE (3,20) RATIO, SUM, ADD
20      FORMAT ('0', 3F8.5)
        END
```

6) What FORTRAN control record would be necessary to make the 1132 printer print the complete program of Problem 5 before proceeding to execute it?

7) Even if only one FORTRAN control record card was used, what monitor control record cards would still be required? Can you name the FORTRAN control record card which would be required under all circumstances?

8) What FORTRAN control records help in debugging (checking out) FORTRAN programs? Should these control record cards be included routinely?

9) Ordinarily, variables used in a FORTRAN program are assigned two words of memory. What FORTRAN control record should be used to permit the assignment of three words of memory to each simple variable?

10) What FORTRAN control record is used to save core memory space? Is it advisable to use it in all FORTRAN programs? Should it be used only in FORTRAN programs containing real variables? In FORTRAN programs containing integer variables?

11) The FORTRAN control record message

    ** A COMMENT MESSAGE, ETC.

    is used to provide comments such as program name, the name of the author, dates, and other useful information. Why can't it be replaced with the usual FORTRAN comment below?

    C-----A COMMENT MESSAGE, ETC.

12) Could portions of your program be separated by blank lines? By blank lines with a C in column 1? By blank lines with ** in columns 1 and 2? By lines containing 72 asterisks (*)? Are there other ways to make your program listing more readable?

CHAPTER 5: MORE FORTRAN

5-1   Subscripted Variables

The variables presented in Chapters 3 and 4 are scalar variables; each variable represents the value of a single number. Many computing applications, however, can be programmed more easily if a variable name represents a list of numbers, a table of numbers or a three-dimensional block of numbers. We might want to find the area resulting from each of a list of ten diameters or the size of loan payments from a table whose rows represent various interest rates and whose columns represent the number of payments required to pay off the loan. Or we might want to compute statistical functions of a distribution of wind velocities contained in an array so that each value of wind velocity was identified by coordinates in three-dimensional space.

Ordinary mathematical notation involving subscripts could be used to represent these variables. We might write A_i for the ith value of AREA, $P_{j,k}$ for the payment of interest rate j and number of payments k, or $V_{l,m,n}$ for the wind velocity at space coordinates l, m and n. In FORTRAN we might write these variables as AREA(I), PAYMT(J, K) and VELOC(L,M,N). The second AREA could be written as AREA(2), the payment in the fourth row and third column as PAYMT(4, 3) and the wind velocity at coordinates 21, 53 and 9 as VELOC(21, 53, 9).

The subscripted variables in the preceding paragraph describe groups of scalar variables arranged in a particular order. *In FORTRAN terminology all subscripted variables may be referred to as arrays,* representing one-, two- or three-dimensional groups of scalar variables. A particular scalar variable, such as PAYMT (4, 3), would be referred to as an element of the PAYMT array.

Since subscripts are used only to indicate the position of an element within an array, all subscripts in FORTRAN must have the values of positive integers (not zero). Subscripts may be written as integer constants, integer variables or simple integer expressions of the type

$$N1 * J \pm N2$$

where N1 and N2 are unsigned integer constants and J is an unsigned integer variable. J may be negative or zero in value, but the expression must be a positive integer. The form of the expression, constant times variable plus or minus constant, must be followed to produce a subscript acceptable to the FORTRAN compiler. The constants or the variable or both may be absent from the expression without violating the form of the expression. Thus A(K), A(9*K), A(K-5), A(9*K-5) and A(K, 9*K, 9*K-5) are all examples of valid subscripting, while the examples shown on the following page are not.

Invalid Subscripted Variable	Explanation
A(−5)	Negative subscript
A(8+K)	Should be K+8
A(M*6−3)	Should be 6*M−3
A(J+K)	Two variables in one subscript
A(−7*N)	Constant must be unsigned
A(I+6.)	Contains floating-point constant
A(J(K))	Contains subscripted subscript

Each subscript is enclosed in parentheses, with the left parenthesis adjacent to the subscripted variable name. Two- and three-dimensional subscripts are separated by commas within the parentheses.

Subscript expressions containing a variable provide the ease of notation for which FORTRAN subscripting has been designed; the subscripts in subscripted variables like PAYMT(J,K) may be changed repeatedly to refer to different values of PAYMT. Suppose that we wish to set each element of the array PAYMT(J,K) to zero, and that we have 20 rows, or values, of J, and 50 columns, or values, of K. The total number of elements in the PAYMT array is 20*50 or 1000 elements. If constants were used as subscripts it would be necessary to write the following 1000 statements:

```
PAYMT(1,1) = 0.
PAYMT(2,1) = 0.
       *
       *
       *
PAYMT(20,1) = 0.
PAYMT(1,2) = 0.
PAYMT(2,2) = 0.
       *
       *
       *
PAYMT(20,2) = 0.
PAYMT(1,3) = 0.
PAYMT(2,3) = 0.
       *
       *
       *
PAYMT(20,50) = 0.
```

In this example all 20 values of J were used as subscripts with K equal to one. Then K was set equal to two and all 20 values of J were used again. The process was repeated until K equaled 50. Using variable subscripts, we can do the same procedure in only seven statements with the IF statement and the program looping technique introduced in Section 3-13:

```
         K = 1
3        J = 1
1        PAYMT(J,K) = 0.
         J = J + 1
         IF (J-20) 1, 1, 2
2        K = K + 1
         IF (K -50) 3, 3, 4
4        go on with the rest of the program at this point.
```

Here we initialize K and J to one, set PAYMT(1,1) to zero at statement 1, then increment and test J. If J exceeds 20, we increment and test K and reset J to one at statement 3. If J does not exceed 20, we simply go to statement 1 to set the next element of the PAYMT array equal to zero. Notice that a floating-point zero is used, since PAYMT is a real or floating-point variable unless specified as an integer. The use of a DO statement would perform this entire procedure in only three statements, as we will see in Section 5-3.

The restriction against subscripted subscripts can easily be overcome by calculating the subscripts from other subscripted variables in a separate statement. The statements

```
         M1 = NOW(J3)
         IF (MOVE(M1)) 23, 5, 23
```

are equivalent in function to

```
         IF (MOVE(NOW(J3))) 23, 5, 23
```

which is illegal because it contains a subscripted subscript. The technique of calculating subscripts from subscripted variables is known as subscript promotion.

5-2   Array Storage and the DIMENSION Statement

The elements of FORTRAN arrays are stored in descending memory locations in core storage. For example, an integer array named JOB consisting of ten elements would be stored so that JOB(1) was in the highest numbered memory location or address used by the array and JOB(10) was in the highest numbered memory location less nine, if the control specification * ONE WORD INTEGERS were in force. If JOB(1) were in memory location 3000, then JOB(10) would be in memory location 2991. When the elements of JOB are used in computations, the current value of the subscript is calculated and subtracted from one plus the address of JOB(1) to get the address of the specific element required.

When two- or three-dimensional subscripting is used, the leftmost subscripts always change more rapidly than the rightmost subscripts if we examine the storage of the resulting arrays in core memory. The ten elements of the JOB array would be

74

stored in ascending core locations as follows: JOB(10), JOB(9), JOB(8), JOB(7), JOB(6), JOB(5), JOB(4), JOB(3), JOB(2) and finally JOB(1).   The three-by-two array named PART would be stored in ascending core locations as PART(3,2), PART(2,2), PART(1,2), PART(3,1), PART(2,1) and finally PART(1,1). The three-by-two-by-two array named B would be stored in ascending core locations as B(3,2,2), B(2,2,2), B(1,2,2), B(3,1,2), B(2,1,2), B(1,1,2), B(3,2,1), B(2,2,1), B(1,2,1), B(3,1,1), B(2,1,1) and finally B(1,1,1). Real elements in arrays will occupy two or three words of memory per element, depending upon the absence or presence of the * EXTENDED PRECISION control record.

Obviously the FORTRAN compiler must have some way of determining how much memory will be required for each array in a FORTRAN source program, so that the correct number of core memory locations can be set aside to contain the values of the elements of the array when the program is executed. The programmer must tell the FORTRAN compiler exactly how many elements are needed in each array (and whether one-, two- or three-dimensional subscripting will be used) by fur- nishing DIMENSION statements at the beginning of the FORTRAN program. Consider the following DIMENSION statements:

DIMENSION AREA(10), PAYMT(20,50), VELOC(25,60,10)
DIMENSION A(1000), JOB(10), PART(3, 2), B(3, 2, 2)

In a DIMENSION statement the array name is followed by constant subscripts indicating the number of subscripts and the largest value that each subscript can attain. Any number of arrays, separated by commas, can be described in a single DIMENSION statement.

If the array name appears in a type statement (Section 3-4), the size of the array must appear in the type statement instead of in a DIMENSION statement. All type statements in a FORTRAN program must appear at the beginning of the program, followed by the DIMENSION statements (if any), followed by the executable state- ments. DIMENSION and type (and FORMAT) statements are not executable, because these statements simply furnish information to the FORTRAN compiler and do not cause the compiler to generate instructions to be executed in the object program.

Each array should be dimensioned to the largest number of elements which will be needed at any point in the execution of the program. However, arrays can take up a lot of memory in a hurry, so arrays should not be made unnecessarily large. Any two- or three-dimensional array can be treated as a one-dimensional array by the programmer, and this will occasionally save appreciable amounts of both memory and execution time. For example, an array which might ordinarily be dimensioned TABLE (20,4) could be dimensioned as TABLE(80). A single subscript N could be calculated from the two subscripts J and K of the 20-by-4 table using the statement

$$N = 20 * (K-1) + J$$

Thus program references to TABLE(J,K) could be replaced by TABLE(N). If execution speed were critical, TABLE(N) dimensioning would result in a faster running program than TABLE(J,K) dimensioning because the computer has to execute more instructions to calculate the current value of a two-dimensional subscript in the object program.

5-3   The DO and CONTINUE Statements

When looping programs were introduced in Section 3-14 it was pointed out that each loop must perform four loop control functions: initialization of the loop index or counter, incrementation of the index, testing to see if the upper limit of the index has been reached, and transferring to the beginning of the loop if the upper limit has not been reached. *The DO statement is designed to perform all of these functions in a single statement,* making the DO statement one of the most powerful statements in the FORTRAN language. A typical DO statement is

DO 100 I = J, K, L

where 100 is the number of the statement which will terminate the loop and I is a nonsubscripted integer variable which will be the loop index or counter. J, K and L are either nonsubscripted integer variables or unsigned integer constants (not zero). J represents the initial value of the loop index, K represents the last or upper limit value of the loop index, and L, if present, represents the incremental quantity to be added to the loop index after each computation of the loop. If L is not furnished in the DO statement and the comma after K is omitted, then the increment is assumed by the compiler to be one.

In summary, the DO statement above can be read as "do all statements from here through statement 100 for all values of I from J to and including K, incrementing I by L each time through the loop."

Section 5-1 contains a seven-statement program to set each element of the 20-by-50 array named PAYMT equal to zero. The same program could be programmed using DO statements in only three executable statements as follows:

```
        DIMENSION PAYMT(20,50)
        DO 1 K = 1, 50
        DO 1 J = 1, 20
1       PAYMT(J, K) = 0.
```

Here we have a DO nest consisting of two DO's, one inside the range of the other. The range of a DO includes all statements after the DO down to and including the terminal statement whose number was contained in the DO statement. Up to 25 DO's may be nested together. After each execution of statement 1, control will go to the nearest unsatisfied DO (the nearest DO which has not reached its upper limit). Control will

76

go to the DO statement with index J until J reaches 20. Then control will go to the DO statement with index K, K will be incremented by one, J will be reset to one and the J loop will be executed 20 times before K changes again. After K has been incremented to 50 (and J has been incremented to 20 a total of 50 times) control will pass on to the statement after statement 1 and at this point both DO's are said to be satisfied.

The place in the program where each function occurs will become obvious when one studies the program of Section 5-1, which is set up to duplicate the sequence of operations of the two DO loops. Initialization of the DO index actually takes place only when the DO statement is executed; the functions of incrementing, testing and transferring are all performed immediately after execution of the terminal statement of the DO (statement 1). After the DO is satisfied (after the upper limit has been surpassed by the DO index) the statement following the terminal statement will be executed, and the program will proceed to any other statements.

In Section 3-14, a program of eight statements was developed to calculate ten areas of circles from ten diameters. As a further example of DO programming, here is how that program would look using the DO statement:

```
10      FORMAT (F10.3)
11      FORMAT (' FOR A DIAMETER OF', F10.3, ' THE AREA IS', F10.3)
        DO 1 NUMBR = 1, 10
        READ (2,10) DIAM
        AREA = 3,1416 * (DIAM * 0.5) ** 2
1       WRITE (1,11) DIAM, AREA
        STOP
        END
```

The program has been reduced from eight executable statements to five. In the preceding example the DO terminated on an arithmetic statement, PAYMT(J,K) = 0., but here the DO terminates on a WRITE statement. NUMBR is not used as a subscript, but merely serves to count the ten times through the loop as NUMBR did in Section 3-14.

Any statement may be used inside the range of a DO except statements which would change the value of the DO index or any of the DO parameters (the initial value, the upper limit and the incremental value). The statement that terminates the range of the DO must be an executable statement (not a FORMAT statement) and must not be a transfer (IF or GO TO) statement or a STOP, PAUSE, RETURN, or another DO statement. The first statement after the DO must not be a FORMAT statement. A transfer statement would transfer control to some other statement before execution of the additional instructions provided at the end of each DO loop by the FORTRAN compiler to increment and test the DO index.

Since the statements in the range of a DO will be executed several times, statements which need to be executed only once (such as statements which initialize the DO) should not be placed inside the range of the DO; otherwise computer time will be wasted in the repeated execution of DO initialization statements.

Sometimes it is desirable to terminate a DO loop with an IF statement, as when going through a list of values searching for a match or an equality in the list. These cases can be handled by the *CONTINUE statement, a dummy statement which simply serves as a terminal statement for DO loops* which would otherwise terminate on a transfer statement. For example, given a TABLE of 100 elements and a variable named ENTRY, find the subscript of the element in TABLE which is equal to ENTRY:

```
      DO 1 J = 1, 100
      IF (ENTRY – TABLE(J)) 1, 2, 1
1     CONTINUE
      J = 101
      WRITE (1, 3)
3     FORMAT ('CANNOT FIND ENTRY IN TABLE')
2     WRITE (1, 4) J
4     FORMAT ('J =  ', I4)
```

The above DO loop will check ENTRY against each value of TABLE. If ENTRY is found to be equal to the Jth element of TABLE, control will go to statement 2 where the value of J will be printed by the WRITE statement. If no element in TABLE is found which is equal to ENTRY, control will go to statement 1 to CONTINUE the DO loop. The CONTINUE statement is simply the place where the FORTRAN compiler will insert the instructions to increment and test the DO index.

After 100 values of TABLE have been tested without finding an equality the DO loop will be satisfied and control will pass to the statement following CONTINUE, where J is set to 101 and the message CANNOT FIND ENTRY IN TABLE is printed. It is essential in any complete program to provide instructions to handle the situation when a DO loop is satisfied, even if you are quite sure that the situation will never occur. Sometime, perhaps due to bad input data or some other error, the DO loop will be satisfied, in which case you may have a difficult debugging job on your hands.

When a DO loop is satisfied, the value of the DO index is no longer defined; then it is necessary to redefine J as equal to 101. If an exit from the DO loop is made before the DO is satisfied, however, the DO index remains at its last value and can be used in subsequent computation. The rule that a DO index is undefined after the DO is satisfied is a basic rule of the FORTRAN language and is necessary to achieve compatibility with other FORTRAN systems on other types of computers.

The initial value of the DO index must not be set equal to zero, because there is no zeroth subscript in FORTRAN. Since all incrementation and testing takes place at the terminal statement, all the statements within the range of the DO will be executed at least once, even if the upper limit of the DO index is less than the initial value.

Restrictions have been established to limit certain tyeps of transfers in and out of the ranges of DO's. These restrictions are as follows:

1) Do not transfer into the range of a DO without executing the DO statement.

2) Transfers out of the range of a DO can be made at any time, but after a transfer out, a subsequent transfer back into the range of a DO can only be made if none of the DO parameters (the DO index, initial value, incremental value and upper limit) have been altered and if the DO either is not in a nest of DO's or is the innermost DO in a nest of DO's.

If the value of the increment is not a factor of the upper limit minus the initial value of the DO index, it is possible to satisfy a DO loop before the upper limit is reached. The DO statement

DO 50 I = 1, 15, 5

will be executed only for values of the DO index I of 1, 6 and 11 since the next value, 16, exceeds the upper limit. One must be careful that this situation does not occur by accident.

5-4   Input and Output of Arrays

Array names may be included in the list of variables furnished as part of a READ or WRITE statement. The FORTRAN compiler is able to identify the name of an array because the array name and the size of the array appeared at the beginning of the program in a DIMENSION or type statement. If PART has been dimensioned as a three-by-two array, the statements

```
      WRITE (1,50) X, Y, PART, Z
50    FORMAT (9F6.0)
```

would cause data to be printed in the sequence X, Y, PART(1,1), PART(2,1), PART(3,1), PART(1,2), PART(2,2), PART(3,2), Z. Notice that this sequence corresponds to the sequence in which the array is stored in core memory in descending core storage locations, and that the leftmost subscript varies most rapidly. A READ statement with a list containing the array name PART would cause the elements of PART to be read into core memory in the same sequence.

Subscripted variables may be indexed within READ and WRITE lists using a notation similar to that of the DO statement. If JOB is a ten-position array and we

79

desire to read only the first six elements of JOB, the statement

READ (2,50) (JOB(N), N = 1,6), X, Y, Z

will cause the first six elements of JOB, followed by X, Y and Z, to be read into core memory. The indexing of JOB is contained within parentheses. The statement may be interpreted as "Read JOB sub N, where N varies from one to six, followed by X, Y and Z."

A third parameter may be added to the indexing to specify the increment to be added to the index after each element is read or written. If only the odd (first, third, fifth, seventh, etc.) elements of JOB are wanted, the statement

READ (2,50) (JOB(K), K = 1, 10, 2)

will cause the odd elements to be read. The full flexibility of DO statement notation is now available.

Two- and three-dimensional arrays are handled in a similar manner. To read in all the elements of the PART array (dimensioned as PART(3,2)) the statement

READ (2,50) PART

or the statement

READ (2,50) ((PART(L,M), L = 1,3), M = 1,2)

will produce identical results, but the first statement is simpler and will take up less memory in the computer. Double parentheses are used to indicate that the first subscript, L, will vary more rapidly than the subscript M.

Two or more arrays can be read or written with interspersed elements. The statements

WRITE (1,51) (JOBA(I), JOBB(I), I = 1, 10)
51   FORMAT (2F12.3)

will cause two columns, one containing the ten-element array JOBA and the other containing the ten-element array JOBB, to be printed. Since the FORMAT statement provides for only two variables, a new line of print or output record will be generated for each pair of variables produced by the WRITE statement.

5-5   Multiline and Nested Formats; X, A, T and H FORMAT Conversion

The ability to skip groups of characters during READ operations or generate blank characters during WRITE operations is provided by X conversion in FORMAT statements. X, A and H conversion are additions to the I, F, E and quote conversions discussed in Chapter 3. The general form used to specify X conversion is nX, where n is the number of characters or columns to be skipped or blanked. If, for example, it is necessary to ignore the contents of the first 30 columns of a card to be read while picking up 10 5-column integers from the remaining 50 columns of the card, the format statement

      100   FORMAT (30X, 10I5)

will do the job when combined with a suitable READ statement. The FORMAT statement

      101   FORMAT (5X, 10I5)

will provide five blank characters to the left of the ten integers when combined with a WRITE statement to a suitable output unit. The same result can be obtained, of course, by using the FORMAT statement

      101   FORMAT (I10, 9I5)

H Conversion

H conversion operates the same as quote conversion except that the programmer must count up the exact number of alphameric characters in each phrase or message to be read or written. If H conversion were used the FORMAT statement 11 from Section 3-1 would be programmed as

      11   FORMAT (17HFOR A DIAMETER OF, F10.3, 12H THE AREA IS, F10.3)

Notice that both quote and H specifications are separated from each other and from the other specifications in the FORMAT statement by commas, and that the specifications are all enclosed in a pair of parentheses.

H conversion is useful for lining up column headings, but any error in counting the number of characters in an H specification will usually result in a program the computer will not execute.

A Conversion

A conversion is used to transmit alphameric characters to and from integer and real variables. In quote and H conversions, the alphameric characters are stored in the FORMAT statement, but in A conversion the alphameric characters are stored in either real or integer variables, permitting the characters to be individually altered by the program to create different messages as the program is executed.

If FORMAT statement 11 from Section 3-1 were written using A conversion, variables would have to be allocated to store the characters in the FORMAT statement.

The characters are stored in EBCDIC code, which requires eight bits per character. Each integer variable occupies a single 16-bit word in memory, so an integer variable can contain only one or two eight-bit characters. A real variable in standard precision occupies two words in memory, and contain up to four characters. The specification 5A2 would allocate five variables, each to contain two characters, and the variables could be either real variables or integers. The specification 10A4 would allocate ten variables, each to contain four characters, and the variables in this case would have to be real variables.

If it is desired to manipulate individual characters as data in the program, only one character should be placed in each word. The specification 25A1 would allocate 25 variables (which could be either real or integers) each to contain a single character. If the specification calls for more characters than the variable can hold (such as A8) then the rightmost characters will be placed in the variable from right to left until the variable is full and the leftmost characters will be lost. If the specification calls for fewer characters than the variable will hold (such as A1) then the extra character positions on the left side of the variable will be filled with blanks.

The READ statement which references the FORMAT statement must contain a list of variable names including the variables containing the characters. A WRITE statement and a FORMAT statement which would duplicate the performance of the WRITE statement used with FORMAT statement 11 in Section 3-1 would be

```
       WRITE (1,11) V1, V2, V3, V4, V5, DIAM, V6, V7, V8, AREA
11     FORMAT (4A4, A1, F10.3, 3A4, F10.3)
```

The real variables V1 through V8 are used to contain the characters in the messages FOR A DIAMETER OF and THE AREA IS. Since FOR A DIAMETER OF contains 17 characters, the specification 4A4, A1 is used to write this message from variables V1 through V5. V1 through V4 will contain four characters each, while V5 will contain a single character. In a similar manner the variables V6 through V8 will contain the 12-character message (including a leading blank) THE AREA IS, according to the specification 3A4.

The only way to get characters into real and integer variables (short of using the DATA statement in Section 5-10) is to read the characters into core memory with a READ statement. The example of FORMAT statement 11 would only work if the characters had been previously read into variables V1 through V8 using another FORMAT statement, such as

```
        READ (2,100) V1, V2, V3, V4, V5, V6, V7, V8
100     FORMAT (4A4, A1, 3A4)
```

with the characters FOR A DIAMETER OF THE AREA IS punched in the first 29 card columns of the card being read.

Nested format specifications are an extension of the repeat specification option discussed in Section 3-9 (where the addition of an unsigned integer to the left of a specification caused the specification to be repeated automatically). The addition of a pair of parentheses permits groups of specifications to be nested together and repeated under the control of an unsigned integer to the left of the left parenthesis. The FORMAT statement

102   FORMAT (2X, I5, 2X, I5, 2X, I5, 3X, I4, 3X, I4)

can be compressed to the nested form

102   FORMAT (3(2X, I5), 2(3X, I4))

which is easier to read and takes less memory in the computer.

Multiline formats can be written using a slash character (/) to indicate a skip to the next line on typewriters or line printers. Several slashes can be grouped together to indicate that several lines are to be skipped. The slashes are separated from other specifications in a FORMAT statement by commas. The multiline FORMAT statement

103   FORMAT (4I10, /////, 6I12, /////)

will cause four integers to be printed, four lines to be skipped, six more integer variables to be printed, then four more lines to be skipped, if the FORMAT statement is referenced by a WRITE statement to a typewriter or line printer. Notice that the number of lines skipped is one less than the number of slashes or next-line skips in the FORMAT statement.

When multiline formats are used with READ statements, the slash provides a means of skipping several entire punched cards or paper tape records in a single FORMAT statement. The FORMAT statement 103 will read four integer variables from a punched card, pass the next four cards through the card reader without reading them, read six variables from the next card, then pass over four more cards without reading them, if FORMAT statement 103 is referenced by a READ statement to the 1442 Card Read Punch. Again the number of cards skipped will be one less than the number of slashes, since each slash causes a skip to the next card.

It is not necessary that the number of variables named in a READ or WRITE list correspond to the number of variable conversion specifications in a FORMAT statement. Consider the statements

        WRITE (1, 104) A, B, C, D, E
104   FORMAT (2F15.4)

These statements will cause A and B to be typed on one line, followed by C and D on the next line, followed by E on the next line, all in a format of F15.4. If the number of variables in the list exceeds the number of specifications, the FORMAT statement is simply repeated from the beginning as many times as required until the entire variable list has been converted. Consider the statements

READ (2, 105) A
105 FORMAT (6F15.4)

Here the number of variables is less than the number of specifications, and the FORMAT statement will be processed from left to right until the entire variable list has been converted, even though extra format specifications will remain unused. In this way a single FORMAT statement can be used with many READ and WRITE statements referring to different numbers of variables, significantly reducing the number of FORMAT statements required in large programs and saving core memory.

T Conversion

The ability to start reading or writing at any position within a record is provided by the T conversion code using the general form Tn (n–1 characters at the beginning of the record will be skipped over). Printing will begin at position n. The operation of T conversion is similar to X conversion. For example, to skip over the first 30 columns of a card and then read ten 5-column integers from the rest of the card, the FORMAT statement

100 FORMAT (T31, 10I5)

will do the job. T format became available in 1967 as an extension to the FORTRAN language for 1130 systems with disk storage.

5-6 Carriage Control on Printers

In addition to the use of slashes to skip lines when printing, the 1132 and 1403 Printers normally interpret the first character of any line to be printed as a carriage control code. The code is as follows:

blank	Single space before printing the line
0	Double space before printing the line
1	Jump to the next page before printing
+	Do not space at all before printing

Care must be taken to make sure that the first character of any format to be printed on the line printers conforms to the above code or unexpected carriage movements will occur. The FORMAT specifications 1H, 1H0, 1H1 or 1H+ can be placed at the left of line printer formats to provide carriage control. The code of "1" actually causes a skip to the next hole in a paper tape positioned to accommodate various form sizes.

5-7   The Computed GO TO Statement

The IF statement (Section 3-13) provides a two- or three-way transfer based upon a high, equal or low comparison. *The computed GO TO provides a many-branched transfer* which can be used to branch to one of many parts of a program and make other decisions involving transfers to more than three different program areas. A typical computed GO TO is

GO TO (9, 67, 43, 107, 7682, 21), NUMBR

where the parentheses contain a list of statement numbers separated by commas and NUMBR is a nonsubscripted integer variable. The value of the variable determines the statement to which control will be transferred: in the example if NUMBR is 4 we will transfer to statement 107 and if NUMBR is 5 we will transfer to statement 7682.

Any number of statement numbers may be enclosed within the parentheses. Obviously NUMBR must fall in the range of one to six to transfer to one of the six statement numbers in the example. If the variable is less than one or greater than the number of statement numbers in the parentheses the resulting transfer will have unpredictable results, causing an error that will be particularly hard to diagnose.

5-8   PAUSE, STOP and END Statements

These statements are usually written as single word commands:

    PAUSE
    STOP
    END

The PAUSE and STOP statements may also be written with an integer constant, such as PAUSE 42 or STOP 1234. The constant must be unsigned and no greater than 9999. The constant will then be displayed at the computer console in the accumulator register to permit the programmer to determine which PAUSE or STOP has occurred.

The PAUSE statement will cause the computer to stop, presumably so that the operator can place more cards in the card reader or perform some other manual supporting function. *The program will continue* with the statement following the PAUSE if the START button at the console is depressed. Excessive use of PAUSE should be avoided as this tends to slow down the overall operation of the system.

The STOP statement will cause a final stop in the card or paper tape versions of 1130 FORTRAN. Pushing the START button after execution of a STOP statement will not restart the computer. The normal procedure at this point is to reset and load another program as described in Chapter 4. (In the monitor version of

FORTRAN to be discussed in Chapter 7, pushing the START button after execution of a STOP statement will cause an automatic transfer to the next program to be compiled or executed.)

The END statement is the last card or paper tape record in the program and is simply a signal to the FORTRAN compiler that the end of the program has been reached. The STOP statement, if used, is the last statement executed by the program, but the card containing the STOP statement might be in the middle of the program card deck. We say that the END statement is physically the last statement in the program and that STOP is logically the last statement in the program. Every program must contain an END statement; the use of PAUSE and STOP is optional. End is not an executable statement; PAUSE and STOP are executable.

5-9   The DATA Statement

Many programs refer to large data tables which are not changed by the program; these tables can be read as input data whenever the program is executed, but it is often more convenient to specify the data as part of the program itself when the program is written. *The DATA statement was added to disk-oriented 1130 systems in 1967 to make it possible to specify data in a FORTRAN program.*

The general form of the DATA statement is a list of variable names separated by commas followed by a list of data values separated by commas, with the list of data values enclosed by slashes. For example:

DATA A, B, J, KLAST/5.63, 2., 438, –10/, VEL, NEXT/–3., 87/

will initialize the variable A to 5.63, B to 2., J to 438, KLAST to –10, VEL to –3. and NEXT to 87. As shown in the example, multiple lists of variables and data may be specified in a single statement. Integer values should be specified for integer variables and real values specified for real variables.

A multiplying constant may be used to repeat a data value for several variable names. For example the statements

DIMENSION GROUP (10)
DATA GROUP/10*1./

will cause all ten variables of the array named GROUP to be set to a value of one. The multiplying constant, which must be less than 4,096, is separated from the data value by an asterisk. Arrays may be specified entirely, as shown, or individually subscripted elements of an array may be specified.

Hexadecimal values may be specified as the letter Z followed by one to four hexadecimal digits. For example:

86

DATA JWORD, KWORD/Z1C, Z1/

will initialize JWORD to the hexadecimal value 1C (which is 11100 in binary or 28 in decimal) and will initialize KWORD to a value of one. Hexadecimal values can only be specified for integer variables.

Alphameric characters (called literal values) may be specified for both real and integer variables by enclosing the characters within quote marks, such as

DATA DOG, CAT, MOUSE/2*'WXYZ', 'A '/

which will initialize DOG to contain the characters WXYZ, CAT to contain WXYZ and MOUSE to contain Ab where b is a blank character. It is assumed that DOG and CAT are standard precision (two-word) real variables capable of containing four characters (32 bits).

The DATA statement is a specification statement and so must be placed ahead of the executable statements in a program. The DATA statement cannot be intermixed with EQUIVALENCE statements (Section 6-8).

5-10   READ and WRITE without Data Conversion

FORTRAN programs compiled under 1130 Disk Monitor control may include READ and WRITE statements which do not provide data conversion through the use of a FORMAT statement. Examples are

READ (NREAD) V1, V2, V3, V4
WRITE (NWRIT) V1, V2, V3, V4
READ (NREAD)

The first READ statement will read a record into the core memory occupied by the variables V1, V2, V3 and V4 in core image format (no data conversion). The amount of data read is controlled by the length of the variable list, which must be equal to or shorter than the length of the record to be read. Excess data in the record will be skipped; the next READ statement will read at the beginning of the next record. NREAD is an integer variable or constant that specifies the unit number of the device to be read.

The WRITE statement in the example will write a record consisting of the variables in the list in core image format upon the device whose unit number is NWRIT. The second READ statement shows how a READ statement without a variable list may be used to skip over an entire record; in this example a record will be read but no data will be stored in core memory.

87

5-11   Summary

All of the 1130 FORTRAN statements have now been discussed except statements involving the use of subroutines and disk storage control (Chapters 6 and 7). The problems which follow can accordingly be used to practice a variety of FORTRAN programming techniques.

5-12   Problems

1)   Write a FORTRAN program to read all 80 columns of a card and then print the 80 columns in reverse order; print the contents of column 80, then column 79, down to column 1. Write the program

   a)   using IF statement logic only,

   b)   using DO loops,

   c)   using indexing within READ and WRITE statements.

   Hint: Use a format of 80A1.

2)   Are the following two program segments equivalent?

```
         .
         .
         .

C-----SEGMENT 1
         .

         DO 5 M = 1, 20, 2
5        READ (2,10) (KOST(L,M), L = 1, 15, 2)
         .
         .


         .
         .
         .

C-----SEGMENT 2
         .

5        READ (2,10) ((KOST(L, M), L = 1, 15, 2), M = 1, 20, 2)
```

3)   Are the two following FORMAT statements equivalent?

```
215   FORMAT(I6, I6, F7.3, I6, I6, F7.3, //////////, I5, I5, I5)
216   FORMAT (2(2I6, F7.3), 10(/), 3I5)
```

4) The following brief program contains one error. Correct it.

```
        READ (2,100) IABC
100     FORMAT(A2)
        WRITE (3,200) IABC
200     FORMAT('+', I2)
        END
```

Note that there are two "obvious" ways of correcting the error. Explain why one way of correcting should be favored over the other and give the circumstances.

5) If the operation of X and T conversions is similar, can you think of any programming situations where one would be preferable over the other? Consider the example:

```
Columns:            1111111111222222222233333333334
           12345678901234567890123456789012345678 90 . . . . .

        SMITH, JOHN              350 PARKWAY ROAD
        SMITH, RICHARD           44 LAKESIDE AVENUE
        SMITH, TOM               1009 23D STREET
        SMYTHE, ALEXANDER        78 SUNSET STRIP
```

Note that the starting positions for printing are easier to identify with the aid of the T-conversion code: these are T1 and T22, and they remain the same throughout the entire printing process. On the other hand, each new line requires a new X code: 10X, 7X, 11X and 4X respectively in the above example. Can you cite an example where the opposite choice of codes would be recommendable? Can you derive from the above example and yours a general rule that would indicate when to use the X code and when to use the T code?

6) Besides the four standard carriage control codes (blank, 0, 1 and + (see Section 5-6)), individual 1130's may have additional carriage control codes built in. For example, a minus sign (–) may possibly mean "triple space before printing the line"; other possible codes are the nonbinary digits (2, 3, . . . , 9) and certain special characters. Check the available codes on your 1130 and make yourself a table of their meanings.

7) In Section 5-7 it is discussed that a complicated error may occur when the index variable of the computed GO TO falls out of its allowable range. Can you think of any simple safeguards? Is the following example an adequate safeguard?

```
            IF ((NUMBR-1) * (6-NUMBR)) 5,10,10
    5       WRITE (3, 6)
    6       FORMAT(' THE INDEX VARIABLE IS OUT OF RANGE')
    7       PAUSE
    10      GO TO (9, 67, 43, 107, 7682, 21), NUMBR
                    .
                    .
                    .
```

8) A good precautionary measure to keep in mind is the maximum number of words (in the 1130's memory) which is available for your FORTRAN program. The total memory capacity of your 1130 will usually not be available to you, for the FORTRAN compiler will take a certain amount of memory space. You should have a clear knowledge of how much computer memory will actually be available under various programming conditions. Estimating how many words of memory are taken up by your program is a relatively easy task. Approximately how many words will be required by a program consisting of no more than 25 statements and having the following dimension and type declarations?

> DIMENSION AXE(10, 10), REST(50), FIRST(24, 36)
>
> REAL LAST(12, 52), MONEY(5,30), NEXT(7,365)
>
> INTEGER ONE, TWO, GET, SET

Will this hypothetical program fit into a 4K 1130? Into an 8K 1130?

9) Write a program to read 100 real numbers and compute and print the biggest (BIG), the smallest (SMALL) and the average (AVG). Write this program first using IF statements and then using a single large DO loop, and prepare a flow diagram for the IF statement version.

10) A straightforward way to sort a list of 100 numbers into sequence so that the small numbers are at the beginning of the list and the large numbers are at the end is to make a series of scans through the list, examining the numbers two at a time and exchanging the positions of the numbers if the number of lower subscript is larger than the number of higher subscript. Compare the first number with the second and exchange them if the second number is smaller, then compare the second number with the third and exchange them if the third number is smaller, etc. When a scan through all the numbers does not result in any exchanges the whole list will be in sequence. Prepare a flow diagram and write a program to do this.

11) Write a program to determine the day of the week that any date in the twentieth century will fall upon, given three integers for day, month

and year. Print out the full name of the weekday in English from a single FORMAT statement, using a two-dimensional array in A format to store the letters of the weekday names, and calculating one of the subscripts of the array from calendar information.

12) If no better method is available it is always possible to find the square roots and the cube roots of a number by trial and error (iteration), by picking a trial number, squaring or cubing it, comparing the result with the given number and adjusting the trial number up or down until the result agrees with the given number to within a given tolerance. Prepare a flow diagram and write a program to find the square root (ROOT2) and the cube root (ROOT3) from a GIVEN number and a tolerance (TOL).

13) The sine of an angle X is equal to

$$\text{Sine } X = X - \frac{X^3}{3!} + \frac{X^5}{5!} - \frac{X^7}{7!} + \frac{X^9}{9!} - \cdots$$

Prepare a flow diagram and write a program to calculate the sine of angles from zero to 360 degrees in increments of ten degrees. X in the above equation must be in radians, where one radian equals 57.29578 degrees. Calculate the sines in a two-dimensional array dimensioned SINE(37,4), where the four columns contain the sine computed using two, three, four and five terms of the equation to show the increase in accuracy produced by additional terms. Print the entire array with the appropriate angle beside each row in both degrees and radians.

14) Using the series equation of Problem 13, calculate a table of the angles and the sines of angles from one to 360 degrees in five-degree increments (dimensioned ANGLE(73) and SINE(73)) and use this table to look up the sine of real angle variables (such as 11.362 degrees) to be read in from cards. Use straight-line interpolation to handle fractions of degrees. A good statement for this interpolation is

ANSER = (ATEST – ALOW) * (SHIGH – SLOW) / (AHIGH – ALOW) + SLOW

where ANSER is the sine of ATEST, ATEST is the angle being looked up, AHIGH and ALOW are adjacent angle values (such as 30 and 25) which ATEST falls between, and SHIGH and SLOW are the sine values from the table corresponding to AHIGH and ALOW values of the angle. In a DO loop, proceed down the ANGLE list until an ANGLE is found which is bigger than ATEST; call that angle AHIGH and interpolate as above. Include tests for angles greater than 360 degrees or less than zero degrees. Prepare a flow diagram before writing the program.

15) The table look-up procedure of Problem 14 could be speeded up considerably by not examining every angle in the table. One way to do this is to jump down the list, several angles at a jump, and then home in on a group of angles containing the desired value. Such a method consists of a gross search followed by a fine search. A good jump size for the gross search is approximately the square root of the number of entries in the table, 73 in this case, so the jump size could be 9. Using two DO statements, rewrite Problem 14 to make a fine search inside a gross search as follows:

DO 10 I = 1, 73, 9

(test for an ANGLE bigger than ATEST, if so go to 11, otherwise continue)

10   CONTINUE

(write error message here indicating an angle over 360 degrees, restart)

11   K = I − 8
        DO 12 J = K, I

(test for an angle bigger than ATEST, if so interpolate as in Problem 14)

12   CONTINUE

Notice that the DO index I is used as the upper limit on the second DO loop. This is possible since I is preserved in a transfer out of the first DO loop.

16) An even better method of speeding up (optimizing) table look-up operations is the binary search method. In the binary search method the table entries are split in half (approximately), a test is made to see in which half ATEST lies, that half is then split in half again and the process continues until the proper entry is found. Given a table of 73 entries where the desired entry happens to be entry 12, the following entries (with test results in parentheses) might be tested in homing in on entry 12 through repeatedly halving the size of the table: 36 (high), 18 (high), 9 (low), 13 (high), 11 (low) and finally 12 (that's it). To halve an odd number like nine, simply divide by two in integer arithmetic and the result (four in this case) is the new table interval. Rewrite the program of Problem 15 using the binary search method. Be sure to handle the problems of error messages and the end points of the table.

17)   Prepare a flow diagram and write a completely general program to read the number of elements in a talbe, then read the table elements in two lists. The first list contains arguments, corresponding to the angles of Problem 16. The second list contains results, corresponding to the sines of Problem 16. Using the binary search method and straight-line interpolation as described in the preceding problems, read a series of arguments for this table and print out the interpolated results.

CHAPTER 6: FUNCTIONS, SUBROUTINES AND SUBPROGRAMS

6-1 The Need for Subroutines

Consider a program in which the answers are angles calculated in degrees, such as 41.567, 128.65 and 8.946 degrees. Suppose that we wish to express these answers in degrees, minutes and seconds instead of decimal fractions of degrees. (Sixty seconds equal a minute and sixty minutes equal a degree.) This can be accomplished in four statements which include rounding off to the nearest second:

```
IDEGS = ANGLE
TEMP = 60. * (ANGLE – IDEGS)
MINS = TEMP
ISECS = 60. * (TEMP – MINS) + .5
```

In this example ANGLE is an angle to be converted, and IDEG, MINS and ISECS are the resulting degrees, minutes and seconds in integer format. The statement IDEGS = ANGLE converts ANGLE to an integer by dropping any fractional part of ANGLE. The second statement retrieves the fractional part by subtracting the integer IDEGS from the real variable ANGLE. Multiplication by 60. produces a real variable TEMP equal to the number of minutes, with a fractional part representing the number of seconds.

The third statement converts TEMP to an integer MINS, the number of minutes. The fourth statement retrieves the fractional part of TEMP, multiplies it by 60. to get seconds, and rounds up by adding .5 or half a second. *This rounding technique is known as half adjusting.* Since the fractional part is then dropped upon conversion to the integer ISECS, adding .5 causes the resulting value of ISECS to be increased by one if the fractional part of the expression was .5 or more, and does not affect the value of ISECS if the fractional part was less than .5. ISECS then becomes the value of seconds rounded to the nearest second. TEMP is a temporary variable used to store the integer and fractional parts of the number of minutes. The fourth statement is in mixed mode, since MINS and TEMP are present to the right of the equal sign.

Suppose that three different angles, ANG1, ANG2 and ANG3, are calculated during the course of the program execution. The four statements of the minutes and seconds procedure (hereafter called the MNSEC procedure) could simply be inserted into the program three times for a total of twelve statements used for the same purpose, or a computed GO TO could be used to permit one set of the four statements to be used three different times for different values of angles as follows:

```
(calculate ANG1)
ANGLE = ANG1
NTEST = 1
```

```
             GO TO 10
     21      (print IDEGS, MINS and ISECS for ANG1, then calculate ANG2)
             ANGLE = ANG2
             NTEST = 2
             GO TO 10
     22      (print IDEGS, MINS and ISECS for ANG2, then calculate ANG3)
              ANGLE = ANG3
             NTEST = 3
             GO TO 10
     23      (print IDEGS, MINS and ISECS for ANG3)
             STOP
     C-----MNSEC PROCEDURE FOLLOWS
     10      IDEGS = ANGLE
             TEMP = 60. * (ANGLE - IDEGS)
             MINS = TEMP
             ISECS = 60. * (TEMP - MINS) + .5
             GO TO (21, 22, 23), NTEST
             END
```

*The variables used as input to a procedure such as MNSEC are called the arguments
of the procedure;* the argument of MNSEC is obviously ANGLE. Accordingly the
value of each angle (ANG1, ANG2 and ANG3) must be placed in ANGLE before the
MNSEC procedure can be executed. It is also necessary to establish where control
of the program will go upon each completion of MNSEC. This is done by setting
NTEST to control a computed GO TO at the end of MNSEC. All this amounts to
about as many extra statements as were saved by writing only one set of the statements in the MNSEC procedure. Another difficulty is that the results of the MNSEC
procedure IDEGS, MINS and ISECS will always appear in the same three variables.
These three variables must be made available whenever the procedure is used.

The idea of setting up a procedure such that it can be used by different
programmers or in different places in a single program is one of the most powerful
ideas in programming. A procedure that can calculate results from arguments and
automatically return to the right place in any program which might use the procedure
is called a subprogram. We say that a program which uses a subprogram "calls" the
subprogram, and, upon completion, the subprogram "returns" control to the calling
program. Besides being able to execute the procedure for which it was designed, a
subprogram must be able to accept arguments from the calling program, to transmit
results to the calling program and, finally, to return control to the place in the calling
program where the call occurred. The FORTRAN system for the 1130 furnishes
three types of statements which provide the linkage between subprograms and calling
programs. These statements are the statement function, the function subprogram
statement and the CALL statement.

6-2   The Statement Function

The statement function handles procedures which have only one result variable and which can be expressed in a single arithmetic FORTRAN statement using nonsubscripted variables. Consider a procedure to take the average of three real variables, which would consist of adding the variables together and then dividing by three. This procedure can be defined as a statement function in the form

$$AVG3(A, B, C) = (A + B + C)/3.0$$

AVG3 is the name of the statement function, and AVG3 must follow the rules for naming a FORTRAN variable. The mode (real or integer) of the function statement may either be implied by the first letter of the name, or be specified by a type statement. The parentheses after AVG3 enclose the three arguments of AVG3. The arithmetic expression to the right of the equal sign is the procedure for calculating AVG3. Up to 15 arguments may be used in a function definition statement, and any FORTRAN arithmetic expression may describe the procedure. The arguments used in a function definition must be nonsubscripted variables.

The definition of a statement function must be located in the program before the first executable statement, right behind the type and DIMENSION statements if any. Once it is defined, a function like AVG3 can be used many times in different arithmetic statements like the following:

$$X = AVG3(Y1, BCELL, Y2) + BASE$$
$$Z = (AVG3(V1, V2, V3) + AVG3(V4, V5, V6))/2.0$$

Notice that the second statement above takes the average of the six variables V1 through V6 by taking half of the average of V1 through V3 plus the average of V4 through V6. The variable names used in the function definition are really dummy variables because any variables or constants of the same mode can be named when the function is used in a program. If one desired to take the average of six variables at several different places in the program, an AVG6 function could be defined in terms of the previously defined AVG3 as follows:

$$AVG6(F, E, D, C, B, A) = (AVG3(F, E, D) + AVG3(C, B, A))/2.0$$

Actually it would be more efficient (because of less division) to define AVG6 as

$$AVG6(F, E, D, C, B, A) = (F+E+D+C+B+A)/6.0$$

The definition of a statement function can contain another statement function if the contained statement function has been defined in a preceding function definition statement.

Another example of a procedure that can be expressed in a statement function is the box function

$$NBOX(NUMBR, NSIZE) = (NUMBR + NSIZE - 1)/NSIZE$$

which calculates the number of boxes, NBOX, required to hold a NUMBR of items if the items can be packed to a quantity of NSIZE items to each box. Constants may be used in the definition of a statement function.

After defining the box function as above we could then calculate the total number of boxes required to hold NPCH peaches at three dozen per box plus NPRU prunes at six dozen per box plus NMEL melons at five per box in a single FORTRAN statement:

$$NTOTL = NBOX(NPCH, 36) + NBOX(NPRU, 72) + NBOX(NMEL, 5)$$

Obviously the statement function enables a programmer to do a maximum of computing with a minimum of programming.

The definition of a statement function may also contain variables which are not arguments; these variables are called the parameters of the function. For example, consider the function definition

$$CROSS(X) = A * X + B$$

where A and B are parameters to be used as normal variables in evaluating the function CROSS. After the definition of CROSS, the statement

$$Y = CROSS(PURCH) - TAX$$

would produce the same result as the statement

$$Y = A * PURCH + B - TAX$$

The dummy names used to define arguments may be used for actual variables in the calling program; the names used to define parameters must be used for actual variables in the calling program. The arguments used in calling a statement function may be subscripted or nonsubscripted variables, constants or arithmetic expressions, including the results of other statement functions as shown in the next section.

When a function is encountered during the execution of a FORTRAN program, program control is transferred to the instructions that have been compiled to calculate the procedure defined by the function. These instructions appear at only one place in the memory of the computer. The result of the procedure then becomes the value of the function just as if the function itself were a FORTRAN variable, and the value of the function is then available for further calculations in FORTRAN arithmetic statements.

6-3   Functions Supplied by the FORTRAN Compiler

A library of useful functions is provided by IBM. The library functions summarized in Figure 6-1 can be used without definition in the calling program.

Name	Function Performed	No. of Arguments	Type of Argument(s)	Type of Function
SIN	Trigonometric sine	1	Real	Real
COS	Trigonometric cosine	1	Real	Real
ALOG	Natural logarithm	1	Real	Real
EXP	Argument power of e (i.e., e^x)	1	Real	Real
SQRT	Square root	1	Real	Real
ATAN	Arctangent	1	Real	Real
ABS	Absolute value	1	Real	Real
IABS	Absolute value	1	Integer	Integer
FLOAT	Convert integer argument to real	1	Integer	Real
IFIX	Convert real argument to integer	1	Real	Integer
SIGN	Transfer of sign (Sign of Arg_2 times Arg_1)	2	Real	Real
ISIGN	Transfer of sign (Sign of Arg_2 times Arg_1)	2	Integer	Integer
TANH	Hyperbolic tangent	1	Real	Real

Figure 6-1   Functions Supplied by FORTRAN

The library functions can be used to advantage in statement functions defined by a programmer. For example the hyperbolic sine and cosine may be defined as

$$SINH(X) = .5 * (EXP(X) - EXP(-X))$$
$$COSH(X) = .5 * (EXP(X) + EXP(-X))$$

Since TANH(X) is supplied by FORTRAN, the above two statements at the beginning of any program will give that program a working set of hyperbolic functions.

Both library functions and statement functions can be nested together to create extremely powerful FORTRAN statements, since the argument of one function may be the result of another function. For example:

$$X = SQRT(ABS(SIN(ANGLE)))$$

means "Take the square root of the absolute value of the sine of ANGLE and name the result X."

$$Z = \text{SIGN(SQRT}(A + B), C)$$

means "Take the square root of the sum of A and B, and assign the sign of C to the result, and call the result Z." The following statements are taken from a program used as an example in Chapter 8:

$$\text{PAR} = \text{ALOG(COSHP} + \text{SIGN(SQRT(COSHP*COSHP-1.), PHI))}$$
$$\text{PHI} = \text{ATAN((P*ECC*SIN(THETA))/(R *(1.+ECC*COS(THETA))**2))}$$

COSHP is a variable, not a function, in the above statements. All the normal rules for FORTRAN arithmetic expressions, including the balancing of parentheses, must be observed. The result is that the power of the language is increased several fold over that of a simple arithmetic statement, however.

We might well ask how a digital computer can compute transcendental functions such as sines and tangents. Certainly no table look-up technique is used, since an accurate table of sines and tangents alone would occupy many thousands of words. The functions are calculated from truncated Taylor's series (see Problem 6, Chapter 5), rational functions or polynomial equations, using only enough terms to provide accuracy to the resolution of the floating-point format specified (6.9 digits for standard precision floating-point, 9.3 for extended precision). There are two sets of functions in the FORTRAN library, one for standard precision and the other set for extended precision floating-point format. The FORTRAN compiler inserts a function from the appropriate set depending upon which precision is to be used by the program being compiled.

The arguments provided in calling a FORTRAN library or statement function may be subscripted or nonsubscripted variables, constants or arithmetic expressions which may involve the results of other functions.

6-4   Function Subprograms and the RETURN Statement

The function subprogram handles procedures which have only one result variable but which require several FORTRAN statements for procedure definition. Function subprogram procedures may involve the use of arrays or the results of other function subprograms. Each function subprogram is programmed and compiled as a separate FORTRAN program.

Consider the procedure required to find the largest number in a list of real variables. A function subprogram to execute this procedure might be called in the form BIG(A, N), where BIG is the name of the subprogram, A is the name of a one-dimensional array containing the list of real variables, and N is the number of real variables in the list. The FORTRAN program for the function subprogram might be as follows:

```
          FUNCTION BIG(A, N)
          DIMENSION A(100)
          BIG = A(1)
          DO 2 I = 2, N
          IF (BIG – A(I)) 1, 2, 2
     1    BIG = A(I)
     2    CONTINUE
          RETURN
          END
```

The above procedure consists of setting BIG equal to the first element of the array A
and then testing the other elements to see if any of them are larger than BIG. If so,
BIG is set equal to the new larger element at statement 1. When the DO loop is satisfied, BIG will contain the value of the largest element. The DO loop will only compare
elements through A(N), where N is an integer variable. The FUNCTION statement
tells the FORTRAN compiler that the program which follows is a subprogram and
lists the number and mode of the arguments. The DIMENSION statement identifies
A as an array to the FORTRAN compiler, and is required if any of the arguments
are arrays. A should be dimensioned large enough to contain any size list which
might be used by the subprogram. All FORTRAN statements except additional
FUNCTION or SUBROUTINE statements may be used in a subprogram.

*The RETURN statement causes control to return to the place in the calling
program which referred to the BIG subprogram.* The RETURN statement is the
last statement executed in the subprogram, but RETURN need not be the physically
last statement in the program. In the BIG subprogram, statement 1 could have been
taken out of the DO loop and located after the RETURN statement as follows:

```
          RETURN
     1    BIG = A(I)
          GO TO 2
          END
```

The above is not as efficient as the original coding of BIG since an extra GO TO
statement is now required, but the new coding will produce identical results.

Several RETURN statements may be used in the same subprogram if the
program branches into several different logical paths. At least one RETURN statement must be present in each subprogram. Since the single result of the function
subprogram will be assigned to the name BIG, there must be at least one arithmetic
statement in the subprogram where BIG is on the left side of the equal sign. The
arguments of a function subprogram must not appear to the left of an equal sign in
the subprogram (they must not be changed by the subprogram).

The BIG subprogram may be executed by compiling the BIG subprogram,
then compiling a FORTRAN main program which calls the BIG subprogram, and
then executing the main program. When the main program is loaded for execution

the loader will also load the object program for the BIG subprogram from disk storage into core memory so that BIG can be executed with the main program, as described in Chapter 7.

   The form used to call a function subprogram is similar to the form used to call a statement function. The following examples show how the BIG subprogram might be called from other programs:

   TOTAL = BIG(BLIST, 50) + BASE
   FINAL = BIG(BILLS, 75) + BIG(EXTRA, 10)
   WHICH = 10. * BIG(BLIST, IABS(J + K – 3))

The last statement may be read as "Set WHICH equal to ten times the largest element in BLIST measured from the beginning of BLIST through the subscript equal to the absolute value of J plus K minus 3." The arguments used to call a function subprogram may be subscripted or nonsubscripted variables, array names, constants or arithmetic expressions which may involve the results of other sub-programs. The arguments must agree in number, mode and sequence with the arguments in the FUNCTION statement, but different variable names may be used. The calling statements may combine the results of several subprograms.

   When a function subprogram is encountered during the execution of a FORTRAN program, program control is transferred to the subprogram instructions. *The single result of the subprogram is calculated and assigned to the name of the subprogram* (such as BIG), and the subprogram name becomes available for use in FORTRAN expressions. Finally, control is returned to the statement that originally called the subprogram. The subprogram instructions appear only once in the object program regardless of how many times the subprogram may be called from different places in the calling program or in other subprograms. A subprogram may call other subprograms.

   The name of a function subprogram may be used as an argument to another function subprogram. This technique requires the use of an EXTERNAL statement as described in Section 6-6.

   The mode of a function subprogram result is implied by the name of the subprogram itself; the mode will be real unless the name begins with I, J, K, L, M or N, in which case the mode will be integer. It is possible to specify the mode of a function subprogram explicitly in the FUNCTION statement, by preceding the word FUNCTION with either REAL or INTEGER. Thus the statement

   REAL FUNCTION MAXOF(A, B, C)

will produce a real result in spite of the function name, and

   INTEGER FUNCTION BOX(K, L)

will produce a result in integer mode.

As a final example of the programming power of function subprograms, consider the problem of iterating a solution for equations which cannot be solved directly. The equation x = a * sin(x) + c cannot be solved directly for x, but a solution can easily be found by repeated evaluations of trial values (or guesses) of x. We shall develop a subprogram to automate the selection of such trial values. The subprogram, called TRIAL, will handle the selection of trial values for equations which have been manipulated into the form

$$x = f(x)$$

where f(x) is a single-valued function of x which does not involve complex numbers. It is permissible, however, that f(x) involve table look-up procedures or other complications requiring several FORTRAN statements.

Consider three values of x (x_1, x_2 and x_3) and three values of the function f(x) which correspond to the three values of x. Call the three function values f_1, f_2 and f_3. Let us assume for the moment that f(x) has constant slope (i.e., that it is a straight line) in the region containing the above three values. The assumption of constant slope is an approximation that will allow us to make a good selection of the next trial value for x.

From the assumption of constant slope, we can write an equation

$$\frac{f_3 - f_2}{x_3 - x_2} = \frac{f_2 - f_1}{x_2 - x_1} \qquad (6\text{-}1)$$

which simply states that the three points are on a straight line. Let x_1 and x_2 represent the two guesses for x, and let x_3 represent a third guess or trial value which we wish to select. If x_3 were the solution to the equation x = f(x), then

$$x_3 = f_3 \qquad (6\text{-}2)$$

Let us define the slope parameter s as

$$s = \frac{f_2 - f_1}{x_2 - x_1} \qquad (6\text{-}3)$$

Substituting equations (6-2) and (6-3) into equation (6-1) and solving for x_3 (eliminating f_3) produces

$$x_3 = \left[\frac{s}{s - 1}\right] x_2 + \left[1 - \frac{s}{s - 1}\right] f_2 \qquad (6\text{-}4)$$

Equation (6-4) can be used to calculate a new trial value x_3 from the last two trial values x_1 and x_2 and their calculated functions. The trial value x_3 will probably not be an exact solution since the function f(x) is probably not a straight line, but x_3 will be a well-calcualted step in the direction of the solution and can then be used as a basis for further trials until a solution of x = f(x) is found to any desired degree of accuracy. Note that there is no requirement that x_2 be greater than x_1 or that x_3 lie between the values of x_1 and x_2. It is required that x_2 not be equal to x_1. The slope parameter s must not be equal to one, as this would indicate an infinite number of possible solutions.

Various other schemes for selecting trial values, such as the methods of Newton, Horner or Graeffe, can be found in texts on numerical analysis. We have had considerable success with the above method, known as Wegstein's method, for many years. Some methods converge on the solution faster than others, and many will not converge at all on certain functions. At times the function may have a solution at several different values of x, some of which may not be pertinent to the problem at hand. Complications such as these are beyond the scope of this text.

The function subprogram TRIAL can now be written as follows:

```
        FUNCTION TRIAL(N, X, FX)
C-----N IS THE NUMBER OF TRIALS WHICH HAVE BEEN MADE.
C-----SOLUTION IS X = F(X).  X AND FX ARE CURRENT VALUES.
C-----XLAST AND FLAST ARE PREVIOUS VALUES.  TRIAL IS THE NEW X
C-----VALUE.
        IF (N - 1) 1, 1, 2
C-----CHECK FOR NO PROGRESS, IF SO, RETURN
2       IF (X - XLAST) 3, 1, 3
3       SLOPE = (FX - FLAST)/(X - XLAST)
        DENOM = SLOPE - 1.
        IF (DENOM) 4, 1, 4
4       FACTR = SLOPE/DENOM
        TRIAL = FACTR * X + (1. - FACTR) * FX
5       XLAST = X
        FLAST = FX
        RETURN
C-----SET TRIAL EQUAL TO FX AND TRY AGAIN.
1       TRIAL = FX
        GO TO 5
        END
```

Arguments for TRIAL include N, the number of trials which have been made on the equation currently in process, and X and FX, the current values of x and f(x). First a check is made to see if N is one; if so, X and FX are stored in XLAST and FLAST, and FX becomes the new value of TRIAL. This is necessary since the subprogram needs two values of X and FX to utilize equation (6-4). If N is greater than one, the subprogram proceeds to evaluate equation (6-4), checking to see that X does not equal XLAST and that the SLOPE is not one, either of which would cause equation (6-4) to divide by zero. If a divide by zero condition exists, the iteration is reinitialized by setting TRIAL = FX.

The number of trials or iterations is presumably under the control of a DO loop in the calling program. Notice that the current values of X and FX are stored in

XLAST and FLAST after each calculation of TRIAL, so that the subprogram is always working with the two latest sets of values. The calling program must count the number of iterations (N) and stop if a solution is not reached in some acceptable number of trials (say 25). The calling program must also test the difference between X and FX and stop when the difference is acceptably small (say less than .00001). The calling program must calculate the value of FX corresponding to each X furnished by the subprogram, and furnish the initial value of X to start things rolling. For the function x = a * sin(x) + c, all of this can be done in five statements:

```
        X = START
        DO 10 J = 1, 25
        FUNCT = A * SIN(X) + C
        IF (ABS(FUNCT - X) - .00001) 11, 10, 10
10      X = TRIAL(J, X, FUNCT)
        (Here is where you will be if 25 trials don't get a solution)
11      (Here is where you will be when you get a solution)
```

The variable START is any reasonable value of X used as a starting point. In the example above, five or six iterations were enough to get a solution to .00001 in most cases. Notice that the variable names J, X and FUNCT in the calling program are not the same as the names N, X and FX used in the subprogram. The number, sequence and mode of these variables must correspond between the calling program and the subprogram, but any names may be used in the calling program.

6-5   Subroutine Subprograms and the CALL Statement

Subroutine subprograms are similar to function subprograms except that *subroutine subprograms may return several different results in several different variables from a single call.* Any or all of the arguments presented with a SUBROUTINE statement may be used to return results to the calling program. Since the name of a subroutine subprogram does not contain the value of the result, the name may be in any mode.

Consider a subroutine subprogram to take decimal fractions of angles in degrees and convert the angles to degrees, minutes and seconds as discussed in Section 6-1:

```
        SUBROUTINE MNSEC(IDEGS, MINS, ISECS, ANGLE)
C----- CONVERT ANGLE IN DEGREES TO IDEG DEGREES, MINS MINUTES, AND
C----- ISECS SECONDS, ROUNDING (HALF-ADJUSTING) TO THE NEAREST
C----- SECOND.
        IDEGS = ANGLE
        TEMP = 60. * (ANGLE - IDEGS)
        MINS = TEMP
        ISECS = 60. * (TEMP - MINS) + .5
        RETURN
        END
```

The use of the RETURN statement is identical to the use of RETURN in function subprograms. IDEGS, MINS and ISECS are obviously the results of the subprogram, since they appear to the left of equal signs in the subprogram. ANGLE is an argument to the subprogram, since ANGLE does not appear to the left of an equal sign. The arguments and results listed in the SUBROUTINE statement must be nonsubscripted variable names or array names or (as described in Section 6-6) they may be the names of other subprograms. It is not necessary to have any arguments at all.

Subroutine subprograms are called by a CALL statement. Examples of a CALL statement for the MNSEC subprogram are

> CALL MNSEC(ID, MN, IS, DEGS)
> CALL MNSEC(IDS, MNS, ISS, 57.29578*ATAN(A/B))

The second CALL statement points up the ability to use arithmetic expressions containing the results of function subprograms as arguments to a subroutine subprogram. (In this case the argument in degrees will be the arctangent of A over B converted to degrees by the constant 57.29578.) The arguments and results listed in a CALL statement must agree in number, sequence and mode with the arguments and results listed in the referenced SUBROUTINE statement. The variable names need not be the same. The arguments and results in the CALL statement may be subscripted or nonsubscripted variables or array names. The arguments (but not the results) may be arithmetic expressions, constants or subprogram names, as described in Section 6-6.

The programming required to convert three angles (ANG1, ANG2 and ANG3) in the example of Section 6-1 can now be reduced to the following:

> (Calculate ANG1)
> CALL MNSEC(IDEGS, MINS, ISECS, ANG1)
> (Print IDEGS, MINS, ISECS for ANG1, then calculate ANG2)
> CALL MNSEC(IDEGS, MINS, ISECS, ANG2)
> (Print IDEGS, MINS, ISECS for ANG2, then calculate ANG3)
> CALL MNSEC(IDEGS, MINS, ISECS, ANG3)
> (Print IDEGS, MINS, ISECS for ANG3)
> STOP

The problems of transmitting the arguments and results, transferring control to the subprogram and returning control to the calling program are all handled automatically by the CALL statement.

As a final example of subroutine subprograms, consider a customized arc tangent routine. The FORTRAN library arc tangent function ATAN accepts as an argument the tangent of the angle and produces as a result the value of the angle in radians. While this appears to be only too reasonable, in practice the ATAN function produces many agonizing debugging sessions because the tangent function starts repeating itself every 180 degrees. The ATAN function will produce the equivalent of a 45 degree angle in radians for the arc tangent of 1.000; actually the arc tangent of 1.000 could be either 45 degrees or 225 degrees or, in the general case, 45 plus or minus n * 180 where n is any integer. Since the sine and cosine functions repeat themselves every 360 degrees, the FORTRAN statement

ALPHA = SIN(ATAN(1.000))

is particularly perilous. If the angle is 45 degrees, the sine is approximately +.70711; if the angle is 225 degrees, the sine is -.70711. The expression SIN(ATAN(1.000)) will produce a result of +.70711 every time.

What we need to resolve this dilemma is an arc tangent subroutine which can distinguish angles over a full 360-degree range. The basis for such a subroutine is shown in Figure 6-2.

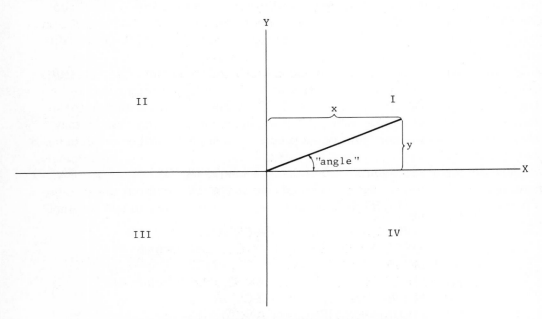

Figure 6-2   Arc Tangent of an Angle from Coordinates

Consider the arc tangent to be calculated by taking the arc tangent of y/x, where y and x are the coordinates of a point on a radius vector from the origin of coordinates, and the angle is measured between the radius vector and the X axis of coordinates as in Figure 6-2. The four quadrants in which the radius vector may lie are numbered in Roman numerals. An angle of 225 degrees would lie in quadrant III and have equal but negative values of y and x; an angle of 45 degrees would lie in quadrant I and have equal and positive values of y and x. Upon further inspection it can be seen that the proposed subroutine must distinguish all combinations of sign of y and x and must also handle the cases of x = 0 and x = y = 0. The case of x = 0 corresponds to a tangent of infinity and would cause division by zero; the case of x = y = 0 corresponds to a radius vector of zero length and an indeterminate angle.

We can now set up a decision table (Figure 6-3) to show how the angle can be computed for all of the above situations. Notice that once we have determined the quadrant in which the angle lies we can use the ATAN function inside the subroutine to compute the arc tangent, as long as x is not zero.

x conditions read across y conditions read down	x negative	x near zero	x positive
y positive	3.1415926+ATAN(Y/X)	1.5707963	ATAN(Y/X)
y near zero	3.1415926+ATAN(Y/X)	0.	6.2831852+ATAN(Y/X)
y negative	3.1415926+ATAN(Y/X)	4.7123889	6.2831852+ATAN(Y/X)

Figure 6-3   Decision Table for Arc Tangent Subroutine

We must test for x near zero rather than x = 0 since roundoff errors in extensive calculations might make it impossible to get an exact value of zero. Accordingly, we will test the expression ABS(X)-.001; if this expression is negative, we will consider the variable X to be zero for purposes of this subroutine. Without the absolute value function ABS in the FORTRAN library it would be necessary to test for small values of X on both sides of zero.

A subroutine subprogram can now be written to implement the decision table of Figure 6-3:

```
        SUBROUTINE ARCTN(ANGLE, Y, X)
C-----THIS PROGRAM FINDS ANGLE = ATAN(Y/X) FOR ANGLES FROM 0 TO
C-----2 PI.
        ANGLE = 0.
        IF (ABS(X)-.001) 2, 9, 9
9       IF (X) 1, 3, 3
3       IF (Y) 4, 5, 5
4       ANGLE = 6.2831852
        GO TO 5
1       ANGLE = 3.1415926
5       ANGLE = ANGLE + ATAN(Y/X)
        RETURN
2       IF (ABS(Y)-.001) 8, 10, 10
10      IF (Y) 6, 7, 7
6       ANGLE = 4.7123889
```

```
             RETURN
7            ANGLE = 1.5707963
8            RETURN
             END
```

The ARCTN subroutine has three RETURN statements as written. ANGLE is the only result of the subroutine, since X and Y do not appear to the left of any equal signs in the subroutine. X and Y are the arguments to the subroutine. ARCTN could be called by the following statements:

```
             CALL ARCTN(THETA, ORDNT, ABCSA)
             CALL ARCTN(ANG1, YVAL(J), WIDTH + BASE – 5.0)
```

6-6   The EXTERNAL Statement

It is possible to use a subprogram name as an argument to be transmitted to a function subprogram or a subroutine subprogram. The subprogram name will replace a dummy subprogram name in the subprogram to be executed. An EXTERNAL statement must then be furnished at the beginning of the calling program (between the type statements and any DIMENSION statements) to tell the FORTRAN compiler that the named subprogram must be loaded into core memory with the calling program when the calling program is executed. Otherwise the FORTRAN compiler would consider the subprogram name to be the name of an ordinary variable.

Consider the following subprogram which contains a subprogram name in its argument list:

```
             FUNCTION SCALE(A, PROGM)
             DIMENSION A(10)
             SCALE = 0.
             DO 1 L = 1, 10
1            SCALE = SCALE + A(L)
             SCALE = PROGM(SCALE)
             RETURN
             END
```

The SCALE subprogram sums the ten values of the array A and takes the PROGM function of the sum to be the result of SCALE. Now consider the following calling program which will use the SCALE subprogram:

```
             EXTERNAL SQRT, ABS
             DIMENSION B(10)
1            FORMAT (10F7.2, I7)
             READ (2, 1) B, NUMB
             GO TO (2, 3), NUMB
2            ANSER = SCALE(B, SQRT)
             GO TO 4
3            ANSER = SCALE(B, ABS)
```

```
4       WRITE (1, 1) B, NUMB, ANSER
        STOP
        END
```

The calling program will calculate either the square root of the sum of the B array or the absolute value of the sum of the B array, depending upon whether NUMB is equal to one or to two. Either SQRT or ABS will replace the dummy function name PROGM when the SCALE subprogram is executed. The program which calls SCALE shows the use of subprogram names in argument lists and an example of the EXTERNAL statement. Subprogram names used as arguments by a calling program must appear in a list, separated from each other by commas, in an EXTERNAL statement as shown in the example.

6-7   The COMMON Statement

The preceding sections have shown how subprograms with large numbers of arguments and results can be called by FORTRAN programs. Frequently it develops that several of the arguments to a subroutine or a function subprogram do not change each time the procedure is used, and that programming could be simplified if it were not necessary to refer to all the arguments in the list each time the subroutine is called. A subroutine may only need to refer to certain arguments the first time the subroutine is called, for initialization purposes. Some of the arguments transmitted to a subroutine may only be needed for subsequent transmittal to another subroutine, and much writing of repetitive argument lists could be avoided if a group of subroutines could be given automatic access to a common list of arguments. Such automatic access is provided by the COMMON statement.

The COMMON statement is a specification statement (nonexecutable) which must be located at the beginning of a FORTRAN program or subprogram immediately after the REAL, INTEGER, EXTERNAL and DIMENSION statements if any. A typical COMMON statement is

$$\text{COMMON ANGLE, DOG(5, 5), TABLE(100), D, E, F} \qquad (6\text{-}5)$$

containing a list of variables, including subscripted array names, separated by commas. (In the above example, D, E and ANGLE could be array names whose sizes were specified in a preceding DIMENSION statement. DOG and TABLE are array names whose size is specified in the COMMON statement. Either method of specifying array dimensions is acceptable.)

The COMMON statement causes core memory locations for the variables in the COMMON list to be assigned to a "common area" which will also be used to store variables listed in COMMON statements from other programs and subprograms to be executed together. Memory locations in the common area are assigned to decreasing storage addresses in the same sequence as the variables listed in the COMMON statement. The common area in core memory is a part of the regular core memory of the computer used in a special way by the FORTRAN compiler.

The common storage allocation caused by statement (6-5) consists of a variable location for ANGLE, followed by 25 variable locations for DOG, followed by 100 variable locations for TABLE and 3 variable locations for D, E and F. The number of words required for each variable location will depend upon whether the variables are one- or two-word integers, two-word standard precision real variables or three-word extended precision real variables. A subprogram to be executed with the program containing statement (6-5) might contain the COMMON statement

$$\text{COMMON DEGS, CAT(25), ALIST(100), G} \tag{6-6}$$

The COMMON statements (6-5) and (6-6) in a calling program and a subprogram will cause ANGLE in the calling program to occupy the same memory location as DEGS in the subprogram, the 25 variables in DOG to occupy the same locations as CAT, TABLE to occupy the same locations as ALIST and D to occupy the same location as G. If the calling program assigns a value of 5.76 to ANGLE by execution an arithmetic statement such as ANGLE = 5.76, then the variable DEGS in the subroutine will have the value 5.76 even though DEGS is not listed in the CALL statement for the subroutine.

The variables in COMMON statements (6-5) and (6-6) have different names, but they must correspond in mode and number of words per variable. If CAT were an integer array while DOG were a real array, then CAT and DOG could not be used interchangeably because they would have different formats in core memory. Several COMMON statements can be used in a single program to extend the size of the common area. The statements

COMMON A, B, C
COMMON D, E, F

are equivalent to the statement

COMMON A, B, C, D, E, F

However, COMMON statements in any one program must not refer to the same variable name more than once. The statements

COMMON A, B, C
COMMON D, A, F

are invalid because the variable A is included twice. Any variable name which appears in a FUNCTION or SUBROUTINE statement in a program cannot be used in a COMMON statement in that program.

Notice that the array DOG(5,5) in statement (6-5) and the array CAT(25) in statement (6-6) are of the same length and implied mode but are dimensioned differently. This shows one way to change two-dimensional array notation to one-dimensional notation. Since arrays are all stored in sequence in descending core locations and because the leftmost subscript varies most rapidly (Section 5-2), the array element DOG(3, 2) will be stored in the same location as the array element CAT(8). If J and K are the dimensions of a two-dimensional array, then any subscript (j, k) of the two-dimensional array can be converted to a subscript (n) of a one-dimensional array through use of the equation

$$n = J(k - 1) + j \qquad (6\text{-}7)$$

The equivalent conversion equation for a three-dimensional array of dimensions (I, J, K) converted to a one-dimensional subscript n is

$$n = IJ(k - 1) + I(j - 1) + i \qquad (6\text{-}8)$$

As an example of the use of COMMON statements, consider a set of three subroutines to be used for graph plotting on the 1132 Printer. The three subroutines include a SETUP subroutine to initialize each graph and compute a scale factor, a SCALE subroutine to insert characters into each line of the graph, and a GRAPH subroutine to write each completed line. Each value to be plotted is scaled to an integer between zero and 119, since there are 120 print positions in each line. The integer is then used as a subscript to locate a subscripted character in the line. The line is then printed after any other necessary characters have been inserted, and the line is then reinitialized to blank characters. The three subroutines are coded as follows:

```
        SUBROUTINE SETUP
        INTEGER BLANK, PLOT
        COMMON LINE(120), BLANK, PLOT, XMIN, XMAX, SPAN
        SPAN = 120./(XMAX – XMIN)
        DO 1 I = 1, 120
   1    LINE(I) = BLANK
        RETURN
        END
```

XMAX and XMIN are the maximum and minimum values which may be assumed by X, the variable to be plotted. BLANK is a character used to clear the LINE before inserting characters; BLANK could be read from cards or tape by the calling program in A1 format.

```
        SUBROUTINE SCALE(X)
        INTEGER BLANK, PLOT
        COMMON LINE(120), BLANK, PLOT, XMIN, XMAX, SPAN
        IX = SPAN * (X – XMIN) + 1.5
        IF (IX) 1, 1, 2
   1    IX = 1
   2    IF (IX – 120) 4, 4, 3
   3    IX = 120
```

111

```
4       LINE(IX) = PLOT
        RETURN
        END
```

Here SPAN is the scaling factor previously computed by SETUP. The statement containing SPAN scales any value of X between XMIN and XMAX into an integer between zero and 120. A series of IF statements are then used to determine that the value of X was in range. Finally the integer value IX is used as a subscript to insert the character PLOT at the correct place in LINE. PLOT, like BLANK, could be read from cards or tape in A1 format by the calling program.

```
        SUBROUTINE GRAPH
        INTEGER BLANK, PLOT
        COMMON LINE(120), BLANK
7       FORMAT (1H, 120A1)
        WRITE (3, 7) LINE
        DO 1 I = 1, 120
1       LINE(I) = BLANK
        RETURN
        END
```

Notice that the COMMON list for the GRAPH subroutine need only contain LINE and BLANK because these are the only variables used in common with the other subroutines and the calling program, and are the very first variables in the common area. The GRAPH subroutine writes the LINE and then reinitializes LINE to a string of BLANK characters.

The calling program should contain an * IOCS record specifying all input-output devices used by the calling program and the subroutines to be called; * IOCS records are not used with subroutines.

A calling program which uses the SETUP, SCALE and GRAPH subroutines might contain the following code:

```
        INTEGER BLANK, PLOT
        COMMON LINE(120), BLANK, PLOT, XMIN, XMAX, SPAN
C-----READ CHARACTERS FOR BLANK AND PLOT, ESTABLISH XMIN AND XMAX.
1       FORMAT (2A1)
        READ (2, 1) BLANK, PLOT
        XMIN = -1.0
        XMAX = 1.0
C-----SETUP THE GRAPH AND GO TO THE TOP OF THE NEXT PAGE ON THE
C-----PRINTER.
        CALL SETUP
2       FORMAT (1H1)
        WRITE (3, 2)
C-----PLOT FUNCTION Y = SIN(X), USING DO LOOP FROM 0 TO 2 PI.
        DO 3 I = 1, 100
```

112

```
                CALL SCALE(SIN(0.0628318*I)
      3         CALL GRAPH
                STOP
                END
```

All variables except the value to be plotted are conveyed to the subroutines through the use of COMMON statements, and the value to be plotted is transmitted as the single argument of the SCALE subroutine, equal to the sine of 0.0628318*I, where 0.0628318 is simply pi/50. The resulting graph consists of 100 lines, each containing one PLOT character. Each line represents an increase in angle of pi/50; the whole graph covers a range of two pi. The position of the PLOT character in each line is proportional to the sine of I/100, where I is the line number.

The SCALE subroutine could be called several times before the GRAPH subroutine is called, with the SCALE subroutine causing several plotted characters to appear on each line of the finished graph. The GRAPH subroutine reinitializes the line after each use by filling the LINE array with BLANK characters. Although the subroutines in this example use identical variable names in COMMON for increased readability, it is not necessary to use the same names. Only subroutine subprograms may change the values of variables in COMMON; any attempt to change COMMON variables in a function subprogram will result in an error message during compilation. COMMON variables cannot be initialized with a DATA statement.

6-8   The EQUIVALENCE Statement

Occasionally two or more programmers may work on parts of a single program or subroutine and find that they have used different names in referring to the same variable. Sometimes it will be found that a particular array is only needed for input operations and that another array is only used for output; in this case the two arrays could share the same locations in core memory with the result that several memory locations could be saved or used for other purposes. *The COMMON statement provided a method for sharing memory locations between variables in different programs; the EQUIVALENCE statement provides a means of sharing memory locations between variables within a single program or subroutine.* EQUIVALENCE statements must be placed immediately behind the COMMON statements in any program.

A typical EQUIVALENCE statement is

EQUIVALENCE (A, B, C), (TABLE(1), ALIST(1)), (D, E)

The variables named in an EQUIVALENCE statement are either subscripted or scalar variables, but never unsubscripted array names. Each pair of parentheses (except the subscript parentheses) encloses a list of variables which are to occupy the same memory locations. In the example the variables A, B and C will occupy the same

113

locations, the arrays TABLE and ALIST will occupy the same locations, and the variables D and E will occupy the same locations. Note that A, TABLE(1) and D will be in different locations since these variables are in different EQUIVALENCE lists within the same EQUIVALENCE statement. Since all the elements of an array are still stored in descending adjacent memory locations, equivalencing TABLE(1) and ALIST(1) will cause each element of TABLE to be equivalenced to the corresponding element of ALIST if the two arrays are of equal size.

The following rules should be observed in the use of the EQUIVALENCE statement. Although any number of variables may appear in a single EQUIVALENCE list and any number of lists may appear in a single EQUIVALENCE statement, the variables in a single list must all be of the same mode (real or integer). Within a single list there must not be more than one variable name which has appeared in another EQUIVALENCE list or in a COMMON statement.

An EQUIVALENCE statement may extend the size of the previously established COMMON area. For instance, the statements

```
DIMENSION LIST(5)
COMMON ITEM, JOBNO
EQUIVALENCE (LIST(1), ITEM)
```

will cause the entire array named LIST to be located in the COMMON area, with LIST(1) in the same location as ITEM, LIST(2) in the same location as JOBNO, and LIST(3), LIST(4) and LIST(5) also in the COMMON area.

An EQUIVALENCE statement must not be used in such a way as to change the starting location of the COMMON area. The statements

```
DIMENSION LIST(5)
COMMON ITEM, JOBNO
EQUIVALENCE (LIST(3), ITEM)
```

would cause LIST(1) and LIST(2) to extend past the beginning of the COMMON area (which started with ITEM, now equivalenced to LIST(3)).

Equivalencing subscripted variables from the same array is not permitted. Equivalencing subscripted variables from different arrays is permitted, subject to the above restrictions, and may be used to convert two- or three-dimensional arrays into one-dimensional arrays. The statements

```
DIMENSION BLOCK(10, 10), GROUP(100)
EQUIVALENCE (BLOCK(1, 1), GROUP(1))
```

will cause each element of BLOCK to be equivalenced to the corresponding element of GROUP. The subscript of GROUP which corresponds to each subscript of BLOCK can be determined from equations (6-7) and (6-8) of Section 6-7.

6-9   The Sequencing of Specification Statements

Specification statements, including DATA, REAL, INTEGER, EXTERNAL, DIMENSION, COMMON and EQUIVALENCE statements, must all appear before the first executable statement and before the first FORMAT statement in a program. The last statement in the program must be END. FORMAT statements may appear anywhere in the program after the specification statements, except as the last statement of or the first statement following a DO loop.

The specification statements must appear in the following sequence at the beginning of the program:

> REAL and/or INTEGER statements
> EXTERNAL statements
> DIMENSION statements
> COMMON statements
> EQUIVALENCE statements
> DATA statements

6-10   The PDUMP Subroutine

A subroutine in 1130 disk-oriented FORTRAN systems provides for dumping of several blocks of data from core memory by a single FORTRAN statement. The subroutine can dump arrays, constants and variables upon the line printer in hexadecimal, integer or floating-point format. The general form of the CALL statement is

CALL PDUMP(A1, B1, F1, A2, B2, F2, A3, B3, F3, A4, B4, F4 . . .)

where each group of three arguments (A_n, B_n and F_n) consists of the variable names of the first and last variables to be dumped (A_n and B_n) followed by a format integer F_n equal to zero for the hexadecimal format, four for integer format or five for floating-point format. To dump all variables from DOG to CAT in hexadecimal format we might write

CALL PDUMP(DOG, CAT, 0)

which will dump all variables from DOG through CAT regardless of whether DOG had a higher core memory address than CAT or vice versa.

6-11   Summary

This chapter on subroutines completes the presentation of the basic FORTRAN language for the 1130 system. The subroutine concept remains perhaps the most important concept in programming, and the extensive use of subroutines has come to be the hallmark of the experienced programmer. The use of subroutines allows the programmer to break up large programming assignments into many smaller pieces which can be debugged as independent units, greatly simplifying checkout. The core memory which can be saved through the use of subroutines makes it possible to program many applications which could not be handled at all without subroutines. The COMMON statement, which permits variables to be shared among different programs and subroutines, and the CALL statement, which establishes an automatic linkage from a calling program to a subroutine and transmits argument and result locations to the subroutine, can be made to serve as the two most powerful statements in the FORTRAN language.

6-12   Problems

1)   In each of the following statement functions, identify the name of the function, the names of the arguments of the functions, the names of the parameters of the function (if any), and any constants present in the statement definition.

    SUMOF(A, B, C) = A + B + C
    POWER(WIDTH, DEPTH) = WIDTH * DEPTH * X + 5.0
    ANY(X, Y, Z) = (X + A) ** 3 + Y/Z
    BFUNC(BETA) = BETA/6. + ALPHA − 3.1416

2)   A subroutine must be able to accept arguments from a calling program, transmit results back to the calling program and return control to the place in the calling program from which the call occurred. Describe how these functions are provided by the CALL and RETURN statements. Why must a function subprogram have only a single result?

3)   Suppose a call is made to a subroutine subprogram; can this subroutine, in turn, call a function subprogram? Give an example. Now suppose a function subprogram is called; can this function, in turn, call a subroutine? Give an example. Since subroutine subprograms may or may not return values, why is there a need for function subprograms?

4)   Consider the statement function statement:

    AVG3(A, B, C) = (A + B + C)/3.0

Could this be written as a function subprogram? Would the following subprogram accomplish the same effect?

    FUNCTION AVG3(A, B, C)
    AVG3 = (A + B + C)/3.0
    RETURN
    END

5) Is the following a valid function subprogram?

```
FUNCTION EMPTY(X)
RETURN
END
```

6) Is the following a valid subroutine subprogram?

```
SUBROUTINE EMPTY
RETURN
END
```

7) What does the following function subprogram accomplish?

```
      FUNCTION TRICK(X)
      IF(X) 5, 10, 15
5     TRICK = -X
      RETURN
10    TRICK = 0.
      RETURN
15    TRICK = X
      RETURN
      END
```

Is there a simpler way of accomplishing this effect? Hint: Check the 1130 library of FORTRAN compiler-supplied functions.

8) Write a program using *all* specification statements in their correct sequence.

9) The volume of a cylinder of radius R and height H is equal to 3.1416 * R * R * H. Write a statement function to find the volume VOL. Then write a function subprogram and a subroutine subprogram to do the same job. In each case, show examples of the statements which might be used to call the function or subroutine.

10) Write a function subprogram named SMALL to find the smallest element in a one-dimensional array of 100 variables named LIST. Why is it not possible to write SMALL as a statement function?

11) Draw a flow diagram for the TRIAL subprogram of Section 6-4. Why does this subprogram have more than one RETURN statement? Could TRIAL be rewritten so as to have only one RETURN statement?

12) Write a subroutine subprogram named MINMX to find both the smallest and the largest element in a one-dimensional array using a single DO loop. Draw the flow diagram.

117

13) What is the difficulty in using the ATAN function to determine the arc tangents in all four quadrants? How does the ARCTN subroutine subprogram solve this difficulty? Draw a flow diagram for the ARCTN subprogram.

14) Using the SETUP, SCALE and GRAPH subprogram of Section 6-7, write a calling program which will use these subprograms to plot a graph of the function $y = x^n$, where n is an input variable read from punched cards.

15) Rewrite the calling program of Problem 14 without using the COMMON statement, changing the subprogram SUBROUTINE statements to include the necessary arguments.

16) Draw flow diagrams for the SETUP, SCALE and GRAPH subprograms of Section 6-7. Explain how the SCALE subprogram locates each plotted character in the line to be plotted.

17) The following represents an invalid use of the EQUIVALENCE statement. Why? (Two errors are present.)

```
DIMENSION BLOCK(100)
EQUIVALENCE (DOG, BLOCK(50))
COMMON CAT, DOG, MOUSE
```

18) Draw a map of the COMMON area showing the relative locations of the variables described by the following:

```
DIMENSION AREA(25)
COMMON ALPHA, BETA, GAMMA
EQUIVALENCE (BETA, AREA(1))
```

19) Develop a calling program and one or more subprograms that will illustrate a valid use of the EXTERNAL statement.

CHAPTER 7:   DISK STORAGE AND MONITOR OPERATION

7-1   The Importance of Disk Storage

From a programmer's point of view, disk storage with interchangeable cartridges is the most valuable optional feature on the 1130 system. Disk storage makes it possible to execute programs of enormous size, programs of tens of thousands of FORTRAN statements; disk storage permits the manipulation of huge data files running into millions of characters; disk storage allows us to compile and execute a main program and related subprograms automatically without punching an object deck or tape; finally, *disk storage allows us to progress automatically from one job to the next, compiling and executing one program after another, without manual intervention.*

The presence of disk storage transforms the 1130 system into a vastly larger, more powerful computing system. It has been estimated that due to the relatively low cost of disk storage on the 1130, 90 percent of the installations of these computers will eventually acquire the programming power that disk storage provides.

This chapter describes the arrangement of data on disk storage, the operation of the 1130 Disk Monitor to automate a sequence of compilations and executions, and the FORTRAN statements provided to manipulate disk storage.

7-2   Disk Storage Organization and Timing

Disk storage is random access storage, as opposed to magnetic tape which is referred to as sequential storage. To read data which are on a magnetic tape at some distance from the data currently being read, we must pass all of the intervening tape through the reading mechanism of the tape drive or else rewind the entire reel of tape. To read data from disk storage at a distance from data currently being read, we simply retract the read/write head, jump it across the disk to the data to be read, and lower the head into place to read the desired data. The magnetic tape drive can move very quickly to the next block of data in sequence but the tape drive will require many seconds to get to information at the other end of the tape reel. The disk storage is able to get from the middle of the disk to data on any other part of the disk in less than a second. The data capacity of a reel of magnetic tape, however, is usually much larger than that of a disk cartridge.

Each type 2315 Disk Cartridge (used on the 1130 system) can hold 512,000 16-bit words of program instructions and data. The disk inside the cartridge resembles a phonograph record: it has two surfaces (top and bottom), each covered with a magnetic oxide into which a pattern of bits may be recorded. Each surface is divided into 200 tracks, and each track is further divided into four sectors of 320 usable words each. *The two read/write heads are positioned over two tracks on opposite sides of the disk at all times. The two tracks are said to form a cylinder of data consisting of eight sectors.* The total capacity of the disk is thus 320 words per sector times eight sectors per cylinder times 200 cylinders per disk, or 512,000 words.

The disk revolves at 1500 revolutions per minute and so requires 40 milliseconds (ms) for each revolution. The read/write heads take 15 ms to jump either one or two tracks, so a jump across all 200 tracks would require 1500 ms. In addition, 20 ms of settling time is required after each jump before the read/write heads can transmit data, and the time required to wait for the desired data to rotate to a position under the heads averages half a revolution or an additional 20 ms. Thus the total average time required to jump across ten tracks and then start reading data would be 5 * 15 + 20 + 20 or 115 ms, about one-tenth of a second.

7-3   Changing the Disk Cartridge

The disk cartridges are interchangeable, making it possible to have a whole library of disk cartridges for different applications, with each cartridge containing half a million words of information. The following procedure should be used to change a disk cartridge:

1)   Open the hinged cover of the disk storage drive.

2)   Turn off the disk drive motor, using the ON-OFF switch located beside the disk storage drive mechanism.

3)   Wait for the disk to stop rotating, then release the latch and remove the disk cartridge from the drive.

4)   Insert the new cartridge. Close the latch to lock the cartridge in place.

5)   Restart the disk drive motor and close the hinged cover. The disk cartridge can be read or written by the computer as soon as it comes up to speed. A light on the console will come on to signify "Disk Ready."

7-4   The 1130 Disk Monitor

The 1130 Disk Monitor is a collection of programs, supplied by IBM, which control the compilation, assembly and execution of programs on 1130 systems equipped with disk storage. The Disk Monitor also provides programs to control the storage and retrieval of both programs and data files, using disk storage to form a library of programs and data supplied by the user. *The Disk Monitor divides disk storage into four different functional areas:*

Area on Disk Storage	Contents
System Area	IBM-supplied programs
Fixed Area	Programs and data in fixed locations
User Area	Programs and data in variable locations
Working Storage	Remaining available empty space

The System Area includes the following major program groups:

System Area Program	Function
Supervisor	Processes monitor control records
DUP (Disk Utility Program)	Stores and retrieves programs and data
FOR (FORTRAN Compiler)	Compiles FORTRAN source programs
ASM (Assembler)	Assembles programs in assembly language
System Library	Library of IBM-supplied subroutines
Core Load Builder	Organizes programs for execution

The System Area also includes several other programs and data blocks, including the DCOM communications area, the core image loader, the core image buffer, and a cold start program to initialize monitor operations. Further detail on these programs can be found in the *IBM 1130 Disk Monitor System Reference Manual*, forms C26-3750 and C26-3717.

The Supervisor program reads all monitor control records and then transfers control of the computer to one of the other programs in the System Area to compile, assemble, store, retrieve or execute the programs or data which follow the monitor records.

The DUP program stores and retrieves programs and data to and from disk storage, as specified by DUP control records. The various DUP functons and control records are discussed in Section 7-6.

The FOR program compiles FORTRAN source programs as specified by the FORTRAN control records described in Section 4-1.

The ASM program assembles source programs written in assembly language as specified by the Assembler control records described in Section 12-7.

The System Library consists of many subroutines to handle input/output operations, data format and code conversions, and arithmetic routines including exponentiation, logarithms and trigonometry. The FORTRAN subroutines are described in Section 6-3; the assembly language subroutines are described in Chapter 13.

The Core Load Builder collects the various subroutines required by a main program and assigns addresses for the subroutines relative to the main program so that the subroutines can be loaded into core memory along with the main program and subsequently executed. The resulting group of main program plus subroutines is called a core load.

An 1130 system can have as many as five disk storage units, but only one disk storage unit will drive the system disk cartridge which contains the System Area programs. The other disk cartridges are called nonsystem cartridges, and they may contain the System Library programs but no other System Area program groups.

The Fixed Area is set aside for data and programs to which the user wishes to assign permanent disk addresses. The user can define the Fixed Area as two or more cylinders, and can then increase or decrease the size of the Fixed Area at any later time. If a program or data block is deleted from the Fixed Area, the specific sectors involved become available for other programs or data which may be added later by the user. Thus the user may establish unused sectors inside of the Fixed Area.

The FLET (Fixed Location Equivalence Table) is a location index for the contents of the Fixed Area on a specific disk cartridge. Each entry in FLET includes the name, format and size of a program or data file in disk blocks. A disk block is equal to one sixteenth of a sector or 20 words.

The User Area is reserved for programs and data which will be referred to by name and which do not require permanent disk addresses. The User Area and the Working Storage area share the sectors left over after the Fixed Area (if any) has been defined. As new programs or data are added to the User Area, the size of Working Storage is reduced accordingly. As programs or data are deleted from the User Area, the remaining programs and data are packed together to eliminate any unused sectors and the size of Working Storage is increased. The User Area normally contains the programs written by the user; the Fixed Area usually contains such data as inventory records, payroll master files, and other data which would be randomly accessed by referring to permanent disk addresses. Notice that the User Area is packed together after each deletion to eliminate any unused sectors, although unused sectors are allowed to remain in the Fixed Area after a deletion.

The LET (Location Equivalence Table) is a location index for the contents of the User Area on a specific disk cartridge. Each entry in LET includes the name, format and size in disk blocks (20 words each) of a program or data file.

The Working Storage area is a temporary storage area used by the FORTRAN compiler, the Assembler and the various program loaders. During a FORTRAN compilation the Working Storage must be large enough to contain the compiled object program prior to loading the object program into core memory.

122

The Supervisor of the 1130 Disk Monitor operates by reading monitor control records which call into action other IBM programs. These other programs (DUP, FOR, ASM, etc.) then read additional control records which further define the operations to be performed. After new programs are compiled or assembled, control of the computer may be turned over to the compiled or assembled programs for immediate execution, or another IBM program or a user-written program may be loaded into core from the disk and executed. The transfer of control from one program to the next is made automatically by the Supervisor as specified by the monitor control records. The automatic compilation and execution of a sequence of unrelated programs is called batch processing.

7-5   Batch Processing Under Monitor Control

The following monitor control records are used to control the sequence of compilations, assemblies and executions required to process a batch of jobs:

Monitor Control Record	Function
// *ANY COMMENT MESSAGE	Any comment message to the computer operator
// JOB T	Beginning of a job deck (T means temporary and is optional)
// ASM	Load the assembler and start assembling
// FOR	Load the FORTRAN compiler and start compiling
// RPG	Load the RPG compiler and start compiling
// PAUS	Wait for the operator to push the START button
// TYP	Next control record will come from the keyboard
// TEND	End of keyboard input; next control record will come from the principal input device
// DUP	Load the DUP program to manipulate disk storage
// XEQ MNAME	Load and execute the main program named MNAME
// EJECT	Cause the principal print device to skip to a new page and print the page header
// END	End of all monitor control records

All monitor control records must have // in columns one and two, a blank in column three, and a left-justified operation code in columns four through seven. If the first character of the operation code is an asterisk, the control record is considered a comment for the operator; it is printed immediately and the next record is read.

The JOB record defines the beginning of a new job deck or tape to be processed, which may contain several compilations and assemblies. If any program in a JOB deck will not compile, none of the programs in that JOB deck will be executed. The letter T in column eight of the JOB record indicates that the job is to be stored on the disk temporarily while the job is being processed; after processing, all programs or data files stored on the disk by DUP for this job will be deleted from the disk. If columns 11 through 14 of the JOB record contain a left-justified disk storage identification name, this name is compared with the name written upon the first sector of the disk, and operator intervention is required if the two names are not identical. The disk storage identification is originally written upon each disk by the Disk Cartridge Initialization Routine (DCIR), an IBM-supplied utility program used to clear and initialize each new disk cartridge.

If additional disk cartridges are needed, their identification names may be punched in columns 16-19, 21-24, 26-29 and 31-34. Processing can be speeded up by locating the core image buffer (CIB) and/or Working Storage upon cartridges other than the system cartridge. If this is done, the identification name of the cartridge to be used for the CIB is punched in columns 36-39 and the identification name of the cartridge for Working Storage in columns 41-44. Columns 46-53 may contain header data to be printed at the top of every listing page.

The ASM record instructs the monitor to load the assembler program into core memory, and should be followed by assembler control records and assembler source statements. The operation of the assembler is described in Chapter 12.

The FOR record causes the loading of the FORTRAN compiler and should be followed by FORTRAN control records and FORTRAN statements. The FORTRAN control records are listed in Section 4-1.

The RPG record similarly causes loading of the RPG compiler. See Chapter 14.

The PAUS record halts the computer to allow the computer operator to put a new card deck in the hopper of the card reader, change the setting of the console switches or otherwise adjust the computer controls. The monitor will proceed to read the next control record as soon as the PROGRAM START button is pushed.

The TYP record instructs the monitor to read the next control record from the console instead of from cards or paper tape. Subsequent control records will continue to be read from the console (keyboard or console printer) until a TEND record is read.

The TEND record simply causes the monitor to return to the principal input device to read subsequent control records. The principal input device is chosen to be either cards or paper tape when the monitor is initialized on a disk cartridge.

The DUP record causes the DUP program to be loaded into core memory. DUP will then read the DUP control records discussed in Section 7-6, which describe how programs and data are to be moved between disk storage and core memory, punched cards, paper tape and the various printers. The DUP record must be followed by DUP control records.

The XEQ record causes the program whose name appears left-justified in columns 8 through 12 to be loaded into core memory and executed immediately. If no name is punched in these columns, the program which has just been compiled or assembled into working storage will be executed. If column 14 contains an L, a core map showing the core address of the main program and all subroutines and subprograms required by the main program will be printed. Columns 16 and 17 must contain the number of LOCAL, NOCAL, FILES and G2250 records, if any, which will follow this XEQ record; the use of these records to control programs and data in disk storage from a FORTRAN program is discussed in Section 7-9. If no LOCAL, NOCAL, FILES or G2250 records are used, the XEQ record is followed by the data records to be processed by the program to be executed. Column 19 of the XEQ record may be used to specify which of three disk input-output subroutines will be used by assembly language programs; column 19 is ordinarily left blank when used with FORTRAN programs.

The comment record is identified by an asterisk in column four; any monitor control record starting with // * will be printed immediately as a comment to the computer operator and ignored by the monitor program. Comment records may not follow immediately after ASM, FOR, RPG or XEQ records as these records must be followed by additional control records defining the specific ASM, FOR, RPG or XEQ function to be performed (or, in the case of XEQ, followed by data to be processed).

As an example of a simple FORTRAN program to be compiled and executed, consider the area program of Section 4-1. A complete listing of this program with all necessary 1130 monitor and FORTRAN control records might appear as follows:

```
// JOB T
// FOR
**  AREAS PROGRAM, WRITTEN BY JOHN DOE, 9/30/67.
*  NAME AREAS
*  IOCS (CARD, TYPEWRITER)
*  LIST ALL
```

```
C-----THIS PROGRAM COMPUTES THE AREAS OF TEN CIRCLES FROM THEIR
C-----DIAMETERS.
        NUMBR = 1
1       READ (2, 10) DIAM
        AREA = 3.1416 * (DIAM * 0.5) ** 2
        WRITE (1, 11) DIAM, AREA
        NUMBR = NUMBR + 1
        IF (NUMBR - 10) 1, 1, 345
345     CALL EXIT
10      FORMAT (F10.3)
11      FORMAT (' FOR A DIAMETER OF', F10.3, ' THE AREA IS', F10.3)
        END
// XEQ
bbb632.491
bbbbb46.05
bbbbb2.414
```

(followed by seven more data cards, then)

```
// JOB
```

The JOB record identifies the start of a new job, and the FOR record causes the FORTRAN compiler to be loaded into core memory from disk storage. The T in the JOB record identifies what follows as a temporary job. The FORTRAN control records, consisting of comment, NAME, IOCS and LIST, are described in Section 4-1. The program listing is identical to that of Section 3-13 except for the CALL EXIT statement (discussed in Section 7-7), which will return control of the computer to the disk monitor after ten areas have been computed.

Because the XEQ record does not contain any program name the AREAS program will be executed, since AREAS is the last program to be compiled into the working storage area. The XEQ record is followed by the data, consisting of ten diameters, one per card, in F10.3 format (b indicates a blank character). After reading the tenth data record, the AREAS program will execute the CALL EXIT statement as indicated by the IF statement. The disk monitor Supervisor will then be loaded back into core memory and will read the next record, which should be the JOB card for the next job to be processed.

7-6   DUP Control Records and Operation

The DUP control records which control the storing, deleting and transmitting of programs and data to and from disk storage use the following format:

Column Positions in the Record	Function
1	Asterisk
2-12, left-justified	DUP function name
13-14	"From" device
17-18	"To" device
21-25, left-justified	Program or data file name
27-30, right-justified	Count field for data
31-34	ID name of "from" cartridge
37-40	ID name of "to" cartridge
41-80	User's comments

The following codes are used to indicate "from" and "to" devices:

Device Code	Device Description
CD	Card reader (or paper tape if the monitor has been loaded from tape)
FX	Fixed Area on the disk
PR	Principal printing device
PT	Paper tape
UA	User Area on the disk
WS	Working Storage area on the disk

The count field in columns 27 through 30 is a decimal, right-justified field which describes the number of records to be moved from the "from" device to the "to" device during data movements only; the count field is left blank for DUP operations involving the movement of programs. If the "from" device is disk storage, the count field should contain the number of sectors to be moved; otherwise the count field contains the number of cards or paper tape records to be moved. Notice that DUP control records, unlike FORTRAN control records, require left- or right-justified fields in specific card columns. In particular, the DUP function name must start in column two.

If the ID names of the cartridges are omitted, then the LET and FLET tables of each cartridge attached to the system and searched for the program or data file name. This search can be eliminated by providing the ID names, saving time if several cartridges are on line (attached to the system). The use of cartridge ID names makes it possible to transfer programs and data files from one cartridge to another.

The following table lists the DUP control records by function and indicates what information fields must be supplied for each function. If a field is used only

127

under certain conditions, that field is marked with a number in parentheses and explained at the end of the table.

Function	From	To	Name	Count	From ID	To ID
Columns:	13-14	17-18	21-25	27-30	31-34	37-40
*DUMP	Yes	Yes	(1)		Option	Option
*DUMPDATA	Yes	Yes	(1)	Yes	Option	Option
*DUMPDATAE	Yes	Yes	(1)	Yes	Option	Option
*DUMPLET			(2)		Option	
*DUMPFLET			(2)		Option	
*STORE	Yes	Yes	(3)		Option	Option
*STOREDATA	Yes	Yes	(3)	Yes	Option	Option
*STOREDATAE	Yes	Yes	(3)	Yes	Option	Option
*STOREDATACI	Yes	Yes	(3)	(4)	Option	Option
*STORECI	Yes	Yes	Yes	Yes	Option	Option
*STOREMOD	Yes	Yes	Yes		Option	Option
*DELETE			Yes		Option	
*DEFINE FIXED AREA				Yes	(5)	Yes
*DEFINE VOID ASSEMBLER						
*DEFINE VOID FORTRAN						
*DEFINE VOID RPG						
*DEFINE PRINC PRINT			(6)			
*DEFINE PRINC INPUT			(6)			
*DWADR						Yes

NOTES:

(1)   Not required when dumping from Working Storage to a printer.

(2)   Use of a name causes only the entry for that name to be dumped.

(3)   Not required if storing to Working Storage.

(4)   Count not required if storing from Working Storage.

(5)   Requires minus sign in column 31 if Fixed Area is being decreased.

(6)   The machine type number (1132, 1403, 2501, 1442, 1134) is required.

In performing the required functions, the DUP program automatically converts data and programs from one format to another to accommodate the formatting requirements of the various input-output devices. The names and abbreviations of the formats are as follows:

Format Name	Abbreviation
Disk System Format	DSF
Disk Data Format	DDF
Disk Core Image Format	DCI
Card System Format	CDS
Card Data Format	CDD
Card Core Image Format	CDC
Paper Tape System Format	PTS
Paper Tape Data Format	PTD
Paper Tape Core Image Format	PTC
Printer Data Format	PRD

Complete details on these formats and their restrictions can be found in the *IBM 1130 Disk Monitor System Reference Manual,* form C26-3717. The information from punched cards and paper tape is stored on the disk in a "bit image" format such that every four card columns (48 punches) become the contents of three words on disk storage (48 bits), and two eight-hole frames of paper tape (16 holes) become the contents of one word on disk storage (16 bits). The card format of three 16-bit words for every four columns allows 54 words to be packed into the first 72 columns of each card; columns 73-80 are used for identification and deck sequence numbers in conventional IBM card code.

The use of a bit image format for card data by DUP means that data cards cannot be read by DUP to be stored in disk storage for later processing by FORTRAN programs; instead a user-written FORTRAN program should be used to read the data cards and write their contents upon the disk, using the disk WRITE statement of Section 7-8.

The DUMP, DUMPDATA and DUMPDATAE functions move programs and data from the User Area, Fixed Area or Working Storage to punched cards, paper tape or a printer. DUMP, DUMPDATA and DUMPDATAE can also be used to move programs and data from the User Area or the Fixed Area to Working Storage. DUMPDATA and DUMPDATAE require a count field containing the number of sectors to be dumped.

The DUMPLET and DUMPFLET functions print the entire LET and FLET tables upon the principal printer of the system. If a cartridge ID name is specified, only that cartridge LET and FLET will be dumped; otherwise the LET and FLET of all on-line cartridges will be dumped.

129

The STORE function moves programs from cards, paper tape or Working Storage to the User Area or Working Storage. A program name is not required if the "to" area is Working Storage. The STORECI function moves programs only from cards, paper tape or Working Storage to the User Area or the Fixed Area. STORECI converts all programs to an absolute "core image" format which loads into core memory faster than the relative or relocatable format used by STORE. After a program has been moved by STORECI, all the subroutines required by the program have been added to the program so that no additional references to the subroutine library need be made the next time that the program is loaded into core memory. A program that has been moved by STORE contains only linkages to any required subroutines which will be obtained from the library on other parts of the disk when the program is loaded. Thus the program moved by STORE takes less space on the disk but requires a few extra seconds to load. STORECI requires that the number of any FILES to be used by the program must be in the count field. (FILES are discussed in Section 7-9.)

The STOREDATA function moves data from cards, paper tape or Working Storage to the User Area, to Working Storage or to the Fixed Area on the disk. Each data file to be moved must start at the beginning of a sector and the count field must contain the number of cards, paper tape records, or sectors to be moved. The data file need not be named if it is going from cards or paper tape to Working Storage. The output from STOREDATA is always in disk data format. The STOREDATACI function is similar except that output is always in core image format (as in STORECI). STOREDATA expects input in a non-core-image format; STOREDATACI expects input in one of the core image formats. STOREDATAE is to STOREDATA as DUMPDATAE is to DUMPDATA.

The STOREMOD function is used to move either a program or data from Working Storage to the User Area or to the Fixed Area, overlaying and thus replacing a program or data file of the same name in the User Area or the Fixed Area. The new program or data to be moved must not be longer (occupy more sectors) than the program or data to be replaced. If the name of the program to be replaced cannot be found in the LET or FLET tables, then STOREMOD operates like the STORE function and finds additional space for the new program.

The DELETE function is used to delete programs or data from the User Area or the Fixed Area. The name of the program or data file is deleted from LET or FLET, and the User Area is packed together to eliminate any unused sectors resulting from the deletion. The Fixed Area is not packed, and a dummy entry (1DUMY) is placed in the FLET table in place of the deleted name.

The DEFINE function is used to initiate or increase the size of the Fixed Area, to delete the assembler program from the disk, or to delete the FORTRAN or RPG compiler from the disk. The assembler and FORTRAN programs cannot be deleted if a Fixed Area has previously been defined on the same disk. The Fixed

Area must be defined (if at all) to be at least two cylinders, with the number of cylinders right-justified in the count field. Subsequent use of the DEFINE FIXED AREA function will increase or decrease the Fixed Area by the number of cylinders in the count field. Deleting the assembler or FORTRAN will make more space available for the Working Storage, User Area and Fixed Area.

DEFINE PRINC PRINT and DEFINE PRINC INPUT are used to define the input-output devices to be used by the Disk Monitor program for dumps, error messages, etc.

The DWADR function writes the address of each sector in Working Storage upon a specifically reserved word in the sector. This function is used to repair and restore correct disk addresses whenever the addresses have been destroyed during execution of a user's program. The contents of Working Storage are destroyed by the operation of DWADR.

Each DUP function causes some information to be printed on the principal printer, usually the address and length of the program, the data file or the disk area being processed by the function involved. Some DUP functions, such as DELETE, may require minutes since much of the disk may have to be repacked. *All DUP functions must be allowed to complete their operations without interruption, or the LET or FLET tables may be left in an unusable state.*

The DUP functions of primary interest to the FORTRAN programmer are the STORE and DELETE functions. STORE is used to store programs and sub-programs in the User Area after compilation for later use with a main program, and DELETE is used to delete these subprograms from the User Area at the conclusion of the job if the subprograms are not to become a permanent part of the user's library. As an example, consider the ORBIT program developed in Chapter 8. The ORBIT program consists of a main program (named ORBIT) which calls two sub-programs (ARCTN and TRIAL), all written in FORTRAN. A card deck sequence of monitor control records, FORTRAN control records and DUP control records which will cause ORBIT, ARCTN and TRIAL to be compiled and executed might be as follows:

```
// JOB
// FOR
** ORBIT ANALYZER PROGRAM, 6/21/67.
* NAME ORBIT
* IOCS (CARD, 1132 PRINTER)
* ONE WORD INTEGERS
* LIST ALL
```
(FORTRAN statements for ORBIT, terminating with an END statement)
```
// DUP
*STORE      WS  UA  ORBIT
// FOR
```

```
**  ORBIT ANALYZER PROGRAM, 6/21/67.
*  ONE WORD INTEGERS
*  LIST ALL
         SUBROUTINE ARCTN(ANGLE, Y, X)
```

(FORTRAN statements for ARCTN, terminating with an END statement)

```
// DUP
*STORE      WS  UA  ARCTN
// FOR
**  ORBIT ANALYZER PROGRAM, 6/21/67.
*  ONE WORD INTEGERS
*  LIST ALL
         FUNCTION TRIAL(N, X, FX)
```

(FORTRAN statements for TRIAL, terminating with an END statement)

```
// DUP
*STORE      WS  UA  TRIAL
// XEQ ORBIT
```

(Data cards, if any, for the ORBIT program would go here)

```
// DUP
*DELETE               ORBIT
*DELETE               ARCTN
*DELETE               TRIAL
// JOB
```

The JOB and FOR monitor control records are followed by the FORTRAN control records and FORTRAN statements for the ORBIT program, after which DUP is called to store the compiled object program for ORBIT from Working Storage to the User Area. The same sequence of operations is then repeated for the two subprograms, ARCTN and TRIAL. ARCTN and TRIAL have no * IOCS or * NAME control records because they are subroutines; only main programs use these records. Notice also that the DUP functions STORE and DELETE must start in column two of the control record.

The XEQ monitor control record then causes the ORBIT object program to be loaded into core memory. During the loading process, the ORBIT program will cause ARCTN and TRIAL (plus any other required subroutines from the subroutine library) to be loaded. The XEQ card is followed by the data cards for ORBIT to be read by the ORBIT program directly, instead of by the monitor. The last data card is followed by a call for DUP to delete ORBIT, ARCTN and TRIAL from the User Area. Finally, another JOB card initializes the Disk Monitor to begin whatever job may appear next at the card reader.

Two steps may be taken to shorten the sequence of control records used to compile and execute the ORBIT program. First, a "T" in column eight of the JOB record would make it unnecessary to delete ORBIT, ARCTN and TRIAL at the end of the job. The "T" would cause the whole job to be considered temporary by the monitor and the programs stored as part of the job would be automatically deleted at the end of the job. Second, if ORBIT is compiled last after ARCTN and TRIAL it is not necessary to store ORBIT in the User Area. An XEQ record with a blank name field immediately behind the ORBIT program END statement would then cause ORBIT to be loaded directly from Working Storage for execution. Since ARCTN and TRIAL had been previously stored in the User Area, they would be loaded with ORBIT because they are called in the ORBIT program. Eliminating the store operation for ORBIT would save several seconds of computer time.

7-7   FORTRAN Disk Commands: CALL LINK and CALL EXIT

In Section 7-1 it was mentioned that disk storage permits the execution of programs of immense size, running to thousands of FORTRAN statements; the statement which makes all this possible is the CALL LINK statement. *Using CALL LINK we can take a very large main program and break it up into many smaller programs,* each a main program to the compiler. The various program segments are then compiled separately and stored in the user area of the disk. CALL LINK permits any program or segment to call another segment, which will then be loaded into core memory together with any required subprograms or subroutines and given control of the computer. *The format of the CALL LINK statement is*

CALL LINK (NAME)

where NAME is the name of any main program residing in disk storage. NAME must be one to five alphameric characters where the first character is a letter. Program control is transferred to the first executable statement in the named program, after the program is loaded into core memory from the disk.

As an example, consider a program named DOG which must be segmented into four parts to make it small enough to fit into core memory. We will call these parts DOG1, DOG2, DOG3 and DOG4, compile them as separate main programs and store them in the User Area. At the logical end of DOG1 we would have the statement

CALL LINK(DOG2)

to transfer control to DOG2. At the end of DOG2, the statement

CALL LINK(DOG3)

would take control to DOG3, at the end of which the statement

CALL LINK(DOG4)

would cause DOG4 to be loaded and executed. Any main program may call any other main program on the disk in this manner: DOG4 may call DOG1 to repeat the entire sequence, or DOG3 might call DOG2 to recalculate part of the data involved.

Depending upon data considerations, DOG1 might call any of the other three programs. We might have a variable NUMB such that control should go to DOG2 if NUMB is one or two, to DOG3 if NUMB is three, and to DOG4 if NUMB is four. The statements

```
      GO TO (31, 31, 51, 61), NUMB
31    CALL LINK(DOG2)
51    CALL LINK(DOG3)
61    CALL LINK(DOG4)
```

will handle the situation nicely.

Different programs connected by CALL LINK can use the same variables in COMMON, since COMMON is not changed by the loading operation caused by CALL LINK if the incoming program has a COMMON area of the same size as the outgoing program. If the new COMMON area is not the same size as the old, then the size of COMMON is determined by the incoming program.

The CALL EXIT statement is used to return program control to the Disk Monitor when a program is finished executing; CALL EXIT thus replaces the STOP statement used to end a program in the card and paper tape systems. Notice that every program written for Disk Monitor control must assume that another program is stacked up in the card or paper tape reader right behind it. Each program should identify its own last data card (perhaps by reading a zero in a field that could not be zero, such as a date field) and then CALL EXIT to return control to the monitor, which will then read the monitor control cards for the next program and process the next program accordingly.

The format of CALL EXIT is simply

    CALL EXIT

Notice that although CALL EXIT will be the last program statement to be executed it is not necessarily the physically last statement in the program; other blocks of statements representing various transfers from IF and GO TO statements may well come after the CALL EXIT statement in the program listing.

7-8   FORTRAN Disk Commands: READ, WRITE, FIND and DEFINE FILE

As the CALL LINK statement provides a method of getting to other programs on the disk, so READ, WRITE and FIND statements are used to read and write data to and from the disk. First it is necessary to define the location and arrangement of the data on the disk, through use of the DEFINE FILE statement. The DEFINE FILE statement by itself only refers to files of data in Working Storage, but DEFINE FILE may be combined with the *FILES control record (Section 7-9) to refer to files in the User Area or the Fixed Area. A typical DEFINE FILE statement is

DEFINE FILE 132 (50, 300, U, NEXT), 57 (27, 80, U, NREC)

where the statement contains one or more lists contained within parentheses. Each list is preceded by an integer, ranging from 1 to 32,767, which is a symbolic file number to be referenced in subsequent READ, WRITE and FIND statements. Inside each list are two integers, the letter U and an integer variable, all separated by commas. The first integer (50 and 27 in the example) defines the number of file records in each symbolic file. The second integer (300 and 80 in the example) defines the number of words of memory in each file record, which must not be greater than 320 words. The number of sectors in a defined file, which is the number of file records divided by the number of records which can be contained in one 320-word sector, must not exceed 1600. The letter U must always be present to indicate that these files will be handled by READ and WRITE statements which do not change the format of the data. The final integer variable (NEXT and NREC in the example) is the number of the next available file record after the execution of each READ or WRITE statement affecting the disk. It is not necessary to initialize this last integer variable to any particular value prior to executing a READ or a WRITE. Any number of lists in parentheses may be included in a single DEFINE FILE statement to define any number of different symbolic files in Working Storage.

The example thus defines file 132 as 50 records of 300 words each and file 57 as 27 records of 80 words each. Since records are assigned to sectors on the disk so as not to overlap sector boundaries, file 132 will have 50 sectors of one record per sector with 20 unused words in each sector, and file 57 will have six sectors of four records each plus one sector containing three 80-word records and 80 words unused. Since floating-point variables occupy two or three words each, this fact must be taken into account when determining the size of disk records which must contain floating-point variables. Also the different programs which may use a single symbolic file should all be of the same precision; if one program is using EXTENDED PRECISION or ONE WORD INTEGERS control records then all programs should do so.

The DEFINE FILE statements in a program should appear before statement functions and before the first executable FORTRAN statement in the program, behind the specification statements (Section 6-9). DEFINE FILE should only be used in main programs; subprograms will then use the files defined by the main program which called the subprograms.

The disk READ, WRITE and FIND statements all use a similar format, of which an example is

```
READ (50' NREC) ABLE, BAKER, CHARL
WRITE (J4' 1) DELTA, GAMMA, THETA, XI
FIND (57' 41)
```

where the two integer variables or unsigned constants in parentheses and separated by an apostrophe are the symbolic file number and a record number within that file where transmission of data to or from core memory will begin. The record number (NREC in the first example) could also be an integer expression. The list of variables which follows specifies the variables in core memory to be written from or read into. All the list options of normal FORTRAN READ and WRITE statements may be used. These variables will frequently be array names, in which case the entire arrays would be read or written. Data transmission always starts at the beginning of a record and continues until enough words of data have been transmitted to fill or empty the list of variables. Again it must be emphasized that floating-point variables will occupy two or three words in a disk record or in core memory.

The FIND statement causes the read/write heads of the disk storage to jump to the place on the disk where the specified record in the specified file is stored while the FORTRAN program simultaneously proceeds to execute the subsequent statements, thereby saving an appreciable fraction of a second if the FIND can be executed many FORTRAN statements ahead of the statement which will READ or WRITE into the specified record. The time saved by FIND will be lost, however, if any other disk operation (such as CALL LINK or a call to a LOCAL program) occurs between the execution of the FIND and the subsequent READ or WRITE. The use of FIND is optional, but optimal use of FIND can greatly reduce the running time of large disk applications.

As an example of the use of disk READ, WRITE and DEFINE FILE statements, consider a program to read 120 cards, store all 80 columns of each card upon the disk in 20A4 format, and then read the cards back into core memory and print each card on the console typewriter. All necessary 1130 monitor and FORTRAN control records are included with the program listing.

```
// JOB T
// FOR
**  READ, FILE, AND PRINT 120 CARDS USING SYMBOLIC FILE NUMBER 30
*  NAME CARD1
*  IOCS (CARD, DISK, TYPEWRITER)
*  LIST ALL
        DEFINE FILE 30 (15, 320, U, NREC)
        DIMENSION CARDS (20, 8)
C-----EACH RECORD IS 320 WORDS, 8 CARDS AT 20 VARIABLES PER CARD
C-----SO 15 RECORDS ARE NEEDED TO HOLD 120 CARDS
1       FORMAT (20A4)
C-----READ AND STORE 120 CARDS
        DO 2 NCNT = 1, 15
        READ (2, 1) CARDS
2       WRITE (30 ' NCNT) CARDS
C-----NOW READ FROM THE DISK AND PRINT 120 CARDS
        DO 3 NCNT = 1, 15
```

```
          READ (30 ' NCNT) CARDS
3         WRITE (1, 1) CARDS
          CALL EXIT
          END
// XEQ
```

(The 120 data cards would go here)

```
// JOB
```

Notice that to create a 320-word record (the maximum possible size) we are storing eight cards per record and processing 15 records. There are many other record arrangements that could have done the job here. The DO index NCNT is used in the disk READ and WRITE statements to specify which record in file number 30 will be read or written next.

This particular program will be speeded up by the use of FIND to overlap the card reading and console typing operations with the job of finding the next record. Use can be made of the NREC variable from the DEFINE FILE statement to provide the record number of the next record. The new program listing is identical with the old listing through statement 1, so starting with statement 1 the new program using FIND is as follows:

```
1         FORMAT (20A4)
C-----READ AND STORE 120 CARDS
          DO 2 NCNT = 1, 15
          READ (2, 1) CARDS
          WRITE (30 ' NCNT) CARDS
2         FIND (30 ' NREC)
C-----NOW READ FROM THE DISK AND PRINT 120 CARDS
          DO 3 NCNT = 1, 15
          READ (30 ' NCNT) CARDS
          FIND (30 ' NREC)
3         WRITE (1, 1) CARDS
          CALL EXIT
          END
// XEQ
```

(The 120 data cards would go here)

```
// JOB
```

Notice that in every case FIND is executed immediately after the disk READ or WRITE statement to provide as much time as possible to find the next record on the disk before that record must be read or written. Since the variable NREC appears only in the DEFINE FILE statement of the main program, NREC must appear also in COMMON if NREC is to be used by subprograms.

Four additional control records are provided to modify the XEQ monitor control record. The first of these control records is LOCAL, which stands for "load on call."

LOCAL identifies subprograms and subroutines to be loaded into core memory only when called by a main program rather than being loaded into core along with the main program and thus reducing core memory available to the main program. For example, if a program will call one of five different subprograms depending upon the data involved, all five subprograms can be made LOCAL, so that only one of the five will be in core memory at any one time, reducing the space required for the five subprograms in core to that of the space required for the largest subprogram of the five. A typical LOCAL control record would be

*LOCALMNAME, SUB1, SUB2, SUB3, SUB4, SUB5

where MNAME is the name of the main program that will call the five subprograms, named SUB1 through SUB5. (Note that no blanks are permitted in a LOCAL record.) If several main programs will be executed as a result of a single XEQ record, then several LOCAL records may be used after the same XEQ record to list the subprograms to be called as LOCAL routines by each main program. If the last subprogram name in a LOCAL record is followed by a comma, then the next record (if a LOCAL record) is considered a continuation of the preceding LOCAL and the name of the main program need not be repeated. Several different LOCAL records may be used to describe the subprograms which will be LOCAL to a single main program. If the XEQ record contains no program name because the program is to be executed from Working Storage, then the main program name in the LOCAL record may be replaced with a comma, resulting in

*LOCAL, SUB1, SUB2, SUB3, SUB4, SUB5

Certain programming restrictions must be observed in connection with LOCAL subprograms and subroutines. No LOCAL routine may call another LOCAL routine or call any other subprogram which might cause a LOCAL routine to be called, because this would cause the first LOCAL routine to be overwritten in core memory before it had completed execution. If routine A calls routine B which calls routine C, and if A is a LOCAL, then neither B nor C may be LOCAL routines for the same main program that designated A as a LOCAL.

The second type of control record that may follow an XEQ record is the NOCAL record, which has the same format as the LOCAL record and must not contain any embedded blanks. *NOCAL specifies subprograms and subroutines which, although not called anyplace in a main program, must be loaded into core memory with the main program.* An example of such routines would be trace and dump routines that might be called from the computer console. If the five subprograms

SUB1 through SUB5 were all to be loaded though not called by the main program MNAME, the NOCAL control records would be

*NOCALMNAME,SUB1,SUB2,SUB3,SUB4,SUB5

All other rules which apply to LOCAL routines also apply to NOCAL routines.

The third type of control record that may follow an XEQ record is *the FILES record, which sets up an equivalence between the symbolic files defined by the DEFINE FILE statement (Section 7-8) and the named files which have been previously established in the User Area and the Fixed Area of the disk by DUP.* The DEFINE FILE statement only provides access to temporary files in Working Storage; the FILES record makes it possible for FORTRAN programs to read and update files in the User Area and the Fixed Area.

Suppose that symbolic file 47 is to be equivalenced to a parts inventory file stored by DUP in the Fixed Area under the name PARTS, and suppose that symbolic file 31 is to be equivalenced to a plant payroll master file stored by DUP in the Fixed Area under the name PAYRL. The FILES record to establish this equivalence is

*FILES(47,PARTS),(31,PAYRL)

where each symbolic file number from a DEFINE FILE statement is enclosed in. parentheses with the name of a previously defined disk data file. A single record may contain several such pairs enclosed by parentheses and separated by commas as shown. Again embedded blanks are not permitted.

If the files are not located on the system cartridge, a third parameter (in addition to the file number and file name) must be enclosed within the parentheses. The third parameter is the cartridge identification name (ID). If the file name is omitted, the file will be located in Working Storage on the specified cartridge.

The fourth type of control record that may follow an XEQ record is the G2250 record, which provides graphic capabilities. See IBM form numbers C26-3717 and C27-6934.

Any number of LOCAL, NOCAL, FILES and G2250 records may follow an XEQ record, but all the records of one type must be grouped together (two FILES records cannot have a NOCAL record between them). The sum of all the FILES records for a single XEQ record cannot exceed 640 units, counting the symbolic file numbers as one unit and the file names as two units each. The sum of all the LOCAL and NOCAL records for a single XEQ record cannot exceed 640 units, counting the subprogram names as two units and the mainline program names as three units. Notice that LOCAL, NOCAL, FILES and G2250 records must be read behind the XEQ record each time the program is executed.

If a given main program is too large to fit into the available core memory, the Disk Monitor will try to squeeze it in through the use of SOCALS, system overlays. Various combinations of the floating-point arithmetic subroutines and the input-output subroutines necessary to execute FORTRAN statements are grouped together as a kind of automatic load-on-call arrangement so that all the subroutines do not have to be in core memory at any one time. Obviously this arrangement will save some memory at the expense of increased execution time and increased disk activity as the various subroutine groups are alternately called in from the disk. If a given FORTRAN subroutine is one that would have been made a SOCAL routine by the Disk Monitor, the subroutine will still be called as a LOCAL if so specified in a LOCAL record. In other words, LOCAL records override any SOCAL groups which may be set up by the monitor.

7-9.1 The EQUAT Control Record

The EQUAT control record, available to 1130 users operating under DMS V2L4 or higher, when present immediately follows the JOB monitor control record which must have punched, right-adjusted in columns 60 and 61, the number of EQUAT records which follow it. Each EQUAT record has the form

*EQUAT(SUB1,SUB2),(SUB3,SUB4), . . . ,(SUBM,SUBN)

with no embedded blanks. SUB1, SUB3, etc., are the names of subprograms referenced in the job. When a core load is built, the EQUAT record causes references instead to the subprograms SUB2, SUB4, etc., respectively, and causes them to be loaded into core instead of SUB1, SUB3, etc. The calling sequence (number and, usually, mode and role of arguments, etc.) for SUB2 must be the same as the calling sequence for SUB1; the sequence for SUB4 must be the same as for SUB3, etc. Use of the EQUAT record enables a programmer to substitute various subprograms for others without having to recompile or reassemble the calling program.

7-10 The ORBIT Program with LOCAL Subprograms

The ORBIT program, discussed in Section 7-6, consists of a main program ORBIT (developed in Chapter 8) and two subprograms, ARCTN and TRIAL. Actually ORBIT calculates satellite trajectories which fall into several types or kinds depending upon the initial velocity of the satellite. Each kind of orbit is then calculated by a separate set of equations which may involve the use of ARCTN and TRIAL. Let us examine the control records which would be required to execute six kinds of orbital calculations as LOCAL routines called by the ORBIT main program. We will name the LOCAL routines KIND1 through KIND6.

The subprograms ARCTN, TRIAL, and KIND1 through KIND6 would be compiled first and stored in the User Area through the use of DUP and STORE control records. Then ORBIT would be compiled into Working Storage, and the following XEQ and LOCAL records would follow the END statement in ORBIT:

```
// XEQ        01
*LOCAL,KIND1,KIND2,KIND3,KIND4,KIND5,KIND6
```

The "01" in columns 16 and 17 of the XEQ record indicates that one LOCAL, NOCAL or FILES record will follow the XEQ record. The name of the main program ORBIT does not appear in the LOCAL record because ORBIT is to be executed from Working Storage.

A decision frequently must be made as to whether a program should be segmented through the use of LOCALs or CALL LINK statements. Since the average LOCAL subroutine is smaller than the average core load brought into core by a CALL LINK, the LOCAL will load faster. If several LOCALs are involved which must be loaded repeatedly, however, it may be faster to create a second core load involving all the subroutines (which will need to be loaded only once through the use of CALL LINK).

In Chapter 8 ORBIT is programmed as a large main program without the use of LOCAL routines; the incorporation of LOCAL subprograms is left as an exercise for the reader.

7-11   Simulating Magnetic Tape on Disk Storage

The BACKSPACE, REWIND and END FILE statements are available on 1130 disk systems to manipulate disk storage in a way that simulates magnetic tape processing. If the user defines a data file in the Fixed Area with a file name of $$$$$, this file can then be used to simulate magnetic tape operation. The tape unit number is replaced by the logical unit number of the disk storage dirve, zero through four. The statement

BACKSPACE 3

will then backspace disk storage drive 3 for one record toward the front of the file. The statement

REWIND 2

will return to the front (beginning) of the file on drive 2 so that the first record in the file will be the next record to be read. The statement

END FILE 0

will cause an end-of-file record to be written on drive 0.

The READ and WRITE statements used to manipulate the $$$$$ file are described in Section 5-10.

7-12   Summary

The ability to create and maintain large files of data is central to many commercial and scientific computing applications. This ability is best provided in the 1130 system through the use of disk storage and the techniques of naming and defining data files. Extremely large programs can be executed via disk storage through the use of the CALL LINK statement and LOCAL control records. Finally, disk storage provides an automatic batch-processing capability through the "hands off" compilation and execution of long strings of different jobs, each consisting of several main programs and subprograms. For these reasons, disk storage is the programmer's most important hardware option.

As this book goes to press various additions are being proposed for the 1130 monitors, and a programmer requiring the full range of monitor functions should refer to the latest version of the IBM manual *IBM 1130 Disk Monitor System Reference Manual* (form C26-3750).

7-13   Problems

1) If the characters from all 80 columns of 50 punched cards are stored on the disk in A1 format, how many sectors will be required? How many cylinders? (Assume that each card is stored entirely within a single sector, but that a sector may contain more than one card.)

2) How many sectors and cylinders will be required for the solution of Problem 1 if A2 format is used?

3) How much time would be required to move the disk read/write heads to a 3,000-word program located 50 tracks from the present position of the heads and then read the program into core memory?

4) Is it advisable to use the LOCAL control record in all programs containing subprograms? (Refer to Problem 3 of Chapter 6.)

5) Can the same subprograms be both LOCAL and NOCAL when they are to be called by the same mainline program?

6) What is the difference between the STOP statement and the CALL EXIT statement?

7)   Refer to Problem 8 of Chapter 5. If the program described in that problem is too large for your 1130, what FORTRAN disk command would you use in order to run it without overloading the available core memory?

CHAPTER 8: FLOATING-POINT MANIPULATION IN FORTRAN

8-1   Statement of the Problem

This chapter contains the development of a FORTRAN program to calculate the orbital motion of small satellites in the gravitational field of a large planetary body, given the initial altitude and velocity of the satellite and the radius and mass of the planet. The program is typical of many floating-point parameter studies in scientific computing applications where it is necessary to calculate a large number of solutions to a set of equations in order to describe the operation of a system, and the program is able to use many of the FORTRAN statements described in previous chapters. The program includes the use of tables indexed by the name of a planet, includes decisions as to which equations to use (based upon the current values of certain parameters), and includes the extensive use of the TRIAL and ARCTN subprograms developed in Chapter 6.

The input data for each orbit consist of the name of the planet, the satellite's initial altitude above the surface of the planet, the satellite's initial velocity and direction of motion, the time interval to be used between successive calculations of the satellite's position, and the total span of time over which the orbital calculations are to be performed. Before computing any orbits the program will read in a table of the names of the planets, the corresponding values of the diameter of each planet and the acceleration due to gravity at the surface of each planet. The table permits the program to calculate the gravitational field strength of a planet in the table whose name is presented with the input data.

The output data for each orbit include a printout of all the input data, followed by a value for the type of orbit involved, the escape velocity, and the circular orbit velocity. The escape velocity is that velocity great enough to permit the satellite to escape from the planet's gravitational field. The escape velocity is a function of the gravitational field of the planet and the altitude of the satellite: the higher the altitude, the lower the velocity required to escape. Satellites whose initial velocity is less than escape velocity usually move in elliptical or circular orbits which will repeat over and over again (unless the orbital path intersects the surface of the planet). Satellites whose initial velocity is equal to or greater than escape velocity move in parabolic or hyperbolic orbits which will not repeat, and the satellite moves away from the planet at a continually decreasing rate (again, unless the surface of the planet gets in the way).

The equations used to calculate orbital motion will differ depending on whether the initial velocity of the satellite is less than, equal to or greater than the escape velocity. The equations also depend on whether or not the satellite's initial direction of motion lies on a straight line through the center of the planet (i.e., on whether or not the satellite is initially moving straight up or down). The program

144

must select one of six sets of equations to use in calculating the orbit depending on which of the following six types of orbits are encountered:

Type	Straight Up or Down?	Initial Velocity	Resulting Orbit
1	Yes	Less than escape	Straight line
2	Yes	Equal to escape	Straight line
3	Yes	Greater than excape	Straight line
4	No	Less than escape	Ellipse or circle
5	No	Equal to escape	Parabola
6	No	Greater than escape	Hyperbola

The circular orbit velocity included in the output data is that required to achieve a circular orbit around the planet at the initial altitude, assuming that the initial direction is parallel to the surface of the planet. The circular orbit velocity, like the escape velocity, is a function of the planet's gravitational field and the satellite's altitude. The velocity required to maintain a circular orbit decreases as the altitude increases.

At the end of each time interval the program calculates and prints the current values of elapsed time (since the first time interval), altitude above the planet's surface, angular position in orbiting around the planet (assuming the initial angle to be zero), pitch direction (whether the satellite is ascending or descending), absolute velocity, circumferential velocity (parallel to the surface of the planet), radial velocity (rate of climb from or descent to the planet's surface), radial distance from the center of the planet to the satellite, the X and Y coordinates of the satellite (with the center of the planet taken as the origin), and an intermediate parameter (called PAR). After this printout the program tests to see if the current value of altitude is less than the radius of the planet; if so, impact has occurred and an appropriate message is printed. The program then tests to see if the total span of time specified with the input data has elapsed; if so (or if impact has occurred), calculation of the orbit is terminated and input data for another orbit is read into the computer.

8-2   Assumptions, Units and Nomenclature

The method used in calculating the orbits rests on four assumptions:

1) The gravitational acceleration of each planet varies with altitude but the acceleration is constant all around the planet at any one altitude.

2) The radius of the planet is a constant (i.e., the planet is completely spherical).

3) The mass of the satellite is negligible compared with the mass of the planet.

4) Atmospheric drag is negligible.

Distances are expressed in miles and time in seconds, so all velocities are expressed in miles per second. (These units permit the use of convenient number ranges throughout the program; for example, the escape velocity at the surface of the planet Earth is 6.95 miles per second.) Angles are computed in radians and printed in degrees.

The following list includes the names of all program variables in the order of their appearance in the program.

Initialization variables:

NCR — card reader unit number, equal to 2.

NTYP — 1132 Printer unit number, equal to 3.

TABLE — 3 x 10 table of planet names, planet diameters and gravitational accelerations, read into memory before computing any orbits.

Input variables for each orbit:

NAME — name of the planet for the current orbit.

ALT — initial altitude of the satellite above the planet's surface, in miles.

V — absolute velocity of the satellite in miles per second.

PHID — initial pitch angle in degrees. See Figure 8-1.

SECS — time interval between positions to be calculated, in seconds.

TMAX — total elapsed time to last position to be calculated, in seconds.

Intermediate and output variables:

RADUS — radius of the planet in miles, looked up from TABLE.

K — gravitational constant of the planet, in miles$^{3/2}$ per second.

RZERO — initial radius from center of planet to the satellite, in miles.

KSQR — K squared (named separately to avoid repeatedly squaring K).

VESCP — escape velocity in miles per second at the initial altitude.

VCIRC — circular orbit velocity in miles per second at the initial altitude.

PHI — pitch angle in radians.

146

TIME — elapsed time in seconds since the initial position.

VLEFT — equal to V minus VESCP, in miles per second.

VR — radial velocity component in miles per second.

VTHET — circumferential velocity component in miles per second.

THETA — angular position around the planet in radians. See Figure 8-1.

RMAX — maximum distance from satellite to center of planet in miles.

C1, C2, C3, SINHP, COSHP, P, A, Q, ECC1 — intermediate parameters.

PAR — a parameter to be iterated using the TRIAL subprogram.

FPAR — the function of PAR to be iterated using TRIAL.

TRIAL — an iteration subprogram developed in Section 6-4.

ARCTN — an arc tangent subprogram developed in Section 6-5.

KIND — the type of orbit, one through six, described in Section 8-1.

R — the current distance from the satellite to center of planet, in miles.

TZERO — time at initiation since the perihelion point or the closest point of the orbit to the center of the planet, in seconds.

H — twice the area swept by the radius R in square miles per second.

ALPHA — angle of initial displacement from the perihelion of the orbit.

ECC — eccentricity (out of roundness) of the orbit.

ESQR — ECC squared.

TD — THETA in degrees, ready for printing.

PD — PHI in degrees, ready for printing.

X — the x coordinate of the satellite, origin at center of the planet.

Y — the y coordinate of the satellite, origin at center of the planet.

Figure 8-1 shows the orientation of the satellite and some of the geometric variables at the initial position. Any orbit resulting from the initial position and velocity will lie in a plane defined by the initial velocity vector of the satellite and the center of the planet. As a convention, we always place the satellite above the planet at the initial position with angle THETA equal to zero, and consider any rotation of the satellite around the planet to occur in a clockwise direction. This convention simplifies the notation and places no restrictions on the types of orbits that can be handled. Thus THETA will increase positively as TIME increases and PHID will only assume values from −180 degrees to +180 degrees.

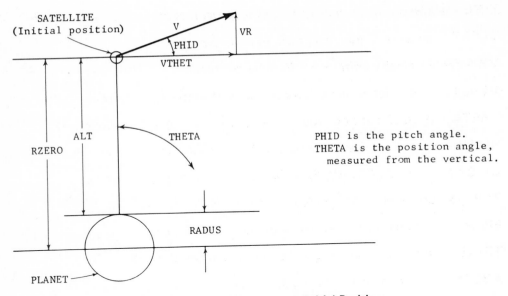

Figure 8-1   Orbital Geometry at Initial Position

PHID is the pitch angle.
THETA is the position angle, measured from the vertical.

8-3   Development of the Primary Equations

Early in the seventeenth century the astronomer Johannes Kepler concluded from many observations that Earth and the other planets followed elliptical orbits about the sun, or type 4 orbits as listed in Section 8-1. In 1684 Sir Isaac Newton, working from Kepler's rules about type 4 orbits, conceived his famous law of universal gravitation: The gravitational force between two bodies is proportional to the product of their masses and inversely proportional to the square of the distance between them. The differential equations describing Newton's law of gravitation cannot be programmed directly in FORTRAN, however.

It is possible to solve the differential equations of orbital motion on a digital computer by taking very small increments of time and stepping along the orbital path, predicting where the satellite will be after one time increment and then correcting the predicted position. This approach would result in a fairly short program which would require a significant amount of computing time.

Another approach is to derive the algebraic equations of motion from the differential equations by integrating the differential equations and introducing certain intermediate parameters to facilitate the manipulation of the resulting algebra. This second approach results in a fairly long program which executes very rapidly, and is the mathematical basis of our program.

The integrations required are long and rather devious, and so they have been isolated in Appendix A for those readers who want a more complete mathematical treatment. The algebraic equations resulting from the integrations are incorporated directly into the program as FORTRAN statements, although some of the algebra cannot be solved directly and requires iteration.

The algebraic pattern for each of the six types of orbits involves iterating for a value of PAR, an intermediate parameter, and then solving for the angular position, altitude and velocity of the satellite as functions of PAR. The parameter PAR is used only to permit easier manipulation of the algebraic equations. Orbit type 2 is an exception in that type 2 can be calculated without the use of any intermediate parameter.

8-4 Plan of Attack and Flow Diagram

The main plan of attack consists of reading data for each orbit, determining the type of orbit (by comparing the direction of motion and the velocity to the escape velocity), and transferring to a set of equations which will calculate the satellite's position at the end of each time interval. After each position calculation, tests are made to determine if impact has occurred or if the specified period of time in which the orbit is to be calculated has expired, and, if not, a transfer is made to repeat the position calculation for the next time interval. A flow diagram for this plan of attack is shown in Figures 8-2 and 8-3.

During the first time period it is not necessary to iterate for a value of the parameter PAR, so this iteration is bypassed in the flow diagram. The iteration is performed on all time periods after the first for all types of orbits except type 2, where the equations of motion are simple enough to permit a direct solution.

Notice that only the main computation blocks and program decisions are shown in Figures 8-2 and 8-3; other decisions (IF statements) will be made during the program but these would confuse the logic of the main flow diagram. If necessary, more detailed diagrams can be prepared to supplement the main flow diagram.

149

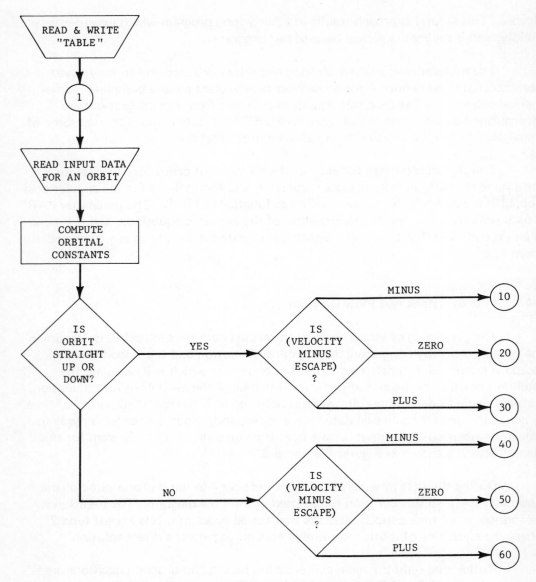

Figure 8-2 Flow Diagram for ORBIT Program, Part I

150

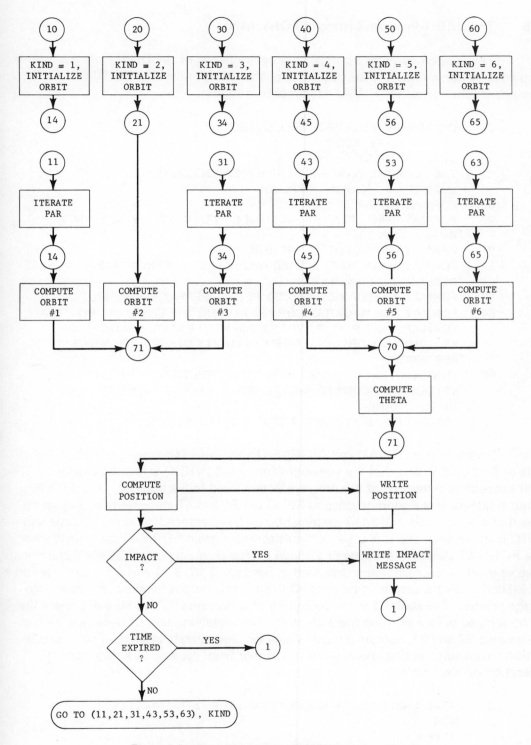

Figure 8-3   Flow Diagram for ORBIT Program, Part II

8-5   The ORBIT Program Listing in FORTRAN

This section contains a complete program listing of the ORBIT program, with explanatory comments. At the beginning of the listing are the TYPE, DIMENSION, statement function and FORMAT statements as follows:

```
C-----ORBIT ANALYZER PROGRAM, 6/21/67.
      REAL K, NAME, KSQR
      DIMENSION TABLE(3, 10)
C-----THE FOLLOWING DEFINES THE HYPERBOLIC SINE OF X
      SINH(X) = .5 * (EXP(X) - EXP(-X))
89    FORMAT (1X, A4, 5X, 2F10.2)
90    FORMAT (60H1 PLANET  ALTITUDE  VELOCITY   PITCH   INTE
     *RVAL    PERIOD)
91    FORMAT (1X, A4, 5H*****, 5F10.3)
92    FORMAT (67H PLANET NAMED ABOVE IS NOT IN NAME TABLE.  PLEASE
     *REPEAT YOUR INPUT.)
93    FORMAT (' ITERATION FAILED, PLEASE REPEAT YOUR INPUT.')
94    FORMAT (46H IMPACT OCCURRED DURING THE LAST TIME INTERVAL)
95    FORMAT(/14H ORBIT IS TYPE, I2, 24H WITH ESCAPE VELOCITY OF,
     *F7.3, 31H AND CIRCULAR ORBIT VELOCITY OF, F7.3, 18H MILES
     *PER SECOND.)
96    FORMAT(/119H     TIME   ALTITUDE   POSITION     PITCH
     *VELOCITY CIRCUM SPD RADIAL SPD    RADIUS   X MILES     Y
     *MILES    PAR)
97    FORMAT (1X, 2F11.0, 2F11.1, 3F11.3, 3F11.0, F8.3)
```

Notice that the REAL and DIMENSION statements follow the sequencing rule of Section 6-9, and that the statement function SINH(X) is located before the first executable statement of the program as described in Section 6-2. Although it is not required, it is a good practice to list all the FORMAT statements of a program together since a single FORMAT statement may be referenced by several READ and WRITE statements, and it is often difficult to find a given FORMAT statement among the FORMAT statements scattered through a large program. The FORMAT statements involve most of the techniques discussed in Sections 3-10, 3-11 and 5-5. Carriage control (Section 5-6) is used in statement 90 to start this output heading on a new page in the printer. The slash (/) at the beginning of statements 95 and 96 will cause a line to be skipped before printing these formats. The remaining output messages, such as statements 92 and 94, contain a blank character immediately after the first H specification to prevent the first character in the format from causing a carriage control operation on the printer.

```
C-----READ TABLE OF PLANETARY DIAMETERS AND GRAVITY
      NCR = 2
      NTYP = 3
      READ (NCR,89) TABLE
```

```
        WRITE (NTYP,89) TABLE
C-----READ INITIAL CONDITIONS FOR AN ORBIT AND LOOK UP PLANETARY
C-----DATA
1       READ (NCR,91) NAME, ALT, V, PHID, SECS, TMAX
        IF (TMAX) 98, 98, 99
98      CALL EXIT
99      WRITE (NTYP, 90)
        WRITE (NTYP,91)NAME, ALT, V, PHID, SECS, TMAX
        DO 2 I = 1, 10
        IF (NAME - TABLE(1, I)) 2, 3, 2
2       CONTINUE
        WRITE (NTYP, 92)
        GO TO 1
```

NCR and NTYP are defined as unit numbers for the card read punch and the printer (Section 3-8). The entire TABLE, ten rows of three columns each, is then read and printed. Each row in TABLE contains the first four letters of the name of a planet followed by the diameter of the planet in miles and the gravitational acceleration at the surface of the planet in feet per second squared. The TABLE entry for the planet Earth appears on the printed output as

```
EART            7926.           32.2
```

and ten cards contain the data for the Sun, Mercury, Venus, Earth, Mars, Jupiter, Saturn, Uranus, Neptune and the Moon, all read by format 89. *It is a good idea to immediately write out input data after the data are read, so that there will be no arguments later about what data the computer was actually using.*

At statement 1 the data for a particular orbit are read. The time during which calculations are to be performed (TMAX) is then used to terminate the program by returning control to the Disk Monitor at statement 98 (CALL EXIT) if TMAX is zero or negative. A blank card placed at the end of the data deck will thus automatically result in a TMAX of zero and terminate the program. In this way the program is set up to handle an indefinite number of orbits and still automatically return to the monitor after calculating the last orbit.

The DO statement referencing statement 2 controls a simple table look-up (Section 5-3) to look up the NAME from the input data in TABLE. Only the first four letters of the name of the planet are used in NAME, since four letters are the most that can be contained in a standard floating-point variable. If NAME is not in the TABLE, format 92 is printed and control goes to statement 1 to read another set of input data, otherwise the program proceeds at statement 3. Equation numbers in parentheses refer to the equations developed in Appendix A.

```
C-----CALCULATE ORBITAL CONSTANTS
3       RADUS = .5 * TABLE(2, I)
```

153

```
          K = RADUS * SQRT(TABLE(3, I)/5280.)                          (8-2)
          RZERO = ALT + RADUS
          KSQR = K * K
          VESCP = SQRT(2. * KSQR / RZERO)                               (8-4)
          VCIRC = VESCP/1.414214
          IF (V) 9, 7, 8
7         PHID = -90.
          GO TO 8
9         V = VESCP
8         PHI = PHID/57.29578
          TIME = 0.
          VLEFT = V - VESCP
          VR = V * SIN(PHI)
          VTHET = V * COS(PHI)
```

The index I is used to pick up the diameter and acceleration from TABLE. Notice that the first column of the TABLE array is alphabetic (A4) format while the other two columns are in floating-point (F10.2) format. Several constants of the orbit are then calculated using the SQRT, SIN and COS functions from the FOR-TRAN library (Section 6-3). If the velocity V is zero, the pitch angle PHID is set to −90 degrees, since the subsequent direction of motion of the satellite must be straight down. If V is negative, V is then set equal to the escape velocity at statement 9. This arbitrary convention enables the escape velocity to be selected for the initial value of V even though the escape velocity may not be known when the data is prepared. The elapsed TIME is set to zero, and the next step is to determine the type of orbit involved.

```
          IF (ABS(PHID) - 90.) 6, 5, 6
5         THETA = 0.
C-----DIRECTION STRAIGHT UP OR DOWN, ORBIT IS A STRAIGHT LINE
          IF (VLEFT) 4, 20, 4
4         RMAX = ABS(2./((2./RZERO) - (V * V / KSQR)))                  (8-5)
          C2 = ((.5 * RMAX)**1.5)/K
          IF (VLEFT) 10, 20, 30
```

If the absolute value of PHID is 90 degrees, then the orbit is type 1, 2 or 3 as described in Section 8-1. If the velocity is not equal to escape velocity, RMAX and C2 can be calculated. Then the velocity is compared with escape velocity (VLEFT) and the orbit type is determined. The next group of statements handles the calculations for orbit type 1 (velocity less than escape and direction straight up or down).

```
C-----STRAIGHT LINE ORBIT, VELOCITY LESS THAN ESCAPE VELOCITY
10        KIND = 1
          CALL ARCTN(PAR, SIGN(SQRT(RZERO), PHI), SQRT(RMAX -
         *RZERO))                                                       (8-7)
          PAR = 2. * PAR
```

154

```
          TZERO = C2 * (PAR – SIN(PAR))                                    (8-8)
          GO TO 14
11        C1 = (TIME + TZERO)/C2
          DO 12 N = 1.50
          FPAR= SIN(PAR) + C1                                              (8-8)
          IF (ABS(FPAR – PAR) – .00001) 14, 12, 12
12        PAR = TRIAL(N, PAR, FPAR)
13        WRITE (NTYP, 93)
          GO TO 1
14        C3 = SIN(.5 * PAR)
          R = RMAX * C3 * C3                                              (8-9)
          V = K * SQRT(ABS((2./R) – (2./RMAX)))                           (8-6)
C------SEE IF THE MAXIMUM ALTITUDE HAS BEEN REACHED
          IF (3.1415926 * C2 – (TIME + TZERO)) 15, 71, 71                 (8-10)
15        PHI = –1.5707963
          GO TO 71
```

The KIND (type) of orbit is established in statement 10. The arc tangent subprogram described in Section 6-5 is then used to calculate the initial value of the parameter PAR. This statement may be read as "PAR is the arc tangent of the square root of RZERO, using the sign of PHI, divided by the square root of RMAX minus RZERO"; it is a good example of the result of one subroutine (SQRT) used as an argument for another subroutine (SIGN) whose result is then used as an argument for a subprogram (ARCTN).

For the first calculation of the orbit (at TIME = 0.) the integration constant TZERO can be calculated directly from PAR, followed by a transfer to statement 14 for the direct calculation of R and V. For subsequent calculations when TIME is not zero it is necessary to iterate, using the TRIAL subroutine described in Section 6-4, to find a value for PAR as a function of TIME. The iteration is controlled by the DO referencing statement 12, permitting up to 50 iterations. If the iterations are unsuccessful, format 93 is written at statement 13 and control goes to statement 1 to read in data for another orbit. Notice that the constant C1 is calculated outside the DO loop so that the computer will not waste time repeating the calculation of C1 each time the iteration is performed.

If the iteration is successful, control goes to statement 14 where R and V can now be calculated directly. A test is then made to see if the maximum altitude (apogee) has been reached; if so, PHI is set to –1.5707963 in radians which corresponds to a straight down direction. Control then goes to statement 71 at the end of the program to print the calculated values of R and V and other parameters of the orbit.

Continuing with the program listing, we find orbit type 2 calculated as follows:

```
C-----STRAIGHT LINE ORBIT, VELOCITY EQUALS ESCAPE VELOCITY
20      KIND = 2
        C2 = 1.414214/(3. * K)
        TZERO = SIGN(C2 * RZERO**1.5, PHI)                        (8-12)
21      R = (ABS(TIME + TZERO)/C2)**.6666667                      (8-12)
        V = SQRT(2. * KSQR / R)                                   (8-13)
        GO TO 71
```

Orbit type 2 does not require the use of an intermediate parameter (such as PAR) or the use of iteration. After the direct calculation of R and V, control goes to statement 71 to print the results. Notice that the expression represented by the constant C2 appears in the equations of TZERO and R. Therefore C2 is calculated in a separate statement to avoid repetitive calculation. We can now calculate orbit type 3.

```
C-----STRAIGHT LINE ORBIT, VELOCITY EXCEEDS ESCAPE VELOCITY
30      KIND = 3
        SINHP = SIGN(SQRT(RZERO/RMAX), PHI
        PAR = 2. * ALOG(SINHP + SQRT(SINHP * SINHP + 1.))         (8-15)
        TZERO = C2 * (SINH(PAR) - PAR)                            (8-16)
        GO TO 34
31      C1 = (TIME + TZERO)/C2
        DO 32 N = 1, 50
        FPAR = SINH(PAR) - C1                                     (8-16)
        IF (ABS(FPAR - PAR) - .00001) 34, 32, 32
32      PAR = TRIAL(N, PAR, FPAR)
        GO TO 13
34      C3 = SINH(.5 * PAR)                                       (8-15)
        R = RMAX * C3 * C3
        V = K * SQRT((2./R) + (2./RMAX))                          (8-14)
        GO TO 71
```

Orbit type 3 follows a calculation procedure similar to orbit type 1. When TIME equals zero, PAR and TZERO can be calculated directly, after which control goes to statement 34. On subsequent calculations (TIME not zero) it is necessary to iterate on the hyperbolic sine of PAR to get PAR as a function of TIME. The iteration is controlled by the DO that references statement 32. If the iteration is not successful, control goes back to statement 13, where format 93 is printed, and control goes back to statement 1; otherwise R and V are calculated at statement 34 and control goes to statement 71 to print the results.

The program listing next considers orbit type 4.

```
C-----CURVED ORBIT, VELOCITY LESS THAN ESCAPE, ORBIT IS AN ELLIPSE
40      KIND = 4
        C3 = 1. - RZERO/A
```

```
         CALL ARCTN(PAR, SIGN(SQRT(ABS(ESQR – C3 * C3)), PHI),
        *C3)                                                          (8-30)
         TZERO = C2 * (PAR – ECC * SIN(PAR))                          (8-33)
         GO TO 45
43       C1 = (TIME + TZERO)/C2
         DO 44 N = 1, 50
         FPAR = ECC * SIN(PAR) + C1                                   (8-33)
         IF (ABS(FPAR – PAR) – .00001) 45, 44,44
44       PAR = TRIAL(N, PAR, FPAR)
         GO TO 13
45       CALL ARCTN(THETA, ECC1 * SIN(.5 * PAR), COS
        *(.5 * PAR))                                                  (8-32)
         R = A * (1. – ECC * COS(PAR))                                (8-31)
         V = K * SQRT((2./R) – (1./A))                                (8-29)
         GO TO 70
```

Again a procedure similar to type 1 is used. When TIME is zero, PAR and TZERO are calculated directly using the ARCTN subprogram of Section 6-5. The statement which calls ARCTN may be read as "PAR is the arc tangent of the square root of the absolute value of ESQR minus C3 squared, using the sign of PHI, divided by C3." On subsequent calculations (TIME not zero) the usual iteration is required, with control going either to statement 13 if the iteration is not successful or else to statement 45. At statement 45 THETA, R and V are calculated directly, with THETA requiring the use of the ARCTN subprogram.

Orbit type 5 appears in the listing as follows:

```
C-----CURVED ORBIT, VELOCITY EQUALS ESCAPE, ORBIT IS A PARABOLA
50       KIND = 5
         Q = .5 * P                                                   (8-34)
         IF (PHID) 51, 52, 51
52       PAR = 0.
         GO TO 56
51       PAR = SIGN(SQRT(RZERO/Q – 1.), PHI)                          (8-36)
56       C2 = (1.414214 * Q ** 1.5)/K
         TZERO = C2 * (PAR + PAR ** 3 / 3.)                           (8-39)
         GO TO 55
53       C1 = (TIME + TZERO)/C2
         DO 54 N = 1, 50
         FPAR = C1 – PAR**3/3.                                        (8-39)
         IF (ABS(FPAR – PAR) – .00001) 55, 54, 54
54       PAR = TRIAL(N, PAR, FPAR)
         GO TO 13
55       CALL ARCTN(THETA, PAR, 1.)                                   (8-38)
         R = Q * (1. + PAR * PAR)                                     (8-37)
         V = K * SQRT(2./R)                                           (8-35)
         GO TO 70
```

The procedure is similar to type 1. If PHID is zero, PAR is set to zero; otherwise the initial value of PAR is calculated from statement 51. On subsequent calculations PAR as a function of TIME is a cubic equation iterated by the TRIAL subprogram. THETA, R and V are then calculated directly at statement 55.

```
      C-----CURVED ORBIT, VELOCITY EXCEEDS ESCAPE, ORBIT IS A HYPERBOLA
      60    KIND = 6
            COSHP = (RZERO/A + 1.)/ECC
            PAR = ALOG(COSHP + SIGN(SQRT(COSHP * COSHP -1.),
           *PHI))                                                        (8-43)
            TZERO = C2 * (ECC * SINH(PAR) - PAR)                         (8-46)
            GO TO 65
      63    C1 = (TIME + TZERO)/C2
            DO 64 N = 1, 50
            FPAR = ECC * SINH(PAR) - C1                                  (8-46)
            IF (ABS(FPAR - PAR) - .00001) 65, 64, 64
      64    PAR = TRIAL(N, PAR, FPAR)
            GO TO 13
      65    CALL ARCTN(THETA, ECC1 * TANH(.5 * PAR), 1.)                 (8-45)
            IF (PAR) 66, 67, 66
      66    R = A * (ECC * SINH(PAR)/TANH(PAR) - 1.)                     (8-44)
            GO TO 68
      67    R = A * (ECC - 1.)                                          (8-44)
      68    V = K * SQRT((2./R) + (1./A))
```

The procedure is again similar to type 1. Since the hyperbolic tangent of zero is zero, a test is made to see if PAR is zero before division by TANH(PAR) in statement 66. If PAR is zero, an alternate equation (statement 67) is used. (Any variable which can become zero should be tested each time the variable is used as a divisor to prevent division by zero.)

Iteration for type 6 handles the hyperbolic sine of PAR. THETA, R and V are then calculated directly starting at statement 65. As all six types of orbits have now been taken care of in the program listing, we are ready to calculate and print all the results at one time interval.

```
      C-----CALCULATE AND PRINT POSITION AT THE CURRENT TIME INTERVAL
      70    THETA = 2. * THETA
            PHI = ATAN((P*ECC*SIN(THETA))/(R*(1.+ECC*COS(THETA))**2))
            THETA = THETA + ALPHA
      80    IF (THETA) 77, 71, 78
      77    THETA = THETA + 6.2831852
            GO TO 80
      78    IF (THETA - 6.2831852) 71, 79, 79
      79    THETA = THETA - 6.2831852
            GO TO 78
      71    X = R * SIN(THETA)
```

```
          Y = R * COS(THETA)
          VTHET = V * COS(PHI)
          VR = V * SIN(PHI)
          ALT = R - RADUS
          TD = THETA * 57.29578
          PD = PHI * 57.29578
          IF (TIME) 75, 75, 76
75        WRITE (NTYP, 95) KIND, VESCP, VCIRC
          WRITE (NTYP, 96)
76        WRITE (NTYP, 97) TIME, ALT, TD, PD, V, VTHET, VR, R, X, Y, PAR
```

The value of THETA calculated for orbit types 4, 5 and 6 is only one-half of the true value of THETA, which is corrected in statement 70. THETA is then adjusted into the range of zero to 6.2831852 radians by the IF statements 80 and 78. Beginning at statement 71 the other output parameters are calculated. If TIME is zero, the heading formats 95 and 96 are printed; otherwise the parameters are printed without a heading at statement 76. All that remains is to test to see if impact has occurred or if the prescribed amount of time has elapsed.

```
          IF (ALT) 72, 72, 73
72        WRITE (NTYP, 94)
          GO TO 1
73        TIME = TIME + SECS
          IF (TIME - TMAX) 74, 74, 1
74        GO TO (11, 21, 31, 43, 53, 63), KIND
```

If impact has occurred a message is printed at statement 72, and control goes to statement 1 to read data for another orbit; otherwise the TIME is incremented at statement 73 and a test is made to see if TMAX has been exceeded, in which case control goes to statement 1. If TMAX has not been exceeded, a computed GO TO takes control of the program to statement 11, 21, 31, 43, 53 or 63, depending upon the KIND (type) of orbit currently being calculated.

We still need a few more statements to decide (at statement 6) whether or not we have an ellipse, a parabola or a hyperbola for an orbit.

```
6         H = RZERO * VTHET                                      (8-17)
          C3 = VTHET - KSQR/H
          CALL ARCTN(ALPHA, -VR, C3)                             (8-25)
          ECC = H * SQRT(VR * VR + C3 * C3)/KSQR
          P = H * H/KSQR
          IF (VLEFT) 601, 50, 601
601       A = ABS(P/(1.-ESQR))
          ECC1 = SQRT(ABS((1.+ECC)/(1.-ECC)))
          C2 = (A**1.5)/K
          IF (VLEFT) 40, 50, 60
          END
```

159

After calculating several intermediate results for later use a transfer is made to statement 40, 50 or 60 as VLEFT, the velocity in excess of escape velocity, is negative, zero or positive. VLEFT thus establishes the type of orbit as an ellipse, a parabola or a hyperbola.

8-6   Input Data Required for ORBIT

The input data consist of ten cards in (1X, A4, 5X, 2F10.2) format containing the TABLE array, followed by one in (1X, A4, 5H*****, 5F10.3) format for each orbit to be calculated. The TABLE cards appear as follows:

SUN	864100.	900.3
MERCURY	3194.	12.9
VENUS	7842.	28.9
EARTH	7926.	32.2
MARS	4263.	12.9
JUPITER	89229.	86.8
SATURN	74937.	38.6
URANUS	33181.	32.2
NEPTUNE	30882.	47.0
MOON	2159.9	5.47

The data cards for each orbit appear as follows (three examples shown):

EARTH	1000.	3.	45.	100.	5000.
EARTH	1000.	0.	0.	100.	5000.
EARTH	1000.	9.	90.	100.	5000.

The first orbit above starts at an altitude of 1000 miles, a velocity of three miles per second, a pitch angle of 45 degrees above the horizontal, using time increments of 100 seconds, and a total time duration of 5000 seconds. The second orbit starts at an altitude of 1000 miles, a velocity of zero, a pitch angle of zero, the same time increment, and the same time duration. The third orbit starts at an altitude of 1000 miles, a velocity of nine miles per second, a pitch angle of 90 degrees (straight up), and the same time increment and duration. The first orbit turns out to be a type 4 which impacts the Earth's surface after about 2000 seconds; the second simply falls straight down (type 1) to an impact after less than 700 seconds; the third goes straight up at a velocity in excess of escape velocity and is still traveling at a velocity of 6.8 miles per second at the end of 5000 seconds. Figure 8-4 shows the printed output for the first orbit.

8-7   Memory Requirements

The ORBIT program contains 163 FORTRAN statements which require 1798 words of core memory, or an average of about 11 words per statement. In addition, 164 words are required to store all the variables referenced in the program for a total memory requirement of 1962 words. The ARCTN and TRIAL subprograms require an additional 106 and 110 words respectively. Since the ORBIT program uses almost every subroutine in the FORTRAN library, the combined programs are a little too large to fit into a 4K (4096-word) memory but will fit easily into an 8K memory.

8-8   Summary

The ORBIT program is designed to show the analysis which must ordinarily precede the programming of a scientific problem in FORTRAN, that a few FOR-TRAN statements can possess enough flexibility to handle a wide range of calculations, and that a large amount of FORTRAN programming can be packed into a relatively small amount of core memory. The ratio of 11 words of memory per FORTRAN statement is typical of scientific problems on the 1130 system.

8-9   Problems

1)   Statement 45 in the ORBIT program as written causes the computer to calculate the expression (.5 * PAR) twice, which is inefficient. Rewrite statement 45 to eliminate this inefficiency. (Hint: It will be necessary to replace 45 with two other statements.)

2)   The ORBIT program could be run on a 4K computer if it could be broken up into several pieces through the use of LOCAL programs. Where are the best places to break up the program? Why?

```
     PLANET    ALTITUDE    VELOCITY    PITCH    INTERVAL    PERIOD
     EARTH     1000.000     3.000     45.000    100.000    5000.000

ORBIT IS TYPE 4 WITH ESCAPE VELOCITY OF 6.212 AND CIRCULAR ORBIT VELOCITY OF 4.393 MILES PER SECOND.
```

TIME	ALTITUDE	POSITION	PITCH	VELOCITY	CIRCUM SPD	RADIAL SPD	RADIUS	Y MILES	X MILES
0.	999.	359.9	44.9	2.999	2.121	2.121	4962.	4962.	-0.
100.	1197.	2.3	41.9	2.742	2.040	1.833	5160.	5156.	211.
200.	1367.	4.5	38.3	2.518	1.975	1.561	5330.	5313.	422.
300.	1510.	6.6	34.1	2.323	1.923	1.304	5473.	5437.	630.
400.	1628.	8.5	29.3	2.159	1.882	1.056	5591.	5528.	834.
500.	1722.	10.4	23.8	2.024	1.851	0.817	5685.	5590.	1033.
600.	1792.	12.3	17.7	1.920	1.829	0.584	5755.	5622.	1227.
700.	1839.	14.1	11.0	1.848	1.814	0.354	5802.	5626.	1415.
800.	1863.	15.9	4.0	1.811	1.807	0.128	5826.	5603.	1596.
900.	1864.	17.6	-3.1	1.809	1.806	-0.097	5827.	5552.	1770.
1000.	1843.	19.4	-10.1	1.841	1.813	-0.324	5806.	5474.	1934.
1100.	1799.	21.2	-16.8	1.908	1.826	-0.553	5762.	5370.	2090.
1200.	1732.	23.1	-23.0	2.008	1.848	-0.786	5695.	5238.	2234.
1300.	1642.	24.9	-28.6	2.139	1.878	-1.024	5605.	5080.	2368.
1400.	1527.	26.9	-33.5	2.300	1.917	-1.270	5490.	4894.	2488.
1500.	1387.	29.0	-37.8	2.490	1.967	-1.526	5350.	4679.	2594.
1600.	1221.	31.1	-41.4	2.710	2.030	-1.795	5184.	4436.	2683.
1700.	1028.	33.5	-44.6	2.963	2.081	-2.081	4991.	4161.	2754.
1800.	804.	36.0	-47.2	3.252	2.208	-2.388	4767.	3855.	2804.
1900.	549.	38.8	-49.4	3.585	2.333	-2.722	4512.	3515.	2829.
2000.	259.	41.9	-51.1	3.971	2.493	-3.091	4222.	3137.	2824.
2100.	-70.	45.6	-52.3	4.428	2.704	-3.506	3892.	2720.	2784.

IMPACT OCCURRED DURING THE LAST TIME INTERVAL

Figure 8-4 Printed Output from the ORBIT Program

CHAPTER 9: INTEGER MANIPULATION IN FORTRAN

9-1   Statement of the Problem

This chapter contains the development of a complete FORTRAN program (named TTT3D) to play three-dimensional tic-tac-toe against a human opponent. The ORBIT program of Chapter 8 consisted of many floating-point calculations and a few decisions; TTT3D consists of many decisions and integer calculations but no floating-point calculations. In the ORBIT program the notation used came easily from the physics of the problem; in TTT3D the choice of an appropriate notation is one of the most difficult steps in planning the program.

The TTT3D program is similar in structure to a large class of strategy problems which occur in the analysis of military situations, in planning the competitive strategy of a business or in almost any situation where the solution of a problem depends on outwitting one or more intelligent opponents. Strategy problems are usually more interesting to program, due to the competitive aspect of the solution, than are scientific parameter studies such as ORBIT.

Many games, including chess, checkers, bridge, twenty-one, poker, TTT3D and ordinary tic-tac-toe have been programmed for digital computers. The most complex of these games cannot yet be played economically upon computers, if by economically we mean that the computer must play as fast as a human opponent and at about the same cost per move as a skilled opponent might charge (say ten dollars per hour as a base rate). The simplest games can be handled by pure learning programs where the computer simply keeps track of all games it has played and repeats those combinations of moves that won while avoiding those combinations that lost. At an intermediate level of complexity we find games like TTT3D, games which would take a long time and millions of games to learn by a pure learning technique devoid of any initial strategy but which can be played economically by strategy programs on fast, low cost computers like the 1130. To the best of my knowledge TTT3D is an indeterminate game, meaning that there is no perfect strategy except a completely exhaustive analysis of all combinations of future moves. The number of possible future moves is high enough to make exhaustive analysis impractical, so it is necessary to devise some clever but nonoptimum strategy in order to play the game economically as defined above. Continued progress in both computer performance and programming technique makes it possible that even the most complex games such as chess will be played economically upon digital computers within a few years.

The idea of a computer which can play and win relatively complex games against human opponents is occasionally propounded as an argument for the possibility of artificial intelligence. We tend to consider a solution "intelligent" if we do not quite understand how the solution was obtained, and the moves which a

163

computer makes as a result of a complex game strategy may not be understood and thus appear "intelligent" to an observer. When the strategy program is thoroughly understood the aura of intelligence disappears as each move is seen to be the result of combining millions of rather trivial decisions. Understanding how a good strategy program works, however, is not usually enough to win against it.

TTT3D is played upon a four-level board where each level consists of a four-by-four grid of 16 squares, for a total of 64 squares or possible moves (Figure 9-1). Either of the two players (the computer or the opponent) can move onto any unoccupied square. The players move alternately, using two different symbols such as X and 0 to record and distinguish their moves upon the board. The game is won by that player who first establishes four of his symbols in a straight row, either horizontally, vertically or diagonally. Inspection of the four-level board reveals that there are a total of 76 rows upon which a win might be established. There are ten rows on each of the four levels, 16 vertical rows, 16 semidiagonal rows contained in planes parallel to an edge of the board, and four true diagonal rows passing from one corner of the board at the top level to the diagonally opposite corner of the board at the bottom level. Some squares appear on more of the potentially winning rows than do other squares. The eight squares grouped around the center of the board on levels two and three and the eight squares which form the corners of the board on levels one and four each appear on seven of the 76 winning rows. These 16 squares we will call prime squares. All of the other 48 squares on the board (all 48 of them) each appear on only four of the 76 winning rows.

The TTT3D program will describe the game to the human opponent, explain how to play if requested to do so, accept and print the opponent's name, give the opponent his choice of the first move, recognize and print messages for won games, lost games, tie games and illegal moves (such as moves upon squares already occupied) and win the game in most cases. Now let us see how all this may be accomplished through programming.

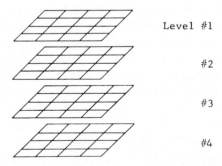

Level #1

#2

#3

#4

Figure 9-1   Playing Board for the TTT3D Program

The board is represented by the array called MOVE which contains an integer variable for each of the 64 squares on the board. Each square in the MOVE array which contains a move made by the computer is set to the value of five; each square where the opponent has moved is set to one. Blank or unoccupied squares are set to zero. This notation was chosen to provide a unique meaning for the sum of the square values for each of the 76 rows. A row whose sum was four would indicate that the opponent had four moves (and had just won the game) in that row; a row whose sum was 15 would indicate that the computer had three moves in that row (and could win immediately if it was the computer's turn to move). The sum of each of the 76 rows is kept in the array called SUM.

The subscripts of the four squares which make up each of the 76 rows are kept in the ROW array, of which the first four values are the subscripts of the first row, the next four values are the subscripts of the second row, etc. (The ROW array was originally dimensioned ROW(4, 76) but it was found that the computation proceeded much faster if the ROW array was singly subscripted, since several seconds were being used in each move to compute and recompute the subscripts.) The sequence of rows in the ROW array is set up so that rows containing a maximum number of prime squares are at the beginning of the array, so that these more important rows will be checked first.

To make things easy for the human opponent all moves will be read by the computer in player code, a three-digit integer where the first digit describes the level of the move, the second digit describes the row position on the level and the third digit describes the column position in the row. For example, 312 would mean third level, first row and second column. It is not necessary to define the precise orientation of levels versus rows versus columns because all such conventions are equivalent as long as the conventions are consistently followed. When the move is analyzed by the computer, however, it is convenient to consider the move as the subscript of one of the 64 squares in the MOVE array. The player code of 312 is convered to a move code of 34 by a block of FORTRAN statements starting with statement 29 in the TTT3D program listing. After the computer determines an appropriate next move, the move is converted from move code to player code by the BOARD subprogram before the move is printed on the output typewriter.

The entire TTT3D program consists of the TTT3D main program, the STRAT strategy subprogram, and the BOARD code conversion subprogram. All variables in these programs are integer variables; no floating-point variables are used. The TTT3D and STRAT programs use COMMON storage to transmit the necessary arguments to the STRAT subprogram as described in Section 6-7.

The following list includes the names of all program variables in the order of their appearance in the program.

NTYP — output typewriter unit number, equal to 1.

NCARD — card reader unit number, equal to 2.

KEYBD — console keyboard unit number, equal to 6.

MOVE(64) — the 64 squares of the TTT3D board.

SUM(76) — the sum of the move values for each of the 76 rows.

ROW(304) — the subscripts of the four squares in each of the 76 rows.

WAIT(20) — the subscripts of prime squares to be used as waiting moves.

TEST(3, 14) — a table describing 14 situations to be tested.

M1 — the subscript of a move recommended by the STRAT strategy
     subprogram.

M2 — another move discovered by the STRAT subprogram.

M3 — the strategy or situation level at which STRAT found the move M1.

LAST(4) — the four moves of the winning row.

NAME(10) — the opponent's name in 10A2 format.

YE — the two letters "YE" to identify a yes answer to questions.

ANS — the first two letters of yes or no answers.

BLANK — two blank characters in A2 format.

K1 — an intermediate parameter used to convert player code to move code.

K2 — same as K1.

K3 — same as K1.

NEXT — the next move in player code coming in from the console keyboard.

The following variables are used only by the STRAT strategy subprogram:

STRAT — the name of the strategy subprogram which determines the next
     move to be made by the computer.

TEST1 — the first test to be made for the situation being processed.

TEST2 — the second test to be made for the current situation.

TEST3 — the third test to be made for the current situation.

J1, J2, K2, L2, J3, K3, L3, J4, J5, K5, L5, J6, J7, J8, K8, L8 — indexing and
     subscripting parameters used by STRAT.

166

The following variables are used only by the BOARD subprogram:

BOARD — the name of a subprogram which converts move code to player code.

L1, L2, L3 — three intermediate parameters used to convert move code to player code.

9-3   Development of the TTT3D Strategy

The TTT3D playing strategy used by the computer, as executed by the STRAT subprogram, consists of looking for certain interesting situations or combinations on the four-level board whenever it is the computer's turn to move and moving in response to the highest priority situation discovered. The interesting situations are recognized by certain combinations of row values as stored in SUM. A total of 13 different situations are examined in priority sequence, and the first situation found to exist on the board causes the computer to make an appropriate response.

As an example of an interesting situation, consider a SUM of four. The discovery of this situation indicates that the opponent has won the game on the last move, and the computer should graciously concede. A SUM of 15 indicates that the computer has three in a row and can win on the current move. A SUM of three indicates that the opponent has three in a row and must be blocked or the game is lost. These three situations are obviously of highest priority and must be checked first. A SUM of 20, indicating that the computer won on the last move, will never occur because the computer (or rather the program) would have discovered a SUM of 15 on the previous move and declared that the game was over.

Consider a situation where each of two rows is found to have a SUM of ten and there is a blank or zero square common to both of the rows. By moving on the blank square the computer can execute a trap. The computer will then have two rows each with a SUM equal to 15, and the opponent can only block one of them on the next move. Obviously this is a situation worth looking for.

What if two rows exist each with a SUM of two and a blank square in common? Then the opponent is about to spring a trap by moving onto the blank square and creating two rows with a SUM of three, only one of which could be blocked by the computer. Obviously here is another interesting situation.

Next consider a more difficult situation where a row with SUM = 10 has a blank square in common with a second row of SUM = 5, and the second row contains another blank square in common with a third row of SUM = 10. By moving onto the common blank square in the first row, the computer will force the opponent to move onto the remaining square in the first row. The opponent will then be confronted with a trap consisting of the second and third rows, each now with a SUM of ten. By moving onto the blank square common to the second and third rows on the following move, the computer will have two rows each of SUM = 15 and must win in one more move. This situation is thus a trap which will win the game three moves in the future. The opponent can create an equivalent situation involving his own moves which the computer must guard against.

A notation of three test numbers suffices to describe any of the above strategy situations. We will call the three test numbers T1, T2 and T3, and the task of the STRAT subprogram is essentially as follows:

"Find on the board a row of SUM = T1 such that the row has a blank square (called M1) in common with a second row of SUM = T2, such that the second row has a blank square (called M2) in common with a third row of SUM = T2. The next move for the computer will be the square M1. The squares M1 and M2 may be the same square."

The numbers T1, T2 and T3 are transmitted to STRAT to indicate the SUM values of rows which the STRAT subprogram will attempt to find upon the board. To permit the simpler situations to be expressed in the three test-number notation, we will adopt the convention that negative test numbers will terminate the search. For example, the test numbers 3, –1, –1 would cause the STRAT subprogram to simply find a row of SUM = 3 and then find a blank square on that row.

We can now list each of the 13 interesting situations in terms of test-number notation and in priority sequence. At each move the computer searches the board for the first situation, then for the second situation, etc. If any situation is found to exist the search is over and a move (or at least a note conceding the game) will immediately be printed. A sketch of typical row values and row intersections (M1 and M2) is shown to clarify each of the 13 situations. Although the sketches show only a single level of the board for simplicity, the search carried out by STRAT will range over all four levels looking for all intersections in three dimensions.

In Strategy Situation 1 the opponent has won the game and all that is left is to concede. In Situation 2 the computer has three in a row, and a move at M1 will win the game. The opponent has three in a row and must be blocked immediately at square M1 in Situation 3. In Situation 4 the computer has a trap consisting of two rows of SUM = 10 with a blank square in common at M1. A move at M1 will produce two rows of SUM = 15, ensuring a win on the next move.

In Situation 5 the computer has a trap consisting of a row of SUM = 10 with a blank square M1 in common with a second row of SUM = 5 which has a blank square M2 in common with a third row of SUM = 10. A move at M1 will produce Situation 4 involving the second and third rows and the blank square M2. In Situation 6 it is necessary for the computer to go on the defensive and look for an opponent's trap equivalent to Situation 4. In Situation 7 the computer must look for an opponent's trap equivalent to Situation 5. Situation 8 may develop into Situation 7 in several different ways, and so must be found and blocked if present.

Situation 9, consisting of a blank row which intersects two rows of SUM = 2, may develop into Situation 7 in several ways and so must be blocked. For example, if the opponent is not blocked and subsequently moves to the square between M1 and M2, the computer will be trapped. In Situation 10 the computer goes on the offensive again, searching for a pattern to develop into Situation 4 or Situation 5. In Situations 11 through 13 the computer is simply looking for situations which may be developed into the traps of Situations 4 and 5.

1	1	1	1

Figure 9-2 Strategy Situation 1, Test Numbers 4, -1, -1

		5	
		5	
		5	
		M1	

Figure 9-3 Strategy Situation 2, Test Numbers 15, -1, -1

1			
	1		
		1	
			M1

Figure 9-4 Strategy Situation 3, Test Numbers 3, -1, -1

5		M1	5
		5	
		5	

Figure 9-5 Strategy Situation 4, Test Numbers 10, 10, -1

5		5	M2
5			
	5		
M1			

Figure 9-6 Strategy Situation 5, Test Numbers 10, 5, 10

1			
	M1		
	1		
	1		1

Figure 9-7 Strategy Situation 6, Test Numbers 2, 2, -1

M2			
1			
1	1	M1	
			1

Figure 9-8   Strategy Situation 7, Test Numbers 2, 1, 2

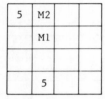

Figure 9-11   Strategy Situation 10, Test Numbers 5, 5, 10

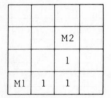

Figure 9-9   Strategy Situation 8, Test Numbers 2, 1, 1

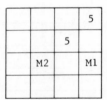

Figure 9-12   Strategy Situation 11, Test Numbers 5, 5, 5

	M2		
	1		
M1	1	1	

Figure 9-10   Strategy Situation 9, Test Numbers 2, 0, 2

			5
		5	
	M2		M1

Figure 9-13   Strategy Situation 12, Test Numbers 5, 0, 10

		5	
	M1	M2	

Figure 9-14   Strategy Situation 13, Test Numbers 5, 0, 5

170

During the course of the game the opponent's moves and the defensive moves generated by the computer will create many new and unexpected situations, and both the computer and the opponent must be able to respond appropriately in the new situations. The computer always examines up to 13 situations throughout the whole board at every move to detect any situations created by the opponent's last move. The sequence of the ROW array has been selected so that the computer will first examine those rows containing prime squares to enable it to control the largest possible number of rows if the same situation level occurs in two different places on the board.

It is not known if the list of situations presented here is an optimum list or if the sequence of situations is optimum, but the present situation list has been quite successful in winning games. If the computer loses a game it is necessary for the programmer to analyze the situation which caused the loss and consider adding the losing situation to the list of situations which the computer will examine at every move, at an appropriate priority within the list. Notice that the computer never uses an offensive situation with a first test number of ten unless the situation is a trap, because this would cause the computer to get three in a row before a trap play existed and thus waste a perfectly good row.

The TTT3D program prints out the situation number and the blank square M2 at each move so that the progress of the game can be studied. If blocking the opponent is not necessary, the computer will proceed through successively lower situation numbers to a successful trap at Situation 4 or 5. The opponent's moves and resulting blocking moves will cause the situation level to oscillate as the computer goes on the offensive, then on the defensive, then on the offensive again.

At the beginning of the game and occasionally during the middle of a game none of the situations described above will exist. Under these conditions the program executes a waiting move from the WAIT list. To add a random flavor to the waiting moves, the subscript of the first waiting move is K1, a parameter varying from one to four as a function of the opponent's last move. If the first waiting move references an occupied square, the other waiting moves in the WAIT list are examined in turn. If all of the squares in the wait list are occupied, a tie game is declared and the program restarts, but the restart is rarely necessary. The WAIT list contains 20 squares in a sequence of the 16 prime squares.

The search for all the blank squares on all of the 76 rows in up to 13 increasingly complex situations requires the execution of perhaps a million IF statements in the STRAT subprogram. Only 14 IF statements appear in the subprogram, and the highly repetitive use of these statements is controlled by eight nested DO loops. The time required for an 1130 to go all the way through all eight loops is 30 to 40 seconds, which is the longest time that the opponent will have to wait for the computer to make a move.

9-4   Plan of Attack and Flow Diagram

The TTT3D program is organized so that the main program TTT3D handles input and output and keeps track of the moves upon the board, the STRAT subprogram calculates the next move based on a search of the 13 situations and the BOARD subprogram converts the move calculated by STRAT into player code. In this way it was possible to debug the program in three relatively small pieces, each of which is a logically complete program. The basic flow diagrams for TTT3D, STRAT and BOARD are shown in Figures 9-15, 9-16 and 9-17.

Certain conventions are required to permit the opponent to select who will move first, to terminate a game and start another, and to terminate execution of the TTT3D program by returning control to the Disk Monitor. The computer will ignore a move of zero and allow the opponent to skip the first move or any other move at any time. Any negative move such as –11 will terminate the game in progress, and a move of 999 will terminate the program.

The STRAT program consists primarily of eight nested DO loops, terminating on statements 21, 22, 23, 24, 25, 26, 27 and 28. In the flow diagram, the DO indexing is summarized in brackets next to each of the terminating statements. The DO loop to statement 21 controls the situation being examined, 22 controls finding a row with a SUM equal to the first test number, 23 controls finding a blank M1 on the first row, 24 controls finding a second row with SUM equal to the second test, 25 controls finding the blank M1 on the second row, 26 controls finding a blank M2 on the second row, 27 controls finding a third row with SUM equal to the third test, and 28 controls finding the blank M2 on the third row.

9-5   The TTT3D Program Listing in FORTRAN

The program listing includes all necessary monitor control records to permit TTT3D to be compiled and executed under control of the 1130 Disk Monitor. COMMON storage is used to transmit arguments and results between the TTT3D and STRAT programs. The type, DIMENSION, COMMON and FORMAT statements appear at the beginning of the listing.

```
// JOB
// FOR
**  THREE-DIMENSIONAL TIC-TAC-TOE PROGRAM, 8/16/66.
*  NAME TTT3D
*  IOCS (CARD, KEYBOARD, TYPEWRITER)
*  ONE WORD INTEGERS
*  LIST ALL
        INTEGER SUM(76), ROW(304), WAIT(20), TEST(3, 14), YE, ANS, BLANK
        DIMENSION MOVE(64), LAST(4), NAME(10)
        COMMON MOVE, SUM, ROW, WAIT, TEST, M1, M2, M3
```

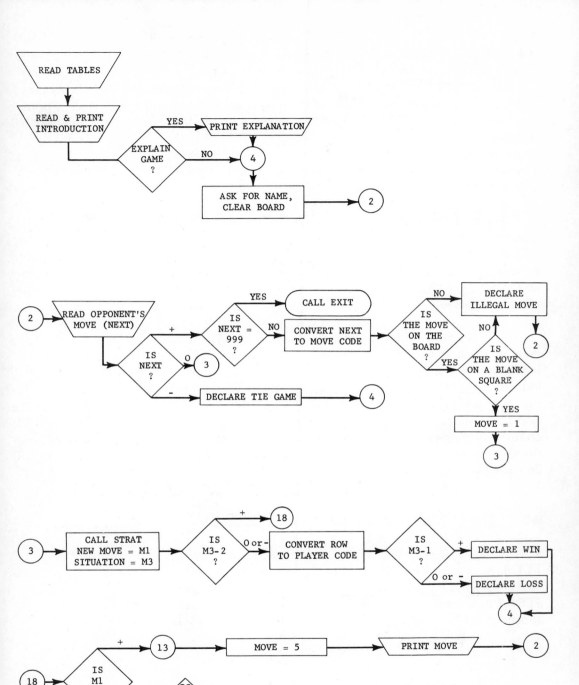

Figure 9-15 Flow Diagram for the TTT3D Program

173

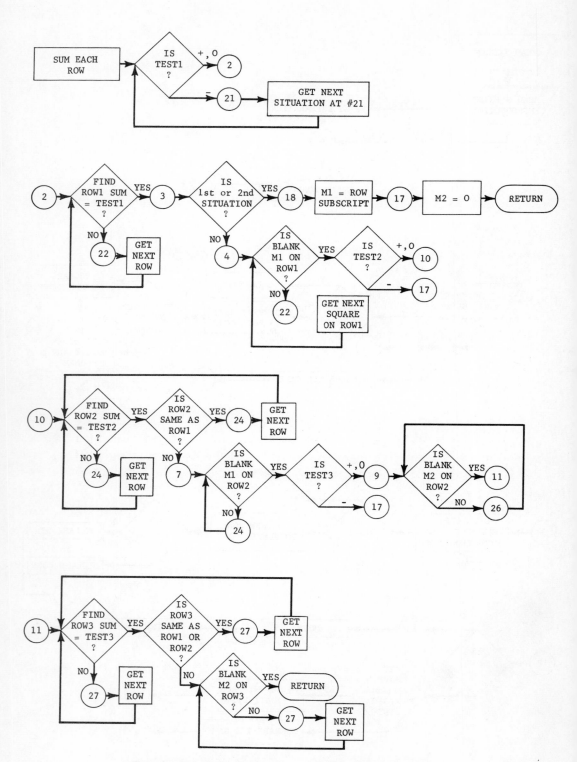

Figure 9-16   Flow Diagram for the STRAT Subprogram

174

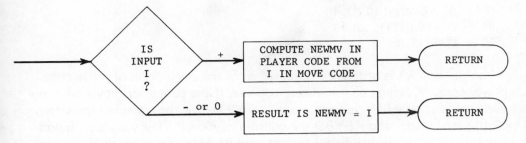

Figure 9-17   Flow Diagram for the BOARD Subprogram

```
89    FORMAT (54H
90    FORMAT (24I3)
91    FORMAT (11H YOU WIN ON, 4I4, 2H,  , 10A2)
92    FORMAT (9H I WIN ON, 4I4, 2H,  , 10A2)
93    FORMAT (14H COME ON NOW,  , 10A2, 22H, THAT MOVE IS ILLEGAL)
94    FORMAT (/17H TYPE YOUR MOVE,  , 10A2)
95    FORMAT (//26H TYPE IN YOUR NAME, PLEASE)
96    FORMAT (23H TIE GAME, RESTARTING,  , 10A2)
97    FORMAT (10A2)
98    FORMAT (11H MY MOVE IS, I4, 12H ON STRATEGY I4, I3)
99    FORMAT (13H YOUR MOVE IS, I4)
```

Notice that all variables are dimensioned in the first statement in which they appear and that DIMENSION statements are not needed for the variables listed in the INTEGER statement. The following statements provide initialization of the program:

```
        NTYP = 1
        NCARD = 2
        KEYBD = 6
C-----K1 INDEXES THE WAIT LIST, INITIALIZE K1 = 1
        K1 = 1
C-----READ ALL DATA TABLES
        READ (NCARD, 90) ROW, WAIT, TEST
        READ (NCARD, 97) YE, BLANK
C-----READ AND PRINT THE INTRODUCTION TO THE PROGRAM
        DO 5 I = 1, 5
        READ (NCARD, 89)
5       WRITE (NTYP, 89)
C-----SEE IF EXPLANATION IS REQUIRED
        READ (KEYBD, 97) ANS
C-----EXPLAIN HOW TO PLAY IF REQUESTED
        DO 10 I = 1, 8
        READ (NCARD, 89)
```

175

```
        IF (YE–ANS) 10, 21, 10
21      WRITE (NTYP, 89)
10      CONTINUE
```

The variable K1 is ordinarily obtained from the calculation of move code from player code. K1 must be initialized, because, if the computer moves first, no move code calculation will have been made. NTYP is now the console typewriter, NCARD the card reader and KEYBD the console keyboard. The variable YE consists of the two letters YE read in A2 format, and BLANK is two blank characters in A2 format. ROW, WAIT and TEST occupy 16 data cards in 2413 format, for a total of 366 variables. Five introductory cards in 54H format are read and printed by the DO loop at statement 5. The two-letter variable ANS is then read and eight explanation cards are read by the DO loop ending at statement 10. Printing of the eight cards depends on whether ANS equals the variable YE. Here we are using an IF statement to compare a variable to see if the variable equals the two letters YE.

```
C-----GET OPPONENT'S NAME
4       DO 20 I = 1, 10
20      NAME(I) = BLANK
        WRITE (NTYP, 95)
        READ (KEYBD, 97) NAME
C-----CLEAR THE BOARD
        DO 1 I = 1, 64
1       MOVE(I) = 0
```

Statement 4 is the starting point for each new game. The NAME array is cleared to blanks and replaced with the opponent's name, which must be of 20 characters or less (10A2 format). The 64 squares of the board are cleared to zero in the MOVE array. We are now ready to accept the opponent's first move.

```
C-----READ OPPONENT'S MOVE, CHECK FOR END OF GAME (-) OR NO
C-----MOVE (0)
2       WRITE (NTYP, 94) NAME
        READ (KEYBD, 90) NEXT
        WRITE (NTYP, 99) NEXT
        IF (NEXT) 19, 3, 6
C-----RETURN TO DISK MONITOR IF MOVE IS 999
6       IF (NEXT - 999) 29, 28, 28
28      CALL EXIT
C-----CONVERT TO MOVE CODE (1-64) AND CHECK RANGE
29      K1 = NEXT/100
        K3 = NEXT - 100 * K1
        K2 = K3/10
        K3 = K3 - 10 * K2
        IF (K1) 8, 8, 22
22      IF (K1-4) 23, 23, 8
23      IF (K2) 8, 8, 24
```

```
24      IF (K2-4) 25, 25, 8
25      IF (K3) 8, 8, 26
26      IF (K3-4) 7, 7, 8
7       NEXT = 16*(K1-1) + 4*(K2-1) + K3
C-----MAKE SURE THAT NEW MOVE IS ON BLANK SQUARE
        IF (MOVE(NEXT)) 9, 9, 8
8       WRITE (NTYP, 93) NAME
        GO TO 2
```

At statement 2 the program requests the opponent's move and prints it immediately to verify that it was entered correctly. If the move (NEXT) is negative, control
goes to statement 19 to start a new game. If NEXT is zero, control goes to statement
3 where the computer will make a move. Otherwise control goes to statement 6 where
control is returned to the Disk Monitor if NEXT is 999. If not, the three digits of
NEXT are separated into K1, K2 and K3. K1 becomes the hundreds digit, K2 the
tens digit, K3 the units digit. The absence of a remainder in integer division in FOR-
TRAN makes the separation possible. The reader should work through a specific
example to see how these statements work. Statement 28 allows control to be
returned to the Disk Monitor to terminate a series of games.

Six IF statements are then used to check that each of the three digits is in the
range of one to four, as otherwise the digits cannot represent moves on the playing
board, which is four-by-four-by-four squares. If any digit is out of range, control
goes to statement 8 to print an illegal move message and then to statement 2 to
request another choice of move from the opponent. Otherwise NEXT is converted
to an integer ranging from 1 to 64 in move code at statement 7.

The program now tests to see if the square in MOVE subscripted by NEXT is
a blank (unoccupied) square. If it is not, the illegal move message is printed. If so,
control goes to statement 9.

```
C-----SET OPPONENT'S MOVE EQUAL TO 1
9       MOVE(NEXT) = 1
C-----CALL STRAT FOR SITUATION ANALYSIS, M1 = BEST MOVE, M2 =
C-----ALTERNATE
C-----M3 IS THE SITUATION LEVEL
3       CALL STRAT
```

At statement 9 the MOVE array is updated by the opponent's latest move,
set equal to one, and subscripted by the move location NEXT. The STRAT subprogram is then called to determine the computer's next move. STRAT has access to all
the variables in COMMON and so needs no argument list. The results of STRAT are
placed in the variables M1, M2 and M3. If STRAT returns at situation levels one or
two (as indicated by the variable M3), then the game is over and M1 contains the row
subscript (1 through 76) of the winning row. Otherwise M1 contains the move subscript of the recommended move, which must be placed in the MOVE array and
printed for anlaysis by the opponent.

177

```
C-----TEST FOR SITUATION LEVEL 1 OR 2, END OF GAME
      IF (M3-2) 17, 17, 18
17    K3 = 4*(M1-1)
      DO 11 I = 1, 4
      K2 = I + K3
11    CALL BOARD(ROW(K2), LAST(I))
      IF (M3-1) 15, 15, 16
C-----HERE PROGRAM HAS LOST
15    WRITE (NTYP, 91) LAST, NAME
      GO TO 4
C-----HERE PROGRAM HAS WON
16    WRITE (NTYP, 92) LAST, NAME
      GO TO 4
```

The calculation at statement 17 computes the subscript of the first square of the winning row in the ROW array, which contains the subscripts of each of the four squares making up each of the 76 possible rows for a total of 304 words of memory. The BOARD subprogram is then called at statement 11 in a DO loop to convert the subscripts of each of the four squares in the winning row to player code and store the player codes in the LAST array. Depending upon whether M3 was two or one, a message of victory or defeat is then printed. The programming for the other situation levels follows.

```
C-----TEST FOR NO SITUATION LEVEL, IF SO USE A WAITING MOVE
18    IF (M1) 12, 12, 13
12    DO 14 I = K1, 20
      M1 = WAIT(I)
      IF (MOVE(M1)) 13, 13, 14
14    CONTINUE
C-----IF WAIT LIST IS EXHAUSTED WE HAVE A TIE GAME
19    WRITE (NTYP, 96) NAME
      GO TO 4
C-----WE HAVE A SITUATION LEVEL, SO COMPUTER'S MOVE EQUALS 5
13    MOVE(M1) = 5
      CALL BOARD(M1, M1)
      CALL BOARD(M2, M2)
C-----PRINT COMPUTER'S MOVE
      WRITE (NTYP, 98) M1, M2, M3
      GO TO 2
      END
```

If M1 is zero the program makes a waiting move, because none of the situations examined by STRAT existed on the board. The WAIT list, consisting of the subscripts of the prime squares, is searched by the DO loop starting at statement 12. The search starts with the subscript K1, which may be any value from one to four and thus randomizes the computer's choice of a first move on the second and subsequent games. If all the squares in the WAIT list are occupied, the program will

178

declare a tie game via the message at statement 28, after which control goes to statement 4 to start a new game.

At statement 13 we have a situation which is not Situation 1 or 2. Here M1 and M2 are converted to player code by the BOARD subprogram and the computer's move (M1, M2 and M3) is printed. Control then goes to statement 2 to read the opponent's next move.

```
// DUP
*STORE     WS     UA     TTT3D
```

The only remaining statements are the // DUP and *STORE cards which cause TTT3D to be stored on the disk in the User Area.

9-6   The STRAT Subprogram Listing in FORTRAN

Starting as before with monitor control cards and specification statements:

```
// FOR
**  THREE-DIMENSIONAL TIC-TAC-TOE PROGRAM, 8/16/66.
* ONE WORD INTEGERS
* LIST ALL
        SUBROUTINE STRAT
        INTEGER SUM(76), ROW(304), WAIT(20), TEST(3, 14), TEST1, TEST2, TEST3
        DIMENSION MOVE(64)
        COMMON MOVE, SUM, ROW, WAIT, TEST, M1, M2, M3
C-----THIS SUBROUTINE FINDS A BLANK SQUARE M1 ON A ROW OF SUM=TEST1,
C-----SUCH THAT ANOTHER ROW OF SUM=TEST2 CONTAINS M1 AND ALSO
C-----CONTAINS A SECOND BLANK SQUARE M2 WHICH IS ON A THIRD ROW OF
C-----SUM=TEST3. NEGATIVE TESTS ARE SKIPPED. IF SITUATION IS 1 OR
C-----2, ANSWER IS A ROW SUBSCRIPT, ELSE ANSWER IS M1. M1 AND M2
C-----MAY BE IDENTICAL. FIRST CALCULATE THE SUM VALUE FOR EACH ROW
        DO 15 J1 = 1, 76
        SUM(J1) = 0
        K2 = 4*J1
        L2 = K2 -3
        DO 15 J2 = L2, K2
        J3 = ROW(J2)
15      SUM(J1) = SUM(J1) + MOVE(J3)
```

The double DO loop terminating at statement 15 sums all the move values in the four squares making up each of the 76 rows, using the subscripts of the squares obtained from the ROW array. Notice that the COMMON statement includes the same list of variables as the COMMON statement in TTT3D, ensuring a one-for-one correspondence in the COMMON area.

179

```
C-----START STRATEGY TESTS FOR THE FIRST SITUATION
         DO 21 J1 = 1, 14
         M3 = J1
         TEST1 = TEST(1, J1)
         IF (TEST1) 21, 2, 2
2        TEST2 = TEST(2, J1)
         TEST3 = TEST(3, J1)
C-----FIND A ROW WHOSE SUM = TEST1
         DO 22 J2 = 1, 76
         IF (SUM(J2) – TEST1) 22, 3, 22
3        IF (J1–2) 18, 18, 4
C-----FIND A BLANK SQUARE M1 ON THE ROW WITH SUM = TEST1
4        K3 = 4*J2
         L3 = K3–3
         DO 23 J3 = L3, K3
         M1 = ROW(J3)
         IF (MOVE(M1)) 23, 5, 23
5        IF (TEST2) 17, 10, 10
```

The DO loop terminating at statement 21 picks up the three test numbers for the situation currently being examined. The test numbers are stored in TEST1, TEST2 and TEST3 to eliminate the time required to repeatedly reevaluate the subscripts of the test numbers in the TEST array. If TEST1 is negative the current situation is skipped; otherwise the program proceeds to look for a row whose sum is equal to TEST1. If such a row is found and the situation level (J1) is one or two, control goes to statement 18; otherwise the program looks for a blank square on the row with a sum equal to TEST1. If such a blank square cannot be found, the DO loop logic will return to search for another row whose sum is TEST1. If no such row exists, the DO loop logic will index to the next situation level and start again. At statement 5 the remaining tests for the current situation are skipped if TEST2 is negative.

```
C-----FIND A ROW WHOSE SUM = TEST2
10       DO 24 J4 = 1, 76
         IF (SUM(J4) – TEST2) 24, 6, 24
6        IF (J4 – J2) 7, 24, 7
C-----FIND THE BLANK SQUARE M1 ON THE ROW WITH SUM = TEST2
7        K5 = 4*J4
         L5 = K5 – 3
         DO 25 J5 = L5, K5
         IF (M1 – ROW(J5)) 25, 8, 25
8        IF (TEST3) 17, 9, 9
C-----FIND ANY BLANK SQUARE M2 ON THE ROW WITH SUM = TEST2
9        DO 26 J6 = L5, K5
         M2 = ROW(J6)
         IF (MOVE(M2)) 26, 11, 26
```

At statement 10 the program starts the search for a row whose sum is TEST2. A check is made at statement 6 to make sure that the row equal to TEST2 is not the same row that was previously found to be equal to TEST1. At statement 7 the search for the blank square M1 on the row equal to TEST2 begins. At statement 8 the remaining tests for the current situation are skipped if TEST3 is negative. Otherwise the program starts a search to find any blank square M2 on the row with a sum equal to TEST2 at statement 9.

```
C-----FIND A ROW WHOSE SUM = TEST3
11      DO 27 J7 = 1, 76
        IF (SUM(J7) - TEST3) 27, 12, 27
12      IF (J7 - J2) 13, 27, 13
13      IF (J7 - J4) 14, 27, 14
C-----FIND THE BLANK SQUARE M2 ON THE ROW WITH SUM = TEST3
14      K8 = 4*J7
        L8 = K8 -3
        DO 28 J8 = L8, K8
        IF (M2 - ROW(J8)) 28, 16, 28
28      CONTINUE
27      CONTINUE
26      CONTINUE
25      CONTINUE
24      CONTINUE
23      CONTINUE
22      CONTINUE
21      CONTINUE
```

At statement 11 the search for a row whose sum is TEST3 begins. At statements 12 and 13 the program checks to ensure that the row whose sum is TEST3 is not the same row as the one with a sum of TEST2 or the row with a sum of TEST1. At statement 14 the search to find the blank square M2 on the row with sum equal to TEST3 begins.

The eight CONTINUE statements starting with statement 21 terminate all the searches and shows how the various searches are nested. If any search completes its DO indexing without success, control goes back to the immediately previous search (the last unsatisfied DO loop) and the program keeps looking. The theoretical maximum number of executions of the innermost DO in the nest (the DO terminating at statement 28) is equal to the product of all the upper limits of the eight DO statements. This maximum is the product of 14, 76, 4, 76, 4, 4, 76 and 4, which is 1,573,289,984. In practice the maximum is much less (usually less than a million) since many of the search conditions are mutually exclusive.

```
C-----IF THIS POINT IS REACHED, NO SITUATION EXISTS
        M1 = 0
        GO TO 17
C-----SITUATION IS 1 OR 2, M1 IS A ROW SUBSCRIPT
```

```
18      M1 = J2
17      M2 = 0
16      RETURN
        END
// DUP
*STORE      WS      UA      STRAT
```

If all of the eight DO loops are satisfied without finding one of the situations in the TEST array, M1 and M2 are set to zero. If Situation 1 or 2 is found, M1 is set equal to the row subscript J2, and M2 is set to zero. If one of the other situations is found, M1 and M2 are set to MOVE subscripts inside the DO loops and the STRAT subprogram simply returns with these values.

The TEST array is dimensioned for a total of 14 situations, although only 13 situations are described in Section 9-3. The fourteenth situation has test numbers of $-1, -1, -1$ and is provided for future expansion of the situation list. Since the first test number is -1, the fourteenth situation is skipped over by the statement immediately preceding statement 2 in STRAT.

9-7   The BOARD Subprogram Listing in FORTRAN

Starting as before with the monitor control statements:

```
// FOR
**  THREE-DIMENSIONAL TIC-TAC-TOE PROGRAM, 8/16/66.
*  ONE WORD INTEGERS
*  LIST ALL
        SUBROUTINE BOARD(I, NEWMV)
C-----THIS SUBROUTINE CHANGES MOVE CODE TO THE EXTERNAL PLAYER
C-----CODE
        IF (I) 1, 1, 2
1       NEWMV = I
        RETURN
2       L1 = (I – 1)/16
        L2 = I – 16 * L1
        L3 = (L2 – 1)/4
        NEWMV = 100*(L1 + 1) + 10*(L3 + 1) + L2 – 4*L3
        RETURN
        END
// DUP
*STORE      WS      UA      BOARD
// XEQ TTT3D
```

The argument I in move code ranging from 1 to 64 is converted into the player code NEWMV unless I is negative or zero, in which case NEWMV is simply set

182

equal to I. A specific example, such as the conversion of the move code 34 into the player code of 312, should be worked out by the reader to understand how integer division is used to effect the conversion.

The XEQ monitor control record will cause the TTT3D program to be loaded into core memory to be executed, and the CALL statements in TTT3D referring to STRAT and BOARD will cause the loading of these programs into core memory along with TTT3D. The input data cards should follow immediately behind the XEQ card.

9-8 Input Data Required for TTT3D

The input data consists of 16 cards in 2413 format, one card containing the letters YE followed by 13 cards in 54H format. The cards in 2413 format contain the 304 numbers of the ROW array, the 20 numbers of the WAIT array, and lastly the 42 numbers of the TEST array. The cards in 54H format contain the introduction to the game and explanatory comments. A complete list of the input data follows. Note that I3 format requires a blank in column 1.

```
22 43 64   1 23 42 61   4 26 39 52 13 27 38 49 16 22 42 62   2 23 43 63   3
23 38 53   8 27 42 57 12 26 38 50 14 27 39 51 15 22 39 56   5 26 43 60   9
22 38 54   6 23 39 55   7 26 42 58 10 27 43 59 11 22 23 24 21 26 27 28 25
22 26 30 18 23 27 31 19 22 27 32 17 23 26 29 20 38 39 40 37 42 43 44 41
38 42 46 34 39 43 47 35 38 43 48 33 39 42 45 36 61   1 21 41 64   4 24 44
49   4 19 34 61 16 31 46 49 13 25 37 52 16 28 40 52   1 18 35 64 13 30 47
49   1 17 33 52   4 20 36 61 13 29 45 64 16 32 48   4   1   2   3 16 13 14 15
13   1   5   9 16   4   8 12 16   1   6 11 13   4   7 10 52 49 50 51 64 61 62 63
61 49 53 57 64 52 56 60 64 49 54 59 61 52 55 58 18 34 50   2 19 35 51   3
21 37 53   5 24 40 56   8 25 41 57   9 28 44 60 12 30 46 62 14 31 47 63 15
 6   7   8   5 10 11 12   9   6 10 14   2   7 11 15   3 18 19 20 17 30 31 32 29
21 25 29 17 24 28 32 20 34 35 36 33 46 47 48 45 37 41 45 33 40 44 48 36
54 55 56 53 58 59 60 57 54 58 62 50 55 59 63 51 22 43 23 42 26 39 27 38
 1 64 13 52   4 61 16 49 22 43 23 42   4 -1 -1 15 -1 -1   3 -1 -1 10 10 -1
10   5 10   2   2 -1   2   1   2   2   1   1   2   0   2   5   5 10   5   5   5   5   0 10
 5   0   5 -1 -1 -1
```

YE
THIS PROGRAM PLAYS THREE-DIMENSIONAL TIC-TAC-TOE ON A
BOARD CONSISTING OF 64 SQUARES ARRANGED ON 4 LEVELS

OF 16 (4X4) SQUARES EACH. IF YOU WANT AN EXPLANATION
OF HOW THE GAME IS PLAYED, TYPE YES. IF YOU KNOW HOW
TO PLAY, TYPE NO AND NO EXPLANATION WILL BE PROVIDED.
THE PURPOSE OF THE GAME IS TO GET 4 MOVES IN A ROW.
WINNING ROWS MAY BE SET UP VERTICALLY, HORIZONTALLY,
OR DIAGONALLY IN ANY DIRECTION. TO ENTER YOUR MOVE,
TYPE IN A 3-DIGIT NUMBER. FOR EXAMPLE, 243 WOULD BE
2ND LEVEL, 4TH ROW, 3RD COLUMN. TO LET ME MOVE FIRST
YOU CAN SKIP YOUR MOVE BY TYPING IN ZERO (000). WHEN
YOU WISH TO START A NEW GAME, TYPE IN A NEGATIVE MOVE
SUCH AS -11. TO GET OFF THE COMPUTER TYPE 999.

9-9   Memory Requirements

The TTT3D program contains 79 FORTRAN statements which require 594
words of core memory, or an average of about seven words per statement. In addition, it requires 510 words to store the variables in COMMON and 18 words to store
the remaining variables. The STRAT subprogram requires a total of 422 words, and
the BOARD subprogram requires 98 words. Since the programs do not use many
library subroutines, TTT3D will fit in a 4K memory. Figure 9-18 shows the printed
output resulting from a typical game.

9-10   Summary

The TTT3D program is designed to show how FORTRAN may be used to
effectively program a strategy problem involving a variety of situations requiring
analysis. This program shows how a very complex decision may be programmed as
the sum of millions of simple decisions, each of which can easily be made by the
computer. It also demonstrates the ability of COMMON to eliminate the
transmission of argument lists in subprogram calling sequences.

9-11   Problems

1)   Use the FORTRAN statements from statement 29 through statement
7 in the TTT3D program listing to convert the following values of
player code into move code: NEXT = 11, 222, 333, 444, 112, 443,
114 and 141.

2)   Use the BOARD subprogram statements to convert the following
values of move code into player code: I = 1, 64, 2, 17, 33, 49 and 63.

THIS PROGRAM PLAYS THREE-DIMENSIONAL TIC-TAC-TOE ON A
BOARD CONSISTING OF 64 SQUARES ARRANGED ON 4 LEVELS
OF 16 (4X4) SQUARES EACH. IF YOU WANT AN EXPLANATION
OF HOW THE GAME IS PLAYED, TYPE YES. IF YOU KNOW HOW
TO PLAY, TYPE NO AND NO EXPLANATION WILL BE PROVIDED.
NO

TYPE IN YOUR NAME, PLEASE
JOHN JONES

TYPE YOUR MOVE
000
MY MOVE IS 222 ON STRATEGY   0 14

TYPE YOUR MOVE
111
YOUR MOVE IS 111
MY MOVE IS 332 ON STRATEGY 223 14

TYPE YOUR MOVE
414
YOUR MOVE IS 414
MY MOVE IS 441 ON STRATEGY 442 12

TYPE YOUR MOVE
441
YOUR MOVE IS 441
COME ON NOW, THAT MOVE IS ILLEGAL

TYPE YOUR MOVE
144
YOUR MOVE IS 144
MY MOVE IS 323 ON STRATEGY 341 11

(after several intervening moves, the output is)

TYPE YOUR MOVE
141
YOUR MOVE IS 141
MY MOVE IS 331 ON STRATEGY 341 5

TYPE YOUR MOVE
411
YOUR MOVE IS 411
I WIN ON 332 333 334 331
JOHN JONES

Figure 9-18 Printed Output from the TTT3D Program

185

3) Why is it desirable to be able to return control to the Disk Monitor by using the CALL EXIT statement after several games have been played?

4) If the opponent types in a move of zero (000) as his first move the computer will move first instead of the opponent. What will happen on subsequent moves if the opponent types in a move of zero?

5) After being defeated by the computer in at least three consecutive games, answer the following question in 50 words or less: Can machines really think?

6) What do you suppose would happen if you programmed your 1130 and someone else's 1130 with a TTT3D program and let your 1130 "play against" the other 1130. Would you have to provide the first move, still? If so, do you think that the outcome (that is, which 1130 wins) will depend on this first move of yours?

7) Finally, could you write a special program which would make your 1130 "play against itself" using the TTT3D program as two identical subroutines that will "call themselves" through this special program and continue to play until "one of them" wins? Is the outcome predictable? Note that there is no actual need to have a duplicate subroutine in storage.

CHAPTER 10: CHARACTER MANIPULATION IN FORTRAN

10-1   The Need for Character Manipulation

In Chapter 8 we discussed a program primarily concerned with floating-point calculation; in Chapter 9 we analyzed a program which exclusively involved integer arithmetic and complex decisions; now we shall examine a set of subprograms designed to manipulate alphameric characters. Such commercial or business-oriented applications as payroll calculations, inventory control and information retrieval demand the ability to move individual characters or strings of characters to form words and sentences, to compare words so as to sort them into alphabetic sequences, to convert strings of digits to floating-point notation and vice versa under program control and to edit combinations of letters, digits and special characters into meaningful combinations like 286-26-8468 (a social security number) or $***394.66– (an asterisk-protected negative dollar field).

We also need to be able to manipulate zone punches, which were introduced in Section 2-6. Since each column of an 80-column punched card contains space for an 11- or 12-zone punch in addition to spaces for the ten digits zero through nine, it is reasonable in commercial applications to use the zone punches (in the same column as a digit punch) to represent special information such as the end of a data field or a minus field or perhaps a card which is to be processed by an alternate set of program instructions. Examination of the table of IBM card codes in Appendix D reveals that the digits 1-9 become the letters A-I with the addition of a 12-zone punch and the same digits become the letters J-R with the addition of an 11-zone punch. The letters S-Z may be similarly formed by adding a 0-zone (zero zone) punch to the digits 2-9, where the 0-zone punch is the punch normally used for the digit zero. When we read a punched card we must be able to sense the presence of zone punches in any card column, to delete or insert zone punches in any card column to be punched by the computer, and thus to convert digits into letters and vice versa.

Another much desired ability for commercial applications is the ability to read a punched card without knowing the format of the card before the card is read. In previous FORTRAN READ statements it has been necessary to refer to a FORMAT statement number, and to do that we had to know the format of the next card to be read by the computer. In many commercial applications it is not practical to know the format of the next card. If, for instance, we are reading payroll time cards interspersed with employee deduction cards, two types of cards will be in different formats and the number of each type of card may vary from one employee to the next (or from one week to the next). It will be impractical to know which type of card will come next in the input data deck. We might solve this problem by punching an 11-zone punch in column 80 of each payroll time card if it were possible to first read the card, then test for the presence of the 11-zone punch and then use one of two different formats.

All of the above operations can be done entirely in FORTRAN through the use of subroutines and subprograms. The remainder of this chapter will be devoted to developing such a subroutine "package." The subroutines in this package have been incorporated, together with other programs, into an IBM library package known as the *IBM 1130 Commercial Subroutine Package* which is described in greater detail in IBM publication number H20-0241.

10-2 A Generalized 80A1 Format

We have previously discussed real or floating-point variables which occupy two or three words of core memory each (in standard or extended precision) and integer variables which occupy one word of core memory each (if the control specification ONE WORD INTEGERS is used). Since the smallest amount of memory which can be referenced by a FORTRAN variable is one word, we shall use a one-word integer variable to store each character. If only one 8-bit character in EBCDIC code (Section 2-5) is stored in each 16-bit memory word, each word will be only half used, but the inefficiency in memory utilization will frequently be compensated by fewer instructions required to manipulate the characters if the characters are stored one per memory word.

Throughout this chapter we shall assume that all data are read into one-dimensional arrays of one word integers such as the following:

```
        DIMENSION JCARD(80), KCARD(80)
1       FORMAT (80A1)
        NCARD = 2
        READ (NCARD, 1) JCARD, KCARD
```

The above coding will place a character from each of the 80 columns of two cards into a separate memory word in the JCARD and KCARD arrays.

10-3 The MOVE Subprogram to Move Strings of Characters

Suppose we wish to move a string of characters from somewhere near the middle of JCARD to a location in KCARD. What information must we furnish to a subprogram to do the job? Obviously the arrays JCARD and KCARD must be named as arguments to the subprogram, and subscripts designating the first and last character positions of the string in JCARD and the first (leftmost) character position in KCARD would also be necessary arguments. The calling statement might read

```
        CALL MOVE(JCARD, J, JLAST, KCARD, K)
```

where J and JLAST are the first and last character positions (subscripts) in JCARD and K is the first position in KCARD. The subprogram will move characters, left to right, from JCARD(J) through JCARD(JLAST) to KCARD(K) and successive words in the KCARD array. Obviously JLAST should be greater than J and K should be at least as far from the right end of KCARD as the quantity JLAST – J. The subprogram can be coded as follows:

```
        SUBROUTINE MOVE(JCARD, J, JLAST, KCARD, K)
        DIMENSION JCARD(80), KCARD(80)
C-----MOVE JCARD(J) THROUGH JCARD(JLAST) TO KCARD(K)
        DO 1 JNOW = J, JLAST
        KNOW = K † JNOW – J
1       KCARD(KNOW) = JCARD(JNOW)
        RETURN
        END
```

As an example, consider moving the characters from JCARD(3) through JCARD(8) to KCARD(5). If the first ten columns of JCARD contain the characters ABCDEFGHIJ and the first ten columns of KCARD contain the characters 1234567890, then after the move the first ten columns of KCARD would contain 1234CDEFGH. Notice that a total of six characters CDEFGH are moved. The calling statement for the example is

```
        CALL MOVE(JCARD, 3, 8, KCARD, 5)
```

10-4 The FILL Subprogram to Fill a Character String with One Character

Suppose now that we wish to fill a character string in JCARD with some arbitrary character. What subprogram arguments will be required? The array name (JCARD), the subscript of the first position in the string (J), the subscript of the last position in the string (JLAST) and the arbitrary character to be inserted are all needed. If the arbitrary character we wish to insert is the character A, we cannot simply write "A" into the subprogram CALL statement; instead we must write an integer constant with the same bit pattern as the character A stored in A1 format.

Consider the EBCDIC code for the letter A, which is 11000001 in binary or C1 in hexadecimal (Section 2-5). When the letter A is stored in a core memory word in A1 format, the EBCDIC code for A will be located in the right side of the word, and the 16-bit word will contain the bit pattern 11000001 01000000 which would be written as C140 in hexadecimal. This bit pattern, however, can also represent the integer –16064 as described in Section 2-2. By writing –16064 in the subprogram CALL statement we can make the letter A available as a program-defined constant. A table of the integer equivalents for EBCDIC characters is in Appendix D.

The coding for the subprogram is

```
        SUBROUTINE FILL(JCARD, J, JLAST, NCH)
        DIMENSION JCARD(80)
```

```
C------FILL JCARD(J) THROUGH JCARD(JLAST) WITH THE CHARACTER NCH
        DO 1 JNOW = J, JLAST
1       JCARD(JNOW) = NCH
        RETURN
        END
```

If we desire to fill the ALPHA array from position four through position eight with the letter B, we might use the calling statement

CALL FILL(ALPHA, 4, 8, –15808)

where –15808 is the integer equivalent for the letter B in EBCDIC code in A1 format as determined from the table in Appendix D. If the first ten characters of the ALPHA array were 9876543210, after execution of the above CALL statement the first ten characters of ALPHA would be 987BBBBB10 with the letter B filled into positions four through eight.

10-5   The NCOMP Function to Compare Two Character Strings

The FORTRAN arithmetic IF statement (Section 3-13) allows us to perform a high, low or equal comparison of two real or integer variables. Now let's write a function to perform high, low and equal comparisons on pairs of character strings of arbitrary length. At first glance all that we need is a DO loop containing an IF statement to compare each pair of characters in A1 format, moving from left to right, until an unequal condition is encountered. This will do the job, but there is a problem of overflow which must be solved.

Suppose that the subroutine is comparing an equal sign character (=) which has an integer equivalent code of 32320 with the letter A which has an integer equivalent code of –16064. The subroutine would then be executing an IF statement equivalent to

IF (32320 – (–16064)) 1, 2, 3

where statement 1 would receive control on a low comparison, 2 on equal and 3 on high. But the effective addition of 32320 plus 16064 would produce an integer larger than 32767, the largest integer which can be represented by a single 16-bit word of memory (Section 2-2).

The overflow problem can be avoided by shifting the 8-bit EBCDIC character code out of the left or high-order bits of the 16-bit word, and in FORTRAN this shifting can only be accomplished by division. If we divide both integers by two before adding, the resulting sum cannot exceed 32767. Notice that division by two always shifts a binary number one bit to the right just as division by ten shifts a decimal number one decimal place to the right. Similarly, multiplication produces

190

a shift to the left. The sign bit in the leftmost bit position of the memory word is not shifted by division or multiplication, of course.

The function can now be coded as follows:

```
      FUNCTION NCOMP(JCARD, J, JLAST, KCARD, K)
      DIMENSION JCARD(80), KCARD(80)
C-----COMPARE JCARD(J) WITH KCARD(K) CONTINUING THROUGH
C-----JCARD(JLAST).
C-----THE RESULT NCOMP WILL BE -, 0 OR + AS (JCARD-KCARD) IS -,
C-----0 OR +.
C-----ASCENDING COLLATING SEQUENCE IS ABCDEFGHIJKLMNOPQRSTUVWXY
C-----Z0123456789 .(+&$*)-/, ' =

      DO 2 JNOW = J, JLAST
      KNOW = K + JNOW - J
      NCOMP = KCARD(KNOW)/2
      NCOMP = JCARD(JNOW)/2 - NCOMP
      IF (NCOMP) 1, 2, 1
2     CONTINUE
1     RETURN
      END
```

The variable NCOMP carries the result of the comparison (high, low or equal) back to the calling program. The collating sequence shows what the result of comparing any two characters will be: the letter B will compare higher than A, the digit 8 will compare higher than 7, etc. The DO loop compares one character from each of the two strings, moving from left to right, until an unequal comparison causes a RETURN to the calling program or until the last character in each string has been compared.

A typical use of the NCOMP subroutine would be inside an IF statement in the calling program such as

```
      IF (NCOMP(JCARD, 1, 10, KCARD, 1)) 10, 20, 30
```

which will cause the first ten characters of JCARD to be compared with the first ten characters of KCARD. If the first ten characters of JCARD were JOHNSONbbb and the first ten characters of KCARD were SMITHbbbbb (where b indicates a blank character), control would go to statement 10 indicating that JOHNSONbbb collates lower than SMITHbbbbb. The NCOMP subroutine thus permits the sequencing of lists of alphameric information.

10-6   The NZONE Subprogram to Manipulate Zone Punches in Cards

As described in Sections 2-6 and 10-1, 12-, 11- and 0-zone punches may be punched in a card column together with digit punches to create codes for letters and special characters. These codes are listed in Appendix D. Examination of the integer equivalent codes in Appendix D reveals that adding 4096 to the integer equivalent code of a character will produce the integer equivalent code for another character having the same digit punch but a different zone punch, provided that the character was a letter of the alphabet. For example, the code for A is –16064. Adding 4096 produces a code of –11968, which is the code for J. The letter A is punched as a digit one punch and a 12-zone punch, while J is punched as a digit one punch and an 11-zone punch.

Let us define a set of index numbers as follows:

Index Number	Characters and Zone Punches
1	A through I, 12-zone and digit punch
2	J through R, 11-zone and digit punch
3	S through Z, 0-zone and digit punch
4	0 through 9, digit punch only
5 or more	Special characters, multiple zone and digit punches

The difference between any two index numbers times 4096 is the amount which must be added to the integer equivalent code of a character associated with the first index number to produce the integer equivalent code of a character having the same digit punch but associated with the second index number. For example, to change a B (index of one) to an S (index of three) we simply add 4096 * (3 – 1) or 8192 to the code for B to get the code for S which is –7616. The index number for any character can be calculated from the integer equivalent code of the character, permitting the identification of zone punches by a subprogram. The index numbers can then be used to add and remove zone punches from the character by altering the integer equivalent code. The NZONE subprogram accomplishes these goals.

It is possible to generate integer equivalent codes which do not correspond to actual characters in the 1130 FORTRAN character set. For example, if 2*4096 is added to the code for the letter A the resulting code will not correspond to any character in the set. A more frequent problem is that of placing an 11-zone punch on the digit zero and producing another illegal character. The NZONE subprogram specifically looks for the 11-zoned zero situation and converts a zero to a solitary 11-zone punch if index two is requested or converts an 11-zone punch (representing a minus sign) to a zero punch if index four is requested. The NZONE subprogram code is as follows:

```
SUBROUTINE NZONE(JCARD, J, NEWZ, OLDZ)
INTEGER OLDZ
DIMENSION JCARD(80)
```

```
C-----OLDZ IS SET TO 1, 2, 3, 4 OR MORE AS JCARD(J) WAS A-I, J-R,
C-----S-Z, 0-9 OR A SPECIAL CHARACTER. JCARD(J) IS THEN ZONED 12
C-----ZONE, 11 ZONE, 0 ZONE, NO ZONE OR LEFT ALONE AS NEWZ = 1,
C-----2, 3, 4 OR MORE. JCARD(J) IS ALWAYS LEFT ALONE IF JCARD(J)
C-----WAS A SPECIAL CHARACTER. ZERO CHANGED TO 11 ZONE BECOMES -, -
C-----CHANGED TO NO ZONE IS ZERO. THE CODE FOR ZERO IS -4032, THE
C-----CODE FOR - IS 24640.
      JTEST = JCARD(J)
      IF (JTEST) 4, 5, 5
4     IF (JTEST + 4032) 8, 6, 8
6     OLDZ = 4
      IF (NEWZ - 2) 2, 7, 2
7     JCARD(J) = 24640
2     RETURN
5     IF (JTEST - 24640) 8, 10, 8
10    OLDZ = 2
      IF (NEWZ - 4) 2, 9, 2
9     JTEST = -12224
3     JCARD(J) = JTEST + 4096 * (NEWZ - OLDZ)
      RETURN
8     OLDZ = 5 + (JTEST - 4096)/4096
      IF (OLDZ - 5) 1, 2, 2
1     IF (NEWZ - 5) 3, 2, 2
      END
```

First the character is stored in JTEST to minimize repeated subscript evaluations, which make extra work for the computer. Before statement 4 we determine whether JTEST is positive or negative, which must be determined immediately because addition to a positive JTEST might cause overflow. If JTEST is the code for zero and the new zone (NEWZ) is to be index two, then the old zone index (OLDZ) is set to four and the character is set to the code for a minus sign. Otherwise, if JTEST is the code for a minus sign, then JTEST is set to -12224, an integer equivalent code for an 11-zoned zero. If either the old zone index or the new zone index is five or more, then the zoning of the character is not changed by the subprogram. If the character is a zero but the new zone index is not two, or if the character is a minus sign but the new zone index is not zero, then the zoning of the character is not changed (to prevent generating codes not in the FORTRAN character set). OLDZ is the result of the subprogram which tells the calling program what zoning was present on the character JCARD(J), and NEWZ is an argument to the subprogram which determines what zoning the character will have after execution of the subprogram.

A typical calling statement for NZONE might be

CALL NZONE(ACARD, 80, 4, NP)

which places the old zone index of the 80th character of ACARD in the variable NP and clears the zone punch if any (index 4). The following table gives additional examples of the operation of the NZONE subprogram.

193

Character Before, NEWZ	Character After, OLDZ
A, 2	J, 1
=, 3	=, 11
M, 1	D, 2
M, 3	U, 2
0, 2	-, 4
-, 4	0, 2

10-7   The GET Function to Get Real Variables from Character Strings

If we could develop a function subprogram to convert character strings into real or floating-point variables, then we could read a punched card in the generalized format 80A1 and pick up variables from any group of card columns at some later time. We would then have the ability to read a card without having to know the format of the card in advance. The GET function performs this conversion.

When we examine the integer equivalent codes for the digits zero through nine we find that there is a relationship between the value of each digit and the code for the digit. The relationship is

$$\text{Digit Value} = (\text{Integer Equivalent Code} + 4032) / 256$$

Given this handy formula, we need only multiply each digit by the appropriate power of ten, sum the products, and, finally, establish the decimal point location. All this is accomplished by the subprogram below.

```
        FUNCTION GET(JCARD, J, JLAST, SHIFT)
        DIMENSION JCARD (80)
C-----GET A REAL VARIABLE FROM JCARD(J) THROUGH JCARD(JLAST).
C-----SHIFT = A MULTIPLICATION CONSTANT TO LOCATE THE DECIMAL POINT.
C-----A NEGATIVE STRING SHOULD HAVE AN 11 PUNCH OVER JCARD(JLAST).
C-----IMBEDDED BLANKS ARE TREATED AS ZEROS.
C-----THE RESULT WILL BE 0. IF OTHER THAN DIGITS AND BLANKS APPEAR
C-----IN ANY POSITION OTHER THAN JCARD(JLAST).
C-----FIRST CLEAR 11 ZONE FROM JCARD(JLAST) IF PRESENT
        CALL NZONE(JCARD, JLAST, 4, NSIGN)
        GET = 0.
C-----START THE MAIN SCAN TO PICK UP THE DIGITS
        DO 3 JNOW = J, JLAST
        JTEST =JCARD(JNOW)
C-----CHECK FOR BLANKS OR OTHER NON-NUMBERIC CHARACTERS
        IF (JTEST) 4, 2, 2
```

194

```
2        IF (JTEST - 16448) 6, 5, 6
5        JTEST = -4032
4        IF (JTEST + 4032) 6, 3, 3
C-----THE CODE FOR A BLANK IS 16448, THE CODE FOR ZERO IS -4032
3        GET = 10. * GET + FLOAT((JTEST + 4032)/256)
C-----NOW SHIFT TO LOCATE THE DECIMAL POINT
         GET = SHIFT * GET
C-----CHECK THE SIGN OF THE STRING, RESTORE 11 ZONE IF NEEDED
         CALL NZONE(JCARD, JLAST, NSIGN, JTEST)
         IF (NSIGN - 2) 7, 11, 7
11       GET = -GET
7        RETURN
C-----SET RESULT (GET) TO ZERO IF ANY NON-NUMERIC CHARACTER FOUND
6        GET = 0.
         RETURN
         END
```

At statement 5 JTEST is given the code for zero if JTEST is a blank character. Notice that the manipulated character is again given the name JTEST to minimize subscript evaluation. The conversion from the integer equivalent code, scaling by a power of ten, and summing up the digits are all performed by statement 3, which produces GET as a floating-point variable. GET is then multiplied by SHIFT to locate the decimal point. Before multiplying by SHIFT, GET is a whole number; if we want to have two digits to the right of the decimal point then SHIFT would have the value of 0.01. To produce four digits to the right of the decimal point SHIFT would require a value of 0.0001.

GET is then given the sign indicated by NSIGN. The 11-zone punch, if present, is restored at JCARD(JLAST) in the character string. At statement 6 GET is set to zero if nonnumeric characters were found in the string. The GET function calls the NZONE subprogram to handle both the testing and restoring of any 11-zone punch at JCARD(JLAST), which would be used to indicate that the character string was negative. If the digit at JCARD(JLAST) is zero, then only the 11-zone punch should appear at that character position since an 11-zoned zero punch is not a legal character for the FORTRAN language on the 1130 computer.

A suggested modification of the GET function would consist of inserting a PAUSE statement after statement 6 to permit the computer operator to repunch the card containing nonnumeric information. Another approach would consist of placing an error indication variable in COMMON to be tested by the calling program. As written, GET will not produce any error indication (aside from setting GET equal to zero) when nunumeric characters are encountered.

GET is ordinarily used in an arithmetic statement such as

TOTAL = GET(RECRD, 1, 5, .01) + GET(RECRD, 6, 10, .001)

If the first ten characters in RECRD are 1375548602, the GET function produces values of 137.55 and 48.602 so that TOTAL assumes a value of 186.152. In a single FORTRAN statement it is now possible to float several character strings from a generalized 80A1 format and to combine the resulting real variables in any arithmetic operations.

10-8 The PUT Subprogram to Put Real Variables into Character Strings

The ability to GET real variables from character strings is, of course, incomplete without the ability to PUT them back. The relationship

$$\text{Integer Equivalent Code} = 256 * (\text{Digit Value}) - 4032$$

is the key to the conversion process. The variable SHIFT now becomes a multiplier to shift the real variable into fractional form, or to locate the decimal point to the left of the high order digit to be placed in the character string. For example, if all the digits of 365.79 are to be PUT, SHIFT would be 0.001 to shift the number into the form .36579.

Another requirement for PUT is the ability to half-adjust the real variable to eliminate truncation errors. If, for example, the number 365.79 represents $365.79 and the amount is the result of several calculations, the number may be carried in core memory as a floating-point number equivalent to 365.78999, which would then be truncated by the PUT subprogram to 365.78, producing an error of one cent. To half-adjust 365.79 we would add .005 to produce 365.795 or 365.79499, either of which would truncate to the correct value of 365.79. The half-adjust fraction is supplied in the calling sequence of the PUT subprogram as the variable ADJST, where ADJST is equal to five positioned one decimal place to the right of the right-hand digit to be PUT, or .005 in the example.

The PUT subprogram must add the half-adjustment fraction ADJST to the variable to be PUT (called VAR) and then multiply by SHIFT to convert VAR to a decimal fraction. Each digit is then PUT into the character string by a succession of shifts to the left (multiplications) and by use of the relationship between digit values and integer equivalent codes.

```
      SUBROUTINE PUT(JCARD, J, JLAST, VAR, ADJST, SHIFT)
      DIMENSION JCARD(80)
C-----PUT VAR INTO JCARD(J) THROUGH JCARD(JLAST).
C-----ADJST = AN ARGUMENT TO HALF ADJUST THE REAL VARIABLE VAR.
C-----SHIFT = AN ARGUMENT TO SHIFT VAR INTO FRACTIONAL FORM.
      NDIG = 0
      DIGS = SHIFT * (ABS(VAR) + ADJST)
C-----NOW PUT THE DIGITS IN THE CHARACTER STRING
      DO 4 JNOW = J, JLAST
```

```
          DIGS = 10. * (DIGS - FLOAT(NDIG))
          NDIG = DIGS
C-----CHECK TO SEE IF OVERFLOW HAS OCCURRED
          IF (NDIG - 10) 4, 5, 5
4         JCARD(JNOW) = 256 * NDIG - 4032
C-----PLACE 11 ZONE PUNCH OVER LAST DIGIT IF NEGATIVE
          IF (VAR) 6, 7, 7
6         CALL NZONE(JCARD, JLAST, 2, NDIG)
7         RETURN
C-----SET ENTIRE STRING TO ASTERISKS IF OVERFLOW OCCURRED,
C-----ASTERISK CODE IS 23616
5         CALL FILL(JCARD, J, JLAST, 23616)
          RETURN
          END
```

Inside the DO loop terminating at statement 4 the digits are picked off one at a time
and converted. Overflow occurs if SHIFT is not a sufficiently low power of ten to
shift VAR into fractional form, and in case of overflow the whole string is filled
with asterisks to indicate an error condition. The NZONE subprogram is used to
place an 11-zone punch over the digit at JLAST if VAR is negative. If the digit at
JLAST is zero and VAR is negative, a minus sign character is placed at JLAST.

PUT is usually called in a statement such as

CALL PUT(ORDER, 3, 7, TOTAL, .005, .001)

If the first ten characters in the integer array ORDER were ABCDEFGHIJ, then
after execution of the above PUT example the characters would be AB18615HIJ if
the current value of TOTAL were 186.152. If TOTAL were 1861.52, overflow would
occur, because multiplication by SHIFT would not shift TOTAL into fractional form,
and the PUT subprogram would fill the string with asterisks. The first ten characters
of ORDER would then be AB*****HIJ. Notice that one plus JLAST minus J specifies the number of digits to be PUT, SHIFT specifies the number of whole number
digits, and the number of fractional digits is determined by the combination of J,
JLAST and SHIFT. The half-adjustment fraction ADJST must agree with the number
of fractional digits to be PUT.

An improved version of the PUT subprogram is distributed with the *IBM 1130
Commercial Subroutine Package*. The improved version involves the use of an additional subroutine written in symbolic assembly language, and the new version provides
greater precision when processing large floating-point numbers. The original version of
PUT is retained in this chapter as an example of character manipulation in FORTRAN,
but it is limited to about seven digits of precision even when using the EXTENDED
PRECISION control record because of the rather large amount of floating-point
manipulation performed within the PUT subprogram.

10-9   The EDIT Subprogram to Produce Edited Output Information

The editing operation consists of merging a string of program constants called a mask field with a string of variable data called a source field. The merged result is located at the mask field and is called the result field. We store the source field, usually consisting of a string of calculated digits, at JCARD(J) through JCARD (JLAST) and we store the mask field at KCARD(K) through KCARD(KLAST). The EDIT subprogram moves the characters from the source field into the mask field while observing certain rules about the replacement of characters in the mask field. The EDIT subprogram is able to produce combinations of digits and special characters, such as 282-26-8468 (a social security number) or ****24.98CR (an asterisk-protected credit field), which are useful in commercial applications.

Some of the characters which may appear in the mask field have special effects as follows:

Blank characters — These are replaced by characters coming from the source field.

Zero character — This character may appear only once in any mask field. It indicates that leading zeros are to be suppressed in the result field to the left of and including the position occupied by the zero character. The leading zeros will be replaced by blank characters.

Asterisk — This character, which may appear only once in a mask field, produces zero suppression as does the zero character except that the leading zeros in the result field are replaced by asterisks, providing what is called asterisk check protection. By filling in leading zeros with asterisks the ability to alter the amount of a check by writing in a high order digit in front of the amount is eliminated.

Dollar sign — This character, which may appear only once in a mask field, produces zero suppression as does the zero character. A dollar sign will also be placed in the result field immeidately to the left of the first nonzero digit or the dollar sign position in the mask field.

Commas — Commas will remain in the result field in the same position which they occupied in the mask field, except that commas to the left of a zero suppression character (0, * or $) will be suppressed and replaced with blanks or asterisks.

CR — The two letters CR are used to indicate a credit or negative field in some commercial applications. If CR appears as the two rightmost characters of the mask, then these characters will be suppressed (blanked out) if the last character of the source field does not contain an 11-zone punch (is not negative), and the characters will be left in the result field if the last character of the source field does contain an 11-zone punch. If the letter C or the letter R appears in any position in the mask except the rightmost positions no special effect will be produced. Only the letter R in the rightmost or last position is actually tested by the EDIT subprogram, so in practice any letter may take the place of C.

Minus sign — A minus sign in the rightmost position of the mask field will have the same effect as the R of CR. This character will be suppressed (blanked) if the source field is positive or left in the result field if the source field is negative.

All other characters including decimal points in any position will not be replaced by characters coming from the source field nor will they be suppressed. The incoming characters from the source field will be moved around these characters, resulting in a merged string of characters in the result field.

Three rules are required for the successful preparation of a mask field. These rules derive from the operation of the special effect characters:

1. There must be at least as many blanks in the mask field as there are characters in the source field.

2. If any zero suppression character is present in the mask field, then the first character in the mask field must be a blank.

3. Only one zero suppression character may appear in a mask field.

The mask field is ordinarily obtained by reading it as input data. Since the mask field is destroyed by each use, the mask field is usually moved into an output array prior to each CALL EDIT statement. The editing operation then takes place in the output array prior to printing or punching the result field.

As the listing is long, it will be discussed in sections.

```
        SUBROUTINE EDIT(JCARD, J, JLAST, KCARD, K, KLAST)
        DIMENSION JCARD(80), KCARD(80)
C-----JCARD(J) THROUGH JCARD(JLAST) IS THE SOURCE FIELD.
C-----KCARD(K) THROUGH KCARD(KLAST) IS THE MASK FIELD.
C-----THE SOURCE FIELD IS EDITED INTO THE MASK FIELD TO PRODUCE
C-----THE RESULT FIELD.
C-----CHECK FOR A NEGATIVE SOURCE FIELD, IF SO CLEAR 11 ZONE
        CALL NZONE(JCARD, JLAST, 4, NSIGN)
        NDUMP = 16448
        MONEY = 16448
        NZRSP = 0
        KNOW = KLAST
        JNOW = JLAST
C-----BLANK = 16448, 0 = -4032, * = 23616, $ = 23360,  , = 27456, - = 24640,
C-----R = -9920
```

199

The preceding statements complete the initialization of the EDIT subprogram. NDUMP, which will contain the blank or asterisk to be dumped in over high order zeros if zero suppression is used, is initialized to the integer equivalent code for a blank. MONEY, which will contain the floating dollar sign if dollar sign zero suppression is used, is also initialized to a blank. NZRSP, the subscript of the position of the zero suppression character if present, is initialized to zero. Since the first scan must proceed from right to left instead of from left to right like all other scans in this package, JNOW is initialized to JLAST and KNOW is initialized to KLAST. We are now ready for the main scanning loop.

```
C-----MAIN SCAN LOOP, INSERT CHARACTERS AND CHECK FOR ZERO
C-----SUPPRESSION
17      KTEST = KCARD(KNOW)
        IF (KTEST) 33, 34, 34
33      IF (KTEST + 4032) 11, 19, 11
34      IF (KTEST - 16448) 13, 20, 13
13      IF (KTEST - 23616) 14, 18, 14
14      IF (KTEST - 23360) 11, 28, 11
18      NDUMP = KTEST
28      MONEY = KTEST
19      NZRSP = KNOW
20      IF (JNOW - J) 11, 26, 26
26      KTEST = JCARD(JNOW)
        KCARD(KNOW)= KTEST
        JNOW= JNOW - 1
        IF (NZRSP) 11, 11, 9
9       IF (KTEST) 35, 36, 36
35      IF (KTEST + 4032) 25, 11, 25
36      IF (KTEST - 16448) 23, 11, 23
23      IF (KTEST - 27456) 25, 11, 25
25      NZRSP = KNOW - 1
11      KNOW = KNOW - 1
        IF (KNOW - K) 27, 17, 17
```

At the beginning of the main scan loop the last character of the mask field is placed in KTEST to minimize repeated subscripting. KTEST is then compared against the zero, blank, asterisk and dollar sign characters and NDUMP, MONEY and NZRSP are set accordingly. The last character of the source field is then placed in KTEST at statement 26, and the new KTEST is placed in the last position of the mask field if this position previously contained a zero, blank, asterisk or dollar sign. If a zero suppression character has been encountered in the mask field, the new KTEST is compared against zero, blank and commas characters and if KTEST is not one of these characters, then the zero suppression position NZRSP is moved one position to the left. Notice that neither JNOW nor KNOW are under DO loop control; since the scan moves from right to left, both variables are decremented in arithmetic statements. The main scan loop moves through successive positions to the left until position K in the mask field has been processed.

```
C-----RESTORE THE 11 ZONE PUNCH IF THE SOURCE FIELD WAS NEGATIVE
27      CALL NZONE(JCARD, JLAST, NSIGN, KTEST)
C-----FILL RESULT WITH ASTERISKS IF MASK FIELD TOO SHORT
        IF (JNOW - J) 29, 21, 21
21      CALL FILL(KCARD, K, KLAST, 23616)
        RETURN
```

Notice that the only characters in the mask field which are replaced by characters from the source field are the zero, blank, asterisk and dollar sign. If there are not at least as many blanks in the mask field as there are characters in the source field, then the mask field will be too short and there will be extra characters remaining from the source field when the last character of the mask field has been examined and processed. In this case the FILL subprogram is called to fill the entire result field with asterisks, indicating an error in setting up the EDIT subprogram mask field.

```
C-----REMOVE CR OR - FROM RIGHT END OF RESULT FIELD IF SOURCE
C-----FIELD POSITIVE
29      IF (NSIGN - 2) 2, 3, 2
2       KTEST = KCARD(KLAST)
        IF (KTEST) 31, 32, 32
32      IF (KTEST - 24640) 3, 5, 3
31      IF (KTEST + 9920) 3, 6, 3
6       KCARD(KLAST - 1) = 16448
5       KCARD(KLAST) = 16448
C-----ZERO SUPPRESSION SCAN, NDUMP IS CHARACTER, NZRSP IS
C-----POSITION
3       IF (NZRSP) 30, 30, 22
22      CALL FILL(KCARD, K, NZRSP, NDUMP)
C-----POSITION FLOATING DOLLAR SIGN OR ASTERISK OR BLANK AT FAR
C-----LEFT
        KCARD(NZRSP) = MONEY
30      RETURN
        END
```

If the CR or minus sign is present at the right end of the mask field it is then blanked at statements 6 and 5 if the source field is positive. The zero suppression is then handled by a single call to the FILL subprogram. The floating dollar sign, which has been stored in MONEY, is positioned at NZRSP if present and the complete editing job is finished.

A typical CALL statement for the EDIT subprogram might be

        CALL EDIT(NDATA, 10, 15, MASK, 1, 12)

If the NDATA and MASK arrays are as shown on the following page, the result field will be stored in the MASK array as shown.

NDATA(10) etc.	MASK(1) etc.	Result Field
01234E	bbb,bb$.bbCR	bbb$123.45bb
01234N	bbb,bb$.bbCR	bbb$123.45CR
01232J	bbbb,bb$.bb–	bbbb$123.21–
282267	bbbbbbb–bb–b	bbbb282–26–7
012345	bbb,bb$.bbCR	bbb$123.45bb
123456	bbb,bb$.bbCR	b$1,234.56bb
012345	bbb,bb*.bbCR	****123.45bb
012345	bbb,bb0.bbCR	bbbb123.45bb
012345	b,bbb,bb0.bb	bbbbbb123.45
ROBERT	bDbAbVblbDbb	bDRAOVBIEDRT
ROBERT	JObHNbSObNbb	************

In the last example, the result field is set to asterisks because there are not at least as many blanks (b's) in the mask field as there are characters in the source field. The mask field is usually established by reading the mask field from a data card, although the FILL or MOVE subprograms could also be used to create the mask.

10-10 An Invoice Program Using the Character Manipulation Package

A typical commercial application is the monthly posting of transactions to a customer's balance sheet and the printing of customer invoices. The input data cards for each customer might consist of a name and master balance card containing the customer's name, address, and the balance owed or credited at the time the last invoice was sent, followed by an indeterminate number of transaction cards describing payments or new purchases by this customer, and finally a blank card which will be punched by the invoice program to create a new master name and balance card to be read in when the program is executed next month. We shall call the invoice program by the name BILLS.

Each master name and balance card thus contains the customer's name in columns 1-20, the customer's address in columns 21-40, the customer's city and state in columns 41-60, the customer's balance in columns 61-68 (with an 11-zone punch in column 68 to represent a credit balance) and a 12-zone punch in column 70 to distinguish master balance cards from transaction cards. Each transaction card contains the customer's name in columns 1-20, the name of the item purchased or returned in columns 21-40, the total value of the transaction in columns 41-48 (with an 11-zone punch in column 48 indicating a credit transaction), the quantity of the item in columns 49-52, and an 11-zone punch in column 70 to distinguish transaction cards from name and master balance cards. The customer's balance and transaction fields are a right-justified string of digits preceded by either blanks or zeros; the dollar value $437.95 is punched in the card field as either bbb43795 or 00043795.

The operation of the BILLS program consists of accumulating transactions and printing the invoice while punching the new master name and balance card for each customer. Next month the new master name and balance card will be followed in the input deck by the transactions for each customer and finally by a blank card to be punched by the program as the master name and balance card for the succeeding month. Each month the program will thus automatically prepare an invoice and a new master name and balance card for each customer using transaction cards accumulated during the current month plus the master name and balance card from the previous month. The program listing, complete with monitor control cards, follows:

```
// FOR
*  NAME BILLS
*  IOCS (CARD, TYPEWRITER, 1132 PRINTER)
*  ONE WORD INTEGERS
*  EXTENDED PRECISION
*  LIST ALL
         DIMENSION INCRD(80), IMASK(13), IPRNT(120),IOTCD(80), ISTOP(5)
1        FORMAT (80A1)
3        FORMAT (1H ,120A1)
4        FORMAT (1H ,22X, 16HPREVIOUS BALANCE, 28X, 13A1)
5        FORMAT (//23X, 5HTOTAL, 39X, 13A1)
9        FORMAT (11X, 109A1)
13       FORMAT (///10X, 3HQTY, 10X, 4HNAME, 46X, 3HAMT)
14       FORMAT (1H1)
17       FORMAT (11H ERROR      , 80A1)
18       FORMAT (10HEND OF JOB)
```

It is necessary to specify ONE WORD INTEGERS for any program which will call the character manipulation subprograms. It is also desirable to specify EXTENDED PRECISION to permit floating-point variables to contain up to 9.3 digits.

```
C------SET I/O UNIT NUMBERS, READ MASK, STOP CODE AND INPUT CARD
         NREAD = 2
         NWRIT = 3
         NPUNC = 2
         READ (NREAD, 1) IMASK, ISTOP
         READ (NREAD, 1) INCRD
```

The first READ statement reads the 13-character mask field, bbbb,bb$.bbCR, used by the EDIT subprogram. The statement also reads a stop code consisting of the characters STOP1 to terminate the execution of BILLS when a card containing the characters STOP1 is read. The use of an arbitrary character string to signify that all input data has been processed is commonly employed in programs required to process an indeterminate amount of input data. The READ statement 2 reads the first data card and stores all 80 columns of information in the INCRD (input card) array.

```
2     K = 1
C-----CHECK IF INCRD CONTAINED THE STOP CODE
      IF (NCOMP(INCRD, 1, 5, ISTOP, 1)) 6, 16, 6
16    WRITE (1, 18)
      PAUSE
      CALL EXIT
C-----CHECK IF MASTER BALANCE CARD OR TRANSACTION CARD IN
C-----COLUMN 70
6     CALL NZONE(INCRD, 70, 5, J)
      IF (J - 1) 10, 20, 10
```

Here we see NCOMP used to check for the presence of the stop code and NZONE used to store the zone punch index from column 70 of INCRD in the variable J. The end-of-job message is written on the console typewriter at statement 16 if the stop code is present. A PAUSE follows to allow the operator to remove the invoice forms from the printer, followed by a CALL EXIT to return control to the monitor. If column 70 of INCRD contained a 12-zone punch, J will be set to one and the IF statement after statement 6 will transfer control to statement 20 to process a master balance card. Otherwise control will go to statement 10 to type an error message, since the master balance card must precede the transaction cards for any one customer.

```
C-----INCRD IS A MASTER BALANCE CARD
20    WRITE (NWRIT, 14)
      WRITE (NWRIT, 9) (INCRD(J), J = 1, 20)
      WRITE (NWRIT, 9) (INCRD(J), J = 21, 40)
      WRITE (NWRIT, 9) (INCRD(J), J = 41, 60)
      CALL FILL(IPRNT, 1, 120, 16448)
      CALL MOVE(IMASK, 1, 13, IPRNT, 100)
      CALL EDIT(INCRD, 61, 68, IPRNT, 100, 112)
      WRITE (NWRIT, 13)
      WRITE (NWRIT, 4) (IPRNT(J), J = 100, 112)
      CALL FILL(IPRNT, 100, 112, 16448)
      TOTAL = GET(INCRD, 61, 68, 0.01)
      CALL MOVE(INCRD, 1, 80, IOTCD, 1)
```

The WRITE statement 20 is simply a carriage control command to get to the top of the next page (next invoice form) on the 1132 Printer. The following three WRITE statements write the customer's name, address, and city and state upon the

204

invoice form. The print line array IPRNT is then filled with blanks (integer equivalent code 16448), and the edit mask IMASK is moved into position in IPRNT. The previous balance from INCRD is then edited into columns 100-112 in IPRNT. Invoice heading information and the previous balance are then printed. IPRNT is refilled with blanks and the GET function is used to store the previous balance in the floating-point variable TOTAL. The entire input card INCRD is then moved to the output card array IOTCD.

```
      C-----NOW READ A TRANSACTION CARD INTO INCRD
      15    READ (NREAD, 1) INCRD
            K = 2
            CALL NZONE(INCRD, 70, 5, J)
            IF (J – 1) 10, 8, 7
      7     IF (J – 2) 10, 11, 10
      C-----CHECK THAT CUSTOMER NAME HAS NOT CHANGED
      11    IF (NCOMP(INCRD, 1, 20, IOTCD, 1)) 10, 12, 10
```

At statement 15 we read either a transaction card for the master name and balance card which has just been processed or else the master card for another customer. The zone punch in column 70 enables the NZONE subprogram to make the distinction. Statement 10 is an error routine to be executed if the zone index is neither one nor two; statement 8 receives control if the new card is a master name and balance card; statement 11 gets control if the new card is a transaction card. The customer's name in the new transaction card is then compared with the name on the master name and balance card, and a transfer is made to statement 10 if the two names are not identical. Otherwise we continue processing the transaction card at statement 12.

```
      12    CALL MOVE(INCRD, 21, 40 IPRNT, 23)
            CALL MOVE(IMASK, 1, 13, IPRNT, 67)
            CALL MOVE(IMASK, 4, 8, IPRNT, 8)
            IPRNT(12) = -4032
            CALL EDIT(INCRD, 49, 52, IPRNT, 8, 12)
            CALL EDIT(INCRD, 41, 48, IPRNT, 67, 79)
            TOTAL = TOTAL + GET(INCRD, 41, 48, 0.01)
            WRITE (NWRIT, 3) IPRNT
            GO TO 15
```

The item name is moved into the print line array at statement 12, after which the edit mask is moved into position to edit the transaction value and a part of the edit mask is moved in to edit the item quantity. A zero (code –4032) is inserted into column 12 of the quantity mask, producing a mask field of b,bb0 from the original mask of bbbb,bb$.bbCR. Then the transaction value and quantity fields are both edited into the two masks in IPRNT, and the transaction value is accumulated into TOTAL. The IPRNT array is written on the 1132 Printer and control goes to statement 15 to read the next transaction or master balance card.

```
C-----NOW PUNCH A NEW MASTER BALANCE CARD
8       CALL PUT(IOTCD, 61, 68, TOTAL, 0.005, 0.000001)
        CALL MOVE(IMASK, 1, 13, IPRNT, 100)
        CALL EDIT(IOTCD, 61, 68, IPRNT, 100, 112)
        WRITE (NPUNC, 1) IOTCD
        WRITE (NWRIT, 5) (IPRNT(J), J = 100, 112)
        GO TO 2
```

Starting at statement 8, the new balance in TOTAL is put into a string of EBCDIC characters, moved into IPRNT and edited, punched into the output card array IOTCD, and finally printed on the invoice. IOTCD contains the complete format of the new master name and balance card. Control then goes to statement 2 to read the master balance card of another customer.

```
C-----ERROR MESSAGE FOR WRONG ZONE IN COLUMN 70 OR WRONG CUSTOMER
10      WRITE (1, 17) INCRD
        GO TO (2, 15), K
        END
```

The error message is typed on the console typewriter together with the entire contents of the input data card. A computed GO TO then transfers control to either statement 2 or 15 depending upon whether a master name and balance card or a transaction card was being processed when the error was discovered. The program listing is now complete. Input consisting of the edit mask and stop code card, followed by a master balance card, followed by four transaction cards for a single customer, might appear as follows:

```
bbbb,bb$.bbCRSTOP1
DAVES MARKET      1997 WASHINGTON ST. NEWTON, MASS.      00011129  A
DAVES MARKET      SUGAR – BAGS            000021020008                J
DAVES MARKET      CHICKEN SOUP – CASES   000038760011                J
DAVES MARKET      TOMATO SOUP – CASES    000030110010                J
DAVES MARKET      SUGAR RETURNED         0000210K0008                J
```

The invoice printed as a result of the input data for Daves Market would appear as shown on the following page.

DAVES MARKET

1997 WASHINGTON ST.

NEWTON, MASS.

QTY	NAME	AMT
	PREVIOUS BALANCE	$111.29
8	SUGAR – BAGS	$21.02
11	CHICKEN SOUP – CASES	$38.76
10	TOMATO SOUP – CASES	$30.11
8	SUGAR RETURNED	$21.02CR
	TOTAL	$180.16

10-11 Memory Requirements

The complete memory requirements for each of the character manipulation subprograms, compiled with ONE WORD INTEGERS and EXTENDED PRECISION, are given below.

MOVE	58 words
FILL	38 words
NCOMP	76 words
NZONE	136 words
GET	150 words
PUT	118 words
EDIT	302 words

The complete memory requirement for the entire package is thus 878 words. Only that part of the package actually called in a main program will take up space in core memory along with the main program, although several of the subprograms call the FILL and NZONE subprograms. The subprograms also make use of several FORTRAN-supplied subroutines such as floating add and multiply, but these subroutines are ordinarily used by most FORTRAN main programs and so are not usually called into memory strictly because of the requirements of the character manipulation package.

207

10-12 Summary

In this chapter we have developed a package of subprograms which radically change both the appearance and the function of the FORTRAN language. The BILLS program consists almost entirely of calls to various subprograms which, in turn, call other subprograms and do all the work of the program; the main program simply determines which subprogram to call next. Although FORTRAN is not particularly well suited to applications requiring extensive character manipulation, the power of the subprogram concept has made it possible to overcome several apparent limitations of the language and create a customized language for a particular application area. The same principle can and should be applied to nearly all application areas. The bigger the programming job, the more profitable it is to ask this question before doing any programming: "How can this job be programmed as a collection of subprograms linked together by one or more main programs?"

One more handy feature for many commercial applications is the ability to select either of the two stackers on the 1442 Card Read Punch, so that some of the cards could be selected into one stack while other cards went into the other stack, all under program control. Here FORTRAN has finally met its match, because control of special input-output functions as well as most bit manipulation operations can only be programmed in symbolic assembly language. However, as we will see in the next two chapters, even these operations can be called by FORTRAN programs once they have been coded in assembly language.

10-13 Problems

1) Write flow diagrams for

    a)   MOVE

    b)   FILL

    c)   NCOMP

    d)   NZONE

    e)   GET

    f)   PUT

2) Write a flow diagram for the EDIT subprogram.

3) Program a function subprogram named IGET to get integer variables from character strings in a manner similar to the way that GET gets floating-point variables from character strings.

4) Program an IPUT subprogram to put integer variables into character strings.

5) Some editing routines for commercial applications convert any plus signs (+) in the source field into blanks in the result field as an arbitrary convention to permit blanks to be located from the source field. Describe how the EDIT subprogram could be modified to include this feature.

CHAPTER 11: SYMBOLIC ASSEMBLY LANGUAGE PROGRAMMING

11-1   Why Assembly Language Programming

Although most of the applications of the 1130 system are written in FORTRAN, knowledge of assembly language programming makes it possible to perform certain manipulations which cannot be expressed in the FORTRAN language. Assembly language also furnishes more detailed insight into how the computer operates than does FORTRAN.

In Section 10-12, we stated that stacker select operations on the 1442 Card Read Punch cannot be programmed directly in FORTRAN. Other input-output devices such as the 1627 Plotter cannot be controlled directly by FORTRAN statements. Applications involving bit manipulation (discussed in Chapter 12) cannot be programmed directly in FORTRAN because FORTRAN is limited to describing data formats consisting of numbers occupying entire 16-bit words or characters occupying 8-bit EBCDIC codes. All these manipulations can be performed by assembly language subprograms which can then be called from FORTRAN main programs.

Assembly language is a symbolic representation of actual machine language instructions (Section 1-5), providing access to the full computing power of the hardware. The major programming systems programs, such as the FORTRAN compiler, were written in assembly language. In Section 1-8 we learned that FORTRAN programs usually require more memory and frequently take longer to execute than the same program written in assembly language by a skilled assembly language programmer.

On the other hand, programs written in assembly language take much longer to code, incorporate many more opportunities for error, and are harder to debug and harder to understand six months later. Programs written in assembly language will require complete reprogramming if it becomes necessary in the future to execute them on other families of computers, such as IBM's System/360, which have different machine language instructions. For these reasons assembly language programming should usually be reserved for those situations where FORTRAN cannot do the job, or where maximum computing speed or minimum use of core memory are critical to the success of the application.

11-2   Instruction Formats in Machine Language

The symbolic assembly language is a symbolic representation of machine language instructions on a one-for-one basis: one statement in assembly language represents one instruction in machine language. The machine language instructions may each occupy either one or two 16-bit words of core memory. The bit patterns within the words are set up as follows:

Bits	Instruction Function
0-4	Operation code of five bits
5	Format bit, indicates one- or two-word format
6-7	Tag bits, indicating the index register used, if any
8-15	Displacement, relative addressing in one-word format
8	Indirect addressing bit in two-word format
9	Branch out of interrupt interpretation of BSC instruction
10-15	Condition indicator bits for BSC and BSI instructions
0-15 (in second word)	Address for a two-word format instruction

When using the coding form shown in Figure 11-1, the symbolic representation of the five-bit operation code is written in columns 27-30, the format indicator in column 32 and the tag bit indicator in column 33. The remaining instruction functions are described in the operands and remarks field starting in column 35. The label field starting in column 21 is used to establish a point of reference to a statement in a manner similar to the use of statement numbers of FORTRAN statements. The use of these fields is discussed in Section 11-4.

11-3   Absolute, Relative, Indexed and Indirect Addressing

The address contained within an instruction represents either the address in core memory (Section 1-4) of the data to be processed (added, subtracted, etc.) by the instruction or *else the address of another instruction* to which control of the computer is to be transferred. The 1130 system provides four methods of address programming: absolute, relative, indexed and indirect.

Absolute addressing consists of using the actual core storage address of the data or instruction required. For example, if the required data were stored in core memory location 257, the absolute address would be 257 in decimal or 00000001 00000001 as a 16-bit binary address. Fifteen bits of a 16-bit word are needed to store absolute addresses ranging as high as 32,767, the maximum address in core memory in a 32K system. Only two-word instructions (format bit = 1) contain enough bits for absolute addressing of the entire memory.

Relative addressing is achieved by forming an address from the eight bits of the displacement field (bits 8-15 in one-word instructions). The relative address may be either positive or negative, and if negative will be carried in twos complement form (Section 2-2). Since only eight bits are available in the displacement field, relative addresses can only range from a high of +127 or 01111111 in binary to a low of –128 or 10000000 in twos complement binary. Relative addresses, however, are interpreted by the computer circuitry to be relative to a 16-bit absolute address contained in either the isntruction address register or an index register.

The instruction address register is a special register or counter inside the computer (but not in core memory) containing the address of the next instruction following the instruction currently being executed by the computer. If the instruction address register (called the IAR) contains an address of 8000, then a relative address of 120 will cause the computer to use an effective address of 8,000 + 120 or 8,120. In the same example, a relative address of –100 will produce an effective address of 8000 – 100 or 7900. Relative addressing via the IAR can be used to refer to words in core memory which are up to 127 words ahead of or up to 128 words behind the next instruction to be executed.

There are three index registers in the 1130 system. Each can contain a 16-bit address which can be inserted, altered or removed by instructions executed during the running of a program. The three index registers are three words (at addresses 1, 2 and 3) in core memory. Relative addressing via an index register (called IR) operates just like relative addressing via the IAR; if an IR contains an address of 8000 and a relative address of 120 is used, the result will be an effective address in the computer of 8120.

Next to the subroutine concept, the concept of indexed instructions is perhaps the most powerful idea in programming. If, for example, we wish to sum up 100 different numbers stored in consecutive core memory addresses, it is only necessary to load the first number into the accumulator register (Section 1-4) and then add each of the remaining 99 numbers to the accumulator. The "add" instruction need only address the first of the 99 numbers relative to an index register. The contents of the index register are then incremented by one after each addition to keep the "add" instruction pointed at the next number to be added. This is, of course, much more efficient than writing 100 "add" instructions. Assembly language instructions would be written to

Initialize the index register

Initialize the accumulator

Add the next number to the accumulator

Increment the index register and test to see if 100 numbers had been added

Transfer to the "add" instruction.

Index registers in assembly language programming commonly perform operations analogous to those performed by subscripting and the DO and CONTINUE statements in FORTRAN programming (Section 5-3). Absolute addresses in two-word instructions may also be indexed, in which case the effective address becomes the sum of the absolute address from the instruction plus the contents of the referenced index register.

Indirect addressing is permitted only in two-word instructions. If bit number 8 (the indirect address or IA bit) is one and bit number 5 (the format or F bit) is also one, then indirect addressing will occur and the effective address used by the computer becomes the contents of the word whose address was contained in the instruction. For example, if the address contained in the second word of the two-word instruction is 5000, and the word at core memory location contains the number 7500, then the effective address used by the computer will be 7500.

Indirect addressing may also be combined with indexing. The contents of the index register are then added to the address in the instruction, and the contents of the indexed instruction address then become the effective address the computer uses to execute the instruction.

Although the various combinations of absolute, relative, indexed and indirect addressing provide considerable programming power for the experienced assembly language programmer, they also provide some fascinating opportunities for error on the part of the novice programmer. The table below summarizes the various address combinations. In the table the format bit (5) is called the F bit; the tag bits (6-7) are called the T bits; IAR stands for the instruction address register; IA stands for the indirect address bit (8); EA stands for the effective address to be used by the computer; IR1, IR2 and IR3 stand for the first, second and third index registers; and DISP stands for the displacement field (bits 8-15).

Effective Address Table

	F = 0 Relative address	F = 1, IA = 0 Absolute address	F = 1, IA = 1 Indirect address
If T = 00	EA = IAR + DISP	EA = address	EA=C(address)
If T = 01	EA = IR1 + DISP	EA = address + IR1	EA=C(address+IR1)
If T = 10	EA = IR2 + DISP	EA = address + IR2	EA=C(address+IR2)
If T = 11	EA = IR3 + DISP	EA = address + IR3	EA=C(address+IR3)

The expression C(address) means "the contents of the word at the address contained within the instruction," and the expression C(address + IR3) means "the contents of the word at (the address contained within the instruction plus the contents of index register 3)."

Addressing in the 1130 system is called wraparound addressing: if the computer has an 8K memory, then the next address after 8191 is zero and if the computer has a 4K memory, the next address after 4095 is zero. In a 4K computer only the least significant 12 bits are used to create an address (in an 8K computer only the least significant 13 bits), so that any calculated address will correspond to some actual address within the computer regardless of the memory size of that particular computer.

11-4   Instruction Formats in Symbolic Assembly Language

A source program in assembly language consists of many statements, each occupying one line on the coding form shown in Figure 11-1 and each corresponding to one punched card or to one paper tape record. On punched cards each statement starts in column 21. The 20 blank columns at the left of each card may contain punches to represent the assembled machine language instruction corresponding to the assembly language statement on the same card after processing by the card Assembler program. Each statement is subdivided into several fields as described below.

Label Field, Symbols

The label field (columns 21-25) is used to describe the location or address of an instruction or data field inside the computer, in the same way that statement numbers in the FORTRAN language are used to describe the location of FORTRAN statements. All data must be labeled if the data is to be directly referenced by a statement. Statements must be labeled if control of the computer will be transferred to them or if their addresses are to be modified by other instructions during the execution of the program. Notice that in FORTRAN it is only necessary to label or assign statement numbers to those statements to which control might be transferred; the assignment of data storage locations is handled automatically by the compiler. However, FORTRAN statements cannot modify other FORTRAN statements during program execution except by changing the values of variables contained within the statements.

A label field may be left blank (if the location need not be referenced by any other statement), may contain an asterisk in column 21 or may contain a symbol. Symbols in assembly language are similar in form to variable names in FORTRAN: each symbol contains one to five letters and/or numbers of which the first character must be a letter ($ # @ count as letters for this purpose). Special characters such

214

as + – * / , are not permitted in symbols. Like FORTRAN variable names, symbols should be chosen for easy readability: VELOC for velocity calculation, ITER for iteration section, or perhaps PRINT for a statement which will produce printed output. Every symbol in the operand field of any statement in a program must also appear in the label field of some statement in the program, just as every FORTRAN statement number used in a FORTRAN statement must appear to the left of some statement in the program. Just as the same FORTRAN statement number cannot be applied to two statements, so the same symbol must not be applied to more than one statement label field. As in FORTRAN, a statement should be labeled only when necessary.

If the label field contains an asterisk in column 21, then the entire statement is considered a comment and is not processed by the Assembler program. (This is analogous to the C for comment in column one of a FORTRAN statement.)

If the label field contains a symbol, the symbol is set equal to the address of the instruction corresponding to the assembly language statement when the program is assembled. This is accomplished through the use of the location counter, which is a counter maintained by the Assembler to count the number of words of memory which are used by statements in an assembly language source program. Special assembly language statements such as ORG (discussed in Chapter 12) are provided to change the setting of the location counter.

Operation Field

The operation field (columns 27-30) usually defines a single machine language instruction to be assembled, but the operation field may also be used to describe data fields, subroutine linkages and special instructions to the Assembler program. All operation codes consist of one to four letters and are punched left-justified in the operation field. Those operation codes which represent machine language instructions are discussed in subsequent sections as load and store instructions, arithmetic instructions, shift instructions, branch instructions and input-output instructions. The operation codes which do not represent machine language instructions are discussed under the headings of program control instructions, data definition instructions, storage allocation instructions, symbol definition instructions and program linking instructions.

Format Field

The format field (column 32) describes whether one or two words of memory are required to store the assembled machine language instruction or data and, in the case of a two-word format, what will be contained in the displacement

215

field of the instruction. Indirect addressing is also indicated by the format field. The format field must contain either a blank, an X, an L or an I as described below.

A blank format field causes bit 5 of the assembled machine language instructions to be set to zero, producing a one-word instruction. A blank format also indicates that any expression or address in the operand field is to be the displacement of the machine language instruction. The Assembler provides automatic relative addressing by subtracting the value of the location counter from the operand field and assembling the difference as the displacement field of the resulting machine language instruction. When this difference is added to the contents of the IAR during the execution of the machine language instruction, the effective address becomes the expression or address originally present in the operand field of the assembly language statement. The location counter is simply a count of the memory locations used by the instructions being assembled; the location counter is used by the Assembler to simulate the IAR, which will keep track of instruction addresses when the assembled program is executed.

Certain machine language instructions, including all the shift instructions, all the conditional branch instructions using the BSC operation code, the load index, load status and wait instructions, do not add the displacement field to the instruction counter during execution. The Assembler recognizes the different addressing technique employed by these instructions and does not subtract the contents of the location counter when these instructions are assembled.

X format is used for one-word instructions which will be moved to another location in memory before execution, since this can only be done if the expression or address in the operand field is the actual displacement value which will be added to the instruction counter upon execution. The use of X format suppresses the automatic relative addressing supplied by the Assembler; the programmer must now determine the relative address himself and include it in the assembly language statement.

Suppose that, at a certain point in a program, we need to branch to either PARTA or PARTB (other locations in the same program) and suppose that we now wish to set the branch instruction to go to PARTA. We can pick up a "branch to PARTA" instruction from some other part of the program and store it at the branch point, but we must make sure that we use X format and use an actual displacement instead of the address PARTA. If the label field of the branch point is BRNCH, then the displacement field must be PARTA – BRNCH – 1. The contents of the IAR will be added to the displacement when the instruction is executed, and the IAR will contain the value BRNCH + 1 at that moment (since the IAR always contains the address of the next memory location after the instruction currently being executed). The effective address after addition of the contents of the IAR will thus be PARTA, which is what we are trying to achieve. We cannot achieve this, however, by specifying PARTA as the operand field. If the instruction were to be assembled at

BRNCH, however, we could use blank format and an operand of PARTA, and the Assembler could automatically calculate the relative displacement value for us.

L format simply indicates a two-word instruction and causes bit 5 of the assembled machine language instruction to be set to 1. The value of the first expression or address in the operand field is then placed in the second word of the assembled instruction. A second operand may be separated from the first operand by a comma. The second operand, if present, designates a value for the displacement field (bits 8-15) of the assembled instruction.

I format indicates an indirectly addressed, two-word instruction. Bits 5 and 8 of the assembled instruction are set to 1. The first operand produces the address for the second word of the assembled instruction; the second operand, if present, furnishes the displacement. Regardless of whether or not a second operand is furnished, bit 8 will remain a one bit to indicate indirect addressing.

Tag (Index) Field

The tag field (column 33) is used to indicate which, if any, of the three index registers is to be used in determining the effective address of the assembled machine language instruction. A blank in column 33 indicates that no index register (IR) is to be used; a 1 indicates IR1; a 2 indicates IR2; a 3 indicates IR3. If a blank tag field is used with load index, store index or modify index instructions, then the instruction counter will be loaded, stored or modified. The effect of the various combinations of indexing with relative or indirect addressing is discussed in Section 11-3.

Operands and Remarks Field, Expressions

The operand and remarks field (columns 35-71) contains expressions describing the address of data or instructions to be processed. In statements using L or I format, two operands may be separated by a comma: the first operand represents values for the second assembled instruction word, and the second operand represents the displacement field in the first assembled instruction word. In statements using blank or X format, a single operand is used to represent a value for the displacement field of the assembled one-word instruction. No blanks may be used within or between operands; the operand field must always start in column 35 of the assembly language statement and go on without blanks until the address or expression representing each operand is completed.

An operand may be a single symbolic address consisting of a symbol: a string of one to five characters where the first character must be a letter. An operand may also be an expression consisting of a single symbol or several symbols and constants connected by arithmetic operators. The first blank character in the operand field signifies the beginning of the remarks field. Remarks, similar to comments in FORTRAN, help explain the program to someone reading the program listing but have no effect upon the assembled program instructions. In FORTRAN it is necessary to isolate comments into separate comment statements; in assembly language it is possible and very desirable to include a comment as part of every single statement. Remember that an entire assembly language statement can be set aside for comments by placing an asterisk in column 21 of the label field.

11-5 Constants, Symbols and Operators in Expressions

The constants in an expression may take the form of decimal constants in the range of -32,768 to 32,767 or hexadecimal numbers in the range of 0 to 8000 or single characters. Decimal constants are written like integer constants in FORTRAN without decimal points or imbedded commas. Hexadecimal constants are written with a preceding slash (/) and may consist of one to four characters. In hexadecimal notation (Section 2-3) the digits zero through nine are written as arabic numerals while the letters A through F are used to represent the numbers ten through fifteen. Typical decimal constants as used in expressions would include 3, 46, 129, 5000; hexadecimal constants of the same value would be /3, /2E, /81, /1388.

Character values can also be used as constants in an expression. Any single character, preceded by a period (.), can be represented. Examples are .A or .$ or .. to represent a period. Notice that since the characters are represented in eight-bit EBCDIC code the same bit pattern can often be represented by a decimal constant, a hexadecimal constant or a single character. For example, the character representation .A is equivalent to /C1 in hexadecimal and to 193 as a decimal constant. Since the single characters are stored in the right-hand or low-order eight bits of a memory word, these character values will not be equivalent to the integer equivalent codes developed in Section 10-4. The integer equivalent codes occupy the leftmost or high-order eight bits of each word in the FORTRAN A1 format; the integer equivalent code for A is -16064.

Symbols, hexadecimal and decimal constants, and characters are called the elements of an expression. A final type of element is the asterisk (*) which is used to denote the current value of the location counter. Because the location counter always points to the first word of the next instruction, the asterisk may be combined with constants in an arithmetic expression to indicate the next instruction plus two words (* + 2) or the next instruction minus ten words (* - 10). Addressing via the location counter is dangerous, however, because it may become necessary to add new instructions between the instruction with the asterisk and the intended address, which would invalidate the arithmetic that indicated that the intended address was ten words away (such as * +10).

Three arithmetic operators +, – and * may be used to combine elements into simple expressions similar to the arithmetic expressions in FORTRAN. Such expressions consist of an element followed by an operator followed by an element followed by an operator followed by an element, etc. Each expression must begin and end with an element, and cannot have two operators or two elements adjacent to each other. The asterisk is used both as an element denoting the current value of the location counter and as an operator denoting multiplication, but this presents no confusion (at least to the Assembler) because each expression must begin and end with an element and consist of alternating elements and operators. For example, the expression **/A5 obviously means "the value of the location counter times the hexadecimal constant A5." Notice that the slash always refers to a hexadecimal constant and never to division in assembly language expressions.

Evaluation of expressions proceeds from left to right, using the value of each element encountered. The low-order 16 bits are retained as the product after each multiplication, and negative results are stored in twos complement form (Section 2-3).

11-6   Relocatable versus Absolute Expressions

A program is said to be relocatable if certain addresses within the program can be easily modified so as to permit the program to be executed from different locations in core memory. During relocatable assembly the Assembler always begins with the location counter set to zero; thus the first word in any program is assembled to be loaded into address zero. Even if a main program could be executed from location zero, the subprograms called by that main program would have to be loaded into locations other than zero because they would have to be in core memory at the same time as the main program. Therefore the subprograms must be able to be relocated into different parts of core memory so that they can be executed with different main programs of varying sizes.

The process of relocation simply consists of adding a constant to those addresses in the program which refer to program locations. For example, since the first word of a program is assembled to be loaded at location zero, any address referring to the first word is an address of zero. If the program is relocated to start at location 4000, a constant of 4000 would be added to the address which had referred to the first word of the program, so that the address will now refer to location 4000 (where the first word of the program will now be stored). Relocation is performed by a relocating loader, a program designed to load other programs into core memory and relocate them to start at the next available memory location behind the last program which has been loaded.

The Assembler must set up identifying bits to indicate which addresses are to be relocated by the relocating loader, and so the Assembler must be able to distinguish absolute expressions (which have a constant value) from relocatable expressions (which have a value dependent upon some memory location or address). The location counter and all labels (unless equated to an absolute expression by the EQU instruction) are relocatable elements, whereas all constants are absolute elements. A relocatable element minus another relocatable element becomes an absolute expression.

For example, consider a symbol whose assembled value is location zero minus another symbol whose assembled value is location ten. The difference is ten words, and will remain ten words even if the first symbol is relocated to location 4000 and the second symbol is relocated to location 4010. Thus the difference between two relocatable elements becomes absolute.

More complex expressions can be evaluated as to relocatability by the following procedure: replace all relocatable elements in the expression with the letter R, and then evaluate the expression using the arithmetic operators to see if the R's will cancel out through subtraction. If no R's are left, the expression is absolute. If the result is R plus or minus a constant or R alone, the expression is relocatable. If the result is R times R, R times a constant or – R, then the expression is neither absolute nor relocatable and is incorrect. Such relocation errors are detected by the Assembler.

Consider the expression START–*+6, which includes an asterisk referencing the location counter. Replacing the relocatable statements with R produces R–R+6, which evaluates to 6. No R's are left, so the expression START–*+6 is absolute. The expression START+*+6 produces R+R+6 which evaluates to 2R+6, however, indicating a relocation error. Fortunately the more complex expressions are seldom needed.

11-7   Registers and Indicators in the Computer

Certain registers and indicators in the 1130 processor can be directly manipulated by symbolic assembly language statements although these devices could not be directly manipulated by FORTRAN statements. A summary of the function of these devices follows.

The accumulator register (ACC) is a 16-bit register which contains the results of add, subtract, multiply and divide operations in integer arithmetic, and can be loaded from and stored into core storage and further manipulated by shift and logical operations.

The accumulator extension (EXT) is a 16-bit register which extends the width of the accumulator to 32 bits for arithmetic with 32-bit integers, to hold the low-order bits of the results of multiply and divide operations, and to hold low-order bits developed during some shift operations.

The *instruction address register (IAR)* is a 15-bit register which contains the address of the first word of the next instruction in sequence; it is the instruction counter.

The *index registers* in the 1130 system are three words in core memory used to obtain the effective address of an instruction.

The *carry indicator and the overflow indicator* can be tested to see whether these indicators are ON or OFF. The carry indicator is turned ON when a one bit is the last bit shifted out of the high-order bits of the ACC. The carry indicator is reset at the beginning of each add, subtract or shift left. The overflow indicator is turned ON whenever addition, subtraction or division produces a result too big for the ACC or whenever a load status instruction encounters a one in bit position 15. The overflow indicator is reset only by testing the indicator or by load status and store status instructions.

11-8   The Load and Store Instructions

The *load accumulator instruction (operation code LD,* bit pattern 11000) loads the contents of the core memory location at the effective address (the EA) into the ACC, replacing the previous contents of the ACC. The contents of the EA are not changed by this instruction.

The *load double instruction (operation code LDD,* bit pattern 11001) loads the contents of the EA and the next higher location as well (EA + 1) into the ACC and the EXT, replacing the previous contents of both registers. For normal use of the load double instruction the EA must be an even-numbered memory location. If the EA is odd, then the contents of the EA alone are loaded into both the ACC and EXT. The contents of EA and EA + 1 are not changed by this instruction.

The *store accumulator instruction (operation code STO,* bit pattern 11010) causes the contents of the ACC to replace the contents of the EA. The contents of the ACC are not changed.

The *store double instruction (operation code STD,* bit pattern 11011) causes the contents of the ACC and EXT to replace the contents of the EA and the EA + 1. Again, the EA should be an even-numbered memory location. If the EA is odd, then only the contents of the ACC are stored at the EA and the EXT and EA + 1 are not affected. In any event the contents of the ACC and EXT are not changed.

The *load index instruction (operation code LDX,* bit pattern 01100) causes the contents of the specified index register to be replaced by the EA, not by the contents of the EA. If no index register is specified by the tag bits of the instruction, then the contents of the IAR are replaced by the EA, causing an unconditional transfer of program control to the EA.

The *store index instruction (operation code STX,* bit pattern 01101) causes the contents of the specified index register (or, if no index register is specified, the contents of the IAR) to replace the contents of the EA. The contents of the index register or the IAR are not changed.

The *store status instruction (operation code STS,* bit pattern 00101) causes the status of the carry and overflow indicators (1 meaning ON, 0 meaning OFF) to replace bits 14 and 15 of the contents of the EA. Bits 0-7 of the EA are unchanged and bits 8-13 are reset to zeros. This instruction allows the programmer to store the status of the carry and overflow indicators to be reloaded later by a load status instruction.

The *load status instruction (operation code LDS,* bit pattern 00100) sets the carry and overflow indicators (1 meaning ON, 0 meaning OFF) according to the values of bits 14 and 15 of the instruction. Normally the load status instruction is the EA of a previous store status instruction.

The examples of Figure 11-1 show various types of addressing and the use of the remarks field, which starts after the first blank column after column 35. The LD instruction will load the contents of index register 1 plus a constant of 3 into the ACC. The STO instruction will store at the location whose address is stored at KCARD+1 not at the expression KCARD+1, since indirect addressing is specified. The STD instruction is in two-word format, so ANS will be assembled as a full 16-bit address word. The LDX instruction will load index register 2 with the contents of ARG+5 since indirect addressing is used. (Otherwise the address ARG+5 would have been loaded into index register 2.) The STS instruction stores the status indicators at STAT, which is the address of the LDS instruction that will reload the status indicators. Normally the STS instruction would be written near the beginning of a sequence of instructions affecting the indicators, while the LDS instruction would be near the end of the sequence. Note that the comments for each statement begin immediately after the first blank in the operands and comments field.

11-9   The Arithmetic Instructions

The *add instruction (operation code A,* bit pattern 10000) adds the contents of the EA to the contents of the ACC, and the resulting sum replaces the contents of the ACC. Negative data or a negative sum will be in twos complement form. The contents of the EA are not changed. The carry indicator is reset at the beginning of the execution of each add instruction and is turned on if the sum exceeds the capacity of the ACC (32,767 to –32,768). The overflow indicator is turned on if a carry occurs out of the high-order bit position of the ACC, but is not reset from its previous condition if no overflow occurs.

222

IBM

IBM 1130 Assembler
Coding Form

Form X26-5994-0
Printed in U.S.A.

Program ______

Date ______

Programmed by ______

Page No. 11-1 of ______

Label (21–25)	Operation (27–30)	F (32)	T (33)	Operands & Remarks (35–70)	Identification (75–80)
	LD		1	3 LOAD CONTENTS OF IR1+3	
	LDD			DATA LOAD CONTENTS OF DATA AND DATA+1	
	STO	I		KCARD+1 STORE INTO ADDRESS AT KCARD+1	
	STD	L		ANS STORE INTO ANS AND ANS+1	
	LDX	I	2	ARG+5 LOAD IR2 WITH ADDRESS AT ARG+5	
	STX		3	SAVE3 STORE CONTENTS OF IR3 AT SAVE3	
	STS			STAT STORE STATUS AT STAT	
STAT	LDS			0 LOAD PREVIOUSLY STORED STATUS	

Figure 11-1 Examples of Load and Store Instructions

The add double instruction (operation code AD, bit pattern 10001) adds the contents of the EA and EA + 1 to the ACC and EXT. The resulting sum replaces the contents of the ACC and EXT. Negative data or sum will be in twos complement form. The contents of the EA and EA + 1 are not changed. For normal use the EA must be an even-numbered memory location. If the EA is odd, then the contents of the EA alone are added to both the ACC and EXT. The carry and overflow indicators behave as described in the add instruction in the preceding paragraph.

The subtract instruction (operation code S, bit pattern 10010) subtracts the contents of the EA from the contents of the ACC. If the carry indicator is turned on during execution of this instruction, a borrow beyond the capacity of the ACC has occurred. In all other respects, the subtract instruction operates like the add instruction described previously.

The subtract double instruction (operation code SD, bit pattern 10011) subtracts the contents of the EA and EA + 1 from the ACC and EXT. If the EA is an odd-numbered memory location, then the EA alone is subtracted from both the ACC and EXT. In all other respects, the subtract double instruction operates like the subtract instruction as far as the indicators are concerned and like the add double instruction regarding the use of core memory.

The multiply instruction (operation code M, bit pattern 10100) multiplies the contents of the EA by the contents of the ACC to produce a 32-bit product (in the format described in Section 2-2) which replaces the contents of the ACC and EXT. The contents of the EA are not changed, and the carry and overflow indicators are not affected.

The divide instruction (operation code D, bit pattern 10101) causes the contents of the ACC and EXT acting as a 32-bit dividend to be divided by the contents of the EA, producing a quotient which replaces the contents of the ACC and a remainder which replaces the contents of the EXT. The remainder receives the sign of the dividend. The overflow indicator will be turned on by dividing by zero or by any quotient greater than 32,767 or less than −32,768.

The logical AND instruction (operation code AND, bit pattern 11100) causes each bit of the contents of the EA to be ANDed with the corresponding bit of the contents of the ACC, with the result replacing the contents of the ACC. The contents of the EA are not changed. Each bit position of the result in the ACC will contain a 1-bit if both the ACC and the EA previously contained a 1-bit in the same position; otherwise the result will contain a 0-bit. The carry and overflow indicators are not affected. The following table shows the four types of bit combinations which affect an AND operation.

EA contains	ACC contained	AND result is
0	0	0
0	1	0
1	0	0
1	1	1

The logical OR instruction (operation code OR, bit pattern 11101) causes each bit of the contents of the EA to be ORed with the corresponding bit of the ACC, with the result replacing the contents of the ACC. The contents of the EA are not changed. Each bit position of the result in the ACC will contain a 1-bit *if either or both of the ACC and the EA previously contained a 1-bit in the same position;* otherwise the result will contain a 0-bit. The carry and overflow indicators are not affected. The table below shows the four types of bit combinations which affect an OR operation.

EA contains	ACC contained	OR result is
0	0	0
0	1	1
1	0	1
1	1	1

The logical exclusive OR instruction (operation code EOR, bit pattern 11110) causes each bit of the contents of the EA to be EORed with the corresponding bit of the contents of the ACC, with the result replacing the contents of the ACC. The contents of the EA are not changed. Each bit position of the result in the ACC will contain a 1-bit *if either the ACC or the EA, but not both, previously contained a 1-bit in the same position;* otherwise the result will contain a 0-bit. The carry and overflow indicators are not affected. The table below shows the four types of bit combinations which affect an EOR operation.

EA contains	ACC contained	EOR result is
0	0	0
0	1	1
1	0	1
1	1	0

The examples in Figure 11-2 show further combinations of indexed and indirect addressing. The addressing should be explained by the remarks field; if not, refer to Figure 11-1 for additional examples. The remarks field starts after the first blank column in the operands and remarks field, and should be used to clarify each symbolic assembly language statement (for the programmer, not for the computer).

IBM 1130 Assembler
Coding Form

Program _____

Programmed by _____

Date _____

Label	Operation	F	T	Operands & Remarks	Identification
21 25	27 30	32	33	35 40 45 50 55 60 65 70	75 80
	A			ONE ADD THE CONTENTS OF ONE	
	AD			DATA+3 ADD CONTENTS OF DATA+3, DATA+4	
	S		I	J SUBTRACT CONTENTS ADDRESS AT J	
	SD			DATA SUBTRACT CONTENTS DATA, DATA+1	
	M		1	3 MPY CONTENTS OF (IR1+3)	
	D		11	3 DIV CONTENTS OF ADDRESS AT (IR1+3)	
	AND		11	O AND CONTENTS OF ADDRESS IN IR1	
	OR			N2 OR CONTENTS OF N2	
	EOR			ONES EOR BY CONTENTS OF ONES	

Figure 11-2 Examples of Arithmetic Instructions

11-10 The Shift Instructions

The shift instructions all operate only in one-word format; indirect addressing is not allowed. If no index register is specified, the number of bit positions in
the ACC and EXT to be shifted is designated by the displacement specified by the
operand field; otherwise the number of bits to be shifted is designated by the contents of the specified index register. A shift count of zero produces an NOP (no
operation) which will simply cause the computer to proceed to the next instruction.

The shift left ACC instruction (operation code SLA, bit pattern 00010)
causes the ACC to be shifted to the left by the shift count contained in the displacement field or in an index register, with all vacated positions at the right end of the
ACC set to zeros. The EXT is not shifted by this instruction, and the overflow
indicator is not affected. The carry indicator is turned on by a 1-bit in the last position shifted out of the high-order position of the ACC and is turned off by a 0-bit
in the last position shifted.

The shift left ACC and EXT instruction (operation code SLT, bit pattern
00010) causes the ACC and the EXT to be shifted to the left by the shift count
contained in the displacement field or an index register, with all vacated positions
at the right of the EXT or ACC set to zeros. The carry indicator operates as in the
shift left ACC instruction.

The shift left and count ACC instruction (operation code SLCA, bit pattern
00010) causes the ACC to be shifted left by the shift count contained in the displacement field or in an index register, but if the shift count is contained in an index
register the shift is terminated by either the shift count being decremented to zero or
by a 1-bit being shifted into the high-order position of the ACC, whichever happens
first. The six low-order bits of the index register used end up containing the decremented shift count at the end of execution of the instruction. The overflow indicator
is not affected. The carry indicator is turned on if the shift is terminated by a 1-bit
in the high-order position of the ACC and turned off if the shift is terminated by
decrementing the shift count to zero. If no index register is specified, this instruction
behaves just like the SLA instruction.

The shift left and count ACC and EXT instruction (operation code SLC, bit
pattern 00010) causes both the ACC and the EXT to be shifted left as in the shift
left and count ACC instruction. The high-order bits from the EXT are shifted into
the low-order bit positions of the ACC. Vacated low-order positions of the EXT
are set to zero. The carry and overflow indicators perform as in the shift left and
count ACC instruction. If no index register is specified, this instruction behaves
just like the SLT instruction.

The shift right ACC instruction (operation code SRA, bit pattern 00011)
causes the ACC to be shifted to the right by the shift count contained in the

displacement field or in an index register. Vacated high-order positions are set to zeros. The EXT is not affected, nor are the carry or overflow indicators.

The shift right ACC and EXT instruction (operation code *SRT,* bit pattern 00011) causes the ACC and EXT to be shifted to the right by the shift count contained in the displacement field or in an index register. This shift preserves the arithmetic sign of the ACC; the value of the sign bit in position 0 of the ACC is duplicated in all the vacated bit positions. The carry and overflow indicators are not affected. Low-order bits shifted out of the EXT are lost.

The rotate right ACC and EXT instruction (operation code RTE, bit pattern 00011) causes the ACC and EXT to be shifted to the right by the shift count contained in the displacement field or in an index register, but this time the low-order positions of the EXT are shifted into the high-order positions of the ACC to form a continuous loop arrangement such that no bits are shifted out and lost. The carry and overflow indicators are not affected.

The examples of Figure 11-3 show additional combinations of indexing as explained by the remarks fields.

11-11   The Branch Instructions, Including WAIT

The branch or skip on condition instruction (operation code BSC, bit pattern 01001) causes any combination of six conditions in the ACC (overflow, carry, even number, plus, minus and zero) to be tested with a resulting skip over a one-word instruction or a branch to another address. If the BSC instruction is written *in one-word format,* the operand field contains any combination of the six conditions to be tested and *the next instruction will be skipped if any of the tested conditions are true.* If the BSC instruction is written in two-word format, the operand field contains an address (or expression) separated by a comma from the list of conditions to be tested, as shown in the examples. *In the two-word format, a branch to the EA will occur if all of the tested conditions are false.* The reversed logic between the one-word and two-word formats, combined with all of the options on the EA (indexing plus indirect addressing), make the BSC instruction a primary source of errors for novice programmers.

The following table summarizes the six conditions to be tested which are controlled by the characters Z – + E C O in the operand field of the instruction statement. The bit positions listed refer to bits in the assembled machine language instruction which are set to one to cause the condition to be tested. Figure 11-4 shows examples of the use of the BSC instruction. The characters representing the conditions to be tested may be listed in the operand field in any sequence. Notice that the BSC instruction may be made to act as an NOP or unconditional skip (by listing a combination of conditions, one of which must always be true, such as

IBM

IBM 1130 Assembler
Coding Form

Program _____

Programmed by _____

Date _____

Page No. __11-3__ of _____

Label	Operation	F	T	Operands & Remarks	Identification
21	27 30	32	33	35 40 45 50 55 60 65 70	75 80
	SLA		8	SHIFT ACC LEFT 8 BITS	
	SLT	1	0	SHIFT ACC + EXT LEFT BY CONTENT IR1	
	SLCA	3	0	SHIFT LEFT COUNT ACC BY CONTENT IR3	
	SLC	3	0	SHIFT LEFT + COUNT ACC + EXT IR3	
	SRA	2	0	SHIFT ACC RIGHT BY CONTENTS OF IR2	
	SRT		5	SHIFT ACC + EXT RIGHT 5 BITS	
	RTE		10	ROTATE ACC + EXT RIGHT 10 BITS	

Figure 11-3 Examples of Shift Instructions

+ – Z) or as an unconditional branch (by listing no conditions at all). NOP means no operation. Through the use of indirect addressing, a BSC may be used to branch conditionally to the contents of an address in memory. This technique may be used to return from a subprogram to a calling main program as described in Section 12-4.

Tested Condition	Character	Description	Bit Position
ACC zero	Z	Skip or don't branch if ACC is zero	10
ACC minus	–	Skip or don't branch if ACC is minus	11
ACC plus	+ or &	Skip or don't branch if ACC is plus but not zero	12
ACC even	E	Skip or don't branch if the ACC is even (bit position 15 of ACC is zero)	13
Carry indicator	C	Skip or don't branch if *indicator off*	14
Overflow indicator	letter O	Skip or don't branch if *indicator off*	15

The branch out or skip on condition instruction (operation code BOSC, bit pattern 01001) is identical in form and function to the BSC instruction, except that bit position nine of the assembled machine language instruction is set to one which causes the highest level of priority interrupt on at the moment to be turned off if the skip or branch takes place. This instruction is normally used to exit from a subprogram which will be executed only if an interrupt condition occurs inside the computer. (The programming of interrupts is discussed in Chapter 13.)

Both the BSC and BOSC instructions will reset the overflow indicator if it is tested. The carry indicator and the contents of the ACC are not changed by testing.

The branch and store instruction register (operation code BSI, bit pattern 01000) is used primarily to branch to a subprogram from a main program or from another subprogram. This instruction stores the contents of the instruction address register (IAR) in memory at the EA and then branches to the address EA + 1. Since the IAR contains the address of the next instruction, a later indirect branch to the EA will return program control to the next instruction following the BSI instruction in the calling program. The EA is usually a data word at the beginning of the subprogram, and the EA + 1 is the first executable instruction of the subprogram.

The BSI instruction can be written in either one- or two-word format. In the two-word format the BSI operates conditionally in the same way as the BSC and BOSC instructions. Any combination of the six conditions (zero, minus, plus, even,

IBM

IBM 1130 Assembler
Coding Form

Program _____

Programmed by _____

Date _____

Page No. 11-4 of _____

Label	Operation	F	T	Operands & Remarks
	BSC			Z, SKIP NEXT INSTRUCTION WORD IF ACC 0
	BSC			+- SKIP IF ACC NOT ZERO (PLUS/MINUS)
	BSC			CO SKIP IF CARRY OR OVERFLOW IS OFF
	BSC			+-Z UNCONDITIONAL SKIP, ACC MUST BE
	BSC	L		JCARD,- BRANCH TO JCARD IF ACC + OR 0
	BSC	L		PLACE UNCONDITIONAL BRANCH TO PLACE
	BSC	I		MYBIT BRANCH TO CONTENTS OF MYBIT
	BSC	LI		0,+- BRANCH TO C(IR1) IF ACC ZERO

Figure 11-4 Examples of the BSC Instruction

carry and overflow) are listed in the operand field separated from the EA by commas, and the storage of the IAR and subsequent branch to EA + 1 will occur only if none of the listed conditions is true; otherwise the next instruction after the BSI will be executed.

In practice the subprogram linkage function of the BSI instruction is handled by the CALL and LIBF statements described in Section 12-5, but an understanding of the BSI instruction helps in understanding CALL and LIBF. When using two-word format the BSI instruction will reset the overflow indicator if it is tested; all other indicators and the contents of the ACC remain unchanged.

The modify index and skip instruction (operation code MDX, bit pattern 01110) increments or decrements the IAR (i.e., to branch), an index register, or a word in memory. A subsequent skip over the next instruction will occur if the index register or memory word being modified changes sign or is zero after modification.

In one-word format the MDX instruction adds the 8-bit displacement specified by the operand field to the IAR (if no index register is specified) or to a specified index register. Since the displacement field is only eight bits wide the value of the expression or address in the operand field must fall between +127 and –128, as discussed in Section 11-3. Modifying the IAR will produce a branch or skip to the new value of the IAR. An operand value of zero will produce an NOP.

In two-word format the MDX instruction will cause the second operand (the displacement) to be added to the EA (the first operand) if no index register is specified, regardless of the presence or absence of indirect addressing. If an index register is specified, the EA (a full 16-bit word) is added to the index register. If an index register and indirect addressing are both specified, the contents of the EA are added to the index register.

The carry and overflow indicators are not changed by the MDX instruction. The two-word MDX instruction permits changing the contents of a word in memory without first loading that word into the ACC and so is very valuable for address modification purposes. Both formats of the MDX instruction can be used to modify and test the contents of index registers and so perform the function of the DO statement in FORTRAN.

The wait instruction (operation code WAIT, bit pattern 00110) stops the computer and causes it to wait until an interrupt occurs or until it is started manually from the computer console. Certain input-output operations controlled by cycle stealing channels may proceed during a wait, but no computations involving the ACC will be performed. If the wait is terminated by an interrupt, program control will branch to a subprogram to process the interrupt. The wait instruction does not affect the carry and overflow indicators, needs no operand, and uses only one-word format.

IBM

Form X26-5994-0
Printed in U.S.A.

IBM 1130 Assembler Coding Form

Program _____

Programmed by _____

Date _____

Page No. _11-5_ of ___

Label 21 25	Operation 27 30	F 32	T 33	Operands & Remarks 35 40 45 50 55 60 65 70	Identification 75 80
	BSI			SUB STØRE IAR AT SUB, GØ TØ SUBt1	
	BSI	L		SUBPR,+ GØ TØ SUBPRt1 IF ACC NØT PLUS	
	MDX			PLACE GØ TØ PLACE	
	MDX	L		JCARD,-1 DECREMENT JCARD BY 1	
	MDX	L		KCARD,1 INCREMENT KCARD BY 1	
	WAIT			WAIT FØR INTERRUPT ØR CONSØLE START	

Figure 11-5 Examples of Branch Instructions, Including WAIT

Any operation code which does not match the bit pattern of a legitimate operation on the 1130 system will always produce a wait condition. This means that if you start trying to execute data words as instructions you may get a wait and be able to find out what happened. On the other hand, your data may just happen to match the bit patterns of instructions, in which case you may have a very difficult time determining just where your program ran amok.

11-12 FORTRAN Object Code in Assembly Language

The FORTRAN compiler translates or compiles FORTRAN statements into machine language instructions (called object code or the object program). As examples of symbolic assembly language programming, we can write statements that are equivalent in function to certain FORTRAN statements.

On a few computers the FORTRAN compiler actually compiles assembly language statements which are then assembled into machine language code in a subsequent operation. The 1130 FORTRAN compiler, however, goes directly to machine language instructions, which contributes considerably to the compilation speed of this system.

Consider the FORTRAN statement

MAX = LAST

where both MAX and LAST are integers. In assembly language we can write

```
LD    L    LAST        LOAD LAST INTO THE ACC
STO   L    MAX         STORE THE ACC AT MAX
```

which restates the meaning of the FORTRAN equal sign as "load the variable or expression at the addresses to the right of the equal sign into the ACC and store the contents of the ACC at the address to the left of the equal sign."

The FORTRAN compiler must always use two-word (L) format because the compiler stores all variables at the end of core memory, much more than 255 words away from the memory location of the instructions which use the variables. As we will see in Chapter 12, the assembly language programmer can usually locate his program variables and instructions using the variables close enough together to permit the use of one-word format instructions; this is a primary reason why assembly language programming can usually use less memory than a FORTRAN program written to do the same job.

Now consider the FORTRAN statement

NEXT = MAX – MIN

where again all the variables are integers. In assembly language,

```
LD    L   MAX        LOAD MAX INTO THE ACC
S     L   MIN        SUBTRACT MIN
STO   L   NEXT       STORE THE ACC AT NEXT
```

As before, the FORTRAN compiler must use only two-word format instructions. The compiler scans the statement and determines that MAX must be loaded first and MIN then subtracted from MAX.

Consider the FORTRAN statement

NEXT = MAX/MIN

using integer variables. Now the equivalent assembly language code becomes more complex:

```
LD    L   MAX        LOAD MAX INTO THE ACC
SRT       16         SHIFT ACC + EXT RIGHT FOR DIVIDEND
D     L   MIN        DIVIDE BY MIN
STO   L   NEXT       STORE QUOTIENT IN ACC AT NEXT
```

The SRT instruction shifts the value of MAX into the EXT to permit the divide operation (Section 11-9) to function properly. The quotient ends up in the ACC.

We can now consider the example described in Sections 1-5 and 1-6 involving the integer variables A, B, C and D:

A = B/(C + D)

In assembly language this becomes

```
LD    L   C          LOAD C INTO THE ACC
A     L   D          ADD D
STO   3   -126       TEMPORARILY SAVE (C + D)
LD    L   B          NOW LOAD B INTO THE ACC
SRT       16         SHIFT TO POSITION DIVIDEND
D     3   -126       DIVIDE BY (C + D)
STO   L   A          STORE THE ACC AT ADDRESS A
```

Here we must store a partial result (C + D) and pick it up later to complete the calculation of the FORTRAN statement. The FORTRAN compiler stores (C + D) at the contents of IR3 plus a displacement of −126 (an address which the compiler uses to store the partial results of integer calculations).

Floating-point operations are performed through the use of subroutines provided by IBM; only integer operations can be coded directly as in these examples. The use of subroutines in assembly language is discussed in Chapter 13. The FORTRAN compiler also handles integer multiplication via a subroutine because the linkage instructions to the subroutine actually take less memory than the shift operations required after each multiplication.

Next consider the code required to control a FORTRAN DO loop with a CONTINUE statement, such as

       DO 20 I = J, K
          .
          .
          .
    20   CONTINUE

which compiles to

    START   LD   L   J   PICK UP J
            STO   L   I   STORE IT IN I
             .
             .
             .
            MDX   L   I, 1   ADD 1 TO I
            LD   L   I   PICK UP THE VARIABLE I
            S   L   K   SUBTRACT THE VARIABLE K
            BSC   L   START+4,+   GO TO START+4 IF MINUS OR ZERO

The dots represent the computations inside the DO loop which do not concern us here. At the end of the loop the index I is incremented and compared against the limit variable K, and a branch is made to continue the DO loop if K is not smaller than I.

The computed GO TO statement in FORTRAN has a particularly simple form in assembly language. The FORTRAN statement

       GO TO (41, 42, 43), L

compiles to

            LDX   I1   L   LOAD L VALUE INTO IR1
            BSC   I1   *-1   PRESENT ADDR + L, INDIRECT
            DC   address of 41 ADDRESS OF STATEMENT 41
            DC   address of 42 ADDRESS OF STATEMENT 42
            DC   address of 43 ADDRESS OF STATEMENT 43

See Section 12-3 for a description of DC statements. Notice that a value of L greater than three will cause a branch to some statement or data after the third DC, and the program will run amok. The BSC counts down to the Lth DC statement and transfers to it indirectly, resulting in a transfer to the appropriate FORTRAN statement.

The FORTRAN IF statement is also very simply rendered in assembly language. The IF statement

IF (ITEM) 1, 2, 3

compiles to

```
LD    L    ITEM           LOAD ITEM VALUE INTO ACC
BSC   L    addr of 1,+Z   GO TO #1 IF NOT + OR 0
BSC   L    addr of 2,+    GO TO #2 IF NOT +
BSC   L    addr of 3      GO TO #3 OTHERWISE
```

11-13 Summing 100 Variables in Assembly Language

Consider the problem of summing 100 different numbers stored in consecutive memory locations, where the first (lowest) memory location is given the address ITEM, and we wish to store the sum in a memory location whose address is SUM. If we were summing an array of 100 integers in FORTRAN, where the array was called ITEM, we could simply write

```
      SUM = ITEM(1)
      DO 10 I = 2, 100
10    SUM = SUM + ITEM(I)
```

Here we have initialized SUM with ITEM(1), the first item, and then have added the other 99 items in sequence. In FORTRAN, the DO statement handles both the address modification (subscripting) as we add successive items, tests to see if all 99 have been added, and transfers out of the loop upon completion. An assembly language program to do this could be written as follows:

```
           LD          ADDER        INITIALIZE ADDRESS TO BE ADDED
           STO         NEXT         STORE INITIALIZED INSTRUCTION
           LDX    1    99           LOAD IR1 WITH THE VALUE 99
           LD          ITEM         LOAD THE FIRST ITEM
NEXT       A           0            INITIALIZED INSTRUCTION HERE
           MDX    L    NEXT,1       INCREMENT ADDRESS TO BE ADDED
           MDX    1    -1           DECREMENT IR1, TEST FOR SKIP
           MDX         NEXT         GO TO NEXT IF NO SKIP OCCURS
           STO         SUM          IF SKIP, STORE SUM WHEN DONE
           MDX         DONE         GO TO DONE, PROGRAM COMPLETED
ADDER      A      X    ITEM-NEXT    EA IS ITEM+1, INITIALIZED INSTR
DONE       Continue with other operations from this point.
```

The above program assumes that ITEM is stored near the program instructions so that one-word format instructions can be used. The statement at ADDER is an effective add at the address ITEM+1, using X format (Section 11-4) to permit the statement

237

to be assembled at ADDER and then executed at NEXT. IR1 is initialized to count the 99 subsequent additions, and the ACC is loaded with the first item to be summed. The repeated additions occur at NEXT. The first MDX statement increments the address to be added, creating address of ITEM+2, ITEM+3, etc. The second MDX decrements IR1 by one, which will cause a skip if IR1 changes sign or is zero after decrementing. If no skip occurs, the SUM is stored and control is transferred to DONE. Notice that the statement at ADDER is never executed at ADDER; control is transferred around ADDER.

If we are willing to get a bit trickier and add up the items in reverse sequence, we can achieve substantial savings in memory and execution time. The previous coding took 12 words of memory; the following code does the same job in only seven words.

```
           LDX    1   99          LOAD IR1 WITH THE VALUE 99
           LD         ITEM+99     LOAD THE LAST ITEM
   NEXT    A      L1  ITEM-1      ADD CONTENTS OF (ITEM-1 + IR1)
           MDX    1   -1          DECREMENT IR1, TEST FOR SKIP
           MDX        NEXT        GO TO NEXT IF NO SKIP OCCURS
           STO        SUM         IF SKIP, STORE SUM WHEN DONE
   DONE    Continue with other operations at this point.
```

Here we are using IR1 to modify the address of the item to be added as well as to count the number of additions. To do this we must add the items from the last item backwards to the first item, since the skip caused by the MDX statement will only work if the IR becomes zero or changes sign, and we want IR1 to be zero after the last or 99th addition. The add instruction addresses ITEM-1 because ITEM - 1 + 99 equals ITEM + 98 which is the address of the next-to-the-last item, which is now the first item to be added. IR1 is initialized to 99 because 99 will become zero and cause a skip after IR1 is decremented by one exactly 99 times.

11-14   Extended Mnemonics for BSC, MDX and RTE

The many functions of the BSC and MDX instructions can cause confusion in reading a program listing. This problem was eased in 1967 by the introduction of additional assembly language mnemonics (instruction names) for the 1130 Disk Monitor to encourage more readable (and therefore more error-free) programs. The extended mnemonics do not provide any increased hardware capability because BSC and MDX can do anything that can be done by the extended mnemonics, but the extended mnemonics can certainly reduce errors in programming.

The BSC instruction in one-word format (Section 11-11) can be replaced by the following:

```
           SKP        +           SKIP IF ACC IS POSITIVE
           SKP        +-          SKIP IF ACC + OR -
```

The two-word BSC instruction can be replaced by

B	L	NEXT	GO TO NEXT (LONG FORMAT)
BZ		OTHER	GO TO OTHER IF ACC ZERO
BNZ		OTHER	GO TO OTHER IF ACC NON-ZERO
BN		NEXT	GO TO NEXT IF ACC NEGATIVE
BNN		NEXT	GO TO NEXT IF ACC NOT NEGATIVE
BP		ELSE	GO TO ELSE IF ACC PLUS
BNP		ELSE	GO TO ELSE IF ACC NOT PLUS
BC		SECT	GO TO SECT IF CARRY IS ON
BO		SECT	GO TO SECT IF OVERFLOW ON
BOD		PROG	GO TO PROG IF ACC ODD

The extended mnemonics can be read as skip on condition (SKP), branch unconditionally (B), branch ACC zero (BZ), branch ACC not zero (BNZ), branch ACC negative (BN), branch ACC not negative (BNN), branch ACC plus (BP), branch ACC not plus (BMP), branch if carry indicator on (BC), branch if overflow indicator on (BO), and branch if ACC is odd (BOD). Condition codes (+, −, Z, O, C, E) can be used only with SKP because the other instructions get their condition codes from the mnemonic itself. All of these instructions except SKP and B are assembled as two-word instructions, but the two-word format need not be specified except for B, where a two-word format is assembled as a BSC and a one-word format is assembled as an MDX.

The MDX instruction (Section 11-11) can be replaced by

B	NEXT	GO TO NEXT (SHORT FORMAT)
MDM	COUNT, 100	INCREMENT COUNT BY 100

where the extended mnemonics read as branch unconditionally (B) and modify memory (MDM). MDM is always assembled as a two-word instruction although the two-word format need not be specified.

The RTE instruction (Section 11-10) can be replaced by

XCH	EXCHANGE THE ACC AND EXT

where the extended mnemonic reads as exchange ACC and EXT (XCH). Notice that XCH is written without an operand; it is equivalent to RTE with an operand of 16.

Indexing and indirect addressing may be used with the extended mnemonics except that MDM, XCH, SKP and short format B cannot be indexed and MDM and XCH cannot be indirectly addressed.

11-15 Summary

This chapter has covered the fundamentals of symbolic assembly language programming, but several important topics including input-output operations, data location assignment, subroutine linkages and monitor operations will be covered in Chapter 12. The machine language instructions set and equivalent assembly language operation codes are summarized in Figure 11-6.

Class	Instruction	Indirect Addressing	Mnemonic
Load and Store	Load Accumulator	Yes	LD
	Double Load	Yes	LDD
	Store Accumulator	Yes	STO
	Double Store	Yes	STD
	Load Index	**	LDX
	Store Index	Yes	STX
	Load Status	No	LDS
	Store Status	Yes	STS
Arithmetic	Add	Yes	A
	Double Add	Yes	AD
	Subtract	Yes	S
	Double Subtract	Yes	SD
	Multiply	Yes	M
	Divide	Yes	D
	And	Yes	AND
	Or	Yes	OR
	Exclusive Or	Yes	EOR
Shift	Shift Left Instructions		
	Shift Left Logical (A) *	No	SLA
	Shift Left Logical (AQ) *	No	SLT
	Shift Left and Count (AQ) *	No	SLC
	Shift Left and Count (A) *	No	SLCA
	Shift Right Instructions		
	Shift Right Logical (A) *	No	SRA
	Shift Right Arithmetically (AQ) *	No	SRT
	Rotate Right (AQ) *	No	RTE
Branch	Branch and Store I	Yes	BSI
	Branch or Skip on Condition	Yes	BSC (BOSC)
	Modify Index and Skip	**	MDX
	Wait	No	WAIT
I/O	Execute I/O	Yes	XIO

* Letters in parentheses indicate registers involved in shift operations.
** See the section for the individual instruction (MDX and LDX)

Figure 11-6   The Machine Language Instruction Set

1) If IR1 contains 1000, IR2 contains 2000, IR3 contains 3000, location 1000 contains 56, location 2000 contains 93, location 3000 contains 41 and location 4000 contains 87, find the effective address (EA) resulting from each of the following assembly language statements:

```
LD            1000
LD      L     1000
A       I     1000
S       2     1000
LDX    I 1    1000
LD     L3     1000
LDX     1     1000
STO     3  0
```

2) If the current value of the location counter is 1000 and if DOG corresponds to address 1000, CAT corresponds to address 2000, MOUSE corresponds to address 3000 and START corresponds to address 4000, find the value of each of the following assembly language expressions and determine if each is relocatable:

```
*+DOG-MOUSE
CAT-DOG
MOUSE-/23
*+3000
```

3) Using the index register values and symbolic addresses furnished with Problems 1 and 2, find the effective address of each of the following:

```
LD     L3  START-MOUSE
A      I2  *-MOUSE+2000
STO    1   **2
```

4) If the ACC contains a bit pattern of FFFF in hexadecimal and the variable LOGIC contains the bit pattern 1111 in hexadecimal, what bit pattern will remain in the ACC after each of the following? (Assume that the ACC is reinitialized to FFFF before each instruction is executed.)

```
AND         LOGIC
OR          LOGIC
EOR         LOGIC
SLA         8
SRA         6
```

241

5)   Based upon the examples in Section 11-12, write assembly language statements equivalent to each of the following FORTRAN statements (all variables are integers):

$$MOST = MAX + LEAST$$
$$AVG = (MAX + MIN)/NUMB$$
$$MANY = MAX + MIN - LEAST/MORE$$

6)   Write the example in Section 11-13 (summing 100 integer variables) without using any index registers. (Hint: Use the BSC statement.*)

7)   Based upon Section 11-13, write a program to take the average of 100 integer variables using index registers.*

8)   Based upon Section 11-13, write a program to find both the maximum and the minimum value of 100 integer variables.*

---

*In Problems 6, 7 and 8, assume that the 100 integer variables are stored in consecutive memory locations as in the examples in Section 11-13, and that the first (lowest addressed) variable is to be called ITEM.

CHAPTER 12: MORE SYMBOLIC ASSEMBLY LANGUAGE PROGRAMMING

12-1 Input-Output Instructions

Conspicuously absent from Chapter 11 is any reference to reading or writing data. On the 1130 system the operations of reading and writing are combined in a single instruction, called the execute I/O instruction.

The execute I/O instruction (operation code XIO, bit pattern 00001) contains an effective address (EA) which is the address of two adjacent words in core memory. The two adjacent words are called an input-output control command (IOCC). The computer examines the 32 bits available in each IOCC as a 16-bit address field, a 5-bit area field, a 3-bit function field and an 8-bit modifier field as shown in Figure 12-1. The EA of the XIO instruction (which points to the first word of the IOCC) should be an even memory location.

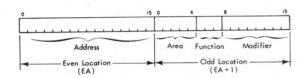

Figure 12-1   Fields in an Input-Output Control Command

There are basically two ways of reading and writing data by the use of an XIO instruction: one word of data per instruction, or many words of data per instruction under data channel control. If only one word is to be read or written, the address field of the IOCC contains the address in core memory from which the word will be written or into which the word will be read. If many words are to be read or written under data channel control, the address field of the IOCC contains the address of a word containing a count of the number of words to be transmitted by a single XIO command. The many words of data will then be written from or read into the core memory locations immediately after the location containing the word count. Transmission under data channel control takes place while the computer goes on to process subsequent instructions, overlapping read/write operations with computation.

The area field of the IOCC identifies the device, such as a card read punch or line printer, which will be controlled during execution of the XIO. In the 1130 the area codes are fixed as follows:

Device	Five-Bit Area Code
1442 Card Read Punch	00010
1132 Printer	00110
Disk Storage	00100
1627 Plotter	00101
Paper Tape Reader	00011
Paper Tape Punch	00011
Console Keyboard	00001
Console Typewriter	00001
Console Entry Switches	00111

The function field of the IOCC selects one of the seven functions described below:

Function	Three-Bit Function Code
Write (one word)	001
Read (one word)	010
Sense Interrupt	011
Control Function	100
Initiate Write	101
Initiate Read	110
Sense Device	111

The function code 000 is not used. The write and read functions cause a single word to be written or read at the core memory location specified by the address field of the IOCC. The sense interrupt function determines which of several devices or conditions might have caused an interrupt signal to the computer (interrupts are further discussed in Chapter 14). The control function causes the computer to interpret the modifier field and to execute a control function such as moving the disk storage read/write head to another track, backspacing magnetic tape, or selecting the alternate card stacker on the card read punch. The initiate write and initiate read functions cause many words to be written or read under data channel control as specified by a word count stored at the address contained in the address field of the IOCC. The sense device function loads a special device status word (DSW) into the ACC. The DSW contains bits which indicate the different status conditions of each of the devices, such as device busy, device not ready, device in an error condition, etc.

The modifier field contains eight bits which define what control operation is to be performed if the control function is present. The bit codes for the various

244

control operations vary with the different devices. The modifier field may also supply additional information as needed for read and write operations.

As an example of an XIO instruction and its associated IOCC, consider the bit patterns involved in selecting the alternate stacker on the 1442 Card Read Punch on an 1130 system. We can name the IOCC IOCC1 to distinguish it from any other IOCC's which may be used in the same program. The XIO can then be written in assembly language as simply

         XIO   IOCC1

if IOCC1 is located close to the XIO instruction to permit the use of a one-word instruction. If not, a two-word XIO involving direct or indirect addressing or indexing could be employed.

The IOCC needs no address field because stacker select is a control operation. On the 1130 system, the area code of the 1442 Card Read Punch is 00010. The function field is control, with a bit code of 100. The modifier field requires a bit in the first or high-order position of the field to cause the control function to be interpreted as stacker select, so the modifier field is 10000000. Using an address field of zero, IOCC1 will consist of two words with bit patterns of 0000000000000000 and 0001010010000000 where the second word consists of 00010, 100 and 10000000 to represent the area, function and modifier fields. IOCC1 is a data word stored at some point in the program where it will not be executed as an instruction.

The real purpose of the IOCC is to create a three-word instruction from the XIO instruction, because there is just too much information required to permit this instruction to be written in two words. The subsequent analysis of the IOCC by the computer uses the ACC register, and we must be careful to remove any valuable data from the ACC before executing an XIO, because any data in the ACC may be lost when the XIO is executed.

In practice very little input-output programming is done through the use of the XIO instruction, because of the program looping required and the necessity of translating the various address, area, function and modifier codes. Most assembly language programmers use the input-output subroutines described in Chapter 13. These subroutines, of course, contain the XIO instructon.

12-2   Examples of Disk Input-Output

As a further explanation of the XIO instruction let us consider the various XIO operations involving disk storage. The organization of data on the disk (Section 7-2) consists of two surfaces (top and bottom) per disk, 200 tracks per surface, four sectors per track and 320 usable words per sector. The total word capacity of a disk is thus 320 * 4 * 200 * 2, or 512,000 words.

Each sector actually contains 321 words, but the first word in each sector is used by the Disk Monitor programs as a sector number, so a programmer cannot alter the first word if he expects to use the Disk Monitor programs. Only the remaining 320 words can be used for data.

Although a word in core memory contains 16 usable data bits, each word on the disk occupies 20 bits. The extra four bits are check bits, created by taking the number of one bits (not the bit value) of the 16-bit word and inserting enough one bits at the end of the word so that the total number of bits is evenly divisible by four. This technique enables the computer to check for missing bits, because the addition or deletion of any bit through an error in the computer will result in a number of bits no longer evenly divisible by four. The check bits are created whenever words are written upon the disk, and may be tested by the computer whenever words are read from the disk into the computer.

The IOCC for an initiate read operaton involving the disk storage includes an address field containing the address of the word count. The word count is the number of words to be read under data channel control, since all read and write operations involving disk storage use data channels. The area field contains the bits 00100 to select the disk input-output device, and the function field contains the bits 110 to indicate the initiate read function. The last three bits of the modifier field indicate the particular sector (out of eight sectors on the two tracks under the disk read/write heads) to be read. The first bit of the modifier field indicates whether the instruction will read the number of words specified by the word count or simply check to see that the number of bits in each word is evenly divisible by four. This IOCC format is shown in Figure 12-2.

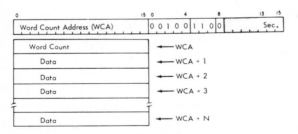

Figure 12-2 IOCC for Disk Storage Initiate Read

If the first bit of the modifier field is zero (bit 8 in the second word of the IOCC), then we have a read operation. Beginning with the first word in the sector, words are read into core memory starting with the first memory location after the word count and continuing until the number of words specified by the word count have been transmitted. A full sector of 321 words is the most that can be transmitted with a single XIO instruction on the 1130 system. An interrupt will occur at the end of the transmission to signal the computer that the operation is completed; the computer will ordinarily be processing other instructions while the transmission takes place.

246

If the first bit of the modifier field is one, then we have a read-check operation. Words are read from the disk as before, but are not stored in core memory. Instead the words are simply checked to see if the number of bits in each word is evenly divisible by four. If any word is not so divisible, a data check indicator bit is turned on in the disk storage device status word, which can then be interrogated by a sense device operation. The contents of disk storage and core memory are not changed by the read-check operation. The contents of disk storage are not changed by the read operation.

The initiate write operation has an IOCC similar to that used in the initiate read except that the function field is now 101 and the first bit of the modifier field is not used. Beginning with the first word after the word count location in core memory, words are written into the sector indicated by the last three bits in the modifier field, starting with the first word in the sector and continuing until the word count is exhausted. As before, a full sector of 321 words is the most that can be transmitted and an interrupt will signal the end of the transmission.

The control operation (function field 100) causes the disk access mechanism to jump a number of tracks specified by the value of the address field. The direction of the jump is controlled by bit position 13 in the modifier field; a zero bit moves the read/write head toward the center of the disk, a one bit moves the read/write head toward the edge of the disk. An interrupt signals the end of the operation unless a movement of zero tracks is specified. Notice that the programmer must know where he is on the disk and where he is trying to go so that he can specify a jump of the correct number of tracks.

The sense device operation (function field 111) causes the disk storage device status word (DSW) to be loaded into the ACC. All of the indicator bits are reset to zero bits if the low-order bit of the modifier field is a one bit. The meaning and position of the various indicator bits are shown in Figure 12-3.

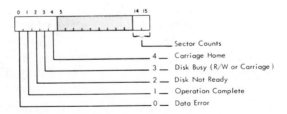

Figure 12-3   Device Status Word for Disk Storage

The carriage home indicator comes on whenever the carriage is at the outermost cylinder on the disk. Disk busy means that the disk is busy reading, writing or seeking another track. Disk not ready means that the disk is busy, or that the disk has just been turned on and has not reached operating speed, or that the disk is not

247

ready for some other mechanical reason. Operation complete means that a read, write or control operation has been completed, and data error means that the division-by-four check has revealed at least one word with incorrect bits. The sector count bits shown in Figure 12-3 indicate the sector number (one through four) of the next available sector on the upper surface of the disk.

In case of an error detected during an input-output transmission the normal practice is to attempt to repeat the transmission three to ten times in order to determine whether the error is transient (in which case it won't happen next time) or is a hard failure (in which case it will happen every time). A transient error can be overcome (for the moment) by repeated trials; a hard error requires that the system be repaired immediately.

Disk file efficiency is heavily dependent upon use of the cylinder concept, which requires that related data be placed to form cylinders of data, each cylinder containing eight sectors on two tracks, one track above the other on opposite sides of the disk. This approach minimizes disk accesses.

Most assembly language programmers use the subroutines of Chapter 13 rather than make direct use of the XIO instruction to control disk storage. For this reason the detailed use of XIO to control other input-output devices will not be described here; a programmer writing new input-output subroutines will normally have access to detailed IBM manuals.

12-3   Data Definition Statements

Special assembly language statements are available to define constant data words such as IOCC's, integer and floating-point numbers, characters and bit patterns.

The define constant statement (operation code DC) is used to define data constants occupying a single word in core memory. The constants are written in the operand field of the statement using the same notation as that developed for elements of assembly language expressions (Section 11-5). Examples of hexadecimal constants could include /3 and /2E and /81 and /805; examples of the same bit patterns written as decimal integer constants are 3, 46, 129 and 2053. A minus sign (–) should precede negative decimal integers. Single characters may be written with preceding periods, as .A, .$, .7 and .. (to represent a period as a character). Expressions involving symbolic addresses (Section 11-5) and other elements may be written in the operand field to create address constants. Further examples are shown at the end of this section. The label field may be used to assign a symbolic address to the constant, so that the constant may be directly referenced by other assembly language statements.

The define decimal constant statement (operation code DEC) is used to define data constants occupying two words of core memory. The constants may be decimal integers for manipulation by the arithmetic instructions using both the ACC and EXT (such as add double, subtract double and divide), or the constants may be floating-point numbers. The floating-point constants may include an exponent (such as E12 or E–4) which represents a power of ten by which the number will be multiplied during conversion to two-word standard precision floating-point format. The floating-point format created in core memory by the DEC statement is identical to that used for standard precision real constants in FORTRAN; these floating-point constants may be processed by either FORTRAN statements or assembly language statements. Examples of DEC integers are 21, –47, 31643 and 0; examples of DEC floating-point constants are 8.87, 887E–2, .0887E2, and 88700.E–4, all of which are different ways of describing the same constant 8.87. Any label assigned to a DEC statement is automatically assigned the value of the next available even-numbered memory location to ensure the correct operation of double word arithmetic.

The DEC statement can produce a third type of constant, called fixed-point binary. The fixed-point binary constant is a number which may contain a decimal fraction stored around a fixed binary point location relative to the 31-bit field contained within two adjacent data words. The binary point location is indicated by the letter B followed by an integer denoting the number of bits which are to represent the whole-number part of the constant. Thus B3 indicates that the three high-order bit positions out of 31 represent the whole-number part of the constant, leaving 28 bit positions to represent the fractional part. The constant is written as a floating-point constant plus the binary point indicator; examples are 9.63B9, 42.5E6B12, .4789B8E3 and 6.487B8. Fixed-point binary constants are seldom used, partly because there is no equivalent representation in FORTRAN. They can be added and subtracted much faster than floating-point numbers, however, so they are used in programs involving decimal fractions where the fastest possible computation speeds are required.

The extended floating constant statement (operation code XFLC) is used to create extended precision floating-point constants occupying three adjacent words in core memory, identical in format to the extended precision real constants used in FORTRAN. The constants are written in the operand field of an assembly language statement exactly like floating-point constants in a DEC statement. Examples are 8.87, 4.56E3, 12.9E–6 and –1467.E–4. Any label present is assigned to the leftmost or first of the three memory words used to store the constant.

The extended binary coded statement (operation code EBC) is used to create a string of words, each containing two 8-bit characters in EBCDIC code. As many as 36 characters may be stored in as many as 18 words by a single EBC statement. The string of characters must begin and end with a period to define the end points of the string; the periods are not stored in memory. Any label used is assigned to the first word in the resulting word string. For example, .NEXT PAGE. would fill five words, with the fifth word containing the E from PAGE and a blank character to fill up the word. As another example, .END OF JOB. would also fill five words, with the last word containing OB.

Further examples of all the data definition statements are shown in Figure 12-4.

12-4   Statements to Control the Assembler, Storage Allocation

The following statements are used to control the operation of the Assembler program; they do not directly create either instructions or data in core memory. Examples of the statements are shown in Figure 12-5.

The assemble absolute statement (operation code ABS) indicates that the assembly language main program which follows the ABS statement is to be assembled as an absolute (instead of a relocatable) program. The ABS statement must be the first statement in the program except for comment statements. An absolute main program is assembled with all addresses converted to absolute values. The first instruction of the program, which would be assigned a location of zero in a relocatable assembly, is assigned an absolute address usually determined by an ORG statement. Any subprograms used by the main program are then relocated into successively higher memory locations after the main program is loaded. Notice that all subprograms must be relocatable. Main programs may be either relocatable or absolute. The advantage of absolute assembly is that the resulting object program can be loaded faster because it is not necessary to calculate the relocated addresses during loading. A program which does not start with an ABS statement is always assembled in relocatable mode, as described in Section 11-6.

The define origin statement (operation code ORG) is used to reset the location counter (Section 11-4) to any desired value. The ORG statement starts the program at a specific memory location in an absolute assembly (in which case the ORG statement should immediately follow the ABS statement) or skips a group of memory locations in a relocatable assembly. For example, an ORG with an operand of *+4 would cause the Assembler to skip the next four words of memory, since the * refers to the next available memory location. An ORG referencing an absolute address in a relocatable assembly is an error and is ignored by the Assembler.

The standard precision statement (operation code SPR) indicates that the program which follows will use standard precision for all arithmetic operations. This enables the Assembler to check that any subroutines called by the program do also involve standard precision arithmetic. (This statement is optional and seldom used in practice.)

IBM

IBM 1130 Assembler
Coding Form

Program _____

Programmed by _____

Date _____

Page No. 12-4 of _____

Label 21 25	Operation 27 30	F 32	T 33	Operands & Remarks 35	Identification 75 80
IOCC1	DC			0 EXAMPLE OF IOCC FOR STACKER	
	DC			/1480 SELECT ON 1442, SECT. 12=1	
DATA1	DC			46 CONSTANT OF 46 IN DECIMAL	
DATA2	DC			/2E CONSTANT OF 46 IN HEXADECIMAL	
DATA3	DC			A CONSTANT CHARACTER A	
DATA4	DEC			-47 12-WORD INTEGER CONSTANT OF -47	
DATA5	DEC			6.53 2-WORD REAL CONSTANT OF 6.53	
DATA6	DEC			9.2B9 2-WORD FIXED POINT BINARY CONST	
DATA7	XFLC			6.53 3-WORD REAL CONSTANT OF 6.53	
DATA8	EBC			.START JOB. 5-WORD CHARACTER STRING	

Figure 12-4 Examples of Data Definition Statements

IBM 1130 Assembler
Coding Form

Form X26 5994 0
Printed in U.S.A.

Program _____

Programmed by _____

Date _____

Page No. _12-5_ of _____

Label	Operation	F	T	Operands & Remarks	Identification
	ABS			SPECIFY ABSOLUTE ASSEMBLY	
	ORG			*+2 ASSEMBLER TO SKIP NEXT 2 WORDS	
	ORG			4000 ASSEMBLER TO START AT 4000	
	SPR			ASSEMBLE WITH STANDARD PRECISION	
	EPR			ASSEMBLE WITH EXTENDED PRECISION	
	END			END OF PROGRAM	
BLOK1	BSS			60 60-WORD BLOCK STARTING AT BLOK1	
BLOK2	BSS	E		60 ASSIGN EVEN ADDRESS TO BLOK2	
BLOK3	BES			60 60-WORD BLOCK ENDING AT BLOK3	
BLOK4	EQU			BLOK1 BLOK4 GETS ADDRESS OF BLOK1	
BLOK5	EQU			BLOK1+30 BLOK5 ADDRESS IS BLOK1+30	

Figure 12-5 Examples of Control and Storage Allocation Statements

An *extended precision statement (operation code EPR)* is also available to indicate that the following program will use extended precision arithmetic exclusively, so that the Assembler program can check that all subroutines also use extended precision. (This statement also is optional and seldom used.)

The *END statement (operation code END)* indicates the end of an assembly language program. It is the last statement in the program, and serves the same purpose as does the END statement in FORTRAN. In an assembly language main program the END statement should contain the address of the first executable instruction in the operands field, to indicate where execution of the program should start after the assembled program is loaded into core memory. It is not necessary to indicate the starting address for subprograms.

It is frequently desirable to assign a single symbolic name to a block or string of data words in memory. In FORTRAN this is handled via the DIMENSION statement; in assembly language it is handled by the block start symbol (BSS) and block end symbol (BES) statements.

The *block start symbol statement (operation code BSS)* contains an absolute value or expression in its operand field to indicate the number of words in the block. The symbol in the label field then becomes the address of the first (lowest addressed) word in the block. The indicated number of words is reserved by the Assembler, but the words are nto cleared to zero or any other initial value. The assembly language program containing the BSS statement must initialize the block. Any symbols appearing in the operand field must have been defined in (appeared in the label field of) previous statements, because the Assembler must be able to determine the size of the block immediately upon encountering the BSS statement.

A letter E in column 32 of a BSS statement will cause the block to start at the next available even-numbered memory location. This facility is useful in setting up blocks to be processed by the double precision arithmetic instructions (Section 11-9). A BSS statement with an operand of zero and an E in column 32 will not reserve any words but will cause the location counter to assign the following statement to an even-numbered location; such a BSS can ensure that a subsequent group of statements will start at an even location.

The *block end symbol statement (operation code BES)* is identical to the BSS statement above except that the symbol in the label field now becomes the address of the word following the last (highest addressed) word in the block.

Notice that arrays in FORTRAN are stored in memory in reverse order; ITEM(50) will be assigned to a location 49 words lower than the location assigned to ITEM(1), assuming that ITEM is an array of one-word integers. In assembly language the storing of data into arrays or blocks is handled directly by the programmer in either forward or reverse order. This can cause problems when arrays created by

FORTRAN programs must be processed by assembly language subprograms unless the programmer is careful to remember that FORTRAN arrays are always stored backwards.

The equate symbol statement (operation code EQU) assigns the value of an address or expression in the operand field to a symbol in the label field. As in the BSS statement, all symbols appearing in the operand field must have appeared previously in the same program as labels. The EQU statement is the only statement which does not cause a symbol appearing in the label field to be assigned a value from the location counter.

12-5   Subprogram Linkage Statements

The CALL statement (operation code CALL) is the primary means of calling a subprogram from an assembly language main program or subprogram. The operand field contains the entry point of the program to be called. The Assembler handles the CALL statement by assembling a two-word BSI to the entry point. The loader then substitutes the relocated address of the subprogram for the entry point name when the subprogram is loaded. A special code is used to indicate to the loader that this instruction is a BSI generated from a CALL statement.

When the CALL statement is executed, the address of the next word following the CALL is stored at location of the subprogram entry point, and execution starts at the word immediately following the entry point. To return to the calling program (which may be in either FORTRAN or assembly language) we need only transfer to the return address stored at the subprogram entry point. If arguments are to be transmitted to the subprogram, they are listed in DC statements immediately following the CALL statement. If arguments are used, it is then necessary to add a constant equal to the number of arguments to the return address stored at the entry point so as to return to the word following the last argument. The return address at the entry point is also used to pick up the argument values for use in the subprogram.

The entry point statement (operation code ENT) defines the entry point(s) of each subprogram. The operand field of each ENT statement contains the symbolic address of the first instruction to be executed when that entry point is called. As we shall see in Chapter 13, it is frequently desirable to combine related subprograms into a single subprogram with several different entry points or several different names by which the subprogram may be called to perform different tasks. Any one subprogram may have up to ten entry points defined by ten ENT statements. All of the ENT statements for a subprogram must be grouped together ahead of all other statements in the subprogram except SPR, EPR and LIBR. The ENT statement is used with all subprograms except for interrupt service subprograms (ISS) and interrupt level subprograms (ILS).

The interrupt service entry point statement (operation code ISS) is used in place of ENT to define the single entry point of a subroutine designed to be executed by the computer when the computer receives an interrupt signal. An interrupt signal usually indicates that something has happened outside of the computer which requires immediate processing. For example, several of the input-output devices send an interrupt signal back to the comptuer to indicate that the devices have completed a transfer of data to or from the computer. Further discussion of interrupts can be found in Section 13-4.

The interrupt level subroutine statement (operation code ILS) is also used in place of ENT to define the single entry point of a subroutine to determine which of several interrupts has occurred. The 1130 provides six different priority levels to determine the relative priority of the different interrupts which may occur. Several different interrupt signals may be wired to the same priority level, so each level requires an interrupt level subroutine to determine which interrupt on that level has signalled the computer. These subroutines are normally part of the IBM program library and a user would not write them unless he wished to change the way in which IBM controlled the input-output devices. Because such a change requires access to various IBM manuals to provide detailed information on how the equipment operates, the details of ISS and ILS programming for the 1130 are not developed in this book.

The call transfer vector statement (operation code LIBF) is another way (besides the CALL statement) to call a subprogram. The LIBF creates a one-word linkage to the subprogram through use of a transfer vector, a table containing the locations of the subprogram (as established by the relocating loader) and the word immediately following the calling statement. The LIBF statement is written with the subprogram entry point in the operand field, just like the CALL statement. Any arguments are listed in DC statements immediately following the LIBF statement. The actual linkage to the subprogram is effected by a BSI executed from the transfer vector. The transfer vector contains the return address of the calling program. The loader stores the address of the transfer vector at the entry point +2 in the subprogram. Thus the second word following the entry point contains the address of the address of the return address or of the first argument. If arguments are used, the return address is incremented by the number of arguments as described under the CALL statement.

The transfer vector requires three words in memory for each subprogram to be called by an LIBF statement. When the subprogram is executed, the first word contains the address of the word following the LIBF call, the second word begins a two-word BSC instruction, and the third word contains the address of the subprogram entry point (the second word of the BSC instruction). The LIBF statement is assembled as a one-word BSI to the appropriate transfer vector location using IR3. For this reason index register 3 is reserved for use by the LIBF linkage and the register must be saved and restored to its initial value before executing any LIBF statement. An easy way around this problem is to avoid using IR3 in any group of linked programs using the LIBF statement.

The transfer vector subroutine statement (operation code LIBR) enables the Assembler and loader to distinguish between subroutines called by the CALL statement and other subroutines called by the LIBF statement. The LIBR statement, containing no operand, must be the very first statement in any subprogram to be called by an LIBF statement. It must not be used in main programs or subprograms to be called by a CALL statement.

All assembly language subprograms called by the FORTRAN CALL statement must be set up for the CALL statement linkage, not the LIBF linkage. Several examples of the CALL statement linkage are presented later in this chapter. A single example of the LIBF linkage is presented here. The LIBF linkage cannot be used with FORTRAN programs except to call programs in the IBM library.

Consider a subprogram called DOG involving two arguments. DOG would be called via an LIBF as follows:

```
LIBF        DOG          CALL THE DOG SUBPROGRAM
DC          ARG1         NAME (ADDRESS) OF 1ST ARGUMENT
DC          ARG2         NAME OF 2ND ARGUMENT
(Program continues here after executing DOG.)
```

The DOG subprogram might be coded as follows:

```
        LIBR                 SPECIFY LIBF LINKAGE
        ENT      DOG         ENTRY POINT MATCHES LIBF CALL
DOG     STX    1 SAVE1+1     SAVE INDEX REGISTER 1
        LDX   I1 0           LOAD TRANSFER VECTOR ADDRESS
        LD    I1 0           LOAD 1ST ARGUMENT INTO THE ACC
        S     I1 1           SUBTRACT 2ND ARGUMENT
        STO   I1 0           STORE DIFF IN 1ST ARG
        MDX    1 2           INCREMENT IR1 BY NO. OF ARGS=2
        STX    1 DONE+1      STORE ADJUSTED RETURN ADDRESS
SAVE1   LDX   L1 0           PICK UP SAVED VALUE IN IR1
DONE    BSC    L 0           RETURN TO CALLING PROGRAM
        END                  END OF THE DOG SUBPROGRAM
```

It can be seen that all the DOG subprogram does is to subtract the value of the second argument from the first argument and store the difference in the first argument. The linkage involves the use of the LIBF, LIBR and ENT statements. The first executable instruction at DOG saves IR1, and the following LDX statement loads IR1 with the address in the transfer vector containing the address of the LIBF+1 which

256

in turn contains the address of the first argument. The indirect LDX followed by an indexed indirect load gets the first argument into the accumulator.

The MDX increments the contents of IR1 by the number of arguments (2). The STX then stores the contents of IR1 as the address of a long BSC instruction, which is executed after restoring the original contents of IR1. The details of saving and restoring the original contents of the index register, picking up the arguments and adjusting the return address are basic to any LIBF subroutine and should be studied carefully.

The DOG subprogram would be coded somewhat differently if it were to be called via a CALL statement. In that case the calling sequence would be as follows:

```
CALL        DOG           CALL THE DOG SUBPROGRAM
DC          ARG1          NAME (ADDRESS) OF 1ST ARGUMENT
DC          ARG2          NAME OF 2ND ARGUMENT
(Program continues here after executing DOG.)
```

The DOG subprogram might now be coded as follows:

```
        ENT        DOG        ENTRY POINT
DOG     DC         0          ADDRESS CALL+1 LOADED HERE
        STX    1   SAVE1+1    SAVE INDEX REGISTER 1
        LDX    I1  DOG        1ST ARGUMENT ADDRESS INTO IR1
        LD     I1  0          LOAD 1ST ARGUMENT IN THE ACC
        S      I1  1          SUBTRACT 2ND ARGUMENT
        STO    I1  0          STORE DIFFERENCE IN 1ST ARGUMENT
        MDX    1   2          INCREMENT IR1 BY NO. OF ARGS=2
        STX    1   DONE+1     STORE ADJUSTED RETURN ADDRESS
SAVE1   LDX    L1  0          PICK UP SAVED VALUE IN IR1
DONE    BSC    L   0          RETURN TO CALLING PROGRAM
        END                   END OF THE DOG SUBPROGRAM
```

The only change in the subprogram caused by the CALL statement is that DOG now receives the address of the address of the first argument, where in the LIBF example the transfer vector held this information. As a result DOG contains a DC which makes it one word longer than the equivalent LIBF subprogram. The LIBR statement is removed, and the three-word transfer vector entry no longer exists.

12-6   Further Examples of FORTRAN Object Code

We are now in a position to examine the assembly language representation of FORTRAN object code involving floating-point variables. Consider the following FORTRAN statement:

A = B

where A and B are real (floating-point) variables. The FORTRAN compiler will
generate the following operations:

```
LIBF     FLD          FLD IS FLOATING  LOAD SUBROUTINE
DC       B            LOAD THE VARIABLE B
LIBF     FSTO         FSTO IS FLOATING STORE ROUTINE
DC       A            STORE THE RESULT IN A
```

The above code simply calls the floating load subroutine from the subroutine library,
loads B, calls the floating store subroutine, and stores the result in A. Subroutines,
required because there are no instructions in machine language to perform floating-
point arithmetic, have been written by IBM to perform all floating-point functions.
The FORTRAN statement

I = A

similarly compiles into

```
LIBF     FLD          FLOATING LOAD SUBROUTINE
DC       A            PICK UP THE VARIABLE A
LIBF     IFIX         CONVERT A TO INTEGER VARIABLE
STO   L  I            STORE THE RESULT IN I
```

Here IFIX is the subroutine to convert real variables to integers. The variable A is
the argument for the FLD subroutine; the IFIX subroutine expects to find its argument in the floating-point pseudo accumulator, a block of three words set aside by
the compiler for floating-point subroutines to use. Thus IFIX has no argument
address and needs no DC statement. Remember that the FORTRAN compiler compiles directly to machine language code; we are examining how this machine language
code might look if it were programmed in assembly language. The FORTRAN compiler does not compile the FORTRAN statements into assembly language form.

Now consider the FORTRAN statement

A = I

which compiles into

```
LD    L  I            PICK UP THE VARIABLE I
LIBF     FLOAT        CONVERT I TO A REAL VARIABLE
LIBF     FSTO         FLOATING STORE SUBROUTINE
DC       A            STORE THE RESULT IN A
```

Multiplication requires a subroutine call from FORTRAN, even in integer
arithmetic, because the needed low-order bits of the product end up in the EXT
register where extra instructions are required to get them out. Accordingly the

258

FORTRAN statement

$$I = J * K$$

compiles into

```
LD     L   J        PICK UP THE VARIABLE J
LIBF       IMUL     INTEGER MULTIPLICATION SUBROUTINE
DC         K        MULTIPLY BY K
STO    L   I        STORE RESULT IN I
```

A floating-point multiplication, such as

$$A = B * C$$

compiles as

```
LIBF       FLD      FLOATING LOAD SUBROUTINE
DC         B        LOAD THE VARIABLE B
LIBF       FMPY     FLOATING MULTIPLY SUBROUTINE
DC         C        MULTIPLY BY C
LIBF       FSTO     FLOATING STORE SUBROUTINE
DC         A        STORE RESULT IN A
```

Now, for a final arithmetic example, consider the FORTRAN statement

$$A = B ** (C+D)$$

which compiles into all of the following:

```
LIBF       FLD      FLOATING LOAD SUBROUTINE
DC         C        LOAD THE VARIABLE C
LIBF       FADD     FLOATING ADD SUBROUTINE
DC         D        ADD THE VARIABLE D
LIBF       FSTO     FLOATING STORE SUBROUTINE
DC         TEMP     STORE RESULT TEMPORARILY (C+D)
LIBF       FLD      FLOATING LOAD SUBROUTINE
DC         B        LOAD THE VARIABLE B
LIBF       FAXB     FLOATING EXPONENT SUBROUTINE
DC         TEMP     CALCULATES B**TEMP
LIBF       FSTO     FLOATING STORE SUBROUTINE
DC         A        STORE RESULT (FINALLY) IN A
```

Notice that FORTRAN object programs consist of one subroutine call after another, with the subroutines doing all the work. The compiler merely figures out the most efficient sequence in which to call the many subroutines.

Subscripts in FORTRAN statements require the use of yet another subroutine to evaluate each variable subscript. The subscript subroutine calculates the number of

259

words which must be added to the base address of the array (the address of the first variable, with a subscript of one) to get the address of a particular subscript combination within the array. Arguments for the subscript subroutine include the current subscript variables plus the original dimensions of the array involved.

Consider the subscripted FORTRAN statement

$$A(I, J) = B(I, J) + C(I, J)$$

which compiles into

LIBF	SUBSC	CALL SUBSCRIPT SUBROUTINE
DC	SGT1	PUT RESULT IN SGT1 AND IN IR1
DC	constant	DIMENSION CONSTANT
DC	I	VALUE OF I SUBSCRIPT
DC	constant	DIMENSION CONSTANT
DC	J	VALUE OF J SUBSCRIPT
DC	constant	DIMENSION CONSTANT
LIBF	FLDX	CALL FLOATING LOAD INDEXED
DC	B	LOAD THE VARIABLE B(I, J)
LIBF	FADDX	CALL FLOATING ADD INDEXED
DC	C	ADD THE VARIABLE C(I, J)
LIBF	FSTOX	CALL FLOATING STORE INDEXED
DC	A	STORE RESULT IN A(I, J)

Notice that, since all the subscripts in the FORTRAN statement are identical, the compiler is smart enough to calculate them only once. This kind of optimization is very difficult to build into compilers, and the early FORTRAN compilers (in the 1950's) tended to produce inefficient object programs through just such inefficiencies as redundantly computing extra subscripts. The above example uses special indexed subroutines to load, add and store, using subscripts previously calculated by the subscript subroutine.

Now let us consider a FORTRAN statement which calls a function subprogram:

$$A = CAT(B + C, D)$$

Here we have a CAT subprogram with two floating-point arguments. The compiled code is as follows:

LIBF	FLD	CALL FLOATING LOAD
DC	B	LOAD THE VARIABLE B
LIBF	FADD	CALL FLOATING ADD
DC	C	ADD THE VARIABLE C
LIBF	FSTO	CALL FLOATING STORE
DC	TEMP	STORE RESULT TEMPORARILY
CALL	CAT	THAT'S RIGHT, CALL CAT

```
DC        TEMP        FIRST ARGUMENT IS TEMP
DC        D           SECOND ARGUMENT IS D
LIBF      FSTO        CALL FLOATING STORE
DC        A           STORE RESULT IN A
```

The CAT subprogram must leave its result in the floating-point accumulator because CAT is a function subprogram, and function subprograms return only a single result. Consider the FORTRAN CALL statement

CALL CAT(B, C + D)

where the result will be stored in the variable B. This compiles to

```
LIBF      FLD         CALL FLOATING LOAD
DC        C           LOAD THE VARIABLE C
LIBF      FADD        CALL FLOATING ADD
DC        D           ADD THE VARIABLE D
LIBF      FSTO        CALL FLOATING STORE
DC        TEMP        STORE RESULT TEMPORARILY
CALL      CAT         CALL CAT SUBPROGRAM
DC        B           FIRST ARGUMENT IS B
DC        TEMP        SECOND ARGUMENT IS IN TEMP
```

FORTRAN READ and WRITE statements are also handled by LIBF calls to subroutines, including subroutines to convert numbers from EBCDIC code to integer and floating-point format and vice versa. As a final example, the FORTRAN READ statement

READ (NREAD, 21) A, I

compiles to

```
LIBF      EREAD       CALL EREAD SUBROUTINE
DC        NREAD       I/O UNIT IS NREAD
DC        21          FORMAT NUMBER 21
LIBF      IOF         CALL FLOATING CONVERSION
DC        A           CONVERT INPUT VARIABLE A
LIBF      IOI         CALL INTEGER CONVERSION
DC        I           CONVERT INPUT VARIABLE I
```

These examples show the compactness and readability of FORTRAN statements as compared to assembly language.

12-7 Assembly Control Records

Source programs consisting of assembly language statements may be assembled into machine language instructions by Assembler programs stored on cards or paper tape or by Assembler programs stored in disk storage under control of the Disk Monitor. Certain control records precede the statements to be assembled to define various options of the assembly process. These control records are similar in purpose to the FORTRAN control records described in Section 4-1.

All of the assembly control records are punched with an asterisk in column 1, followed by the control information in columns 2 to 71. The control records may be in any sequence. The control words should be separated by blanks. A list of the assembly control records follows:

* TWO PASS MODE	(Disk Monitor only)
* LIST	
* LIST DECK	(Disk Monitor only)
* LIST DECK E	(Disk Monitor only)
* PRINT SYMBOL TABLE	
* PUNCH SYMBOL TABLE	(Disk Monitor only)
* SAVE SYMBOL TABLE	(Disk Monitor only)
* SYSTEM SYMBOL TABLE	(Disk Monitor only)
* LEVEL n	
* FILE n	(Disk Monitor only)
* COMMON n	

The * TWO PASS MODE record indicates that two passes (loadings) of the source statements will be made during the assembly process. The Disk Monitor usually requires a single pass, while the card and paper tape assemblers always require two passes of the source statements. This record is not used with card or paper tape system assemblies, since two passes are mandatory. This record is required if * LIST DECK or * LIST DECK E is used.

* LIST causes the assembled machine language instructions to be printed side by side with the source program statements.

* LIST DECK causes the monitor assembler to punch the assembled instructions into columns 1-19 of the source statement cards. If the source statements are on paper tape, then a list deck is not punched. * TWO PASS MODE is required; the assembled instructions are punched on the second pass.

* LIST DECK E causes only the Assembler error codes (Appendix B) to be punched on columns 18-19 of the source statements.

* PRINT SYMBOL TABLE causes the symbol table to be printed, five symbols per line, with multiply-defined symbols preceded by an M and absolute symbols in a relocatable program preceded with an A. (A multiply-defined symbol is one which appears in the label field of two or more statements.)

262

* PUNCH SYMBOL TABLE causes the symbol table to be punched on cards as a set of EQU source cards. These cards can then be used as input for a * SAVE SYMBOL TABLE. A symbol table may also be listed on an off-line printer.

* SAVE SYMBOL TABLE saves the symbol table generated by the current assembly on the disk as a system symbol table which may then be used to permit several programs to exchange data and program locations via a common system symbol table. This record must be used only with absolute assemblies.

* SYSTEM SYMBOL TABLE causes a system symbol table previously saved by a * SAVE SYMBOL TABLE record to be merged with the symbol table generated by the current assembly. The currently assembled program thus has access to all of the symbol definitions saved previously. If the currently assembled program is an absolute program, * SAVE SYMBOL TABLE may also be specified to add the symbols from the current program to the system symbol table. The symbols in the system symbol table will all have absolute values.

* LEVEL n assigns interrupt level n, where n is an integer from zero to five, to the program following. The program must be an interrupt level subroutine (ILS).

* FILE n causes n sectors at the beginning of disk working storage area to be reserved for the program being assembled before any LOCALs or SOCALs are stored. (Not valid for Disk Monitor System Version 2.)

* COMMON n causes n words of the FORTRAN COMMON area to be saved when the assembled program is loaded for execution, so that the assembled program may use FORTRAN variables in the COMMON area of core memory.

No provision is made for naming assembly language programs by an * NAME control record as used in FORTRAN. Assembly language subprograms are named by the first ENT statement, and assembly language main programs are named by the DUP control record *STORE, which assigns a program name of as many as five characters.

12-8 Assembly Under Control of the Card and Paper Tape Systems

Assembly under the card or paper tape systems (without the use of the Disk Monitor) is a multipass operation. First a deck or tape consisting of a loader program, followed by the Assembler program, followed by the source program is fed into the computer. The source program consists of statements in assembly language to be assembled into a machine language program. During the first pass the Assembler creates a symbol table which lists the address (relative to zero) of all symbols used in the source program.

After the computer stops at the end of the first pass, the source program must be fed into the computer a second time. Now the assembled instructions and any resulting error codes are punched into columns 1-20 of the source program cards or tape. The source program can then be listed on an off-line printer (such as an IBM type 407), on the console typewriter or the type 1132 printer through utility programs furnished by IBM. Notice that in the card system the actual source cards contain the assembled instructions, while in the paper tape system the source tape is repunched along with the assembled instructions.

The punched output from the second pass is not yet in a form that can be loaded and executed by the computer. Now we must load a compressor program, followed by the output from the second pass, followed by a deck of blank cards. The blank cards will receive the compressed object program which may then be loaded for execution behind a relocating binary loader program. One more pass is required if we want to get the deck into core image (nonrelocatable) format.

The FORTRAN compiler, by comparison, does all of its work in a single pass. Since one FORTRAN statement does the work of many assembly language statements, the FORTRAN source program contains far fewer statements than an equivalent assembly source program and so will compile even faster than one would assume from the number of passes required. As we will see in the next section, assembly is a one-pass operation under Disk Monitor control. Anyone with much assembly language work to do would be well advised to add disk storage to his computer.

It is poor programming practice to write a single program in assembly language larger than 200 or 300 statements. As in FORTRAN programming, big programs should always be written as collections of small subprograms to facilitate debugging and documentation. If you insist upon writing monster programs, then you may find that you are using more symbols than the Assembler can contain within the symbol table. Approximately 300 symbols can be used in a 4092-word computer, 1600 symbols in 8192 words and 4300 symbols in a 16384-word computer. If you receive an error message that you have exceeded the symbol table capacity, then you must break the program into subprograms and assemble the subprograms separately.

12-9   Assembly Under 1130 Disk Monitor Control

Assembly under monitor control is normally a one-pass operation. The deck or tape to be assembled is preceded by a // ASM monitor control record, as described in Section 7-5. An assembly language main program or subprogram may be part of a job (headed by a // JOB record) which includes other assembly language programs and other FORTRAN programs. As the assembly language statements are read by the Assembler the symbol table is created and the statements are written on

264

the disk, where they can be retrieved by the Assembler a few seconds later to complete the assembly process. After assembly, the programs may be stored on the disk through the use of // DUP and *STORE records identical to those used by FORTRAN. The // XEQ record may be used for execution. A subprogram with several entry points (ENT statements) is always stored by referring to the name of its first entry point.

Three additional statements are available in assembly language programs executed under monitor control. These statements are LINK, EXIT and DSA (define sector address).

The LINK statement (operation code LINK) is used to load and execute another main program from disk storage. The operand field must contain the name of a main program (FORTRAN or assembly language) previously stored and listed in the location equivalence table of the disk. The LINK statement produces four words of object code: two words are used to transfer to the monitor supervisor and the remaining two words contain the program name (in a chopped six-bit EBCDIC code) which the supervisor will use in calling in the next core load. All subprograms required by the new main program will automatically be loaded with it.

The EXIT statement (operation code EXIT) functions just like the CALL EXIT statement in FORTRAN; it simply returns control to the monitor which then processes the next monitor control record and proceeds with the next compilation, assembly or execution. A two-word branch to the monitor supervisor program is produced by the EXIT statement. No operand is required. EXIT returns control to the monitor; LINK passes control to the program named in the LINK statement.

The define sector address statement (operation code DSA) assigns a symbolic name to the disk address of a program or data block. As new blocks of information are added to and deleted from the disk the disk addresses of the remaining blocks change as the working storage area is compacted by DUP. The DSA statement reserves three memory words which are filled in when the program containing the DSA is loaded for execution. The first word contains the length in words of the block to be read, the second word contains the disk sector address of the block, and the third word contains the address within the block at which execution should start if the block is to be executed as a program.

The operand of a DSA statement is simply the name of a program or data block as previously defined by an *STORE operation under DUP control. The DSA statement is normally used with the disk input-output subroutines DISK0, DISK1 and DISKN which are discussed in Chapter 13.

A heading statement (operation code HDNG) is provided on the 1130 system to furnish page headings when the assembled program is printed under monitor control during the assembly process. The operand field in columns 35-71 may contain any desired heading information. When the HDNG statement is encountered by the Assembler, the 1132 Printer ejects to the top of the next page (skips to channel one) and prints the heading information there. The same information will be printed at the top of each succeeding page until another HDNG statement is encountered.

Another option available under monitor control is the list statement (operation code LIST), which can be used to list part of a program during assembly as follows:

1) ON in the operand field will cause the Assembler to start listing with the next statement.

2) OFF in the operand field will cause the Assembler to stop listing.

3) Nothing in the operand field will cause the Assembler to start listing if at the beginning of an assembly, or to stop listing if not at the beginning of an assembly.

The space statement (operation code SPAC) is another monitor option which will space a number of lines on the listing printer equal to the value of the expression in the operand field.

The eject statement (operation code EJCT) is a monitor option which causes the listing printer to jump to the top of the next page to continue the listing at that point.

A dump statement (operation code DUMP) permits a dump of core memory to be made at the end of program execution. Three parameters separated by commas must be specified in the operand field:

1) An expression equal to the lowest addressed core location to be dumped

2) An expression equal to the highest addressed core location to be dumped

3) A format digit, either blank or zero

Regardless of the format digit the dump is 16 words per line in hexadecimal format, with the address of the first word printed at the left. After dumping, a CALL EXIT is executed to bring in the next monitor job.

The ability to dump and then continue execution is provided by the PDMP statement (operation code PDMP), a monitor option similar to DUMP except for the operation code. After PDMP has executed, control goes to the next statement in the program.

The define file statement (operation code FILE) is similar to the DEFINE FILE statement in FORTRAN (Section 7-8) in that it defines the files to be used in a main program and, through the use of *FILES control records, equates the files to previously assigned files in the User Area or the Fixed Area on the disk. Five parameters separated by commas must be specified in the operand field:

1) A file identification number, ranging from 1 to 32767

2) An integer defining the number of records in the file

3) An integer (1-320) defining the number of words in each record

4) The letter U, indicating that the file will be read without conversion

5) The label of a variable which will contain the number of the next available file record after reading or writing to the disk

The FILE statement can only be used in main programs; subprograms must then use the files defined by the main program.

Examples of the monitor assembly statements are shown in Figure 12-6.

12-10 A Stacker Select Subroutine for the 1442 Card Read Punch

As an example of a program which is easy to write in assembly language but almost impossible to write in FORTRAN, consider a subprogram to select the alternate stacker on the 1442 so that all cards containing a one in column 80 will be selected out of a deck of cards passing through the card reader. We shall write this subprogram as part of a job consisting of an assembly language subprogram to select the stacker and a FORTRAN main program to decide when the stacker should be selected, together with the necessary control records for the Assembler, compiler and the Disk Monitor.

The program listing for the complete job is as follows:

```
// JOB T
// ASM
*  LIST
                ENT         STACK      NAME OF ROUTINE IS STACK
        IOCC1   DC          0          FIRST WORD OF IOCC
                DC          /1480      SECOND WORD OF IOCC
        STACK   DC          0          RETURN ADDRESS GOES HERE
                XIO         IOCC1      SELECT THE STACKER
                BSC     I   STACK      RETURN TO CALLING PROGRAM
                END
// DUP
*STORE      WS  UA STACK
```

267

IBM

IBM 1130 Assembler
Coding Form

Program _____

Programmed by _____

Date _____

Page No. 12-6 of _____

Label	Operation	F	T	Operands & Remarks	Identification
	LINK			PROG2 LINK TO PROGRAM 2 (PROG2)	
	EXIT			EXIT TO MONITOR, END JOB.	
LP3	DSA			PROG3 LP3 IS DISK ADDR OF PROG3.	
	HDNG			HEADING INFORMATION IN COLUMNS 35-71	
	LIST			ON START PROGRAM LISTING	
	LIST			OFF STOP PROGRAM LISTING	
	SPAC			15 SPACE LISTING FOR 15 LINES	
	EJCT			EJECT LISTING TO NEXT PAGE	
	DUMP			START,STOP, DUMP FROM START TO STOP	
	PDMP			BEGIN,3000, DUMP FROM BEGIN TO 3000	
	FILE			21,10,200,U,NEXT	

* ABOVE IS FILE 21, 10 RECORDS OF 200 WORDS EACH

Figure 12-6 Examples of the Monitor Assembly Statements

```
// FOR
**  TEST PROGRAM FOR STACKER SELECT SUBPROGRAM
*  NAME TEST
*  IOCS (CARD)
*  ONE WORD INTEGERS
*  LIST ALL
        DIMENSION NCARD(80)
1       FORMAT (80A1)
2       READ (2, 1) NCARD
        IF (NCARD(80) + 3776) 2, 3, 2
C-----THE INTEGER EQUIVALENT CODE FOR 1 IS -3776, SEE SEC. 10-4
3       CALL STACK
        GO TO 2
        END
// XEQ
```

First we start the job with a // JOB T record, indicating that this is a temporary job not to be stored upon the disk for future use. After calling in the Assembler and asking for a listing of the program to be assembled, we can write the stacker select subprogram in seven assembly language statements starting with ENT.

The IOCC consists of a first word which is unused and a second word which contains an area code of 00010 for the 1442, a function code of 100 for control and a modifier field of 10000000 as described in Section 12-1. The second word thus contains the bit pattern 0001010010000000 which is 1480 as a hexadecimal constant. The rest of the assembly language statements constitute the subprogram linkage statements described in Section 12-5 for a subprogram to be called by a CALL statement in either FORTRAN or assembly language.

After temporarily storing the assembled STACK program through the use of a // DUP control record (Section 7-6), we call in the FORTRAN compiler to compile TEST, a program to test the STACK subprogram. The TEST program reads a card at statement 2 and calls the STACK subprogram if the card contains a one in column 80 as determined by the IF statement. The IF statement compares column 80 with the integer equivalent code for a one in A1 format as described in Section 10-4. If the STACK subprogram is called, the card which has just been read will be selected into the alternate stacker when the next card is read. The stacker selection will remain in effect only for a single card.

An // XEQ record causes TEST to be executed, and TEST will automatically load STACK as one of the subprograms called by TEST. The data cards to be stacker selected would follow immediately behind the // XEQ record.

12-11 Additional Data Definition Statements

The 1130 Disk Monitor Version 2 includes two additional data definition statements, define name (DN) and define message (DMES).

The define name statement (operation code DN) is used to pack a name of five characters or less into a two-word (32 bit) constant. If a label is used, the label is assigned the address of the first word of the constant. A special six-bit code is used to express five characters in only two words. Up to five characters may be specified in the operand field. DN may be used to modify LINK statements during execution.

The define message statement (operation code DMES) is used to create a message within a Disk Monitor program in a format that can be used by the printer output subroutines. If a label is used, the label is assigned the address of the first word of the message. The tag bit position (column 33) must be specified as zero for the console printer, one for the 1403 Printer, or two for the 1132 Printer. The operand field may contain any string of message characters, including printer control characters.

The following control characters may be used in DMES statements:

Control Character	Function	Limitation
'X	Blank	Same as space ('S)
'T	Tabulate	Console printer only
'D	Backspace	Console printer only
'B	Black ribbon	Console printer only
'A	Red ribbon	Console printer only
'S	Space	Same as blank ('X)
'R	Carriage return	Console printer only
'L	Line feed	Console printer only
'F	Repeat next character	
'E	End of message	
'b (b=blank)	Continue on next DMES	

The control character 'F applies only to message characters. The control characters can be repeated up to 99 times by placing the number of control functions desired between the apostrophe and the control character. For example, '20L will produce 20 line feeds. The control character 'b will cause the message to continue on a following DMES statement; in this way long messages can be created. The control

270

character 'E should be at the end of each message not continued to another state-ment; if both 'E and 'b are missing, the message will terminate in column 71.

12-12 Summary

This chapter completes our presentation of the elements of assembly lan-guage programming. We are now ready to consider in detail the problems of using assembly language to solve various problems in data manipulation which cannot be solved conveniently in the FORTRAN language. Chapter 13 will provide further examples of assembly language subprograms together with a discussion of the large library of subroutines supplied by IBM to ease some of the burdens of assembly language programming.

12-13 Problems

1)   Assuming an address of 5000 (in decimal) and a modifier field of 00000000 (in binary), write DC statements for the IOCC's which would be required to

     a)   write a word to the 1627 Plotter on an 1130 system

     b)   read a word from the paper tape reader on an 1130 system

     c)   sense the device status word of the console typewriter on an 1130 system

2)   Write data definition (Section 12-3) statements for the following:

     a)   decimal constants of 3, 91, 42, 129 and 3498

     b)   the above decimal constants converted to hexadecimal constants

     c)   floating-point constants of 93.6, −4.0 E03, 5.301 and 10

     d)   the above as extended floating-point constants

     e)   the EBCDIC character string HERE WE GO AGAIN

3)   Why must all assembly language subprograms be assembled in relocatable mode?

4)   In writing an assembly language subprogram to be called exclusively by other assembly language programs, what factors determine whether the subprogram should be called with an LIBF or a CALL statement?

271

5) In the DOG subprogram of Section 12-5, what address is loaded
   into IR1? By which assembly language statement in the subprogram?

6) Write the equivalent assembly language statements for the following
   FORTRAN statements:

   a) A = B + C

   b) I = J * K + L

   c) CALL FUN(A, B)

7) Write the equivalent assembly language statements for the following
   FORTRAN statements:

   a) GO TO (5, 10, 15, 20, 25), I

   b) IF (K–10) 5, 6, 7

   c) DO 100 J = 2, 38, 3

8) Write the equivalent assembly language statements for the following
   FORTRAN statements:

   a) WRITE(3, 5) SUM, PROD, ANSER

   b) READ(2, 4) (ITEM(K), K = 1, 10)

   c) FORMAT(1H1, ' THE ANSWER IS', F8.2)

9) When would the control record * PRINT SYMBOL TABLE be
   useful?

10) Why does assembly under the card and paper tape systems require
    two or more passes?

13-1   A Subprogram to Convert from A1 to A2 Format

In Chapter 10 we discussed an assortment of FORTRAN subprograms to manipulate character strings in A1 format. If many characters must be processed, however, the A1 format wastes memory, because only eight bits of each 16-bit word are used. To put all of the bits back to work we should store the characters in A2 format and convert back to A1 format for actual processing of the characters such as editing and zone manipulation. The use of A2 format is particularly desirable if large files of characters must be maintained upon disk storage for inventory control and other commercial applications.

It is very difficult, but not impossible, to write a FORTRAN program which will convert character strings from A1 to A2 format and vice versa. Such a FORTRAN program is left as an exercise for the reader. The program is fairly simple in assembly language and is much more efficient in both memory required and execution time than is the FORTRAN program. Of course we must be able to convert A1 to A2 and A2 to A1, and we can accomplish this by a single assembly language subprogram with two entry points. (In FORTRAN, two separate subprograms would be needed.) The entry point which converts from A1 to A2 we shall call PACK, while the entry point which converts from A2 to A1 we shall call UNPAC.

As we see from the flow diagram of Figure 13-1, UNPAC and PACK are able to share many of the instructions of the combined subprogram. A switch called SWTCH is used to branch to those instructions that cannot be shared. SWTCH is set separately to either pack or unpack immediately after each of the two entry points.

The PACK routine would be called by a FORTRAN statement such as

CALL PACK (JCARD, J, JLAST, KCARD, K)

to pack characters from JCARD(J) through JCARD(JLAST) from the array JCARD into the array KCARD starting at character position KCARD(K). The array at JCARD consists of singly dimensioned one-word integers in A1 format; the characters transmitted to KCARD are in A2 format. An even number of characters is always packed from JCARD; if an odd number is specified by J and JLAST, one extra character after JLAST is packed. The packed characters occupy half as many words in KCARD as the unpacked characters occupied in JCARD.

The UNPAC routine may be called by a FORTRAN statement such as

CALL UNPAC (JCARD, J, JLAST, KCARD, K)

to unpack characters from JCARD(J) through JCARD(JLAST) in A2 format into the KCARD array, starting with position KCARD(K), in A1 format.

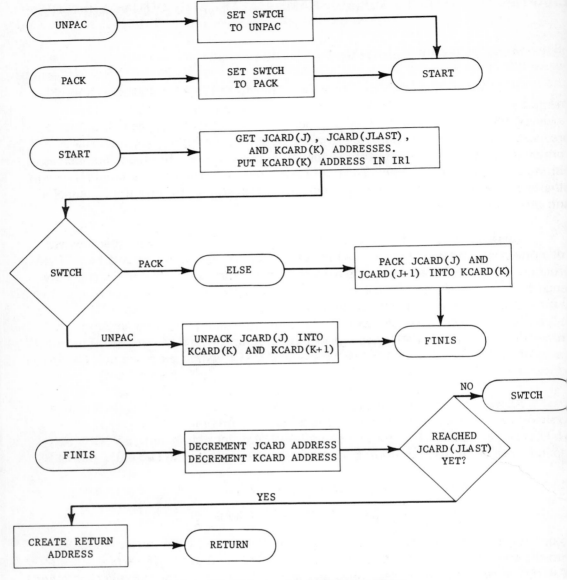

Figure 13-1   Flow Diagram for UNPAC and PACK

Remember that the FORTRAN compiler compiles machine language instructions from the aforementioned FORTRAN CALL statements that are equivalent to the following statements in assembly language:

```
CALL      PACK        (OR CALL UNPAC)
DC        JCARD       ADDRESS OF START OF JCARD ARRAY
DC        J           ADDRESS OF VARIABLE J
DC        JLAST       ADDRESS OF JLAST
```

```
            DC              KCARD          ADDRESS OF START OF KCARD ARRAY
            DC              K              ADDRESS OF K
```

Since we know that the CALL statement in assembly language will execute as a two-word BSI instruction, we know that the address of the first word after the CALL will be transmitted to the entry point of the subprogram when the subprogram is executed. Thus the entry point contains the address of

```
            DC              JCARD
```

which means that the entry point contains the address of the address of the first word in the JCARD array. To get the address of the second argument J, we must increment the address at the entry point by one. The entry point will then contain the address of the address of the variable J.

Now we are ready to take a look at the assembly language statements which comprise the PACK and UNPAC subprogram.

```
            ENT             UNPAC          SUBROUTINE ENTRY POINT
 * CALL UNPAC (JCARD, J, JLAST, KCARD, K)
            ENT             PACK           2ND SUBROUTINE ENTRY POINT
 * CALL PACK (JCARD, J, JLAST, KCARD, K)
UNPAC      DC              0              1ST ARGUMENT ADDRESS GOES HERE
            LD              SW2            PICK UP A NOP INSTRUCTION
            STO             SWTCH          STORE THE NOP AT SWTCH
            MDX             START          GO TO START FOR JOINT ROUTINE
SW1         MDX   X         ELSE-SWTCH-1 SWITCH TO BRANCH TO ELSE
SW2         MDX   X         0              SWITCH TO NOT BRANCH TO ELSE
PACK        DC              0              1ST ARGUMENT ADDRESS GOES HERE
            LD              PACK           PICK UP 1ST ARGUMENT ADDRESS
            STO             UNPAC          PUT ARGUMENT ADDRESS AT UNPAC
            LD              SW1            PICK UP THE BRANCH TO ELSE
            STO             SWTCH          STORE THE BRANCH AT SWTCH
```

All of the above statements are simply overhead required to set up a subprogram with two entry points and a way of switching between them. The two statements that start with asterisks are, of course, comments. Notice that the branch SW1 must use X format (Section 11-4) because this branch must be assembled at one location and then moved to another location to be executed. The PACK routine stores its first argument at UNPAC so that both routines may now use the same statements to pick up the arguments for the subprogram. Continuing with the subprogram statements:

```
START   STX    1   SAVE1+1       SAVE THE CONTENTS OF IR1
        LDX   I 1   UNPAC         PUT 1ST ARGUMENT ADDRESS IN IR1
        LD     1   0             PICK UP JCARD ADDRESS
        A          ONE           ADD CONSTANT OF ONE
```

                                275

```
          S      I1  1        SUBTRACT VALUE OF J
          STO        JCARD+1  STORE JCARD(J) ADDRESS
          LD      1  3        PICK UP KCARD ADDRESS
          A          ONE      ADD ONE
          S      I1  4        SUBTRACT VALUE OF K
          STO        KCARD+1  STORE KCARD(K) ADDRESS
          LD      1  0        PICK UP JCARD ADDRESS AGAIN
          A          ONE      ADD ONE
          S      I1  2        SUBTRACT VALUE OF JLAST
          STO        JLAST    STORE JCARD(JLAST) ADDRESS
KCARD     LDX    L1  0        PUT KCARD(K) ADDRESS IN IR1
```

The above statements initialize the addresses of statements that refer to the arguments of the PACK and UNPAC routines. The address of the address of the first argument (JCARD) is loaded into IR1 after saving the previous contents of IR1, and the arguments are picked up. The previous contents of IR1 may have been in use by the FORTRAN program that called the subprogram, so the contents of any index register used by the subprogram must be saved and eventually restored. Now an indirect load via IR1 will pick up the value of an argument while a direct load via IR1 will pick up the address of the argument. Because this distinction is the cause of many errors in coding assembly language subprograms, the reader should study the subprogram statements until he is sure that he understands how this is accomplished.

The address of JCARD(J) is computed by the program as

JCARD(J) address = JCARD address + 1 – J

This is necessary because all FORTRAN arrays are actually stored backwards in core memory and the address of JCARD is identical to the address of JCARD(1). Therefore we must subtract the value of the subscript J from the address of JCARD and add one to allow for the fact that we are actually starting at the address of JCARD(1). The other array addresses are calculated similarly. After loading the address of KCARD(K) into IR1, we are ready to proceed with the statements that actually do the work of packing and unpacking.

```
JCARD     LD     L   0        PICK UP THE VALUE OF JCARD(J)
SWTCH     MDX    X   0        TO ELSE IF PACK, NOP IF UNPAC
          SRT        8        SHIFT LOW ORDER BITS TO EXT
          SLA        8        REPOSITION HIGH ORDER BITS
          OR         BMASK    PUT BLANK IN LOW ORDER BITS
          STO    1   0        STORE HIGH ORDER IN KCARD(K)
          MDX    1   -1       DECREMENT ADDRESS OF KCARD(K)
          SLT        16       MOVE LOW ORDER BITS FROM EXT
          OR         BMASK    PUT A BLANK IN LOW ORDER BITS
          MDX        FINIS    GO AROUND PACK ROUTINE
```

```
ELSE    SRT        24          SHIFT HIGH ORDER BITS TO EXT
        MDX   L    JCARD+1,-1  DECREMENT JCARD(J) ADDRESS
        LD    I    JCARD+1     PICK UP THE NEXT JCARD(J)
        RTE        8           SHIFT BACK BITS FROM THE EXT
FINIS   STO   1    0           STORE RESULT IN NEXT KCARD(K)
```

The above statements pick up the next value of JCARD(J) and immediately branch to ELSE if the value is to be packed. Otherwise unpacking is required, and the low-order bits (the right-hand character) are temporarily shifted into the EXT and replaced by a blank. The unpacked word in the ACC is then stored at KCARD (K), and the KCARD(K) address is then decremented to point to the next word in the KCARD array. The low-order bits are retrieved from the EXT, a blank is added, and the result is stored at the next word in the KCARD array at FINIS.

If packing is required, we shift the high-order bits at ELSE (the left-hand character) all the way to the low-order positions of the EXT. After decrementing the address of JCARD(J), we pick up the next word to be packed and rotate the high-order bits of the next word into the low-order bits of the ACC while rotating the bits previously stored in the EXT back into the high-order bits of the ACC. The result is stored at KCARD(K) at the statement labeled FINIS.

Notice that all array addresses are decremented rather than incremented, because FORTRAN arrays are stored backwards in core memory so that JCARD(2) occupies an address exactly one word lower than JCARD(1) (assuming that we have one-word integers). Notice also that it is much easier to control the addressing of KCARD(K) through an index register than it is to control the addressing of JCARD (J) through direct address modification in memory.

All that remains now is to test to see if we have reached JCARD(JLAST) and, if so, to return to the calling program. The statements are as follows:

```
        MDX   L    JCARD+1,-1  DECREMENT JCARD(J) ADDRESS
        MDX   1    -1          DECREMENT KCARD(K) ADDRESS
        LD         JCARD+1     PICK UP JCARD(J) ADDRESS
        S          JLAST       SUBTRACT JCARD(JLAST) ADDRESS
        BSC   L    JCARD,-     GO TO JCARD IF + OR 0
        MDX   L    UNPAC,5     GET RETURN ADDRESS
SAVE1   LDX   L1   0           RESTORE CONTENTS OF IR1
        BSC   I    UNPAC       RETURN TO CALLING PROGRAM
BMASK   DC         /0040       MASK FOR LOW ORDER EBCDIC BLANK
ONE     DC         1           CONSTANT OF ONE
JLAST   DC         0           JCARD(JLAST) ADDRESS STORAGE
        END                    END OF PACK & UNPAC SUBPROGRAM
```

277

13-2   A Subprogram to Move Bit Strings within Words

In Chapter 10 we developed a FORTRAN subprogram called MOVE to transmit strings of characters from a group of words in one array to a different position in another array. Now we shall develop a subprogram in assembly language to provide the general capability to move strings of bits within words and thus provide a general bit manipulation subprogram that may be called by FORTRAN programs. The calling sequence in FORTRAN is

CALL MVBIT (JWORD, J, JLAST, KWORD, K)

where JWORD and KWORD are single words in memory (not arrays). We wish to move a string of bits from JWORD to KWORD. The bit string will start with the Jth bit of JWORD and end with the JLASTth bit of JWORD. The bit string will be moved into KWORD starting at the Kth bit position. For example, suppose that JWORD consisted of the bit pattern 1111111111111111 and KWORD consisted of 0000000000000000. The FORTRAN statement

CALL MVBIT (JWORD, 3, 8, KWORD, 9)

will cause bits three through eight of JWORD to replace the bits starting with bit position nine in KWORD, resuting in a KWORD of 0000000001111110. Remember that the first bit position is position zero and that the last bit position in a single word is bit position 15. The contents of JWORD will not be changed by the MVBIT subprogram.

The MVBIT (stands for move bits) subprogram has a single entry point. The subprogram consists of statements to save the index registers and pick up the arguments to the subprogram, more statements to move the bits from JWORD to KWORD as specified by the arguments, and finally a few statements to restore the index registers and return to the calling program. The first group of statements is

```
        ENT         MVBIT        SUBROUTINE ENTRY POINT
*   CALL MVBIT (JWORD, J, JLAST, KWORD, K)
*   BITS J THROUGH JLAST IN JWORD ARE MOVED
*   TO KWORD STARTING IN BIT POSITION K
MVBIT   DC          0            FIRST ARGUMENT ADDRESS GOES HERE
        STX    1    SAVE1+1      SAVE IR1
        LDX   I 1   MVBIT        PUT 1ST ARGUMENT ADDRESS IN IR1
        STX    2    SAVE2+1      SAVE IR2
        LD    I 1   1            PICK UP VALUE OF J
        STO         J+1          STORE AT J
        LD    I 1   4            PICK UP VALUE OF K
        STO         K+1          STORE AT K
        LD          FIFTN        PICK UP CONSTANT OF 15
        A           J+1          ADD VALUE OF J
```

```
       S       I 1   2              SUBTRACT VALUE OF JLAST
       STO           SHIFT+1        STORE COMPUTED SHIFT VALUE
```

As in the case of PACK and UNPAC, we proceed to load IR1 with the address of the address of the first argument (JWORD), then we pick up the arguments. A shift constant equal to 15 + J – JLAST is calculated for future use in the subprogram. We are now ready to move the bits.

```
           LD          ONES      PICK UP MASK OF 1111111111111111
SHIFT      LDX   L2   0          PUT SHIFT CONSTANT IN IR2
           SLA    2   0          SHIFT LEFT BY THE CONSTANT
           STO         TEMP1     STORE THE RESULT TEMPORARILY
J          LDX   L2   0          PUT THE VALUE OF J IN IR2
           SRA    2   0          SHIFT RIGHT J BITS
           AND   I 1  0          AND IN THE CONTENTS OF JWORD
           SLA    2   0          SHIFT LEFT J BITS
K          LDX   L2   0          PUT THE VALUE OF K IN IR2
           SRA    2   0          SHIFT RIGHT K BITS
           STO         TEMP2     STORE THE RESULT TEMPORARILY
           LD          TEMP1     RETRIEVE PREVIOUS RESULT
           SRA    2   0          SHIFT RIGHT K BITS
           EOR         ONES      EOR BY THE BASK 1111111111111111
           AND   I 1  3          AND IN THE CONTENTS OF KWORD
           OR          TEMP2     OR IN THE RESULT FROM TEMP2
           STO   I 1  3          STORE THE FINAL RESULT IN KWORD
```

The above statements isolate the bits J through JLAST of JWORD by shifting a mask of ones in the ACC, picking up the bits from JWORD by an AND statement, shifting these bits to the Kth position of the ACC, and finally clearing a hole in KWORD with an EOR and an AND and inserting the bits from JWORD with an OR. The reader should walk through these instructions with a couple of examples and a pencil and paper to clear up the details of the bit manipulations involved. Notice that IR1 is used to pick up the arguments while IR2 controls the shifts.

Since only one word is processed by MVBIT, there is no loop to repeat and all that remains is to restore the index registers and return to the calling program:

```
           MDX   L    MVBIT,5    GET RETURN ADDRESS (PAST 5 ARGS)
SAVE1      LDX   L1   0          RESTORE IR1
SAVE2      LDX   L2   0          RESTORE IR2
           BSC   I    MVBIT      RETURN TO CALLING PROGRAM
ONES       DC         /FFFF      MASK OF ONES, 1111111111111111
FIFTN      DC         15         CONSTANT OF 15
TEMP1      DC         0          TEMPORARY STORAGE LOCATION
```

```
TEMP2   DC          0               2ND TEMPORARY STORAGE LOCATION
        END                         END OF THE MVBIT SUBPROGRAM
```

The MVBIT subprogram could be used inside a FORTRAN subprogram to do the same job that PACK and UNPAC were designed to do. Since PACK and UNPAC always move and shift exactly eight bits, however, they are considerably faster than MVBIT in converting between A1 and A2 formats. MVBIT can be used to pack and unpack variable-length bit patterns and has much more flexibility than PACK and UNPAC. Here we see the usual choice between a general purpose routine (MVBIT) and a special purpose routine that executes somewhat faster.

13-3   Interpreting Assembly Language Statements in FORTRAN

Before we leave the subject of bit manipulation in assembly language, let us examine how a completely general bit manipulation capability could be provided for use by FORTRAN programs through the use of assembly language subprograms. The most general approach consists of executing the actual assembly language statements (such as AND, OR, EOR and the shift statements) directly in FORTRAN programs. Can this be done? Yes, if we are willing to write subprograms for each of the assembly language statements which we wish to make available in the FORTRAN language.

Consider the FORTRAN statement

JWORD = AND(KWORD, LWORD)

The above statement implies the existence of a function subprogram to perform some function called AND upon two integer variables KWORD and LWORD. The statement will store the result of this function in the variable JWORD. The AND function could simply pick up the arguments and execute an AND statement from assembly language, leaving the result in the ACC to be stored by the FORTRAN statement which called the subprogram. As we shall see, many statements are required in assembly language to perform this simple operation.

Let us first examine a single function subprogram to perform the AND function described above. Such a subprogram could be written as follows:

```
        ENT        AND           SUBROUTINE ENTRY POINT
*  ACC = AND (KWORD, LWORD)
*  THIS IS A FUNCTION SUBPROGRAM TO PROVIDE THE AND STATEMENT
AND     DC         0             FIRST ARGUMENT ADDRESS GOES HERE
        STX    1   SAVE1+1       SAVE CONTENTS OF IR1
        LDX    I 1 AND           FIRST ARGUMENT ADDRESS IN IR1
        LD     I 1 0             PICK UP VALUE OF FIRST ARGUMENT
```

```
            AND   I1   1            AND IN VALUE OF SECOND ARGUMENT
            MDX   L    AND, 2       GET RETURN ADDRESS (2 ARGS)
    SAVE1   LDX   L1   0            RESTORE CONTENTS OF IR1
            BSC   I    AND          RETURN TO CALLING PROGRAM
            END                     END OF AND  FUNCTION SUBPROGRAM
```

The above subprogram contains ten statements and requires 14 words of memory to execute a single statement which might take only one word in assembly language. Similar subprograms can be provided for the OR, EOR, SLA, SRA and any other required assembly language operations, thus elevating some or all of the assembly language statements to the point where the statements could be used individually in FORTRAN programs.

Such a group of subprograms would interpret assembly language statements in FORTRAN, since each function subprogram would transfer to many instructions which would pick up the arguments, execute the desired operation and leave the result in the ACC. At the FORTRAN level many assembly language functions could be nested together, such as

JWORD = AND (OR (KWORD, LWORD), MWORD)

which would cause JWORD to receive the AND function of MWORD with the OR function of KWORD with LWORD.

We can write subprograms to provide entirely new capabilities for FORTRAN, and groups of subprograms can radically expand the list of problems which can be solved easily through FORTRAN programming. Special subprogram libraries can be developed to interpret the specific requirements of applications such as stress analysis or statistical analysis. Although the computing efficiency of such systems may be low, the relative ease of programming may be more important.

There is also no reason why we cannot write programs in FORTRAN or assembly language to interpret new language structures developed for specific applications. Consider the following (which is *not* FORTRAN):

```
        READ AND PRINT 5
        COMPUTE MEAN, MAX, MIN
        HALT
```

The above may be taken to mean "read and print the values of five variables according to some predetermined format, then calculate and print the arithmetic mean, the maximum and the minimum of the five variables." Using the character manipulation subprograms of Chapter 10, a FORTRAN program could be written to pick up the words in the above statements, look up these words in tables and perform the specified operations. A program which did not have to do a table look-up to determine what to do next would execute much faster, but a new, highly simplified language like the example might be just the thing for a statistician who was too busy to even learn the FORTRAN language. These ideas are further developed in *FORTRAN IV, Programming and Computing* by James T. Golden (Englewood Cliffs, N. J., Prentice-Hall, Inc., 1965).

13-4   Input-Output Subroutines for Assembly Language Programs

IBM has provided subroutines to control input-output (I/O) devices such as the 1442 Card Read Punch, the 1132 and 1443 Printers, the 1627 Plotter, disk storage, the console keyboard, the typewriter and paper tape readers and punches. These subroutines are all interrupt service subroutines (ISS).

The basic calling sequence for all of the I/O subroutines is as follows:

```
LIBF     NAME1     CALL NAMED SUBROUTINE
DC       /1234     HEXADECIMAL CONTROL PARAMETER
DC       AREA      ADDRESS OF I/O AREA IN MEMORY
DC       ERROR     ADDRESS OF USER'S ERROR ROUTINE
```

The name of the subroutine consists of four letters followed by either 0, 1 or N. For some devices, such as disk storage, three different routines are available (DISK0, DISK1 and DISKN). For any named subroutine, NAME0 is the simplest and shortest routine, NAME1 is somewhat longer but has more flexibility in handling errors, and NAMEN can operate two or more devices simultaneously or transfer data faster than the NAME0 or NAME1 subroutines.

The control parameter (/1234 in the basic calling sequence) is a four-digit hexadecimal constant in which the individual digits specify the function to be performed (read, write or test the device) and indicate which of several similar devices may be involved.

The read function reads a specified quantity of data in the form of characters or words from a specified input device. Depending on the device, an interrupt will occur at the end of each character or word being read or else at the end of the transmission of the entire specified data quantity.

The write function writes a specified quantity of data on a specified output device. As with the read function, interrupts will occur at the end of each word or character or else at the end of the entire transmission.

The test function tests the status of the specified I/O device to see if the device is busy because a previous operation has not been completed. The return to the user's program from a test function is at LIBF+2 if the device is busy and at

LIBF+3 if the device is not busy. For example, a common use of the test function is

```
CHECK    LIBF      PRNT1          CALL THE PRINT ROUTINE (1132 PRINTER)
         DC        /0000          SPECIFY THE TEST FUNCTION
         MDX       CHECK          BRANCH BACK TO CHECK AGAIN IF BUSY
         LIBF      SETUP          IT'S NOT BUSY SO GO SET UP PRINT LINE
```

Here we see a small program loop which will repeatedly test the 1132 Printer to see if the 1132 is busy and branch back to CHECK to repeat the test. When the 1132 is no longer busy, the return from PRNT1 will be at LIBF+3, the LIBF to SETUP. SETUP is presumably a user-written subroutine to get the line set up for printing. Notice that if the test function is specified, additional arguments to specify an I/O area or an error routine must be omitted from the calling sequence.

Referring back to the basic calling sequence, the I/O area parameter is the address of a table in memory consisting of one or two control words, followed by the actual data words to be written. For input operations the table contains one or two control words, followed by the area in memory into which the incoming words will be read. The control words specify the word count which is the number of words of data to be read or written. If the I/O device is transmitting characters instead of 16-bit words, then the characters or card columns may be packed two per word so that the word count will not equal the number of characters to be processed.

The error parameter in the basic calling sequence transfers control to a user-written error routine to enable the user to decide what action to take if errors are detected by the I/O subroutine while servicing interrupts from the I/O device. Since the I/O subroutine is an interrupt service subroutine, we shall refer to the I/O subroutine as an ISS in the interrupt discussion which follows.

Interrupt servicing of I/O devices permits the user's program to execute instructions while waiting for the I/O device to complete the reading or writing operation. For example, a few milliseconds are available between the reading of adjacent card columns by the 1442 Card Read Punch on the 1130 system. The user's program can execute many instructions during these milliseconds. When an interrupt indicates that the next column is ready to be read, the user's program is interrupted at the end of the isntruction currently being executed. When the card column has been read, control returns to the next instruction in the user's program after the instruction during which the interrupt occurred. The user must be careful not to get ahead of the I/O process by attempting to use data which have not yet been read.

Each ISS actually consists of two subprograms: a call routine to initiate the required I/O operation and an interrupt response routine to handle the subsequent interrupts as each character or record is transmitted by the I/O device. The 1442 Card Read Punch on the 1130 interrupts the computer after each card column is read or punched so that the computer may receive or send out the contents of the next card column. The ISS that handles card reading is a subprogram to call the card reader into operation on the next card plus an interrupt response routine to read the card columns one at a time and transmit them into core storage.

Each call routine first determines if the specified device is busy with a previous operation. After waiting until the device is not busy, the call routine checks to see if the arguments to the call routine are correct and then initiates the requested I/O operation. Control of the computer is then usually returned to the user's program without waiting for the completion of the operation. The assembly language ISS are more sophisticated than the ISS used by FORTRAN programs; FORTRAN READ and WRITE statements usually cause the computer to wait until the I/O operation is completed before the computer can execute any further statements in the user's program. Most of the call routines provide, as an option, the ability to test whether or not the device is busy, permitting the user to perform other processing operations until the device is available.

The call routines thus provide overlapped I/O operations for assembly language programmers. It is possible to initiate printing upon the 1132 Printer, for example, and then read a couple of cards while the printer is actually printing a line. The line of characters to be printed is stored in a different area in memory than are the characters coming from the cards, since otherwise the characters to be printed would be overlaid by the incoming characters from the card reader before the printing operation was completed. To conserve memory, FORTRAN programs use the same area in memory for several different I/O operations; for this reason most FORTRAN I/O operations are not overlapped. As we will see, however, overlapped I/O can be provided for FORTRAN programs through the use of assembly language subprograms.

Each interrupt response routine is executed in response to an interrupt from the specific I/O device serviced by the interrupt response routine. These routines fetch the next character or record to be transmitted, check for any error conditions, and execute retry operations if an error has occurred and the I/O operation needs to be repeated.

If an error is detected by the call routine before the I/O operation is initiated, the address of the subroutine call (an LIBF) in the user's program is stored in core location 40, an error word is stored in the accumulator, and the program waits to retry the operation if the PROGRAM START button is pushed. The first hexadecimal digit in the accumulator will be 1 if the card reader is the source of the error, 2 if the console typewriter, 3 if paper tape, 5 if the disk, 6 if the line printer and 7 if the plotter. The fourth hexadecimal digit of the accumulator will be a 0 if the device is not ready (perhaps not turned on or not attached) or the digit will be a 1 if the arguments to the call routine are incorrect.

If the interrupt response routine detects an error after the I/O operation is initiated, control may be transferred back to the user's program to decide what to do next. The transfer of control is accomplished by means of one of the arguments to the call routine; this error argument is the address of a group of statements that forms the error routine inside the user's program. The user's error routine must end with an indirect BSC to the error argument and must start with a DC to store the return address from the interrupt response routine. An error word will be in the accumulator for possible analysis by the user's error routine; the various error words are listed in Appendix B. If error word is reset to zero by the user's error routine, then the interrupt response routine will terminate the I/O operation and proceed back to the user's calling program. If the error word is not reset, the interrupt response routine will retry the I/O operation, returning to the user's error routine if further error conditions are encountered.

As an example, let us name the error argument ERROR. The following user's error routine would suffice to tell the interrupt response routine to retry the I/O operation:

```
ERROR   DC          0           RETURN ADDRESS GOES HERE
        BSC     I   ERROR       RETURN WITH ACC UNCHANGED
```

To tell the interrupt response routine to terminate the I/O operation:

```
ERROR   DC          0           RETURN ADDRESS GOES HERE
        SRA         16          CLEAR THE ACC TO ZEROS
        BSC     I   ERROR       RETURN WITH ACC CLEARED
```

The user's error routine should not use other I/O subroutines to send out error messages; such messages should be scheduled by setting switches in the user's program which can be checked later after completion of the interrupt response processing. Otherwise the computer may go into an endless loop of recurring interrupts due to interrupts caused by the new I/O operation. The user's error routines for the 1130 system should also avoid using any other subroutines that may possibly have been in use when the interrupt response routine got control of the computer because the return address of the other subroutines would then be lost unless the other subroutines had been specially coded to permit reentry before they had compelted execution.

13-5   Calling Sequences for the Input-Output Subroutines

Two subroutines are available for 1442 Card Read Punch input-output operations on the 1130: CARD0 and CARD1. CARD0 has no error parameter; if an error occurs this subroutine will simply wait for operator intervention. CARD1 is the standard card subroutine; using a user-written error routine as described previously, CARD1 requires more memory than does CARD0.

The calling sequence is

```
LIBF      CARD1      OR CARD0
DC        /J00K      CONTROL, J = FUNCTION, K=DEVICE
DC        AREA       ADDRESS OF I/O AREA
DC        ERROR      ADDRESS OF ERROR ROUTINE
```

The error argument ERROR must be omitted when calling CARD0. The letter J in the control argument should be replaced by the digit 0 for a test function, 1 for a read function, 2 for a punch function, 3 for a card feed function and 4 to select the alternate card stacker. The letter K should be replaced by a 0. For example, the control argument to read a card from the card reader is /1000. If a test function or a stacker select function is specified, both the AREA and ERROR arguments must be omitted. The feed function simply causes a card to feed through the 1442 Card Read Punch to the next station: from the hopper to the reading station, from the reading station to the punching station, or from the punching station to the stacker. The feed function is used to skip over cards without either reading or punching; if the feed function is specified, the AREA argument must be omitted.

The number of card columns to be read or punched is specified by the value of the word at AREA; the words following AREA in memory are the I/O area, one word per card column to be read or punched. The data in the I/O area are in card column code which consists of the 12 high-order bits in each word set to 1 or 0 to represent the presence or absence of punches in the 12 punch positions in each card column (12-zone, 11-zone and the digit positions 0-9). A card code conversion subroutine such as SPEED or HOLEB (described in Section 13-7) must be used to convert the data into card code before punching and to convert from card code to EBCDIC code after reading.

After each card column is read or punched, control is returned to the user's program. An interrupt occurs when the next column reaches the read or punch heads and that column is then processed, after which control again returns to the user's program. An operation complete interrupt occurs after the last column is processed. Reading or punching always starts with column 1 on the card, but fewer than 80 columns may be processed if so specified by the word count at AREA. The entire card will advance one station, however.

Since control goes back to the user's program after each card column is read, the user may start using the data before the whole card has been processed. This is inherently dangerous because, if an error occurs, the I/O subroutine will attempt to reread the card. The user should preferably wait until the operation is complete before using the incoming data, or at least be prepared to pick up the data a second time if an error condition develops. During punch operations it is important not to store new data into the I/O area until the processing of the previous card has been completed.

One subroutine, PRNT1, is available to handle printing and carriage control operations on the 1132 Printer. The calling sequence is

```
LIBF      PRNT1
DC        /JKL0      CONTROL, J=FUNCTION, KL=CARRIAGE
DC        AREA       ADDRESS OF I/O AREA
DC        ERROR      ADDRESS OF ERROR ROUTINE
```

The letter J in the control argument should be replaced by the digit 0 for a test function, 2 to print with normal checking, 3 for carriage control and 4 to print only numeric data. If $J = 3$, then the digit at K indicates a carriage control operation to be performed immediately (before printing the next line); if $J = 3$ and $K = 0$, then the digit at L indicates a carriage control operation to be performed after printing the next line. The hexadecimal digits at K and L are specified as follows:

Digit Value	Carriage Control Function
1-6	Skip to channel 1-6 on the carriage control tape
9	Skip to channel 9 as above
C	Skip to channel 12 as above
D, E, F	Skip one, two or three lines

If $J = 2$ or $J = 4$ (print functions), then the digit at L will cause a space to be taken after printing the line if $L = 0$ or spacing will be suppressed if $L = 1$.

One line is printed by each call to one of the print functions. The data to be printed are stored after the word at AREA in EBCDIC code packed two characters per word. The word count, equal to $[(N+1)/2]$ if N is the number of characters, is stored at AREA. Since control is returned to the user's program after initiating the print operation, care must be taken to avoid replacing the data at AREA until the print operation has been completed (to avoid destroying characters which have not yet been printed). This problem is usually avoided by double buffering: the line of data to be printed is set up somewhere else in memory and moved into AREA by a subroutine which calls PRNT1.

Two subroutines are available to perform read operations from the typewriter keyboard and write operations to one or more typewriters. The subroutines are TYPE0 and WRTY0. The TYPE0 subroutine handles both keyboard input and typewriter output; the WRTY0 subroutine handles only typewriter output. The WRTY0 routine is preferable if keyboard input is not needed because the WRTY0 routine requires less memory than the TYPE0 routine. Since the calling sequences for the TYPE0 and WRTY0 routines are identical, we will discuss the TYPE0 routine.

The calling sequence is

```
LIBF       TYPE0       OR WRTY0 OR TYPEN OR WRTYN
DC         /J0KK       CONTROL, J=FUNCTION, K=DEVICE
DC         AREA        ADDRESS OF I/O AREA
```

Notice that the WRTY and TYPE subroutines have no error argument. The letter J in the control argument should be replaced by the digit 0 for a test function, 1 to read from the keyboard and immediately print each character upon the associated typewriter, and 2 to print upon the typewriter only. The digits at K should both be zero when using the 1130.

If a read-print function (J = 1) is specified, the subroutine first unlocks the keyboard and then returns control to the user's program. As each key is depressed, an interrupt is generated which causes the ISS to read and print the corresponding character. After the specified number of characters has been transmitted, the keyboard is locked and the operation is completed. The print function is similar except that the interrupts are initiated by completion of the printing of the previous character.

If the keyboard is backspaced, the subroutine assumes that the previous character was in error, types a slash (/) over it and replaces it (in memory) with the next character entered. If the "erase field" key is pressed, the subroutine assumes that the whole message is in error, types two slashes and returns the carriage to restart the message at the beginning. The new message overlays the old message, character by character, instead of erasing it. If the "end of message" (EOF) key is pressed, the transmission is ended even though the word count may have indicated a longer message.

The word at AREA contains a count equal to the number of characters involved if a read-print function is specified, or equal to half the number of characters to be printed if the print function is specified. The data to be printed are stored after the count at AREA, packed two characters per word in console printer code.

Two subroutines are available to handle paper tape operations. PAPT1 operates both the paper tape reader and the paper tape punch, but only one at a time. PAPTN operates both devices simultaneously. The calling sequence is

```
LIBF       PAPT1       OR PAPTN
DC         /JK0L       J=FUNCTION, K=CHECK, L=DEVICE
DC         AREA        ADDRESS OF I/O AREA
DC         ERROR       ADDRESS OF ERROR ROUTINE
```

The letter J in the control argument should be replaced by the digit 0 for a test function, 1 for a read function, and 2 for a punch function. The digit at K may be set at 1 to indicate that the subroutine should look for and act upon DEL (delete)

and NL (stop) codes when reading paper tape punched in the PTTC/8 code. If K = 0, no check for these characters is made. If K = 1, the DEL code will not be stored in the computer as it is read and the NL code will terminate the reading of data. If a test function is specified (J = 0), then the digit at L must be 0 or 1 to indicate whether the reader or punch should be tested.

Interrupts occur at the end of each character read or punched as described previously. The word at AREA contains a count equal to half the number of characters to be read or punched. The characters are packed two per word in the words immediately following the count. The eight channels from the paper tape are read into eight bits directly, so any bit pattern may be read or punched.

A single subroutine, PLOT1, is available to operate the 1627 Plotter. The calling sequence is

```
LIBF      PLOT1
DC        /J000        CONTROL, J=FUNCTION
DC        AREA         ADDRESS OF I/O AREA
DC        ERROR        SPACE FOR UNUSED ERROR ARGUMENT
```

No error argument is used, although a nonzero error argument must be present. The letter J in the calling sequence should be replaced by the digit 0 for a test function or by the digit 1 for a write function. The word at AREA contains the number of words of data to be plotted. Each of the four hexadecimal digits in each word in the I/O area produces a separate motion of the plotter, either a short straight-line motion in one of eight directions or repetition of a previous motion. Strings of hexadecimal digits can be used to draw graphs, letters or free-form shapes. A summary and example of the plotter control digits is shown in Figure 13-2.

Two subroutines, DISK1 and DISKN, are provided to perform disk storage operations. DISK1 is used to transmit blocks of any size and DISKN is a larger routine designed to minimize disk read and write times where large data blocks are involved. Both routines have similar error handling procedures.

The calling sequence is

```
LIBF      DISK1        OR DISKN
DC        /J0KL        J=FUNCTION, K=SEEK, L=DISPLACEMENT
DC        AREA         ADDRESS OF I/O AREA
DC        ERROR        ADDRESS OF ERROR ROUTINE
```

The digit at J specifies one of the following I/O functions:

289

Hexadecimal Digit	Plotter Action (See Diagram Below)
0	Pen Down
1	Line Segment = + Y
2	Line Segment = + X,+Y
3	Line Segment = + X
4	Line Segment = + X,-Y
5	Line Segment = - Y
6	Line Segment = - X,-Y
7	Line Segment = - X
8	Line Segment = - X,+Y
9	Pen Up
A	Repeat the previous pen motion the number of times specified by the next digit (Maximum - 15 times)
B	Repeat the previous pen motion the number of times specified by the next two digits (Maximum- 255 times)
C	Repeat the previous pen motion the number of times specified by the next three digits (Maximum- 4095 times)
D	Not Used
E	Not Used
F	Not Used

Figure 13-2 1627 Plotter Control Digits

Value of Digit at J	I/O Function
0	Test
1	Read
2	Write without read-back check
3	Write with read-back check
4	Write immediately (DISKN only)
5	Seek

All of the above functions require the AREA argument; functions 0 and 4 require that the ERROR argument be omitted.

The read function reads the number of words specified at AREA into core memory, starting with the disk sector address stored at AREA+1. As many as 50 retries are made in case of errors, after which control will go to the user's error routine.

The write with read-back check function first checks to see that the specified disk sector address is not in a file-protected area of the disk. If so, the computer waits for operator action. Otherwise writing proceeds for the specified number of words. Each sector is read after writing to ensure that the writing operation was without error; if not, up to 50 retries are made before exiting to the user's error routine. The write without read-back check is identical except that no read-back check is made.

The write immediate function writes data immediately without file protection checks and without repositioning the access arm. One of the eight sectors in the cylinder currently under the read-write head is written as specified by the low-order three bits of the sector address at AREA+1. For all writing operations the subroutine supplies the sector identification word, which is the first word in each sector.

The seek function moves the access arm as specified by the seek option digit at K. If the digit at K is zero, the access arm is moved to the sector address contained in the I/O area; if the digit is one, the access arm is moved to the next cylinder of data toward the center of the disk.

The displacement digit (L in the calling sequence) operates as follows: if the digit is zero, the sector address contained in the I/O area is regarded as the actual disk address to be used; if the digit is one, the sector address in the I/O area is regarded as relative to the first unprotected address on the disk. The address of the first unprotected sector is then added to the address in the I/O area to obtain the actual disk address to be used. Note that file-protected sectors are identified only by a bit in the sector identification word; file protection is handled entirely through programming and not through any hardware devices.

The I/O area at AREA consists of two control words followed by the block of memory which contains the data before writing and after reading. The first control word contains a count of the number of words of data to be transmitted (to or from the disk) and the second control word contains the sector address, ranging from 0 to 1599, indicating at which sector on the disk the transmission will begin. Bits 0-3 of the second word must contain the disk drive number: 0, 1, 2, 3 or 4.

Two subroutines, READ0 and READ1, are available to control the 2501 Card Reader on the 1130 system. Error handling procedures are similar to procedures for CARD0 and CARD1 for the 1442 Card Read Punch. The calling sequence is

```
        LIBF      READ1      OR READ0
        DC        /J00K      CONTROL, J=FUNCTION, K=DEVICE
        DC        AREA       ADDRESS OF I/O AREA
        DC        ERROR      ADDRESS OF ERROR ROUTINE
```

The error argument ERROR must be omitted when calling READ0. The letter J in the control argument should be replaced by a digit 0 for a test function or by a digit 1 for a read function. The letter K should be replaced by a zero. Both the AREA and ERROR arguments are omitted if a test function is specified.

The number of card columns to be read is contained in the word at AREA; the words following AREA in memory will contain the card columns after reading, one column per word in the card column code described for CARD0 and CARD1.

A feed function can be obtained by a read function with a card column count of zero. A read function after the last card in the hopper has been read causes the card to be ejected, followed by a halt for operator intervention.

Two subroutines, PNCH0 and PNCH1, are provided to control the 1442 Model 5 Card Punch. Error handling procedures are similar to procedures for CARD0 and CARD1. The calling sequence is

```
LIBF      PNCH1      OR PNCH0
DC        /J00K      CONTROL, J=FUNCTION, K=DEVICE
DC        AREA       ADDRESS OF I/O AREA
DC        ERROR      ADDRESS OF ERROR ROUTINE
```

The error argument ERROR must be omitted when calling PNCH0. The letter J in the control argument should be replaced by the digit 0 for a test function, 2 for punch or 3 for feed. The letter K should be replaced by a zero. Both the AREA and ERROR arguments are omitted if a test function is specified; AREA is omitted for a feed function.

The punch and feed operations are performed exactly as previously described for CARD0 and CARD1.

A single subroutine, PRNT3, is provided to handle printing and carriage control operations on the 1403 Printer on an 1130 system. The calling sequence is

```
LIBF      PRNT3
DC        /JKL0      CONTROL, J=FUNCTION, KL=CARRIAGE
DC        AREA       ADDRESS OF I/O AREA
DC        ERROR      ADDRESS OF ERROR ROUTINE
```

The letter J in the control argument should be replaced by the digit 0 for a test function, 2 for a print function or 3 for carriage control only. The AREA and ERROR arguments must be omitted for the test and carriage control functions. The digits at K and L control the printer carriage as described previously for PRNT1, except that all 12 channel skips may be produced by hexadecimal values 1 through C (for 12) of the digits at K and L.

The word count, equal to $[(N+1)/2]$ if N is the number of characters to be printed, is stored at AREA. The characters are packed two per word in 1403 Printer code. As in PRNT1, care must be taken to avoid placing new data at AREA until the previous print operation has been completed.

None of the subroutines in this section can be used in assembly language subprograms called by a FORTRAN main program which specifies the same I/O device in its * IOCS control record; for example, CARD1 cannot be used in a subprogram if the calling main program includes * IOCS (CARD). The reason is that FORTRAN programs use simplified input-output subroutines which would compete for interrupt processing with the assembly language subroutines described in this section.

13-6   A Subprogram to Provide Overlapped Printing

Subprograms can be written in assembly language to provide overlapped I/O capabilities for FORTRAN programs. Such subprograms require more memory than the standard FORTRAN I/O subroutines employed by the READ and WRITE statements, but they may double the number of cards or lines per minute produced by programs involving only small amounts of computation. As an example of such a subprogram, consider the following program, which uses the PRNT1 subroutine to control the 1132 Printer on an 1130.

```
           ENT      PRINT          SUBROUTINE ENTRY POINT
*  CALL PRINT(LINE), DIMEN. LINE(121), SUBPROGRAM NAMED PRINT
PRINT   DC        0              ADDRESS OF ARGUMENT ADDRESS
*  TEST FIRST TO SEE IF PRINTER IS BUSY
TEST     LIBF      PRNT1          CALL PRNT1 SUBROUTINE
         DC        /0000          SPECIFY TEST FUNCTION
         MDX       TEST           TEST AGAIN IF BUSY
*  PREPARE TO PACK LINE 2 CHARS/WORD IN REVERSE ORDER
         LD    I    PRINT          PICK UP ADDRESS OF LINE
         STO        LOADI+1        SAVE ADDRESS OF LINE
         STX   1    SAVE1+1        SAVE CONTENTS OF IR1
         LDX   L1   AREA+1         PICK UP I/O AREA ADDRESS
         STX   1    STORE+1        AREA ADDRESS NOW SET UP
LOADI   LDX   L1   0              IR1 CONTAINS THE ADDRESS OF LINE
```

After entering the new subprogram at PRINT we immediately test to see if the PRNT1 subroutine is still busy as the result of a previous operation. If it is still busy, we repeatedly check the busy condition at TEST. When the subroutine is no longer busy we must be ready to pack the characters to be printed two per word, as this is the format required by PRNT1. We must also reverse the sequence of the characters in memory, since the line to be printed (LINE) is a FORTRAN array and is therefore stored backwards in memory. LINE is assumed to be in 120A1 format.

```
* NOW PACK, REVERSE AND BLANK THE WHOLE LINE
PACK    LD      1   0           GET A CHARACTER FROM LINE
        AND         LMASK       DROP 8 LOW ORDER BITS
        STO         TEMP        STORE THE RESULT TEMPORARILY
        LD          BLANK       PICK UP A BLANK (A1 FORMAT)
        STO     1   0           BLANK THE LINE POSITION
        MDX     1   -1          MOVE TO NEXT CHARACTER
        LD      1   0           GET THE NEXT CHARACTER AND
        SRA         8           SHIFT TO RIGHT SIDE OF WORD
        OR          TEMP        MERGE WITH FIRST CHARACTER
STORE   STO     L   0           STORE PACKED CHARS IN AREA
        LD          BLANK       PICK UP ANOTHER BLANK
        STO     1   0           BLANK ANOTHER LINE POSITION
        MDX     1   -1          MOVE TO NEXT CHARACTER
        MDX     L   STORE+1,1   MOVE TO NEXT WORD IN AREA
        LD          STORE+1     GET CURRENT AREA ADDRESS
        S           LAST        COMPARE LAST AREA ADDRESS
        BSC     L   PACK,+      CONTINUE IF NOT YET LAST
```

The above coding, which is similar in some respects to the PACK subprogram of Section 13-1, not only packs and reverses the characters in LINE but also fills the LINE with blank characters after the contents of LINE have been moved to AREA, the I/O area.

```
* NOW INITIATE PRINTING FROM THE I/O AREA
SAVE1   LDX     L1  0           RESTORE CONTENTS OF IR1
        LIBF        PRNT1       CALL PRNT1 SUBROUTINE
        DC          /2000       SPECIFY PRINT FUNCTION
        DC          AREA        ADDRESS OF I/O AREA
        DC          ERROR       ADDRESS OF ERROR ROUTINE
* RETURN TO THE FORTRAN CALLING PROGRAM
        MDX     L   PRINT,1     ADJUST THE RETURN ADDRESS
        BSC     I   PRINT       RETURN TO CALLING PROGRAM
* ERROR ROUTINE PUTS CONTENTS OF ACC INTO LINE(121)
ERROR   DC          0           RETURN ADDRESS LINK
        MDX     L   LOADI+1,-120 GET LINE(121) ADDRESS
        STO     I   LOADI+1     PUT ACC INTO LINE(121)
        SRA         16          CLEAR THE ACC
        BSC     I   ERROR       RETURN TO ISS ROUTINE
```

In case of an error the error routine at ERROR saves the contents of the ACC at LINE(121) so that the FORTRAN program can examine the error indicator from the ACC by means of IF statements. LINE is dimensioned LINE(121) so that 120 characters will constitute a full print line and so that the last word can be used to store any error indications. The error routine then clears the ACC which terminates the operation. All that remains of the program are the program constants.

```
*  ALL PROGRAM CONSTANTS FOLLOW
AREA     DC      60          I/O AREA OF 60 WORDS
         BSS     60          REMAINDER OF AREA
LAST     DC      AREA+60     LAST ADDRESS IN AREA
LMASK    DC      /FF00       MASK OF 1111111100000000
TEMP     DC      0           TEMPORARY STORAGE WORD
BLANK    DC      /4040       BLANK IN A1 FORMAT
         END                 END OF THE PRINT SUBPROGRAM
```

To provide complete control of the 1132 Printer another subprogram, perhaps called SKIP, should be written to provide a range of carriage control functions. The SKIP subprogram could be a second entry point in the PRINT subprogram. We might also want to provide another subprogram, perhaps called BUSY, to allow the FORTRAN programmer to test directly to see if the PRNT1 subroutine was busy as the result of a previous operation. BUSY might be a third entry point in PRINT. These additions are left as exercises for the reader.

Notice that no FORMAT statement is used with PRINT, although FORMAT statements are required for use with WRITE statements in FORTRAN. The LINE to be printed by PRINT must have been previouslly formatted into 120A1 format, perhaps through the use of the MOVE and PUT subprograms of Chapter 10.

13-7   The Code Conversion Subroutines

The various I/O devices use unique codes to represent characters or words of data, and IBM provides subroutines to convert from one code to another as well as to and from the EBCDIC code used to describe characters during normal processing inside the 1130 computer. The different codes are

1. The IBM card code, a 12-bit image in each word of the 12 punches in a single card column

2. The perforated tape transmission code, PTTC/8, an 8-bit image of the punches in a single row of 8-channel paper tape

3. The console printer code, a special 8-bit code representing characters to be printed

4. The extended binary coded decimal interchange code (EBCDIC), an 8-bit code used by FORTRAN to represent A format characters in memory

5. The 1403 Printer code, consisting of two 6-bit plus parity codes packed in bits 1-7 and 9-15 of each word, with each 6-bit code representing a single character.

The code conversion subroutines are

BINDC — to convert binary integers to decimal integers in IBM card code

DCBIN — to convert decimal integers in card code to binary integers

BINHX — to convert binary integers to hexadecimal integers in card code

HXBIN — to convert hexadecimal integers in card code to binary integers

HOLEB — to convert card code to a subset of EBCDIC and vice versa

SPEED — to convert card code to EBCDIC and vice versa, using all codes

PAPEB — to convert PTTC/8 subset to EBCDIC subset and vice versa

PAPHL — to convert PTTC/8 subset to card code subset and vice versa

PAPPR — to convert PTTC/8 subset to console printer code or 1403 Printer code

HOLPR — to convert card code subset to console printer code or 1403 Printer code

EBPRT — to convert EBCDIC subset to console printer code or 1403 Printer code

BIDEC — to convert 32-bit binary integers to decimal numbers in IBM card code

DECBI — to convert decimal numbers in card code to 32-bit binary integers

ZIPCO — to convert from one arbitrary code to another through a customized conversion table

The word subset refers to the fact that all of the subroutines except SPEED will handle only those codes which are listed in the Appendices. In general, any character or bit pattern not in the subset list will be replaced by a blank during the conversion process. The first four subroutines in the list handle one word of data per call; the other subroutines can convert an entire message or block of data through a single call.

The basic calling sequence for BINDC, DCBIN, BINHX, HXBIN, DECBI and BIDEC is

```
LIBF      BINDC      OR ANY OF THE OTHERS
DC        AREA       ADDRESS OF THE I/O AREA
```

where AREA consists of six words for BINDC or DCBIN, four words for BINHX or HXBIN, or 11 words for BIDEC or DECBI, to contain the decimal or hexadecimal data. The single binary word to be converted to or from decimal or hexadecimal is stored in the ACC. The double word for BIDEC or DECBI is stored in the ACC and EXT.

The basic calling sequence for HOLEB, SPEED, PAPEB, PAPHL, PAPPR, HOLPR and EBPRT is

LIBF	HOLEB	OR ANY OF THE OTHERS
DC	/JKLM	CONTROL WORD IN HEXADECIMAL
DC	INPUT	ADDRESS OF INPUT AREA
DC	OUTPT	ADDRESS OF OUTPUT AREA
DC	nnnn	CHARACTER COUNT

The control word /JKLM consists of four hexadecimal digits which specify control options for the subroutine. For example, in SPEED the first digit specifies whether the EBCDIC characters are to be packed two per word (0) or unpacked (1). The fourth digit specifies the direction of the conversion, card code to EBCDIC (0) or EBCDIC to card code (1). The control digits may be summarized as follows:

Subroutine	Digit	Control Function
HOLEB	4th	0=card code to EBCDIC, 1=EBCDIC to card code
SPEED	1st	0=packed EBCDIC (2/word), 1=unpacked EBCDIC
SPEED	4th	Same as HOLEB
PAPEB	3rd	0=initialize case, 1=do not initialize case
PAPEB	4th	0=PTTC/8 to EBCDIC, 1=EBCDIC to PTTC/8
PAPHL	3rd	Same as PAPEB
PAPHL	4th	0=PTTC/8 to card code, 1=card code to PTTC/8
PAPPR	3rd	Same as PAPEB
PAPPR	4th	0=console printer code, 1=1403 Printer code
HOLPR	4th	Same as PAPPR
EBPRT	4th	Same as PAPPR
ZIPCO	1st	1=12-bit card code input, 0=all else
ZIPCO	2nd	1=unpacked input, 0=packed input
ZIPCO	3rd	1=12-bit card code output, 0=all else
ZIPCO	4th	1=unpacked output, 0=packed output

All digit positions not listed above should contain zeros. The initialize case option for the paper tape routines adds a case shift character to the output to initialize the upper and lower case of PTTC/8 to agree with the first character processed.

INPUT and OUTPT in the basic calling sequence contain the addresses of the input and output areas, which do not contain any character count or word count. The count of characters to be processed is written as a decimal integer in place of the argument nnnn. The input and output areas thus contain only the characters before and after processing. All the codes except card code are packed two characters per word in all subroutines except SPEED, where the EBCDIC code may be either packed or unpacked as specified. IBM card code is always stored one character per word because the card code is a 12-bit code which must occupy more than half of a 16-bit word in memory.

The ZIPCO routine also requires an additional CALL statement immediately after the fourth DC statement, of the form

CALL   TABLE   NAME OF CONVERSION TABLE

where TABLE is the name of a conversion table supplied by the user, or else the name of one of the IBM-supplied tables listed below:

  EBCCP — EBCDIC to console printer code

  EBHOL — EBCDIC to card code

  EBPT3 — EBCDIC to 1403 Printer code

  CPEBC — Console printer code to EBCDIC

  CPHOL — Console printer code to card code

  CPPT3 — Console printer code to 1403 Printer code

  HLEBC — Card code to EBCDIC

  HOLCP — Card code to console printer code

  HLPT3 — Card code to 1403 Printer code

  PT3EB — 1403 Printer code to EBCDIC

  PT3CP — 1403 Printer code to console printer code

  PTHOL — 1403 Printer code to card code

The conversion method used by ZIPCO is much faster than that used by the other conversion subroutines because ZIPCO creates the address of the table entry directly from the argument (the code to be converted). Each conversion table consists of 128 words, each containing two 8-bit characters. The seven low-order bits of the argument are used as an address, and the high-order bit is used to indicate which of the two characters in each word are to be used.

13-8 The Arithmetic and Functional Subroutines

A large library of arithmetic and functional subroutines is available to provide the computational capabilities of FORTRAN for direct use in assembly language programs. The basic calling sequence for all of these subroutines is

```
LIBF      NAME        OR CALL NAME
DC        ARG         ADDRESS OF ARGUMENT
```

Some of the subroutines are called with a CALL statement; others are called with an LIBF. Some subroutines require a DC statement containing the address of an argument; others do not. Many of the subroutines can also be written with an X added to the subroutine name to indicate that the contents of IR1 are to be added to the argument address to form the effective address of the argument; these subroutines are indicated by a preceding asterisk in the summary table on the following page. (For example, the indexed name of FADD would be FADDX.)

Those subroutines involving floating-point arithmetic use a floating-point accumulator (called FAC) which consists of three words in memory starting at the address 125 + C(IR3) or 125 plus the contents of IR3 in an 1130. Some of the subroutines require different names for standard and extended precision as noted in the table. Subroutines restricted to extended precision always start with the letter E.

If a subroutine requries two arguments, then one argument will be in either FAC (if floating-point) or the ACC and the other argument must be specified by a DC statement. If a subroutine requires only one argument, then that argument may be in FAC or the ACC, or it may be specified by a DC statement as shown in the table. Exceptions are the XMDS, XMD and XDD subroutines, which require one argument in the ACC and a second argument in the last two words of FAC (at C(IR3) + 126 in an 1130).

The result of each subroutine is stored in FAC (if floating-point) or in the ACC. In subroutines involving subtraction, the argument is subtracted from FAC or the ACC and the difference replaces the contents of FAC or the ACC. In subroutines involving division, FAC or the ACC is divided by the argument. The reverse subtract routine subtracts FAC from the argument. The reverse divide routine divides the argument by FAC. In the exponential routines FAXI, FAXB and FIXI, FAC or the ACC is raised to the power specified by the argument.

The normalizing routine NORM shifts the mantissa of the floating-point number in FAC to the left until bits 0 and 1 are different, while increasing the floating-point characteristic accordingly. NORM is used to shift floating-point variables into normalized format after computation. NORM is called by some of the other subroutines; NORM ordinarily need not be called by a user unless he is manipulating bits inside of the floating-point numbers.

The floating to decimal (FBTD) and decimal to floating (FDTB) subroutines require an argument in the form of a string of EBCDIC characters, one per word in the low-order eight bits of each word, in the form sd.ddddddddEsdd where s is a

Function	Call, Args.	DC	Standard Precision	Extended Precision
Floating add, subtract	LIBF, 2	Yes	*FADD, *FSUB	*EADD, *ESUB
Floating multiply, divide	LIBF, 2	Yes	*FMPY, *FDIV	*EMPY, *EDIV
Load FAC, store FAC	LIBF, 1	Yes	*FLD, *FSTO	*ELD, *ESTO
Floating sine, cosine	CALL, 1	Yes	FSIN, FCOS	ESIN, ECOS
Floating sine, cosine	CALL, 1	No	FSINE, FCOSN	ESINE, ECOSN
Floating arctan, square root	CALL, 1	Yes	FATAN, FSQRT	EATAN, ESQRT
Floating arctan, square root	CALL, 1	No	FATN, FSQR	EATN, ESQR
Floating log e, exponential	CALL, 1	Yes	FALOG, FEXP	EALOG, EEXP
Floating log e, exponential	CALL, 1	No	FLN, FXPN	ELN, EXPN
Hyperbolic tangent	CALL, 1	Yes	FTANH	ETANH
Hyperbolic tangent	CALL, 1	No	FTNH	ETNH
Floating base to integer exp.	LIBF, 2	Yes	*FAXI	*EAXI
Floating base to floating exp.	CALL, 2	Yes	*FAXB	*EAXB
Fix floating to integer	LIBF, 1	No	IFIX	IFIX
Float integer to floating	LIBF, 1	No	FLOAT	FLOAT
Floating normalize	LIBF, 1	No	NORM	NORM
Floating to decimal, reverse	CALL, 2	Yes	FBTD, FDTB	FBTD, FDTB
Floating arith. range check	LIBF, 1	No	FARC	FARC
Fixed integer to integer exp.	LIBF, 2	Yes	*FIXI	*FIXI
Fixed square root	CALL, 1	No	XSQR	XSQR
Fixed fractional multiply	LIBF, 2	No	XMDS	
Fixed dbl-word multiply, div.	LIBF, 2	No	XMD, XDD	XMD, XDD
Floating reverse subtract	LIBF, 2	Yes	*FSBR	*ESBR
Floating reverse divide	LIBF, 2	Yes	*FDVR	*EDVR
Floating change sign	LIBF, 1	No	SNR	SNR
Floating absolute value	CALL, 1	No	FAVL	EAVL
Floating absolute value	CALL, 1	Yes	FABS	EABS
Integer absolute value	CALL, 1	No	IABS	IABS

sign character (+ or –). d is a digit and E represents the beginning of a floating-point exponent. Any blank character will terminate the string; the exponent may be deleted and the number of digits may be fewer than shown. The argument address in the DC statement is the address of the first word of the string.

Many examples of the use of the floating-point subroutines may be found in Section 12-6. The input-output routines used in Section 12-6 are not the assembly language I/O routines used in Chapter 13 but are special I/O routines used only by the FORTRAN compiler.

Several maintenance programs are furnished by IBM to initialize disk sector addresses, create or modify disk ID names, copy the contents of one disk on another disk, and update the various monitor programs. Utility programs are also furnished to reproduce and print out the contents of card decks and paper tapes. These programs are not discussed here, but the reader should be aware of their existence.

13-9 The Dump Subroutines

Four subroutine entry points are available in the 1130 subroutine library to dump selected words of data upon the console printer or the 1132 or 1443 Printers in either decimal or hexadecimal format. The basic calling sequence for these subroutines is

```
CALL      DMTX0      OR DMTD0, DMPX1 OR DMPD1
DC        START      ADDRESS OF 1ST WORD DUMPED
DC        END        ADDRESS OF LAST WORD DUMPED
```

All of the subroutines dump eight words per line with the address of the first word printed to the left of the line. Before dumping the data, each subroutine prints a single line containing the status of the overflow and carry indicators and the contents of the ACC, EXT, IR1, IR2 and IR3.

DMTX0 dumps in hexadecimal on the console printer, DMTD0 dumps in decimal on the console printer, DMPX1 dumps in hexadecimal on the line printer and DMPD1 dumps in decimal on the line printer. Hexadecimal data is printed four characters per word and decimal data is printed five digits plus sign per word. The START and END addresses may be calculated and inserted by the user's program that calls the dump routine, providing the ability to dump various portions of core memory depending upon the conditions encountered by the user's program.

Another subroutine, DMP80, may be called to dump the first 80 words of core memory in hexadecimal format. These words contain information regarding the status of the interrupts which may be useful during debugging. DMP80 prints upon the console printer, using the following calling sequence:

```
CALL      DMP80      DUMP 1ST 80 WORDS IN HEX
```

13-10 Problems

1) Write a FORTRAN program to read a card in 80A1 format, pack columns 1-30 into A2 format using the PACK subprogram of Section 13-1 and then print columns 1-30 in the A2 format.

2) Write a FORTRAN program to do the same processing as in Problem 1, using the MVBIT subroutine of Section 13-2 instead of the PACK routine.

3) Repeat Problem 1 using individual subroutines for the necessary logical and shift operations as described in Section 13-3.

4) Given a line of 80 EBCDIC characters in A1 format, write an assembly language subroutine to print the characters upon the console printer using the WRYTO and EBPRT subroutines (refer to the example of the PRNT1 subroutine in Section 13-6).

CHAPTER 14: RPG

14-1   Introduction to RPG

The computer is no longer a tool reserved for the exclusive use of scientists, mathematicians or engineers. In fact, the computer market has been considerably expanded by the significant increase of business and nonscientific applications developed during the 1960's. These applications have made the computer an indispensable tool in the daily activities of numerous organizations. The availability of many computers of different capabilities and price ranges effectively enables even the smallest organization to own, lease, rent or time-share the computer that best fits its needs.

While the proliferation of computing equipment is the main factor in the acceptance of the computer by the most diverse organizations, the most important development that contributes to this acceptance is the repertoire of problem-oriented programming languages that enable users to "communicate" with their computers. A significant addition to this repertoire is RPG, which stands for Report Program Generator.

Unlike assembly language (or Assembler), RPG is not a machine-oriented language. Although RPG is a problem-oriented programming language, it is not a procedural language; in this respect, it differs markedly from FORTRAN, and the most important difference centers around its unique "specification" approach to programming. As its name indicates, RPG "generates" a program (in machine language) and, were it not for its somewhat limited function, RPG could be considered the highest level programming language used in data processing today. However, many of its features disqualify RPG from a fair comparison with other problem-oriented languages and many computer programmers hesitate to classify RPG as a programming language at all. Future developments in the field of programming languages will undoubtedly resolve the classificational disputes; meanwhile, the reader is encouraged to make a personal judgment by studying this chapter and the one following it.

14-2   RPG Specifications

Unlike FORTRAN programs, which are usually coded on a single form, the writing of RPG programs is almost impossible without several appropriately designed forms. The RPG programmer enters on these forms descriptions and definitions of various classes of instructions; each class of instructions is referred to as a "specification."

A typical program written in RPG consists of the following specifications:

1.   Control Card and File Description

2. Extension and Line Counter

3. Input

4. Calculation

5. Output-Format

These five specification forms, not all of which are required for each RPG program, supply all the information necessary for the 1130 RPG Compiler to generate a program.

In addition to the five specification forms just mentioned, there are two other forms:

6. Printer Spacing Chart

7. Indicator Summary

These seven forms are illustrated in Figures 14-1 through 14-7, as follows:

Figure 14-1: RPG Control Card and File Description Specifications
IBM Form X21-9092

Figure 14-2: RPG Extension and Line Counter Specifications
IBM Form X21-9091

Figure 14-3: RPG Input Specifications
IBM Form X21-9094

Figure 14-4: RPG Calculation Specifications
IBM Form X21-9093

Figure 14-5: RPG Output-Format Specifications
IBM Form X21-9090

Figure 14-6: Printer Spacing Chart
For IBM Printers Models 1132 or 1403

Figure 14-7: RPG Indicator Summary
IBM Form X21-9095

IBM

Printed in U.S.A.

RPG CONTROL CARD AND FILE DESCRIPTION SPECIFICATIONS

Date ____________

Program ____________

Programmer ____________

Punching Instruction	Graphic							
	Punch							

Page (1 2) ____ Program Identification (75 76 77 78 79 80) ____

Control Card Specifications

Line (3 4 5)	Form Type (6)	Core Size to Compile (7 8 9)	Object Output (10)	Listing Options (11)	Core Size to Execute (12 13 14)	Debug (15)	MFCM Stacking Sequence (16)	Sterling: Input--Shillings (17)	Sterling: Input--Pence (18)	Sterling: Output--Shillings (19)	Sterling: Output--Pence (20)	Inverted Print (21)	360/20 2501 Buffer (22)	Number Of Print Positions (23 24 25)	Alternate Collating Sequence (26)	Refer to the specific System Reference Library manual for actual entries. (27–74)
0 1	H															

File Description Specifications

Line (3 4 5)	Form Type (6)	Filename (7–14)	File Type: I/O/U/C/D (15)	File Designation: P/S/C/R/T/D (16)	End of File: E (17)	Sequence: A/D (18)	File Format: F/V (19)	Block Length (20–23)	Record Length (24–27)	Mode of Processing: L/R (28)	Length of Key Field or of Record Address Field (29 30)	Record Address Type: A/K/I (31)	Type of File Organization or Additional Area: I/D/T or 1-9 (32)	Overflow Indicator (33 34)	Key Field Starting Location (35–38)	Extension Code E/L (39)	Device (40–46)	Symbolic Device (47–52)	Labels (S, N, or E) (53)	Name of Label Exit (54–59)	Extent Exit for DAM / Core Index (60–65)	File Addition/Unordered: A/U (66)	Number of Tracks for Cylinder Overflow (67)	Number of Extents (68 69)	Tape Rewind: N/U (70)	File Condition U1-U8 (71 72)	(73 74)
0 2	F																										
0 3	F																										
0 4	F																										
0 5	F																										
0 6	F																										
0 7	F																										
	F																										
	F																										

Figure 14-1

IBM

International Business Machines Corporation

GX21-9091-1 U/M 050*
Printed in U.S.A.
*No. of forms per pad may vary slightly

RPG EXTENSION AND LINE COUNTER SPECIFICATIONS

Date _____
Program _____
Programmer _____

Punching Instruction	Graphic				
	Punch				

Page [ ] [ ]   1 2

Program Identification [ ]

75 76 77 78 79 80

Extension Specifications

Line	Form Type	Record Sequence of the Chaining File	Number of the Chaining Field	From Filename	To Filename	Table or Array Name	Number of Entries Per Record	Number of Entries Per Table or Array	Length of Entry	P = Packed/B = Binary	Decimal Positions	Sequence (A/D)	Table or Array Name (Alternating Format)	Length of Entry	P = Packed/B = Binary	Decimal Positions	Sequence (A/D)	Comments
3 4 5	6	7 8	9 10 11	12 13 14 15 16 17 18	19 20 21 22 23 24 25 26	27 28 29 30 31 32	33 34 35	36 37 38 39	40 41 42	43	44	45	46 47 48 49 50 51	52 53 54	55	56	57	58 59 60 61 62 63 64 65 66 67 68 69 70 71 72 73 74
0 1	E																	
0 2	E																	
0 3	E																	
0 4	E																	
0 5	E																	
0 6	E																	
0 7	E																	
0 8	E																	
0 9	E																	
1 0	E																	

Line Counter Specifications

Line	Form Type	Filename	1		2		3		4		5		6		7		8		9		10		11		12	
			Line Number	FL or Channel Number	Line Number	OL or Channel Number	Line Number	Channel Number	Line Number	Channel Number	Line Number	Channel Number	Line Number	Channel Number	Line Number	Channel Number	Line Number	Channel Number	Line Number	Channel Number	Line Number	Channel Number	Line Number	Channel Number	Line Number	Channel Number
3 4 5	6	7 8 9 10 11 12 13 14	15 16 17	18 19	20 21	22 23 24	25 26	27 28 29	30 31 32	33 34	35 36 37	38 39	40 41 42	43 44	45 46 47	48 49	50 51 52	53 54	55 56 57	58 59	60 61 62	63 64	65 66 67	68 69	70 71 72	73 74
1 1	L																									
1 2	L																									
1 3	L																									

306

IBM

International Business Machines Corporation

RPG INPUT SPECIFICATIONS

GX21-9094-1 U/M050
Printed in U.S.A.

Date _____
Program _____
Programmer _____

Punching Instruction | Graphic | | | |
Punch | | | |

Page | | 1 2

Program Identification | 75 76 77 78 79 80

Line	Form Type	Filename	Sequence	Number (1-N)	Option (O)	Record Identifying Indicator or **	Record Identification Codes 1 Position	Not (N)	C/Z/D	Character	2 Position	Not (N)	C/Z/D	Character	3 Position	Not (N)	C/Z/D	Character	Stacker Select	P = Packed/B = Binary	Field Location From	To	Decimal Positions	Field Name	Control Level (L1-L9)	Matching Fields or Chaining Fields	Field Record Relation	Field Indicators Plus	Minus	Zero or Blank	Sterling Sign Position
3 4	6	7 8 9 10 11 12 13 14	15 16	17	18	19 20	21 22 23 24	25	26	27	28 29 30 31	32	33	34	35 36 37 38	39	40	41	42	43	44 45 46 47	48 49 50 51	52	53 54 55 56 57 58	59	60 61 62	63 64	65 66	67 68	69 70	71 72 73 74
0 1	I																														
0 2	I																														
0 3	I																														
0 4	I																														
0 5	I																														
0 6	I																														
0 7	I																														
0 8	I																														
0 9	I																														
1 0	I																														
1 1	I																														
1 2	I																														
1 3	I																														
1 4	I																														
1 5	I																														

Figure 14-3

307

International Business Machines Corporation

RPG CALCULATION SPECIFICATIONS

GX21-9093-1 U/M 050*
Printed in U.S.A.
*No. of forms per pad may vary slightly

Date _____

Program _____

Programmer _____

Punching Instruction | Graphic | | | | |
Punch | | | | |

Page ☐ 1 2

Program Identification ☐☐☐☐☐☐ 75 76 77 78 79 80

Line			Form Type	Control Level (L0-L9, LR, SR)	Indicators						Factor 1	Operation	Factor 2	Result Field	Field Length	Decimal Positions	Half Adjust (H)	Resulting Indicators			Comments
						And		And										Arithmetic	Compare	Lookup (Factor 2) is	
				N0T		N0T		N0T										Plus Minus Zero	High Low Equal 1>2 1<2 1=2	High Low Equal Table (Factor 2) is	
3	4 5	6	7 8	9 10 11	12 13 14	15 16 17	18 19 20 21 22 23 24 25 26 27	28 29 30 31 32	33 34 35 36 37 38 39 40 41 42	43 44 45 46 47 48	49 50 51	52	53	54 55	56 57	58 59	60 61 62 63 64 65 66 67 68 69 70 71 72 73 74
0 1	C																
0 2	C																
0 3	C																
0 4	C																
0 5	C																
0 6	C																
0 7	C																
0 8	C																
0 9	C																
1 0	C																
1 1	C																
1 2	C																
1 3	C																
1 4	C																
1 5	C																

Figure 14A

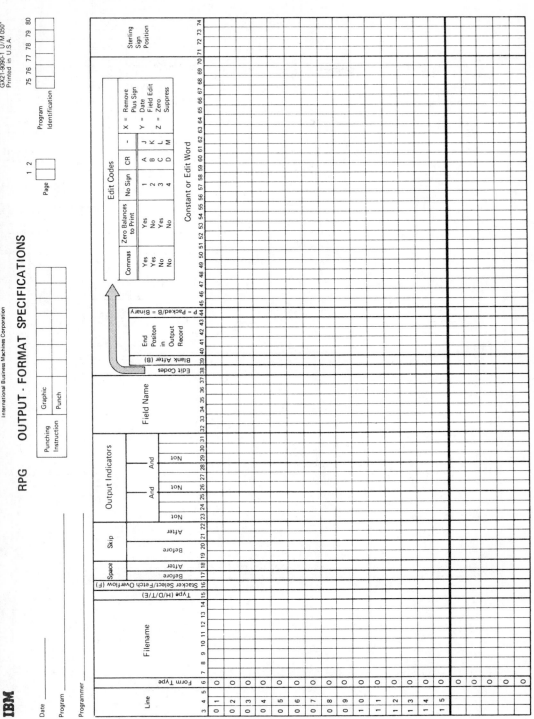

Figure 14-5

309

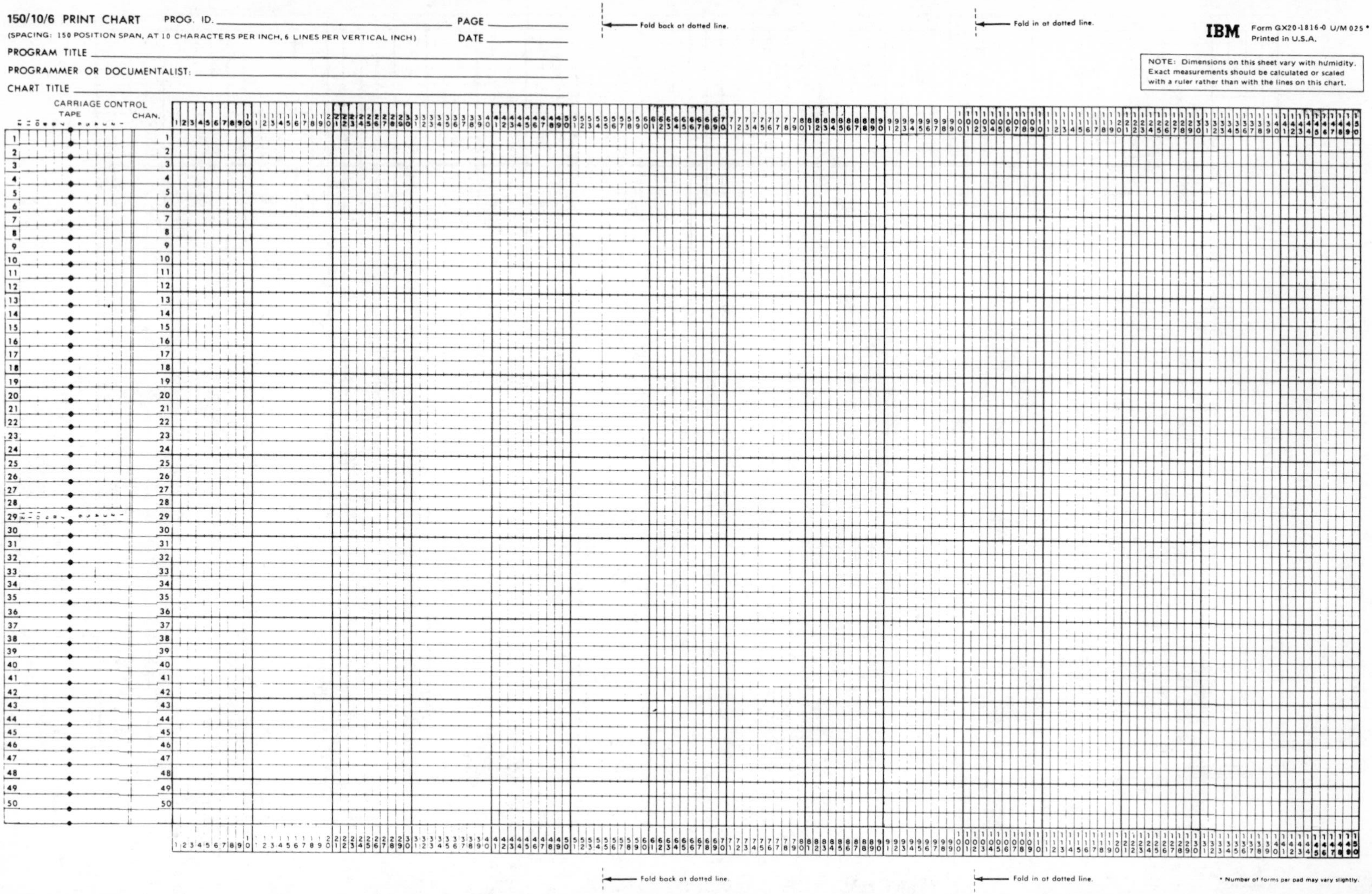
150/10/6 PRINT CHART
PROG. ID.
PAGE
DATE
(SPACING: 150 POSITION SPAN, AT 10 CHARACTERS PER INCH, 6 LINES PER VERTICAL INCH)
PROGRAM TITLE
PROGRAMMER OR DOCUMENTALIST:
CHART TITLE
CARRIAGE CONTROL TAPE
CHAN.
Fold back at dotted line.
Fold in at dotted line.
IBM
Form GX20-1816-0 U/M 025 *
Printed in U.S.A.
NOTE: Dimensions on this sheet vary with humidity. Exact measurements should be calculated or scaled with a ruler rather than with the lines on this chart.
* Number of forms per pad may vary slightly.

Figure 14-6

International Business Machines Corporation

RPG INDICATOR SUMMARY

GX21-9095-0 U/M025
Printed in U.S.A.

Date _____
Program _____
Programmer _____

Punching Instruction	Graphic			
	Punch			

Program Identification: 75 76 77 78 79 80

Page: 1 2

Circle Indicators Used:

01	02	03	04	05	06	07	08	09	10
21	22	23	24	25	26	27	28	29	30
41	42	43	44	45	46	47	48	49	50
61	62	63	64	65	66	67	68	69	70
81	82	83	84	85	86	87	88	89	90
L1	L2	L3	L4	L5	L6	L7	L8	L9	
H1	H2	H3	H4	H5	H6	H7	H8	H9	H0

11	12	13	14	15	16	17	18	19	20
31	32	33	34	35	36	37	38	39	40
51	52	53	54	55	56	57	58	59	60
71	72	73	74	75	76	77	78	79	80
91	92	93	94	95	96	97	98	99	
OA	OB	OC	OD	OE	OF	OG	OV		
U1	U2	U3	U4	U5	U6	U7	U8		

Predefined Indicators:

| M-C: | M1 | M2 | M3 | M4 | M5 | M6 | M7 | M8 | M9 |
| | C1 | C2 | C3 | C4 | C5 | C6 | C7 | C8 | C9 |

Note: All indicators are not valid with all systems.

FUNCTION OF INDICATORS

Indicators:
- Record Identifying
- Input Field
- Calculation Result
- Matching and Chaining
- Control Level, Overflow, Halt and User

Figure 14-7

311

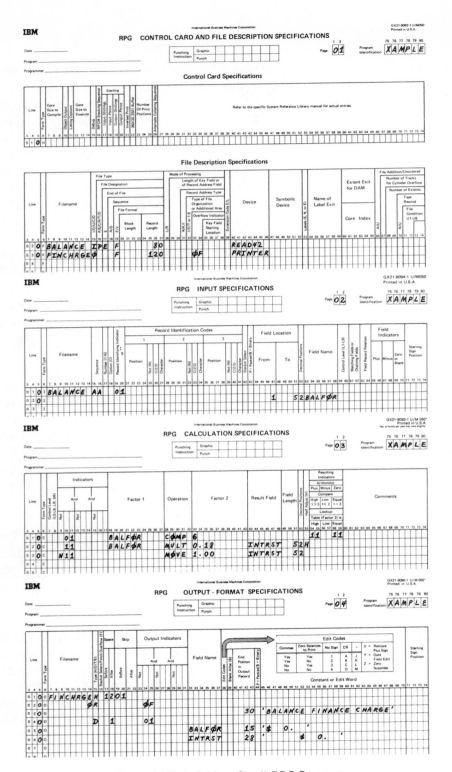

Figure 14-8   A Very Small RPG Program

312

14-3   A Very Small RPG Program

Consider Figure 14-8, which is a complete RPG program. Only four RPG specification forms are used in this brief program, and each form is used only once. Therefore each page is a distinct form, and columns 1-2 of all four forms have the page number in the correct collating sequence. The program has been given a name, XAMPLE, that is entered in columns 75-80 of each one of the forms; the name is chosen by the programmer and serves no other purpose but to identify the program. A total of fourteen (14) lines of coding constitute the entire source program; these lines correspond to the fourteen cards that will be punched. Column 6 of each form has a preprinted one-letter code that defines the form type and the corresponding punched card.

The first line of the first form (Figure 14-8) is the RPG Control Card specification; the punched card would have 01010H in its first six columns and XAMPLE in the last six, all columns in between (7-74) remaining blank. In general, of course, this card may have other entries in columns 11, 17-21 and 26 that are not necessary for this example but will be discussed in Section 14-5. The RPG Control Card is placed at the beginning of the RPG Source deck; because of this it is often called the "Header" card—which explains the one-letter code H in column 6.

The lower portion of the first form of Figure 14-8 has two lines of coding. The two lines contain the names and descriptions of two files. The input file (an I is entered in column 15) is named BALANCE (columns 7-14) and it consists of cards that will be read by the card reader (columns 40-46), with each card's record length not exceeding 80 columns (columns 24-27). The output file (an O is entered in column 15) is named FINCHRG (columns 7-14) and it will appear on printout paper the width of which is 120 columns (columns 24-27), the printing being done, of course, by the printer (columns 40-46).

The next form on Figure 14-8 is used to describe the input in detail. The name of the input file (BALANCE) is again entered (columns 7-14). This file consists of only one data field, named BALFOR (columns 53-58) which is to be located in the first five columns of each input card (columns 44-51 of the form) and which should have two decimal spaces (column 52).

The following form on Figure 14-8 is used to perform the necessary computations with the data. In this example, the first operation consists of comparing the balance forward (BALFOR) to 6 and if it exceeds, or is equal to, six dollars (columns 54-59) proceed with the next line where BALFOR is multiplied by 0.18 (18% annually or 1.5% per month) and the resulting amount is stored in INTRST (columns 43-48). If BALFOR is less than 6, then the second line is skipped and 1.00 is stored in INTRST instead.

The last form on Figure 14-8 is used to describe the output. The name of the output file (FINCHRGE) is again entered (columns 7-14). The output will consist of a heading (H) and details (D), as specified in column 15. Carriage control instructions (columns 17-22) follow; one line is skipped from the top of the print-out page, two lines are skipped after printing the heading, and one line is skipped after printing each detail line (columns 17-18); the paper tape that regulates the printer carriage advances to channel 1 before printing is to begin (columns 19-22). The printout will look like this:

```
        1                  2                  3
        0                  0                  0
  _____
          B A L A N C E   F I N A N C E   C H A R G E
  _____

  _____

  _____
        $   0.xx                  $   0.xx
  _____
        $   0.xx                  $   0.xx
  _____
```

As this quite elementary example demonstrates, writing RPG programs is comparatively easier than programming in other computer languages. In order to learn to program in RPG one must become familiar with the details of the various RPG specification forms involved, and follow the rules governing the filling out of each form. Additional examples illustrating features of each form are given at the end of each of the following sections. A few more complicated examples and additional characteristics are presented in Chapter 15.

14-4   Common Specifications

Although all five RPG specification forms (Figure 14-1 to 14-5) may be used in a program, and although each RPG specification form has numerous fields to be filled out by the programmer, the writing of RPG specifications is not a difficult task. Before considering each specification form by itself, specification items common to all forms will be described. The first *seven* and the last *six* columns of each of the five specification forms mentioned in Section 14-2 have functionally identical entries.

Columns 1 and 2

The specification page number is entered into these two columns. The programmer should assign ascending numbers to the pages of each program speci-fication form set to collate in the sequence listed in Section 14-2.

Columns 3, 4 and 5

Columns 3 and 4 have preprinted first two digits of line numbers (e.g., 01, 02, 03, etc.). Column 5 may be filled in with a digit of the programmer's own choosing; generally, the simplest choice is a 0 (zero), because the line numbers then will be in ascending sequence of tens (e.g., 010, 020, 030, etc.), and also because additional lines which may require insertion between two preprinted lines will be easily identified in their proper sequence (e.g., 010, *014*, *016*, 020, *025*, 030, etc.).

Column 6

This column contains a preprinted one-letter code which must be punched into all RPG specification cards. The codes, which identify the form type, are

H	Header Control Card
F	File Description
E	File Extension
L	Line Counter (not used by 1130 RPG)
I	Input
C	Calculation
O	Output-Format

Column 7

Depending on the form type used, this column may be either left blank (possible in the Control Card and Calculation specification forms) or contain an alpha-betic character (letter) (optional in the Calculation and necessary on all other speci-fication forms). An asterisk (*) in column 7 identifies the given line as a comment line in all specification forms. Thus the programmer may insert explanations and remarks in each specification form. (Two forms permit additional commentary text without the asterisk; it is possible to write comments in columns 58 to 74 of the File Exten-sion specification form and in columns 60 to 74 of the Calculation specification form.)

315

Columns 75 to 80

   Program identification is entered into these six columns on each specification form, if so desired. These columns may be left blank or may contain alphameric characters. Aside from appearing on the program listing, these entries have no other meaning but that of naming or identifying the particular program or subprogram listed. However, the object program name of the RPG source program will be obtained from the entries in columns 75 to 80 of the RPG Control Card; if these columns on the Control Card are left blank, the object program identification RPGOBJ will be used.

14-5   Control Card and File Description Specifications

   The Control Card and File Description Specifications are entered into a single form (see Figure 14-1).

   The Control Card Specifications are written on the line provided at the top of the form, and subsequently punched on one card, called the control or header card. Each RPG program must have one control card; this card must be placed before the RPG source program deck. The contents of the 1130 RPG Control Card are limited to six fields, as summarized below:

   1.   Columns 1-2 and 3-5
        Page and line numbers as described in Section 14-4.

   2.   Column 6
        Already has the preprinted code H, signaling that the card is the control, or header, card.

   3.   Column 11
        Provides the programmer with options for the source program: to compile it only or to list it with or without compiling it.

   4.   Columns 17-20
        These four columns are to be used only when the program has to handle Sterling currency amounts; the programmer has a choice between IBM and BSI (British Standards Institute) formats.

   5.   Column 21
        This column is used only if the European convention of printing is to be adopted (i.e., commas instead of decimal points, and day-month-year instead of month-day-year).

   6.   Column 26
        Allows the programmer to alternate the collating sequence, if necessary.

The remaining columns on the RPG Control Card are ignored by the 1130 RPG Compiler and therefore may be left blank. Columns 75-80 may be used to identify the program with a name, as described in Section 14-4.

The RPG File Description Specifications are entered in 16 fields, many of which, because of their specialized purpose, are not always used. The most important fields (excluding the common entries described in Section 14-4) are summarized below:

1. Columns 7-14
   File names—identifiers with leading alphameric character—chosen by the programmer, are entered into these eight columns; names of distinct files are distinguished on the basis of the identifiers' first five characters, which, because of this requirement, must be unique. Special characters or embedded blanks are not permitted and all identifiers must be left-justified.

2. Column 15
   Used to specify the type of file represented by the identifier; there are only four types: Input, Output, Update and Combined.

3. Columns 24-27
   The programmer should enter here the length of the record to be used; the lengths vary, for example, from a minimum of 1 to a maximum of 80 if the record is a card or a maximum of 120 if the record is printer output paper.

4. Columns 40-46
   Required to specify the input-output device used by each file.

Two columns (6 and 19) should be filled with an F; column 6 identifies the form type (File Description Specifications) while column 19 designates each file as of fixed-length format (variable-length format is not allowed in 1130 RPG).

Four fields are ignored by the 1130 RPG Compiler and may be left blank: columns 20-23, 35-37, 53-65 and 67-74.

Figure 14-9 provides examples of the RPG Control Card and of File Description Specifications.

The maximum number of files that may be specified in an 1130 RPG program is ten. Only one primary file and only one record-address file are allowed; up to eight secondary and up to eight input-table files are permitted; up to two printer output and up to nine nonprinter output files are possible, and up to nine chaining files could be entered. However, the total number of files, regardless of choice or combination, must be ten or less.

317

International Business Machines Corporation

RPG   CONTROL CARD AND FILE DESCRIPTION SPECIFICATIONS

GX21-9092-1 U/M050
Printed in U.S.A.

Date _____
Program _____
Programmer _____

Punching Instruction | Graphic | | | |
| Punch | | | |

Page **01**   Program Identification **TRYØUT**

1 2

Control Card Specifications

Line	Form Type									

Refer to the specific System Reference Library manual for actual entries.

| 3 | 4 5 | Form Type | Core Size to Compile 7 8 9 | Object Output 10 | Core Size to Execute 11 12 13 | Debug 14 15 | MFCM Stacking Sequence 16 | Input–Shillings 17 | Input–Pence 18 | Output–Shillings 19 | Output–Pence 20 | Inverted Print 21 | 360/20 2501 Buffer 22 | Number Of Print Positions 23 24 25 | Alternate Collating Sequence 26 27 |
| 0 1 | O H | | | D | | | | | | | | | | | |

File Description Specifications

Line	Form Type	Filename	I/O/U/C/D	P/S/C/R/T/D	E End of File	File Type A/D	File Format F/V	Block Length	Record Length	L/R	Mode of Processing A/K/I	Length of Key Field or of Record Address Field	Record Address Type I/D/T or 1-9	Type of File Organization or Additional Area	Overflow Indicator	Key Field Starting Location	Extension Code E/L	Device	Symbolic Device	Labels (S, N, or E)	Name of Label Exit	Extent Exit for DAM	Core Index	File Addition/Unordered	Number of Tracks for Cylinder Overflow	Number of Extents	Tape Rewind	File Condition U1-U8
0 2	O F	CRED1ITS	I	P E			F		80									READ42										
0 3	O F	CRED2ITS	I	S			F		80									READ42										
0 4	O F	PAY1RØLLØ					F		120									PRINTER										
0 5	O F	PAY2RØLLØ					F		100	20KI			1					DISK										
0 6	O F	LEDGER	U	C			F		400R18KI			1					DISK										
0 7	O F	REPØRT	Ø				F		60									CØNSØLE										
0 8 0	F	MASTER	C	S		A F	F		80									READ01										
0 9 0	F	MAINFILE	I	R			F		80									EREAD01										
1 0 0	F	DUALFILE	I	T			F		100									EDISK										

Figure 14.0

318

Figure 14-9 Examples of RPG Control Card and File Description Specifications

Line 010—The only entry is a D in column 11 meaning that the source program will be listed but not compiled; a B in the same column would have reversed the option to compilation only without listing, and if the column had been left blank, the program would have both listed and compiled. The rest of the Control Card (except the common entries, columns 1-6 and 75-80) are left blank. However, blank spaces are not devoid of meaning. The absence of any entries in columns 17-20 simply means that the program will not handle any Sterling currency amounts. But a blank column 21 signifies that the domestic convention of printing will be used upon output (if an I had been entered here, the European convention, or "inverted" print option, would have been used). The blank in colum 26 indicates that the regular collating sequence will be followed, as opposed to the alternate collating sequence that requires an A entry here. The rest of the columns must be left blank at all times. Only one Control Card per RPG source program is permitted.

Line 020—The file defined on this line, named CRED1ITS (columns 7-14) is an input (I in column 15) and primary (P in column 16) file; in general, input files may be primary, secondary, chained, record-address, or table-input files, but only one primary file may be defined for an 1130 RPG program, and primary files are always input files. The E in column 17 permits the programmer to ascertain an end-of-job after an end-of-file condition for this file has been reached (i.e., the end of job occurs when this file is depleted). The F in column 19 indicates fixed file format, an entry that is obligatory on each line of the 1130 RPG File Description Specifications form (variable file format is not allowed by 1130 RPG). No entries are required under Block Length (columns 20-23) so that these columns are to be left blank. Since CRED1ITS is an input file, cards (of 80 columns record length, columns 26-27) will be read by the IBM 1442 Reader/Punch (device identified in columns 40-46).

Line 030—Another input file, CRED2ITS, is defined similarly to CRED1ITS, but is a secondary file (S in column 16).

Line 040—An output (O in column 15) file named PAY1ROLL (columns 7-14) is to be processed on the IBM 1132 Printer (device identified in columns 40-46) with a record length of 120 printed columns on the printer output paper (columns 25-27).

Line 050—Another output file, PAY2ROLL, is to be processed on disk (device identified in columns 40-46). The file is index-sequential (I in column 32) and the records are addressed through keys (K in column 31). Each record is 100 characters long (columns 24-27) and the length of the record-address field is 20 (columns 29-30). The key field for indexed-sequential files always begins in position 1 (column 38).

Line 060—An update (U in column 15) file designated as chained (C in column 16) file, named LEDGER (columns 7-14) is to be located on disk (device identified in columns 40-46). The file is index-sequential (I in column 32), and the records are addressed through keys (K in column 31). The processing is random (R in column 28).

Line 070—The records of the output file named REPORT are to be printed on the console printer or typewriter (device identified in columns 40-46).

Line 080—A combined, secondary file (columns 15, 16) named MASTER (columns 7-14) will have its records inputted on the IBM 2501 Reader (columns 40-46). Each record is an 80-column card (columns 26-27). Column 18 has an A, indicating that the matching fields are in ascending order; a specification entry for matching fields will be required in columns 61-62 of the Input Specifications form (Figure 14-3).

Line 090—The records of an input, record-address file (columns 15, 16) named MAINFILE (columns 7-14) will be inputted on the IBM 2501 Reader (columns 40-46). The E in column 39 indicates that other information about this file will be entered on the Extension Specifications form (Figure 14-2); the E entry is only allowed if the file is a chaining file, a record-address file (as in this example), or a table file (as in Line 100, where the input-table file named DUALFILE is processed on disk).

319

14-6   Extension and Line Counter Specifications

The RPG Extension and Line Counter Specifications form (see Figure 14-2) is a dual form. The Line Counter Specifications portion, located at the bottom of the form, is not used in 1130 RPG programs (however, it is used, for example, in System/3 and System/360 RPG programs).

The two main purposes of the RPG File Extension Specifications are the description of tables (of data) and the description of the relationship (if any) among various files, the names of which have been entered in the File Description Specifications form. The most important fields (excluding the common entries described in Section 14-4) are summarized below:

1. Columns 11-18
   Allow the programmer to identify the file that contains the table; this file's name must appear previously in columns 7-14 of the File Description Specifications form.

2. Columns 19-26
   These are used in conjunction with columns 11-18 in order to determine the relationship between two files.

3. Columns 27-32
   The name of the table is entered here; the table must be a function or argument table; its name may consist of four to six characters, the first three being the letters TAB and the last one to three any alphameric characters of the programmer's own choosing.

4. Columns 33-45
   Descriptions of the characteristics of the table identified in columns 27-32 are entered here; the principal characteristics are the number of table entries per record (columns 33-35), the number of entries per table (columns 36-39) and the length of each table entry (columns 40-42).

5. Columns 46-51
   If two tables are necessary, the name of the second (i.e., alternating) table is entered here, following the same rules as for the first table.

6. Columns 52-57
   Descriptions of the features of the second table are entered here in a way entirely similar to those for the first table that were entered in columns 33-45.

7. Columns 58-74
   These 17 columns, ignored by the RPG Compiler, allow the programmer to introduce commentary text.

Figure 14-10 provides examples of the RPG File Extension Specifications as related to the files of Figure 14-9.

14-7   Input Specifications

Figure 14-3 presents the RPG Input Specifications form. As its name suggests, the form is designed to let the programmer describe the process of reading in the program's data. The various groups of data that may comprise the input are usually referred to as *records* (see Section 3-9). In order to fully characterize the input, the programmer must identify the input record and describe this record's fields. The RPG Input Specifications form consists basically of two sections:

> Columns 7-42
> Where the programmer identifies the input record

and

> Columns 43-70
> Where the programmer describes the record's fields.

As in all RPG forms, columns 1-5 are reserved for page and line numbers, column 6 comes preprinted with the form-identifying one-letter code, which in this case is an I (for Input Specifications), and columns 75-80 are used for program identification; in addition to these common specifications, columns 71-74 of the Input Specifications form are used only if the program has to handle Sterling currency amounts.

The record identification section (columns 7-42) is segmented into three principal fields, as summarized below:

1. Columns 7-14
    Where the programmer enters a name for each file that was entered in the File Description Specifications form as an input file, according to the same rules (see Section 14-5).

2. Columns 21-41
    These 21 columns are divided into three identical subfields of seven columns (columns 21-27, 28-34 and 35-41). Entries in these subfields allow the programmer to identify each record type on the basis of special (record identification) codes that appear in specified positions of the input records. The presence of the three subfields permits the programmer to enter up to three identifying codes on one line of the Input Specifications form or more than three by reusing the number of required subfields of subsequent lines (the codes are in an "AND" relationship, i.e., the record is identified by, for example, code 1 *and* code 2 *and* code 3, etc.). Each of the three subfields is

321

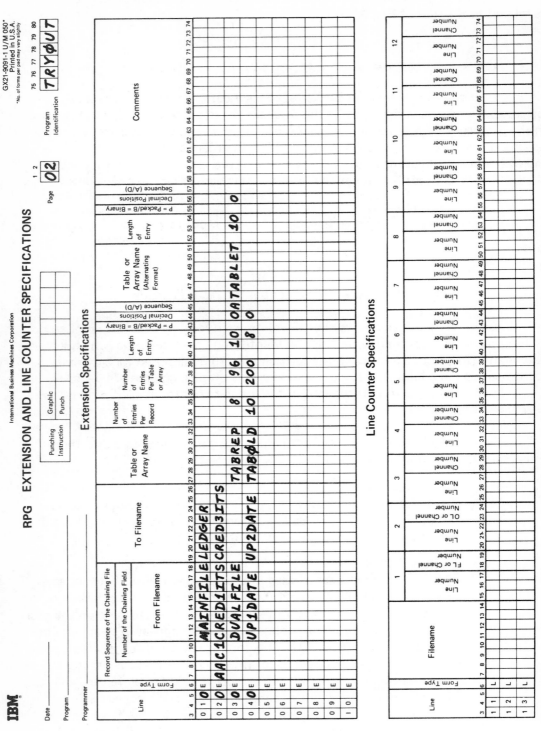

Figure 14-10

322

Figure 14-10 Examples of RPG File Extension Specifications

Line 010—A record-address file, MAINLINE, supplies the addresses of the records to be processed in the indexed-sequential update chained file LEDGER (see Figure 14-9).

Line 020—File CRED1ITS is an input primary card file containing the record key that will be used to process records in the disk file CRED3ITS. In this example, CRED1ITS is the chaining file because it chains (or links) to the CRED3ITS file. Columns 7-10 are used to denote the linking of the files; columns 7-8 contain the code AA (from columns 15-16 of the Input Specifications form) which indicates that the file has only one record type and the input records are not in a predetermined sequence; columns 9-10 contain the code C1, the number of the chaining field, which must also appear in columns 61-62 of the Input Specifications form.

Line 030—An input-table file, DUALFILE (see Figure 14-9), consists of both an argument table and a function table. TABREP contains the arguments that are described in columns 33-45; each record has 8 arguments, and the argument table has 96 arguments of length 10 each; the numerical information in this table has no decimal positions (0 in column 44) and is in ascending sequence (A in column 45). TABLET specifies the functions that are described in columns 52-57; the length of each function is ten characters with no decimal positions. The format of DUALFILE is alternating since entries are arranged in the order argument—function; a very elementary, but good, illustration of this format is a file containing argument and function tables from which determinations of the sales tax based on the sale price of various items can be made.

Line 040—An input-table file, UP1DATE, consists of arguments only, which, once updated, are to be processed (written or punched) by the output-table file, UP2DATE; the arguments, contained in the table named TABOLD, are described in columns 33-45.

segmented into four sections, namely,

Position — which locates the particular identifying code in the corresponding record type,

Not — when an N is entered, the code described must not be present in the defined position else the column is left blank,

C/Z/D — which permits the option of comparing the character in the next (fourth) section of the subfield to the code contained in the record by checking the entire character (C), only the zone portion (Z), or only the digit portion (D), and

Character — which defines the character to be used to identify the type of input record; if the preceding section of the subfield has a C or D, then this may be any one of the 256 EBCDIC characters (see Section 2-5 and Appendix D), or if the preceding section has a Z, the character in this section may be & or A through I (to check the 12-zone), – or J through R (to check the 11-zone), S through Z (to check for the 0-zone) and blank or 0 through 9 (to check for no zone).

3. Columns 15-16, 17, 18, 19-20 and 42
These columns provide additional information concerning the processing of the input records. Depending on whether the input records are or are not in a certain order, the sequence (columns 15-16) may be arbitrary (a two-character alphabetic code is entered) or predetermined (a two-digit numeric code is used). Column 17 may be left blank, or may be filled with a 1 or an N; blank signifies no predetermined sequence, 1 means only one record is present, and N means one or more records are present. If the records are in a predetermined order (and, hence, are sequenced numerically), then column 18 may be entered with an O (Optional) which means that the record of the specified type is not necessarily present; otherwise, column 18 is left blank. Columns 19-20 should be entered with a two-digit indicator (in the range from 01 to 99) to assign a two-digit code for the input record defined in columns 21-41. Finally, column 42, stacker select, should be left blank for single stacker devices and for combined files; otherwise, the number of the stacker to which the cards are to be selectively placed is entered.

The Field Description section (columns 43-70) consists of a number of subsections, the meaning of which is largely self-explanatory. Each line of record identification entries (columns 7-42) may pertain to more than one field and each of the fields is represented by one line of field description entries; thus, several field description lines may correspond to one record identification line.

324

Figure 14-11 provides examples of the RPG Input Specifications as related to the files of Figure 14-9.

The coding of the RPG Input Specifications form may be classified in the range from a virtually effortless filling of the appropriate sections to a rather complicated and error-prone exercise. The difficulties arise in the interrelations of the Input Specifications form with two other forms, Calculation Specifications and Output-Format Specifications, and are chiefly created by the slightly cumbersome RPG logic which may involve many indicators of various kinds per file. Although most of the difficult cases could be illustrated with examples, the treatment of these is beyond the scope of this textbook. Some examples richer in these features are given in Chapter 15; for additional and more detailed discussion of these and other, more specialized, features, the reader is advised to refer to the Bibliography (Appendix G).

14-8   Calculation Specifications

The RPG Calculation Specifications form (Figure 14-4) is, perhaps, after the Control Card, the simplest of the RPG form repertoire. The four main fields (not counting common entries, as in all RPG forms, see Section 14-4) are specific in their purposes.

The conditioning sections (columns 7-17) are used to define the conditions under which the calculations are to be carried out. The calculating sections (columns 18-53) have the obvious purpose and are broken down into four subfields: names of factors involved in the calculations (columns 18-27 and 33-42), name of the operator identifying the operation to be carried out (columns 28-32), name of the variable obtaining (or storing) the result of the calculation (columns 43-48), and incidental computational information which includes field length, number of decimal spaces, and rounding option (columns 49-53). The testing section (columns 54-59) has likewise its obvious purpose of testing indicators or comparing arithmetic values of the two factors. Finally, commentary text may be entered in the comment section (columns 60-74).

Figure 14-12 provides examples of RPG Calculations Specifications. This example provides simple usage illustrations for 13 of the 27 RPG operation codes, including all 7 arithmetic operations. The operation codes not illustrated have more specialized purposes. A few further illustrations of RPG operation codes appear in Chapter 15. The field length, decimal positions, and half-adjust columns (columns 49-53) were left blank in the example in Figure 14-12, but their usage is self-explanatory. A final remark with regard to the sectioning of the RPG Calculation Specifications form may be helpful in remembering the entries: 1) Entries in columns 7-17 define "when to compute"; 2) Entries in columns 18-53 tell us and

International Business Machines Corporation

RPG INPUT SPECIFICATIONS

Date _____
Program _____
Programmer _____

Punching Instruction	Graphic		
	Punch		

Page **03**   1 2

GX21-9094-1 U/M 050*
Printed in U.S.A.

Program Identification (75 76 77 78 79 80): **TRYØUT**

Line	Form Type	Filename	Sequence	Number (1-N)	Option (O)	Record Identifying Indicator	Position 1	Not(N) 1	C/Z/D 1	Char 1	Position 2	Not(N) 2	C/Z/D 2	Char 2	Position 3	Not(N) 3	C/Z/D 3	Char 3	From	To	Dec Pos	Field Name	Control Level	Matching/Chaining	Field Record Relation
010	I	CRED1ITS	AA			01	13		C	L									1	12		CLIENT		C1	
020	I		BB			02	13		D	7	80	N	Z	−											
030	I																		1	3		STATUS			
040	I																		4	6		BUREAU			
050	I																		7	9		DELAYS			
060	I																		10	12		REFERN			
070	I																								
080	I	MAINFILE	CC			25	80		D	1															
090	I		ØR			26	80		D	2															
100	I																		1	35		DATA10	L1		
110	I																		36	70		DATA20	L1		
120	I																		1	20		DATA05	L1		25
130	I																		36	55		DATA15	L1		26
140	I	CRED2ITS	DD			39	76		D	1	77		D	1	78		D	1							
150	I		AND				79		D	1	80	N	Z	&											
160	I																		1	70		ADDRES			

Field Indicators — Plus (65 66), Minus (67 68), Zero or Blank (69 70); Sterling Sign Position (71 72 73 74)

Figure 14-11

*Number of forms per pad may vary slightly

326

Figure 14-11   Examples of RPG Input Specifications

Line 010—The input primary file CRED1ITS (columns 7-14 of this form and in Figures 14-9 and 14-10) contains alphabetic characters that need not be read in a predetermined sequence (AA in columns 15-16); therefore, columns 17, 18 are left blank. Whenever a record from file CRED1ITS is read, the record identifying indicator 01 (columns 19-20) is turned on if an L is found in column 13 of an input card.

Line 020—There is only one field, named CLIENT (columns 53-58) in this type of input record, occupying the first 12 columns of each card to be read; this field chains (C1 in columns 61-62) to file CRED3ITS (Figure 14-10).

Line 030—The record identifying indicator 02 is turned on if column 13 of an input card contains the digit 7 and column 80 does not contain an 11-zone punch.

Lines 040-070—This type of input record has four three-column fields, named STATUS, BUREAU, DELAYS and REFFERN; these fields have alphameric data, hence no decimal positions (column 52) are specified.

Lines 080-090—The records of the input file MAINFILE (Figure 14-9) are distinguished from other records by the presence of the digit 1 or the digit 2 in column 80; since the record identification codes are in an "AND" relationship, an "OR" must be entered in columns 14-15.

Lines 100-130—Four fields are identified in MAINFILE; the last two fields, DATA05 and DATA15, are respective subfields of the first two, DATA10 and DATA20, since, for example, DATA05's location is in the first 20 columns of the card while DATA10's is in the first 35 columns of the same card. Although all four fields have control level indicator L1 (entered in columns 59-60 of this Input Specifications form and also in columns 7-8 of the Calculation Specifications form), the first two fields are disregarded because they are not conditioned by the field-record relation indicators 25 or 26.

Lines 140-150—The records of the input secondary file CRED2ITS (Figure 14-9) are distinguished from other records by the presence of the digit 1 in columns 76, 77, 78 and 79, and the absence of a 12-zone punch in column 80.

327

IBM

International Business Machines Corporation

GX21-9093-1 U/M 050*
Printed in U.S.A.
*No. of forms per pad may vary slightly

Page **04**   1 2

Program Identification   **TRYØUT**   75 76 77 78 79 80

RPG CALCULATION SPECIFICATIONS

Date _____   Program _____   Programmer _____

Punching Instruction — Graphic / Punch

Line	Form Type	Control Level	Indicators	Factor 1	Operation	Factor 2	Result Field	Resulting Indicators
01	C			ADDEN1	ADD	ADDEN2	SUM1	
02	C			INDEX	ADD	1	INDEX	
03	C				Z-ADD	25	SUBTØT	
04	C			X	SUB	Y	Z	
05	C				Z-SUB	VARBLE	VARBLE	
06	C			FACTR1	MULT	FACTR2	PRØDCT	
07	C			TØRIAL	MULT	5	TØRIAL	
08	C			10000000	MULT	10000000	Z	
09	C			FIRST	DIV	SECØND	MAYBE	
10	C				MVR		ANSWER	
11	C				MOVE	25	KEEP	
12	C			CØEFF1	CØMP	CØEFF2	SUBTØT	25 47 68
13	C		25	CØEFF1	SUB	CØEFF2	QUATN	
14	C		47	CØEFF2	SUB	CØEFF1	QUATN	
15	C		68		MOVE	0	QUATN	
16	C			TAXTØT	LØKUP	TABREP	TABLET	
17	C			DATA35	CHAIN	LEDGER		
18	C				GØTØ	STØP		
19	C			STØP	TAG			

Figure 14-12

328

Figure 14-12   Examples of RPG Calculation Specifications

Line 010—The contents of the field or literal in Factor 1 named ADEND1 (columns 18-27) are algebraically added to the contents in Factor 2 named ADEND2 (columns 33-42), and the resulting sum is stored in SUM1 (columns 43-48).

Line 020—Factor 1 named INDEX is incremented by 1.

Line 030—The result field, SUBTOT, is first set equal to zero (initialized) and then 25 is added to it; Factor 1 is not used. For an alternative way of accomplishing this, see Line 110.

Line 040—This line is equivalent to the assignment $Z = X - Y$.

Line 050—The result field, VARBLE, is first set equal to zero and then its own value from Factor 2 is subtracted. Factor 1 is not used. This operation accomplishes the reversal of the sign of a field, e.g., if VARBLE was positive, after this operation it would be negative.

Line 060—FACTOR1 is multiplied by FACTOR2 and the product is stored in PRODCT.

Line 070—TORIAL is multiplied by 5.

Line 080—The product of these two 8-digit numbers will be a 16-digit number, and this will cause problems, as 1130 RPG cannot detect arithmetic overflow. Not more than 14 digits are permitted.

Line 090—FIRST is divided by SECOND and the quotient is stored in ANSWER, if Factor 2, SECOND, is not equal to zero (if the divisor happens to be zero, an error wait occurs, leaving it up to the operator to either continue with a zero in the result field or terminate the job). While the quotient will be stored in ANSWER, the remainder will be lost unless the move-remainder (MVR) operation is specified as the next operation, in which case the half-adjusting (rounding) entry H (column 53) must not be used for the divide (DIV) operation.

Line 100—The remainder of the preceding division is stored in KEEP. Both Factor 1 and Factor 2 must be left blank.

Line 110—The contents of Factor 2 are moved to the result field; SUBTOT obtains the value 25 (compare with Line 030).

Lines 120-150—The literal or contents of Factor 1 are compared against the literal or contents of Factor 2. The operator COMP then turns on the appropriate indicators in columns 54-59. Thus, if COEFF1 is greater than COEFF2, then control is transferred to indicator 25; if COEFF2 is larger, indicator 47 is turned on; and if the two fields are equal, indicator 68 is turned on.

Line 160—The name of Factor 1, TAXTOT, is used to search an argument table, the name of which appears under Factor 2, TABREP (Figure 14-10), and the result field has the name of the function table, TABLET (Figure 14-10).

Line 170—A record, named DATA35 in Factor 1, is retrieved from a disk file named LEDGER (Figure 14-9 and 14-10) in Factor 2.

the 1130 RPG Compiler "what to compute"; 3) Entries in columns 28-32 define "how to compute," i.e., what operation to use; and 4) Entries in columns 54-59 determine "how to test results of the computations."

14-9 Output-Format Specifications

Figure 14-5 presents the RPG Output-Format Specifications form. This form is designed to describe the manner in which output is to be handled. As before, the essential items are files and the main information about these pertains to the positioning (or formatting) of data, results of calculations and special reports. The form itself could be partitioned into three principal sections (excluding common entries, Section 14-4, and the four columns (columns 71-74) reserved for use only if the program has to handle Sterling currency amounts).

1. Columns 7-31
Which allow the programmer to identify the output field and select the proper carriage control for spacing.

2. Columns 32-44
Where the programmer describes the fields with their respective names, concerning the location and appearance of these fields.

3. Columns 45-70
Where the programmer enters numerical constants and/or "edit words" that will add to the comprehension and readability of the output.

The first section (columns 7-31) is used for File Identification and Control. In addition to entering the file name (columns 7-14), the programmer chooses the type file type (Heading, Detail, Total or Exception) by entering one of the four one-letter codes (H, D, T, E) in column 15, and the number of the stacker of the output unit that will accept the selected cards in column 16 (which should have a 1 or be left blank, if the regular stacker is used). Then, carriage control entries (columns 17-22) designate the number of lines to be skipped before printing and the appropriate channel on the paper tape to which the printer carriage will skip before printing. Finally, columns 23-31 are used to enter the output indicators which are going to control the output of the lines specified.

The second and third sections (columns 32-44 and 45-70) are largely self-explanatory; the form has a convenient table of edit codes at the top right corner.

Figure 14-13 provides examples of RPG Output-Format Specifications. As this simple example illustrates, the RPG Output-Format Specifications form is almost self-explanatory. Output indicators are tied in with the RPG program logic. The various edit codes involved are summarized on the form itself.

14-10 Printer Spacing Chart

The Printer Spacing Chart (Figure 14-6) is a very convenient tool in the planning of the physical positioning and appearance of printed records.

The chart is a much larger sized form than the rather "petite" RPG forms. It approximates the dimensions of the actual printout paper. Prior to completing the RPG Output-Format Specifications form, the programmer may wish to organize the layout on the Printer Spacing Chart in a manner identical to the final output desired. Although the chart extends to 144 columns, the line printers associated with the 1130 permit only 120 columns of output. As the vertical size of the paper (or other output media, such as self-sticking labels, for example) may vary, the appropriate paper tape length should be chosen and punched according to the particular output requirements.

An example of a layout of desired output on the printer spacing chart is given in Figure 14-14.

14-11 Indicator Summary Form

As mentioned in Section 14-4, two RPG Specifications forms permit commentary text specifically (the File Extension Specifications form in columns 58-74, and the Calculation Specifications form in columns 60-74); also, all RPG forms allow commentary text on any line of the form if an asterisk (*) is entered in column 7. Comments are optional entries on RPG forms; they will be printed on the source program listing but otherwise will be disregarded by the 1130 RPG Compiler. Since RPG programming requires the filling out of a number of different RPG forms, the addition of comment lines greatly increases the readability of the RPG source program and provides extremely useful documentation for future reference and to other programmers. Therefore, the writing of comments in all RPG forms is to be strongly encouraged.

The RPG Indicator Summary form (Figure 14-7) allows the programmer to list all the indicators used in the RPG program in an organized manner, and thus significantly enhance the program's documentation. Column 7 of the Indicator Summary form contains the asterisk (*) code already preprinted; hence all entries on this form will be treated as comments by the 1130 RPG Compiler and will appear only in the source program listing. The entries on the Indicator Summary form may be punched on cards; it is customary to insert these cards after the File Description Specifications form cards. The usage of the Indicator Summary form is self-explanatory.

An example involving indicators found in the preceding examples is given in Figure 14-15. Figure 14-16 is a composite illustration with tables, describing the uses of all of the fields on the RPG specification forms.

IBM

International Business Machines Corporation

RPG   OUTPUT - FORMAT SPECIFICATIONS

GX21-9090-1 U/M 050*
Printed in U.S.A.

Date _____
Program _____
Programmer _____

Punching Instruction — Graphic / Punch

Page **05**   1 2

Program Identification **TRYOUT**   75 76 77 78 79 80

Edit Codes

Commas	Zero Balances to Print	No Sign	CR	-
Yes	Yes	1	A	J
Yes	No	2	B	K
No	Yes	3	C	L
No	No	4	D	M

X = Remove Plus Sign
Y = Date Field Edit
Z = Zero Suppress

Line	Form Type	Filename	Type (H/D/T/E)	Stacker Select/Fetch Overflow (F)	Space Before	Space After	Skip Before	Skip After	Output Indicators						Field Name	Edit Codes	Blank After (B)	End Position in Output Record	P=Packed/B=Binary	Constant or Edit Word
010	0	PAY1ROLLH					1201		1P											
020	0		OR						OF											
030	0																	67		'COMPANY PAYROLL'
040	0																	109		'DATE'
050	0								01						MONTH			112		
060	0		H OR		2				OF											
070	0														DAY			115		
080	0														YEAR			120		
090	0																	10		'DEPT'
100	0																	40		'NAME'
110	0																	55		'SOC SEC'
120	0																	70		'GROSS SAL'
130	0																	80		'FED TAX'
140	0																	90		'MISC DED'
150	0																	105		'NET SAL'
160	0		D		2				02						DEPT			10		
170	0														NAME			40		
180	0														SOCSEC			55		
190	0																			
200	0																			

*Number of forms per pad may vary slightly

Figure 14-13

332

Figure 14-13   Examples of RPG Output-Format Specifications

Line 010—An output file, named PAY1ROLL (columns 7-14), previously defined (Figure 14-9), is going to be processed. Heading records (H in column 15) are printed first, after one line is skipped from the top of the printout page (column 17) and after the paper tape that regulates the printer carriage has advanced to channel 1 before printing begins (columns 19-20); once the initial headings are printed, two more spaces are skipped (column 18).

Lines 030-070—The heading, COMPANY PAYROLL, is positioned at the top and middle of the printout sheet of 120 columns. At the right top corner, the heading DATE: is followed by the actual entries contained in the fields MONTH, DAY and YEAR.

Lines 100-160—Additional subheadings are printed.

Lines 180 on—The entries under the respective subheadings are printed from the contents of the corresponding fields.

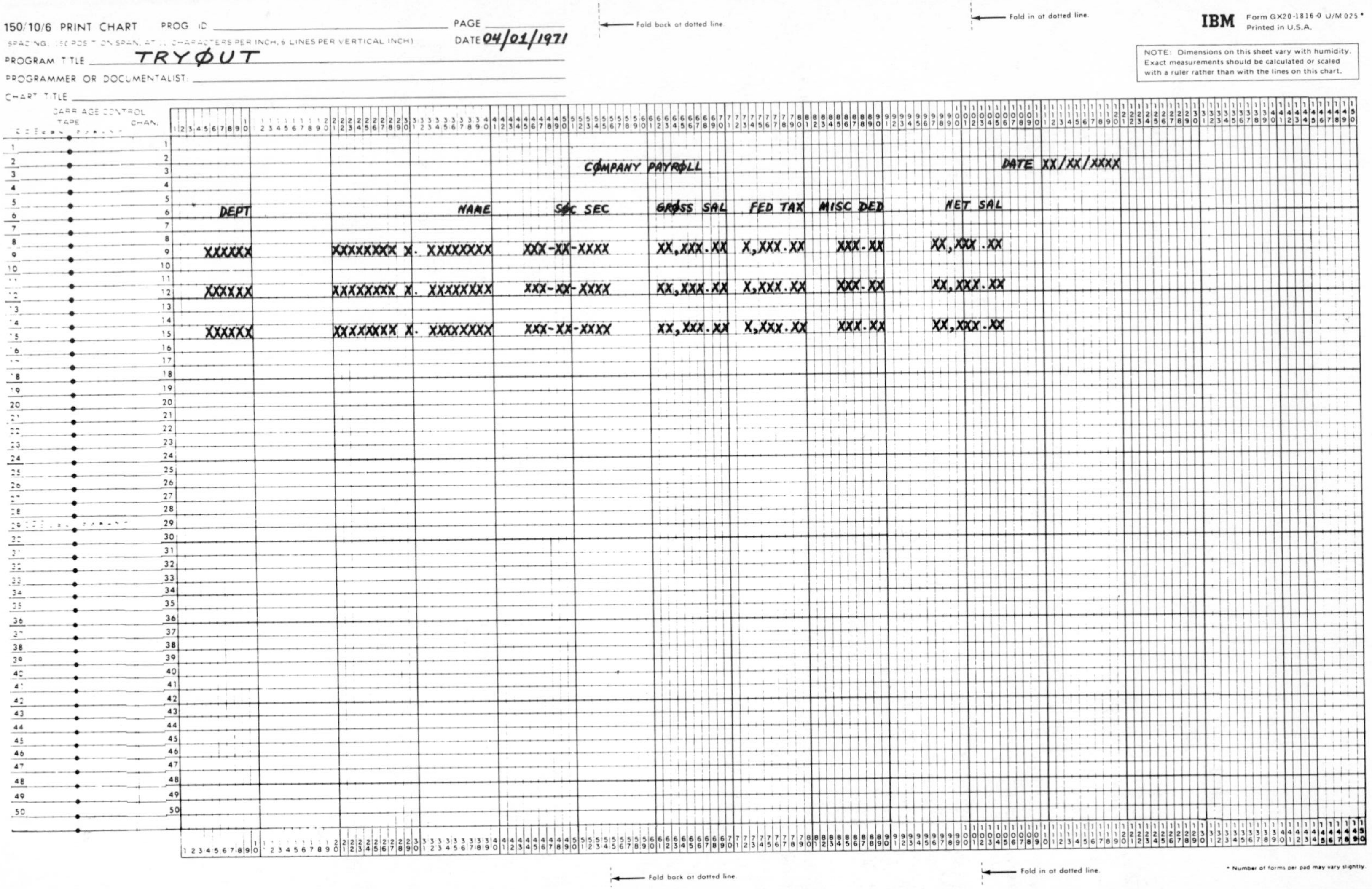

SPACING: 10/25 25 SPAN. / CHARACTERS PER INCH, 6 LINES PER VERTICAL INCH)

PROGRAM TITLE TRYOUT DATE 04/01/1971

PROGRAMMER OR DOCUMENTALIST ___

CHART TITLE ___

IBM   Form GX20-1816-0 U/M 025*
Printed in U.S.A.

NOTE: Dimensions on this sheet may vary with humidity.
Exact measurements should be calculated or scaled
with a ruler rather than with the lines on this chart.

COMPANY PAYROLL   DATE XX/XX/XXXX

DEPT	NAME	SOC SEC	GROSS SAL	FED TAX	MISC DED	NET SAL
XXXXX	X. XXXXXXXX	XXX-XX-XXXX	XX,XXX.XX	X,XXX.XX	XXX.XX	XX,XXX.XX
XXXXX	X. XXXXXXXX	XXX-XX-XXXX	XX,XXX.XX	X,XXX.XX	XXX.XX	XX,XXX.XX
XXXXX	X. XXXXXXXX	XXX-XX-XXXX	XX,XXX.XX	X,XXX.XX	XXX.XX	XX,XXX.XX

* Number of forms per pad may vary slightly.

Figure 14-14

Figure 14-14   Example of Layout of Desired Output on the Printer Spacing Chart

(facing page)

The entries on the Printer Spacing Chart are arranged according to obvious space requirements. This example is based on the example of RPG Output-Format Specifications form entries (Figure 14-13).

Figure 14-15   Example of RPG Indicator Summary Form

(following page)

It is a good idea to keep track of the various indicators used, especially since the RPG program's complexity increases in direct proportion to the number of indicators used. The example given here involves a few of the indicators encountered before, mainly from Figure 14-11.

Figure 14-16   RPG Specification Forms with Field Descriptions

(pages 337 through 346)

The circled numbers and letters shown on the specification forms reference explanatory notes on the pages following.

International Business Machines Corporation

RPG INDICATOR SUMMARY

GX21-9095-0 U/M025
Printed in U.S.A.

Date _____
Program _____
Programmer _____

Punching Instruction	Graphic			
	Punch			

Page **07** Program Identification **TRYOUT**

Note: All indicators are not valid with all systems.

Circle Indicators Used:

01 02 03 04 05 06 07 08 09 10 11 12 13 14 15 16 17 18 19 20
21 22 23 24 25 26 27 28 29 30 31 32 33 34 35 36 37 38 39 40
41 42 43 44 45 46 47 48 49 50 51 52 53 54 55 56 57 58 59 60
61 62 63 64 65 66 67 68 69 70 71 72 73 74 75 76 77 78 79 80
81 82 83 84 85 86 87 88 89 90 91 92 93 94 95 96 97 98 99
L1 L2 L3 L4 L5 L6 L7 L8 L9 0A 0B 0C 0D 0E 0F 0G OV

Predefined Indicators:
1P M1 M2 M3 M4 M5 M6 M7 M8 M9 U1 U2 U3 U4 U5 U6 U7 U8
M-C: M1 H1 H2 H3 H4 H5 H6 H7 H8 H9 H0
LR L0 MR

(Circled indicators: 01, 02, 03, 25, 26, 47, 68, 39, 0F, L1, 1P)

FUNCTION OF INDICATORS

Line	Form Type	Record Identifying	Input Field	Calculation Result	Matching and Chaining	Control Level, Overflow, Halt and User	Function of Indicators
01	*OF	ID	F	C	M	L	CLIENT CARD
02	*OF	01					CREDIT RATING CARD
03	*OF	02					MISCELLANEOUS CREDIT DATA CARD
04	*OF	03					MAINFILE CARDS OR RESULTING INDIC FROM CALCULATION
05	*OF	25		47			MAINFILE CARDS
06	*OF	26		68			ADDRESS CARD
07	*OF	39					RESULTING INDICATOR FROM COMPARISON CALCULATION
08	*OF						SAME AS 47
09	*OF						
10	*OF					L1	MAINLINE FIELDS
11	*OF					1P	FIRST PAGE OUTPUT INDICATOR
12	*OF					0F	OVERFLOW INDICATOR
13	*F						
14	*F						
15	*F						

Figure 14-15

International Business Machines Corporation

GX21-9092-1 U/M050
Printed in U.S.A.

RPG CONTROL CARD AND FILE DESCRIPTION SPECIFICATIONS

Date _____
Program _____
Programmer _____

| Punching Instruction | Graphic | | | | | | |
| | Punch | | | | | | |

Page (1) Program Identification (A)

75 76 77 78 79 80

Control Card Specifications

Refer to the specific System Reference Library manual for actual entries.

Line | Form Type | Core Size to Compile | Object Output | Listing Options | Core Size to Execute | Debug | MFCM Stacking Sequence | Sterling: Input-Shillings / Input-Pence / Output-Shillings / Output-Pence | Inverted Print | Number 360/20 2501 Buffer | Number Of Print Positions | Alternate Collating Sequence

B 1 H (7) (8) (9)

File Description Specifications

| | | File Type | Mode of Processing | | Extent Exit for DAM | File Addition/Unordered |
| | Filename | File Designation / End of File / Sequence / File Format | Length of Key Field or of Record Address Field / Record Address Type / Type of File Organization or Additional Area / Overflow Indicator / Key Field Starting Location | Device | Symbolic Device | Name of Label Exit | Number of Tracks for Cylinder Overflow / Number of Extents / Tape Rewind / File Condition U1-U8 |

Line | Form Type | Filename | I/O/U/C/D | P/S/C/R/T/D | E | A/D | F/V | Block Length | Record Length | L/R | A/K/I | I/D/T or 19 | Extension Code E/L | Device | Symbolic Device | Labels IS, N, or E | Name of Label Exit | Core Index | A/U | N/U

0 2 F (10) (11) (16) (21) (22) (24) (25) (26)
0 3 F
0 4 F (12) (17) (23)
0 5 F (13) (18)
0 6 F
0 7 F (14) (19)
B F (15) (20)

International Business Machines Corporation

GX21-9095-0 U/M025
Printed in U.S.A.

RPG INDICATOR SUMMARY

Date _____
Program _____
Programmer _____

| Punching Instruction | Graphic | | | | | | |
| | Punch | | | | | | |

Page (2) Program Identification (A)

75 76 77 78 79 80

Indicators

Circle Indicators Used:

Note: All indicators are not valid with all systems.

01	02	03	04	05	06	07	08	09	10	11	12	13	14	15	16	17	18	19	20
21	22	23	24	25	26	27	28	29	30	31	32	33	34	35	36	37	38	39	40
41	42	43	44	45	46	47	48	49	50	51	52	53	54	55	56	57	58	59	60
61	62	63	64	65	66	67	68	69	70	71	72	73	74	75	76	77	78	79	80
81	82	83	84	85	86	87	88	89	90	91	92	93	94	95	96	97	98	99	
L1	L2	L3	L4	L5	L6	L7	L8	L9		OA	OB	OC	OD	OE	OF	OG	OV		
H1	H2	H3	H4	H5	H6	H7	H8	H9		U1	U2	U3	U4	U5	U6	U7	U8		

Predefined Indicators: IP L0 LR MR H0

M-C: M1 M2 M3 M4 M5 M6 M7 M8 M9 C1 C2 C3 C4 C5 C6 C7 C8 C9

Line | Form Type | Record Identifying | Input Field | Calculation Result | Matching and Chaining | Control Level, Overflow, Halt and User

0 1 F • ID F C M L **FUNCTION OF INDICATORS**
0 2 F •
0 3 F •
0 4 F • (27)
0 5 F •
0 6 F •
0 7 F •
0 8 F •
0 9 F •
1 0 F •
1 1 F •
1 2 F •
1 3 F •
1 4 F •
1 5 F •
B F •
F •

Figure 14-16 Concordance of Entries on RPG Specifications Forms

International Business Machines Corporation

RPG EXTENSION AND LINE COUNTER SPECIFICATIONS

GX21-9091-1 U/M 050*
Printed in U.S.A.
*No. of forms per pad may vary slightly

Date _____

Program _____

Programmer _____

Punching Instruction — Graphic / Punch

Page **3** Program Identification **A**

75 76 77 78 79 80

Extension Specifications

Line	Form Type	Record Sequence of the Chaining File / Number of the Chaining Field / From Filename	To Filename	Table or Array Name	Number of Entries Per Record	Number of Entries Per Table or Array	Length of Entry	P=Packed/B=Binary	Decimal Positions	Sequence (A/D)	Table or Array Name (Alternating Format)	Length of Entry	P=Packed/B=Binary	Decimal Positions	Sequence (A/D)	Comments
0 1	E															
0 2	E	⊛28 ⊛30	⊛31	⊛32	⊛33 ⊛34		⊛35				⊛39	⊛40				⊛42
0 3	E															
0 4	E	⊛29					⊛36					⊛41				
0 5	E															
0 6	E						⊛37									
0 7	E															
0 8	E						⊛38									
0 9	E															
1 0	E															

Line Counter Specifications   **B**

Line	Form Type	Filename	1 Line Number	FL or Channel Number	2 Line Number	OL or Channel Number	3 Line Number	Channel Number	4 Line Number	Channel Number	5 Line Number	Channel Number	6 Line Number	Channel Number	7 Line Number	Channel Number	8 Line Number	Channel Number	9 Line Number	Channel Number	10 Line Number	Channel Number	11 Line Number	Channel Number	12 Line Number	Channel Number
1 1	L																									
1 2	L																									
1 3	L																									

International Business Machines Corporation

RPG INPUT SPECIFICATIONS

GX21-9094-1 U/M 050*
Printed in U.S.A.

Date _____

Program _____

Programmer _____

Punching Instruction — Graphic / Punch

Page **4** Program Identification **A**

75 76 77 78 79 80

Line	Form Type	Filename	Sequence	Number (1/N)	Option (O)	Record Identifying Indicator or **	Record Identification Codes 1 Position	Not (N)	C/Z/D	Character	2 Position	Not (N)	C/Z/D	Character	3 Position	Not (N)	C/Z/D	Character	Stacker Select	P=Packed/B=Binary	Field Location From	To	Decimal Positions	Field Name	Control Level (L1-L9)	Matching Fields or Chaining Fields	Field Record Relation	Field Indicators Plus	Minus	Zero or Blank	Sterling Sign Position
0 1	I	⊛43	⊛44				⊛48				⊛48				⊛48				⊛52		⊛54			⊛56	⊛57				⊛60			
0 2	I		⊛45				⊛49				⊛49				⊛49				⊛53		⊛55					⊛58						
0 3	I																															
0 4	I		⊛46				⊛50				⊛50				⊛50											⊛59						
0 5	I																															
0 6	I		⊛47				⊛51				⊛51				⊛51																	
0 7	I																															
0 8	I																															
0 9	I																															
1 0	I																															
1 1	I																															
1 2	I																															
1 3	I																															
1 4	I																															
1 5	I																															
B	I																															

*Number of forms per pad may vary slightly

Figure 14-16 (cont.)

International Business Machines Corporation

GX21-9093-1 U/M 050*
Printed in U.S.A.
*No. of forms per pad may vary slightly

RPG CALCULATION SPECIFICATIONS

Date _____

Program _____

Programmer _____

Punching Instruction — Graphic / Punch

Page 5   Program Identification A

Line	Form Type	Control Level (L0-L9, LR, SR)	Indicators And Not / And Not	Factor 1	Operation	Factor 2	Result Field	Field Length	Decimal Positions	Half Adjust (H)	Resulting Indicators / Arithmetic Plus Minus Zero / Compare High Low Equal 1>2 1<2 1=2 / Lookup Table (Factor 2) is High Low Equal	Comments

(Form rows 01–15 and B, all marked with C in Form Type column; circled reference numbers: 61, 62, 63, 63, 64, 65, 66, 67, 68, 69, 70)

International Business Machines Corporation

GX21-9090-1 U/M 050*
Printed in U.S.A.

RPG OUTPUT - FORMAT SPECIFICATIONS

Date _____

Program _____

Programmer _____

Punching Instruction — Graphic / Punch

Page 6   Program Identification A

Edit Codes

	Commas	Zero Balances to Print	No Sign	CR	−	X = Remove Plus Sign
	Yes	Yes	1	A	J	Y = Date Field Edit
	Yes	No	2	B	K	Z = Zero Suppress
	No	Yes	3	C	L	
	No	No	4	D	M	

Constant or Edit Word

Line	Form Type	Filename	Type (H/D/T/E)	Stacker Select/Fetch Overflow (F)	Space Before After	Skip Before After	Output Indicators And Not / And Not / Not	Field Name	Edit Codes	Blank After (B)	End Position in Output Record	Packed/B = Binary	Sterling Sign Position

(Form rows 01–15 and B, all marked with O in Form Type column; circled reference numbers: 71, 72, 73, 74, 75, 76, 77, 78, 79, 80, 81, 82, 83, 84, 85)

*Number of forms per pad may vary slightly

Figure 14-16 (cont.)

339

FOR ALL FORMS:

Codes for column 6:

H	Control Card	I	Input
F	File Description	C	Calculation
E	File Extension	O	Output-Format

Codes for column 7:

Blank or letter (option for all forms)
* The line is a comment

A Used for program identification only. May contain alphameric characters or may be left blank.

B A zero may be entered in col. 5 for each line; if lines need to be inserted, intermediate line numbers may be chosen. For each page number, there is a choice of 999 line numbers (001-999).

1 Pages 01-04

2 Pages 05-09

3 Pages 05-09

4 Pages 10-39

5 Pages 40-69

6 Pages 70-99

CONTROL CARD:

7 B Compile only
   D List only
   Blank—Compile and list

8 I European (inverted print) convention
   Blank—Domestic convention

9 A Alternating collating sequence
   Blank—Regular collating sequence

10 Up to 8 alphameric (letter first) characters, left-justified (first five characters must be unique)

11 I Input file   U Update file
   O Output file   C Combined file

12 P Primary file   R Record-Address
   S Secondary file   (RA) file
   T Table file   C Chained file

13 E End-of-job at end-of-file (input files)
   Blank—End-of-job when all input files have been processed; or random processing of ISAM file; or table or output file

14 A Ascending order of matching fields
   D Descending order of matching fields
   Blank—No matching fields

15 F Fixed-length file format

CONTROL CARD (continued)

16 80—Card
   120—Printer paper
   640—SAM files (disk)
   636—ISAM files (disk)
   Blank—Assumed 80

17 R ISAM file (random processing)
   L ISAM file (processing limits provided by RA file)
   Blank—Cards or SAM (disk) file

18 Length entry made for RA file's address field or ISAM file's key field
   Blank—Otherwise

19 K ISAM file (processed by record key)
   Blank—SAM (disk) file or cards

20 I ISAM file
   2 Two I/O areas used
   Blank—Cards or SAM (disk) file

21 OF or OV—Overflow indicators are used
   Blank—Overflow indicators not used or for console typewriter and nonprinter devices

22 1 ISAM file
   Blank—Cards or SAM (disk) file

23 E RA file, chaining file or table file; additional information provided on File Extension form
   Blank—Otherwise

24 READ42—IBM 1442 Card Read/Punch Model 6 or 7
   READ01—IBM 2501 Card Reader Model A1 or A2
   PUNCH42—IBM 1442 Card Punch Model
   PRINTER—IBM 1132 Printer
   PRINT03—IBM 1403 Printer Model 6 or
   CONSOLE—IBM 1131 Console Printer
   DISK—IBM 2310 Disk Storage Drive Model B1 and B2, or IBM 1131 Internal Disk

25 1-99999 (right-justified)—Number of ISAM file records
   Blank—Otherwise

26 A ISAM file to which new records will be added; column 15 must have letter C, column 28 must be blank, and columns 16-18 of Output-Format form must have ADD entry
   Blank—Otherwise

27 See Indicator Summary Table, pp 343-344

CONTROL CARD (continued):

Entry from columns 15-16 of Input form, used with C1, C2, C3—ISAM files, alternate chaining method
Blank—Otherwise

C1, C2 or C3 entry from columns 61-62 of Input form (if entry is made in columns 7-8 of this form)
Blank—Otherwise

Name of chaining file, or Record-Address (RA) file, or table file

Name of chained file, or file to be accessed, or output file (or blank), respectively to columns 11-18

TABx or TABxx or TABxxx—name of table (from four to six alphameric characters, the first three being TAB)

Right-justified

Right-justified

Right-justified

P Packed data (disk files only)
Blank—Otherwise

0 — Numeric field, no decimals
1-9 — Numeric field, 1-9 decimals
Blank—Alphameric field

A Data in table is in ascending sequence
D Data in table is in descending sequence
Blank—No sequence

See columns 27-32.

Right-justified

See columns 43-45

Commentary text (disregarded by RPG compiler)

INPUT:

Name of files (left-justified) described as input files in cols. 7-14 of File Description form

Unique 2-character code (e.g., AA, BB, CC, GL, SF, etc.)—Unsequenced records or only one type of record (column 17 must be blank)
Unique 2-digit code (e.g., 01, 28, 46, etc.)—Sequenced records (column 17 must not be blank)

INPUT (continued):

45 I One record type (sequenced) is read before other records
    N One or more record types (sequenced) may be read
    Blank—Unsequenced records

46 O (letter) Given record need not be present (is optional (Used only when cols. 16-16 have numeric code)
    Blank—Given record must be present, or records are unsequenced

47 01-99—Choice of 99 indicators; order is of no importance

48 Right-justified

49 N Code (described in columns 26-27, 33-38, 40-41) is absent
    Blank—Code is present

50 C Code is entire character
    Z Code is zone portion only
    D Code is digit portion only

51 Any one of the 256 EBCDIC characters—If columns 26, 33, 40 (respectively) have C or D
    12-zone, 11-zone, or absence of 11- or 12-zone—If columns 26, 33, 40 have Z

52 Blank—For stacker of single-stacker devices or normal stacker of multistacker devices
    Number of chosen stacker—Otherwise

53 P Packed data (disk only)
    Blank—Otherwise

54 Right-justified

55 Blank—Alphameric data
    0—Numeric data, no decimals
    1-9—Numeric data, 1-9 decimals

56 Up to six alphameric (letter first) characters, left-justified

57 L1 (lowest) to L9 (highest) indicators

58 M1-M9—Matching field indicators
    C1-C3—Alternate chaining method indicators

59 Usually record-identifying (01-99) indicators (from columns 19-20) to show relation to fields in different locations

60 01-99 or H1-H9—Plus or Minus is used for numeric fields with respectively positive or negative values; Zero or blank is used for alphameric fields.

CALCULATION:

61   L1-L9—From cols. 59-60 of Input form
LR—Last record indicator
L0—Level zero indicator
SR—Closed (internal) subroutine coding line

62   Any of the indicators may be used

63   Field name—Up to six alphameric characters (letter first) left-justified; must have been defined in columns 53-58 of Input form or as a result field (columns 43-48 of this form)
Literal, numeric—Up to ten characters including one decimal point and/or one sign (plus or minus), left-justified
Literal, alphameric—Up to eight (any of the 256 EBCDIC) characters enclosed in quotes ('), left-justified

64   See Table of Operation Codes, page 345

65   Up to six alphameric characters (letter first), left-justified, or blank

66   1-14 digits—right-justified (numeric field)
1-256 characters — right-justified (alphameric field)
Blank—If already defined elsewhere on this form or on the Input form

67   Blank—Alphameric field
0—Numeric field, no decimals
1-9—Numeric field, 1-9 decimals

68   H Half-adjust (round up) result field
Blank—No half-adjust needed

69   Any of the indicators may be used

70   Commentary text (disregarded by the RPG Compiler)

OUTPUT-FORMAT:

71   Name of files (left-justified) described as output files in columns 7-14 of File Description form

72   H Heading line (titles)
D Detail line
T Total line
E Exception line

73   ADD—ISAM files, records to be added; must have A in column 66 of File Description form
Other entries—Otherwise

74   Blank—For stacker of single-stacker devices or normal stacker of multistacker devices
Number of chosen stacker—Otherwise

75   0, 1, 2 or 3—Lines before printing

76   0, 1, 2 or 3—Lines after printing

77   01-12—Skipping before printing
Blank—No skipping before printing

78   01-12—Skipping after printing
Blank—No skipping after printing

79   Any of the indicators may be used

80   Name of field (left-justified) defined either on the Input or Calculation form

81   See Table of Edit Codes, page 346

82   B Reset alphameric field ot blanks or numeric field to zeros

83   Right-justified

84   P Packed data (disk only)
Blank—Otherwise

85   Constant—Up to 24 (any of the 256 EBCDIC) characters enclosed in quotes (') left-justified
Edit word:
   '*'—Replaces all leading zeros with asterisks (called "asterisk protection")
   '$'—Prints $ to the left of the high-order significant digit
   Other edit words, used for punctuation, zero suppression, etc., enclosed in quotes

Indicator	Where Located	Where Used	Turned On	Turned Off	Notes
Field Indicators 01-99 Zero and Blank Plus Minus	Input form	Indicator (calc.), Output Indicators	By Blank or Zero in specified field; by Plus in specified field; by Minus in specified field	Before this field status is to be tested the next time	Note 1
H1 through H9	Input form Calculation form	Indicator (calc.), Output Indicators	Whenever the specified field status or record identification condition is satisfied	Internal, at the end of the detail cycle	Note 1
LR	Internal	Control Level (calc.), Output Indicators	After processing the last record of the last file (see Column 17 of File Description)	At the beginning of processing	Note 1 Note 2
L0 (Level Zero)	Internal	Control Level (calc.), Output Indicators	At the end of every processing cycle	Is never turned off by RPG	
Control Level Indicators L1 through L9	Input form Columns 59-60	Control Level (calc.), Indicators (calc.), Output Indicators	When the value in a control field changes. All indicators of the lower levels are also turned on	At end of following detail cycle	Note 1
MR (Matching)	Internal	Indicators (calc.), Output Indicators	If the matching-field contents of the record of a secondary file match the matching-field contents of a record in the primary file	When all total calculations and output are completed for the last record of the matching group	
OF/OV	Internal	Indicators (calc.), Output Indicators		After the following heading and detail lines are completed	Note 3

Indicator	Where Located	Where Used	Turned On	Turned Off	Notes
Record Identifying Indicator 01-99	Input form Columns 19-20	Indicators (calc.), Output Indicators Field-Record Relation	When specified record has been read and before total calcula- tions are executed	Before the next record is read during the next processing cycle	Note 1
Resulting Indicators 01-99 Plus Minus Zero Compare operation High Low Equal Lokup operation High Low Equal Testz operation High Low Equal Chain operation	Calculation form	Indicators (calc.), Output Indicators	By a positive balance in field, by a negative balance in field, by Zero balance in field If Factor 1 > Factor 2 If Factor 1 < Factor 2 If Factor 1 = Factor 2 If Table > Factor 1 If Table < Factor 1 If Table = Factor 1 If 12 zone is present If 11 zone is present If no zone is present By a no-record-found condition	The next time a calcu- lation is performed for which the program specifies the indicator as a resulting indicator and the specified con- dition is not satisfied	Note 1
1P (First Page)	Internal	Output Indicators	At beginning of processing before any input records are read	Before the first detail card is read	Note 4

Note 1. Turning indicators on or off can also be accomplished by using SETON and SETOF operation codes.

Note 2. All control level indicators (L1-9) are also turned on when LR is turned on.

Note 3. The OF indicator remains on during the following detail calculations and output cycles.

Note 4. This indicator is used to condition printing of the first page of the report.

Table of Operation Codes

Operations	Control Level	Conditioning Indicators	Factor 1	Operation Codes	Factor 2	Result Field	Field Length	Decimal Positions	Half Adjust	Resulting Indicators
DECIMAL										
Add	0	0	N	ADD	N	N	0	0	0	0
Zero and Add	0	0		Z-ADD	N	N	0	0	0	0
Subtract	0	0	N	SUB	N	N	0	0	0	0
Zero and Subtract	0	0		Z-SUB	N	N	0	0	0	0
Multiply	0	0	N	MULT	N	N	0	0	0	0
Divide	0	0	N	DIV	N	N	0	0	0	0
Move Remainder	0	0		MVR		N	0	0		0
MOVES										
Move	0	0		MOVE	E	E	0	0		
Move Left	0	0		MOVEL	E	E	0	0		
Move High-to-Low Zone	0	0		MHLZO	A	E	0	0		
Move Low-to-High Zone	0	0		MLHZO	E	A	0			
Move High-to-High Zone	0	0		MHHZO	A	A	0			
Move Low-to-Low Zone	0	0		MLLZO	E	E	0	0		
LOGICAL										
Compare	0	0	E	COMP	S					R
Test Zone	0	0		TESTZ		A	0			R
Table Look-up	0	0	E	LOKUP	S	0	0	0		R
SET INDICATORS										
Set Indicators On	0	0		SETON						R
Set Indicators Off	0	0		SETOF						R
FILE										
Chain to a File Randomly	0	0	E	CHAIN	I					0
Branch to Exception Output Line	0	0		EXCPT						
BRANCHING										
Branching or GOTO	0	0		GOTO	L					
Providing Label for GOTO	0		L	TAG						
Branch to Closed Subroutine	0	0		EXSR	L					
Begin Closed Subroutine	SR		L	BEGSR						
End Closed Subroutine	SR		OL	ENDSR						
Exit to a Subroutine	0	0		EXIT	L					
RPG Label	0			RLABL		E	0	0		

KEY:

If the entry is blank it cannot be filled in.

A	=	Required field must be alphameric.
E	=	Required field must be either alphameric or numeric.
I	=	Required file name.
L	=	Required label name.
N	=	Required field must be numeric.
0	=	Optional entry.
OL	=	Optional label entry.
R	=	Required entry.
S	=	Required field must be of the same type (alphameric or numeric) as Factor 1.
SR	=	Required entry in control level columns.

Table of Edit Codes

Edit Codes	Positive Number Two Decimal Positions	Positive Number No Decimal Positions	Negative Number Three Decimal Positions	Negative Number No Decimal Positions	Zero Balance Two Decimal Positions	Zero Balance No Decimal Positions	Negative Number—Two Decimal Positions—End Position Specified as 10 — Output Print Positions								
							3	4	5	6	7	8	9	10	11
Unedited	1234567	1234567	00012ƀ	00012ƀ	000000	000000				0	0	4	1	2	
1	12,345.67	1,234,567	.120	120	.00	0					4	.	1	2	
2	12,345.67	1,234,567	.120	120							4	.	1	2	
3	12345.67	1234567	.120	120	.00	0					4	.	1	2	
4	12345.67	1234567	.120	120							4	.	1	2	
A	12,345.67	1,234,567	.120 CR	120 CR	.00	0				4	.	1	2	C	R
B	12,345.67	1,234,567	.120 CR	120 CR						4	.	1	2	C	R
C	12345.67	1234567	.120 CR	120 CR	.00	0				4	.	1	2	C	R
D	12345.67	1234567	.120 CR	120 CR						4	.	1	2	C	R
J	12,345.67	1,234,567	.120–	120–	.00	0				4	.	1	2	–	
K	12,345.67	1,234,567	.120–	120–						4	.	1	2	–	
L	12345.67	1234567	.120–	120–	.00	0				4	.	1	2	–	
M	12345.67	1234567	.120–	120–						4	.	1	2	–	
X	1234567	1234567	00012ƀ	00012ƀ	000000	000000				0	0	4	1	2	
Y			0/00/12	0/01/20	0/00/00	0/00/00			0	/	4	1	/	2	
Z	1234567	1234567	120	120								4	1	2	

1	Print with commas, print zero balance, suppress sign.
2	Print with commas, suppress zero balance and suppress sign.
3	Print without commas, print zero balance, suppress sign.
4	Print without commas, suppress zero balance and suppress sign.
A	Print with commas, print zero balance, print sign as CR.
B	Print with commas, suppress zero balance, print sign as CR.
C	Print without commas, print zero balance, print sign as CR.
D	Print without commas, suppress zero balance, print sign as CR.
J	Print with commas, print zero balance, print sign as –.
K	Print with commas, suppress zero balance, print sign as –.
L	Print without commas, print zero balance, print sign as –.
M	Print without commas, suppress zero balance, print sign as –.
X	This code is accepted by 1130 RPG, but no function is performed.
Y	Edit date field:

Y — Edit date field:

| 3 digit – (n)n/n | 5 digit – (n)n/nn/n |
| 4 digit – (n)n/nn | 6 digit – (n)n/nn/nn |

The first n will be zero suppressed.

Z — High-order zero suppression and remove sign.

An edit word may be used with a numeric field by leaving this column blank.

The ƀ represents a blank. This is caused by a negative zero not corresponding to a printable character.

If the inverted print option is chosen (I in column 21 of the RPG Control Card), a comma must be used instead of a decimal point in all numeric literals. Edit codes 1 through 4, A through D, J through M will invert commas for decimals and vice versa. The Y edit code will invert periods for slashes.

1)   Why is RPG an important programming language for businesses and other organizations with small computer installations?

2)   What is the minimum number of RPG forms that need to be filled out to produce a meaningful RPG program?

3)   Which RPG form has the most sections and subfields? Which has the least?

4)   What is the normal collating sequence of the RPG forms? Since each form has a page number, how should the forms be numbered?

5)   Is variable file format permissible in 1130 RPG?

6)   Sterling currency fields appear on several RPG specification forms: name the forms. The forms, as designed, handle the "old" Sterling currencies, namely shillings and pence. What simple modification will easily convert them to the decimal Sterling currency adopted when the United Kingdom changed recently to the metric system? Note: In the "old" system, there were 20 pence to a shilling and 12 shillings to a pound. The decimal system has 100 decimal pence to a pound.

7)   Write a brief RPG program which will read a deck of 100 cards and print all the information contained on the cards.

8)   Rewrite the program of Problem 7 by making it print the cards in reverse sequence in which they were read.

9)   Rewrite the program of Problem 7 by making it print only every second card in the deck and skip the other ones.

10)   Rewrite the program of Problem 7 by making it print the number of cards that were processed at the bottom of the output listing.

11)   Rewrite the program of Problem 7 by making it print only certain fields from each card and disregard the rest of the information contained on the cards.

12)   Consider the following entries on the RPG File Description Specifications form:

110FPROBLEM . OP . AF . . . . . 640 . . . . EREAD42

There are five errors in the preceding specification line. Can you spot them?

Hints: Can a primary file be an output file?
Can an output file have a matching fields entry on the Input Specifications form?
Is the record length correct or should the device be changed?
Should further entries be made on the File Extension Specifications form?

13) Consider the following entries on the RPG Input Specifications form:

010IPROBLEMAAN077 .. 80NDA 1

    (continued)   . . 10 . TEST . . L1 . . 7728 . . . .

What features do you notice? Are the data numeric or alphameric? Is the record identification code acceptable? Is there a predetermined sequence to the records of this file or not, and is the coding correct in this respect?

14) Consider the following entries on the RPG Calculation Specifications form:

010C . . . . A . . . . ADD . . . B. . . . . . . .C . . . . 50 . . . .
020C   B   ADD   C   D   50
030C   Z–ADD   5   E   50
040C   F   SUB   G   H   50
050C   I   MULT   J   K   50
060C   Z   Z–SUB   Z   Z   50
070C   FIRST   DIV   ANSWER   50
080C   MVR   SECOND KEEP   50
090C   FIRST   COMP   SECOND   50
100C   0   MOVE   AWAY   50

If A = 10, B = 20, F = 30, G = 4, I = 8, J = 9, what are C, D, E, H and K? What coding mistakes do you notice on lines 060-100? How can these mistakes be corrected?

15) Complete Figure 14-13 using additional RPG Output-Format Specifications forms. Could you reduce the number of specification lines used by reformatting the output?

16) Complete the entries on the Printer Spacing Chart (Figure 14-14) according to the Output-Format specifications of Problem 15.

17) Check if there are other indicators from the examples of RPG specification forms given in previous sections of this chapter that would merit inclusion on the Indicator Summary form.

18) In the following list, which are proper literals? Give reasons.

a) 'APRIL 1, 1971'

b) '04 01 1971'

c) 'SARATOGA'

d) '3.1415926535'

e) 3.1415926535

f) –10.0

19) What would you enter in columns 21-41 of the RPG Input Specifications form to identify the record types with the given identification codes?

a) The word YES followed by three digits in positions 75-80.

b) Any letter of the alphabet in position 80.

c) A zero-zone punch in column 79 but no 12-zone punch in column 80.

20) What is accomplished in the following Calculation Specifications portion of an RPG program?

```
010C . . . . . . . . . . .  ENTRY1 . . . . . .  ADD . .  ENTRY2  . . .  ENTRY2 . . . . .  50 . . . . .
020C . . . 50                               Z–SUB  ENTRY2       ABSENT
030C   N50                                  Z–ADD  ENTRY2       ABSENT
040C                     ABSENT             COMP   NEWENTRY
```

Hint: What relationship does ABSENT have to ENTRY2? What can you say about the algebraic sign of ENTRY 2 as compared to the sign of ABSENT?

21) Write calculation specifications to perform the following operations:

a) Net Salary = Gross Salary – Federal Tax – Misc. Ded.

b) If Federal Tax is more than 50 percent of Gross Salary, or if Federal Tax is zero, stop.

c) If Net Salary is zero or negative, stop. (See Figure 14-13.)

349

CHAPTER 15: MORE RPG

15-1　RPG Programming Concepts

As we showed in Chapter 14, the writing of 1130 RPG programs is a relatively uncomplicated process. In order to attain the techniques necessary to write RPG programs with facility, the programmer should

1)　Learn and become proficient in general computer programming ideas (see Section 1-1).

2)　Get into the habit of laying out the desired output on the printer spacing chart.

3)　Study, practice, and become familiar with the usage of each individual RPG specification form, and learn the logical interrelations among coding lines on different forms.

In essence, then, analyzing the problem and properly coding the various RPG forms required are the two indispensable steps that have to be mastered. Let us review these two steps with regard to the small RPG program introduced in Section 14-3.

Let us suppose that a retailer or a department store bills its credit customers on a monthly basis; a basic charge of $1. is added to each account with a balance below a certain minimum amount outstanding, and 1½ percent per month (or 18 percent annually) interest is computed on balances exceeding that minimum level. Let us design the program that will read the customer's unpaid balance, compare it with an established minimum amount, decide whether to levy the $1. service charge or calculate the 18 percent interest, and print the current balance and interest.

First we need to find the minimum level below which the service charge should be added. This can be done by solving the alternate problem of finding the lowest balance for which the 18 percent "finance" charge will yield less than the minimum $1. "service" charge; letting B be the unpaid balance, and solving

$$\frac{18 \cdot B}{100} < 1$$

we obtain $B < \frac{100}{18}$ = $5.56. This means that for balances above or equal to $5.56, 18 percent interest will result in a charge of at least $1., while for balances below $5.56, the $1. service charge should be used. However, $5.56 is a rather awkward amount, and a "round" number such as $6. may be preferred. The analysis is then as follows:

1) Read the balance;

2) If the balance is greater than or equal to $6., multiply it by 0.18 (18 percent) and thus obtain the interest or finance charge;

3) If the balance is smaller than $6., levy a $1. service charge.

4) Output the balance and the corresponding charge.

These four actions constitute the skeletal solution to the programming problem, and could be easily flowcharted. This solution is transferred to the RPG Calculation Specifications form (see Section 14-3) where the programmer gives names to the fields containing the input data (unpaid balance) and the output data (balance and interest).

The next thing to be resolved is the handling of the input and the output. The RPG Input Specifications form is filled with the name of the input file and the corresponding name of the field containing the input data (as previously entered on the RPG Calculation Specifications form); the RPG Output Specifications form is likewise filled with the name of the output file, the corresponding names of the output fields and the heading titles (a manual, trial layout should be inked on the Printer Spacing Chart first).

Then the programmer reconciles the information about the files that are to be used in this program upon the RPG File Description Specifications form. Finally, an appropriate RPG Control Card specification is prepared, the Indicator Summary form is filled (in this case with the only two indicators used, 01 and 11) and commentary text is inserted wherever it would clarify the forms' contents.

The above approach applies to the preparation of most RPG programs, because the order of the coding steps (and, therefore, of the RPG programming concepts) is, generally, 1) Calculation, 2) Input and Output, 3) File Description (and Extension), and 4) Control Card and Documentation.

In this chapter we will overview a few more advanced RPG features such as the usage of tables, subroutines and disk storage; a more comprehensive example is presented at the end of the chapter. Further details about 1130 RPG can be found in *IBM 1130 RPG Language*, IBM SRL Publication C 21-5002-1 and subsequent technical newsletters.

15-2 Tables

The most general definition of a table is that of an ordered arrangement of information. Produce prices in a supermarket, merchandise in a department store catalog, securities exchange quotations in a financial periodical, and engineering tool size lists are all examples of tables. There is, probably, no human endeavor that does not require the utilization of certain data which are best stored in tabular form. The simplest examples of tables (addition, multiplication, square roots, logarithms, etc.) need not be stored because the arithmetic operations involved are the most fundamental and conventional (see Section 1-8); in general, information that may be calculated (no matter how complicated the actual computations) need not be stored, because the necessary arithmetic may be carried out to obtain the answers when needed. This is not true for information that cannot be generated analytically; and in many cases when a calculation algorithm could be devised, it is far more cost-effective and practical to obtain the information by simply "looking it up" (see Sections 5-3 and 5-12, Problems 14, 15, 16 and 17).

In RPG, tables are classified by their entries, and the two entry types (arguments, functions) engender four types of tables: argument, function, argument-function and function-argument (the latter two are called alternating). The collection of records that provides all of the table entries for a given table is called a table file. Table operations require a table name and a file name. The name of the file appears twice: once on each of the RPG File Description and RPG File Extension Specifications forms. The name of the table will appear on the RPG File Extension Specifications form; this name is four, five or six characters long with the first three being the letters TAB (see Section 14-6). File names of files that contain tables are used to identify (i.e., input) table files, while table names simply name the tables that are stored in these files (a file may have more than one table). The rules for forming tables and creating records containing table entries are summarized below.

1) The file containing the table or tables should be identified in the RPG File Description Specifications form as previously mentioned (Section 14-5) but with two additional entries: T in column 16 (indicating that it is a table file) and E in column 39 (indicating that the same file name is entered upon the RPG File Extension Specifications form).

2) Each line of coding on the RPG File Extension Specifications form must have, in columns 11-18, the file name of the table file identified on the RPG File Description Specifications form; if the table only has arguments or only functions, columns 27-45 should be used; otherwise, if the table is alternating (argument-function or function-argument), then both columns 27-45 and 46-57 should be used.

3) Table entries must be positioned beginning with column 1, and the number of table entries per record must be the same for all records except the last one, which may have any number of entries.

4) Entries in table records must be adjacent and of equal length; no blanks may be contained between entries. For alternating tables, the entries must not be split from record to record, and each record in the file must begin with an entry of the same type (argument or function).

5) The sequence of the table may be in ascending, descending or no order, unless the LOKUP operation is to be performed on the table and high or low indicators are specified, in which case the table must be in either ascending or descending order. For alternating tables, the argument entries will be in some order while the function entries may be in no particular sequence.

6) Table files must be sequential (blank in column 32 of the RPG File Description Specifications form), and the file must contain the exact number of table entries as indicated on the RPG File Extension Specifications form.

7) Table record format must be fixed-length, but records may contain more than one table entry. Alphameric entries must not exceed 248 characters and numeric entries must not exceed 14 digits.

8) A maximum of eight lines of coding for tables is allowed on the RPG File Extension Specifications form; therefore, up to eight table names may be defined for single-entry tables (arguments or functions) and up to 16 table names may be used for alternating (argument-function or function-argument) tables.

The examples given in Figures 15-1, 15-2 and 15-3 serve to illustrate the processing of tables in an RPG program. The argument sequence (column A in Figure 15-1) is in ascending order. Three pairs of alternating tables are entered on the RPG File Extension Specifications form (Figure 15-2):

1) Item number and price per item (TABITM and TABTAG)

2) Item number and code name (TABNUM and TABCOD)

3) Quantity available and code name (TABHAV and TABNAM)

Although TABITM and TABNUM represent a listing of the same entries (item numbers), their usage is slightly different; TABITM's entries are arguments of the alternating argument-function table whose function entries are supplied by TABTAG; both sets of entries are numeric, as indicated by the presence of decimal positions. TABNUM's entries, on the other hand, are numeric literals, and also arguments of the alternating argument-function table whose function entries are supplied by TABCOD. Finally, TABHAV's entries (arguments) are in descending order, which would require alphameric sorting of the data appearing in column C of Figure 15-1 prior to its use in the alternating table whose function entries are provided by TABNAM.

353

A	B	C	D
Item Number (argument)	Code Name (function)	Quantity Available (argument)	Price per Item (function)
10	STAPLERXX	014	0395
12	ENVELOPES	578	0005
15	3RBINDERS	062	0275
27	NOTEPADS7	310	0015
33	BALPTPENS	129	0185
48	CARBPAPER	200	0040
51	GREETCARD	405	0035
64	WRAPPAPER	073	0025
79	TYPRIBBON	026	0115
86	TEMPLATES	031	0060

A.	Item Number	TABITM, TABNUM
B.	Code Name	TABNAM, TABCOD
C.	Quantity Available	TABHAV
D.	Price per Item	TABTAG

Figure 15-1 Contents of Tables

Figure 15-3 exemplifies a few of the simpler procedures with tables. There are four LOKUP ("look-up") operations (lines 010, 030, 050 and 060 of the RPG Calculation Specifications form) and, correspondingly, four search arguments, all identified in columns 18-27 (Factor 1). In the first instance, ITEMNUMBER contains the search argument which is compared to the arguments of the table TABITM; if arguments match, the corresponding function in TABTAG is identified and the indicator 05 is turned on. On the next line, 020, the function located in TABTAG (the price of the item whose number was matched) is multiplied by NUMBER (number of items to be purchased, in Factor 2) and the resulting product is stored in PURCHS. However, if a match is not attained (i.e., the search argument in ITEMNUMBER does not match any of the arguments in the table TABITM), indicator 05 is not turned on and line 020 is bypassed; in this case, the table look-up of TABHAV is carried out with the search argument contained in the field QUANT. Let us assume that QUANT has the numeric literal 885; the table look-up operation LOKUP will discover the fact that all arguments in table TABHAV (column C in Figure 15-1) are lower, and hence indicator 10 will be turned on, which, in turn, will turn on indicator H4 by way of the SETON operation (line 040 of the RPG Calculation Specifications form, Figure 15-3). If QUANT had

354

contained an argument that would provide a match with an argument of TABHAV, line 040 of the RPG Calculation Specifications form would have been bypassed, and the numeric literal 79 would become the next search argument, in a table look-up operation of TABNUM; as is easily seen from the example, a match is produced and the code name TYPRIBBON is identified in table TABCOD. Finally, the search argument contained in QUANT is again used to search the table TABHAV with the intent to identify a code name in TABNAM if a match occurs.

15-3   Subroutines

Subroutines in RPG play a programming role similar to subroutines (or, more generally, subprograms) in other programming languages, such as FORTRAN (see Chapter 6). That certain procedures, among them report headings, common computations, and often replicated program segments of different kinds, are or should be considered standard programming sections (or blocks), is a fact dictated by programming experience and known to all data processing centers. A procedure that can be used in different "main" RPG programs or in many different places of the same "main" RPG program is called an RPG subroutine. There are two kinds of subroutines in 1130 RPG:

1)   *Internal subroutines*, written in RPG, and

2)   *External subroutines*, written in assembly language.

Internal Subroutines

Subroutines written in RPG are called *internal* or *closed subroutines*. These subroutines, entered on the RPG Calculation Specifications form, are written as part of the "main" RPG program that calls them. Three operation codes, EXSR, BEGSR and ENDSR (entered in Operation, columns 28-32 of the RPG Calculation Specifications form) are used.

The EXSR (exit to closed subroutine) code causes a transfer from any point in the RPG program to an internal subroutine the name of which appears on the same coding line in Factor 2 (columns 33-42); control level entry (columns 7-8) and/or up to three indicators (columns 9-17) are optional for EXSR statements but all other columns must be left blank. The EXSR statement may itself be part of an RPG subroutine and may provide a transfer to another subroutine, in which case the control level indicator SR (columns 7-8) must be used. Recursive subroutines (subroutines that call themselves) are not allowed in 1130 RPG; hence the name in Factor 2 must not be the name of the subroutine which contains the given EXSR statement. See examples of EXSR statements in Figure 15-4.

RPG EXTENSION AND LINE COUNTER SPECIFICATIONS

IBM — International Business Machines Corporation
GX21-9091-1 U/M 050* Printed in U.S.A.
*No. of forms per pad may vary slightly

Date _____
Program _____
Programmer _____

Punching Instruction — Graphic / Punch

Page **02**
Program Identification **TABLES**

Extension Specifications

Line	Form Type	From Filename	To Filename	Table or Array Name	Number of Entries Per Record	Number of Entries Per Table or Array	Length of Entry	P=Packed/B=Binary	Decimal Positions	Sequence (A/D)	Table or Array Name (Alternating Format)	Length of Entry	P=Packed/B=Binary	Decimal Positions	Sequence (A/D)
010	E	FILE1TAB		TABITM	1	10	2				OATABTAB	4		2	
020	E	FILE2TAB		TABNUM	1	10	2				ATABCØD	9			
030	O	FILE3TAB		TABHAV	1	10	3				DTABNAM	9			
040	E														
050	E														
060	E														
070	E														
080	E														
090	E														
0I0	E														

Line Counter Specifications

Line	Form Type	Filename	1 FL or Channel Number / Line Number	2 OL or Channel Number / Line Number	3	4	5	6	7	8	9	10	11	12
11	L													
12	L													
13	L													

Figure 15-2 Definition of Tables on the RPG File Extension

356

International Business Machines Corporation

RPG CALCULATION SPECIFICATIONS

Date _____

Program _____

Programmer _____

| Punching | Graphic | | |
| Instruction | Punch | | |

Page **04**   Program Identification **TABLES**

Line	Form Type	Control Level (L0-L9, LR, SR)	Indicators (And Not / And Not / Not)	Factor 1	Operation	Factor 2	Result Field	Field Length	Decimal Positions	Half Adjust (H)	Resulting Indicators
01	C			ITEMNUMBER	LOKUP	TABITM	TABTAG				
02	C		05	TABTAG	MULT	NUMBER	PURCHS	62			05
03	C		N05	QUANT	LOKUP	TABHAV					10
04	C		10		SETON						H4
05	C		N10	'79'	LOKUP	TABNUM	TABCOD				
06	C		N20	QUANT	LOKUP	TABHAV	TABNAM				20
07	C										
08	C										
09	C										
10	C										
11	C										
12	C										
13	C										
14	C										
15	C										

Figure 15-3   Examples of Processing of Tables

357

International Business Machines Corporation

RPG CALCULATION SPECIFICATIONS

GX21-9093-1 U/M 050*
Printed in U.S.A.
*No. of forms per pad may vary slightly

75 76 77 78 79 80
Program Identification R O U T I N

Page 04
1 2

Date _____
Program _____
Programmer _____

Punching Instruction — Graphic ___ Punch ___

Line	Form Type	Control Level (L0-L9, LR, SR)	Indicators	Factor 1	Operation	Factor 2	Result Field	Comments
010	C		10		EXSR	SUB1		
020	C				<other operations>			
030	C		15		EXSR	SUB2		
040	C				<other operations>			
050	C	SR		SUB1	BEGSR			
060	C	SR			<body of subroutine>			
070	C	SR			ENDSR			
080	C	SR			BEGSR			
090	C	SR		SUB2	<body of subroutine>			
100	C	SR			GOTO	OUT		
110	C	SR			.			
120	C	SR	25		ENDSR			
130	C	SR		OUT				
140	C	SR			ENDSR			
150	C							

Figure 15-4   Examples of RPG Closed (Internal) Subroutine Coding

The BEGSR (begin closed subroutine) code defines the entry point or beginning of an internal subroutine. The ENDSR (end closed subroutine) code defines the exit point or end of an internal subroutine. Both BEGSR and ENDSR require the control level indicator SR in columns 7-8. For the BEGSR code, Factor 1 (columns 18-27) must contain the name of the subroutine referred to by the EXSR statement. For the ENDSR code, Factor 1 may contain a name which will serve as the entry point for a GOTO statement within the subroutine (and hence an exit out of the subroutine or a transfer back to the "main" program containing the closed subroutine); when the GOTO operation code is used with the ENDSR code, a TAG code is not needed, thus making it impossible to associate the name in Factor 1 with a GOTO outside the subroutine. With the exception of SR in columns 7-8, the name in Factor 1 (columns 18-27) which is required for BEGSR (the name of the closed subroutine) and optional for ENDSR, and the operation codes BEGSR or ENDSR in Operation (columns 28-32), all other columns must be left blank for these two statements. After the ENDSR statement, control is returned to the specification line immediately following the EXSR statement that called the closed subroutine. Examples of BEGSR and ENDSR statements are shown in Figure 15-4.

The 1130 RPG internal subroutine specifications follow all other calculation specifications on the RPG Calculation Specifications form. The calls to closed subroutines, by way of the EXSR statement, however, may be placed anywhere among the calculation specifications, but the order of execution of the subroutines called will depend on whether the EXSR statement is the first or last detail or first or last total calculation of the RPG program; essentially, if EXSR is the first detail or first total calculation, execution of the subroutine is delayed until the input data becomes available for processing or the record type has been determined and the control field has been tested; if EXSR is the last detail or last total calculation, control is transferred to the specified subroutine before heading and detail records are outputted or before the totals are printed or punched. Any data field that may be referred to by the "main" RPG program may be referred to likewise by the closed subroutine contained in the program.

A few important considerations govern the possibilities for arbitrary transfer of control in an RPG program containing a closed subroutine. First, the name in Factor 1 associated with the BEGSR statement may not be used as a label for a GOTO anywhere in the program (including the subroutine); the only way in which the BEGSR statement may be reached is after the EXSR statement has invoked the call. Second, the GOTO operation code may transfer control to a specification line with a TAG operation, under the following two circumstances: if the TAG operation is located within the subroutine, the associated GOTO must also be within the same subroutine; a GOTO statement located inside a closed subroutine may branch to an outside TAG statement only if the given TAG operation code is not located in another subroutine.

International Business Machines Corporation

RPG CALCULATION SPECIFICATIONS

GX21-9093-1 U/M 050*
Printed in U.S.A.
*No. of forms per pad may vary slightly

Punching Instruction — Graphic / Punch

Page **04** 1 2

Program Identification **ROUTIN**

Date _____ Program _____ Programmer _____

Line	Form Type	Control Level (L0-L9, LR, SR)	Indicators And Not	And Not	And Not	Factor 1	Operation	Factor 2	Result Field	Field Length	Decimal Positions	Half Adjust (H)	Resulting Indicators	Comments
0 1	C							`<RPG PROGRAM STATEMENTS>`						
0 2	C		10				EXIT	SUBR5						
0 3	C						RLABL		PURCHS	62				
0 4	C						RLABL		IN25					
0 5	C						RLABL		COST	42				
0 6	C						`<OTHER RPG PROGRAM STATEMENTS>`							
0 7	C													
0 8	C													
0 9	C													
1 0	C													
1 1	C													
1 2	C													
1 3	C													
1 4	C													
1 5	C													

Figure 15-5. Examples of RPG External Subroutine Coding

External Subroutines

Subroutines written in assembly language (see Chapter 11) are called *external subroutines.* Unlike the internal or closed subroutines, the external subroutines are coded separately, on the IBM 1130 Assembler Coding Form (see, for example, Figure 11-1). External subroutines are usually written to handle standard programming blocks or functions that would be difficult to code in RPG (such as some arithmetic computations, e.g., square roots, logarithms, etc.). The operation codes EXIT and RLABL (entered in Operation, columns 28-32 of the RPG Calculation Specifications form) are used.

The EXIT (exit to external subroutine) code causes a transfer from any point in the RPG program to an external subroutine the name of which is restricted to five alphameric characters (the first one must be a letter) and appears on the same coding line in Factor 2 (columns 33-37); control level entry (columns 7-8) and/or up to three indicators (columns 9-17) are optional for EXIT statements but all other columns must be left blank. If a control level entry or indicators are used, the EXIT statement (in this case called a conditional EXIT operation) is executed only if the indicators are turned on (i.e., the conditions dictated by the indicators are fulfilled). The EXIT statement may also be used within a closed RPG subroutine; both the EXIT and the associated RLABL statements should be entered into a closed RPG subroutine if the same external subroutine is used at several points in the "main" RPG program. The EXIT statement causes an Assembler CALL statement (see Section 12-5) to be generated. Examples of EXIT statements are given in Figure 15-5.

The RLABL (RPG label) code defines the "main" RPG program's fields or indicators that are to be used in the external subroutine named in the EXIT statement. The RLABL statement makes the compiler generate the address of the referenced field or indicator; the address of the field corresponds to the address of the field's control word which can be used to determine the length of the field and to decide whether the field is numeric or alphameric. If a field is to be defined, its name is entered in Result Field (columns 43-48) and (only if not defined previously in the program) its length and number of decimal positions (if the field is numeric) are entered in columns 49-52. If an indicator is to be defined, the code IN followed by the indicator is placed in the first four columns of the Result Field (columns 43-46). All other columns for an RLABL statement must be left blank. RLABL statements must be placed immediately after the EXIT statement with which they are associated. See examples of RLABL statements in Figure 15-5.

The calls to external subroutines, by way of the EXIT statement, may be placed anywhere among the calculation specifications, but the order of execution of the subroutines called will depend on whether the EXIT statement is the first or last detail or first or last total calculation of the RPG program; the situation is entirely similar to the one dictating the execution of closed subroutines, as discussed previously.

361

15-4   Disk Storage

Disk storage concepts have been introduced earlier in this book; see Section 1-3, Chapter 7 and Section 12-2. The disk storage device associated with the 1130 is named DISK in columns 40-46 of the RPG File Description Specifications form. Certain ideas with regard to disk storage pertain specifically to file organization and processing in RPG, and these will be briefly discussed here; for additional information and details, the reader is encouraged to consult the IBM SRL publications *IBM 1130 Disk Monitor System, Version 2: Programming and Operator's Guide* (form C26-3717) and *IBM 1130 RPG Language* (form C21-5002-1).

The methods of handling files can be summarized into two categories: file organization and file processing. File organization is the method of arranging data records on a direct access storage device (DASD) such as disk; file processing is the method of retrieving data records from the file.

There are two kinds of file organization available for use with 1130 RPG: *sequential* and *indexed-sequential.* If data records are arranged sequentially, the file is called sequential-access method (SAM) file; if the arrangement of the records is indexed-sequential, the file is called indexed-sequential-access method (ISAM) file. For each of the two kinds of file organization there are two methods of file processing: *sequential* and *random.*

When a file is arranged sequentially, its records are entered on disk consecutively, in the same order as inputted, one after another; card files are always sequential. For files arranged indexed-sequentially, each record is associated with a record key that determines the *ascending* collating sequence in which the records are entered on disk; the record key, supplied by the programmer, is any identifying data present on each record of the file; the index of an indexed-sequential file is used to locate the required records.

Sequential processing of SAM files consists of processing all records in the order in which they are located on the file, beginning with the first record. Sequential processing of ISAM files is determined by the record key; all records of an ISAM file may be processed in the record key sequence or processing may be limited to only a segment of the entire file with an arbitrary starting point; if only a segment of the entire file is to be processed, another file, called record address (RA) file, has to be created to define the processing limits.

Random processing of SAM files consists of processing records in an order independent of the sequence in which these records are located in the file; record numbers, which determine the relative position or consecutive location of the record in the file, must be supplied to the program if a record is to be found, since the program does not make comparisons by record content. Random processing of ISAM files is done by searching the index with the record key.

Organization of SAM Files

The following three steps are involved in the organization of SAM files:

1) Disk space for a SAM file should be obtained by way of the DUP STOREDATA function which will set aside a specified number of sectors for the file and will record the name of the file (see Section 7-6).

2) The SAM file should be described on the RPG File Description Specifications form with the following entries:

Columns 7-14: The name of the SAM file;

Column 15: The letters I, O or U, depending on whether the SAM file is an input, output or update file;

Columns 24-27: The length of the record (a maximum of 640 characters);

Column 28: Must be left blank when creating the SAM file that will be processed sequentially; if random processing will be used, an R should be entered;

Columns 40-46: The device entry (DISK).

The other columns will be filled in accordance to the programming requirements associated with the usage of the SAM file; the various entries are described in Section 14-5. Columns 16, 17, 18, 28 and 39 may have the appropriate entries, if needed; column 19 must have the letter F to indicate fixed-length format; columns 29-38, 47-52 and 66 should be left blank for SAM files.

3) If the SAM file is to be updated, only those fields that will be changed of the records to be updated need to be specified on the RPG Output-Format Specifications form; the RPG program will incorporate the changed fields with the old unchanged ones and return the updated records into their previous disk locations. Updating may be performed during either detail or total calculations if the SAM file is processed randomly, and only during detail calculations if it is processed sequentially. If a file is to be extended or new records are to be added to it, it is preferable to use an ISAM file, because the SAM file would have to be reloaded in its entirety.

Examples of SAM file organization are given in Figure 15-6.

IBM

International Business Machines Corporation

RPG CONTROL CARD AND FILE DESCRIPTION SPECIFICATIONS

GX21-9092-1 U/M050
Printed in U.S.A.

Date _____
Program _____
Programmer _____

Punching Instruction | Graphic | | | Program Identification | 75 76 77 78 79 80 → F I L E S X
| Punch | |

Page | 1 2 → 0 1

Control Card Specifications

Refer to the specific System Reference Library manual for actual entries.

File Description Specifications

Line	Form Type	Filename	File Type	File Designation	End of File	Sequence	File Format	Block Length	Record Length	Mode of Processing	Length of Key Field or of Record Address Field	Record Address Type	Type of File Organization or Additional Area	Overflow Indicator	Key Field Starting Location	Extension Code E/L	Device	Symbolic Device		Labels (S, N, or E)	Name of Label Exit		Extent Exit for DAM / Core Index		File Addition/Unordered / etc.	U1-U8
0 2	0	F	* SAM FILES																						
0 3	0	F	SAMINPUT	I	P	E	A	F		100							DISK								
0 4	0	F	SAMØUT	Ø				F		80							DISK								
0 5	0	F	SAMUPDT	U	S		A	F		80							DISK								
0 6	0	F	* ISAM FILES																						
0 7	0	F	ISAMINPT	I	P	E	A	F		100	4 K I			1			DISK								
0 8 0		F	ISAMØUT	Ø				F		80	4 K I			1			DISK								
0 9 0		F	ISAMUPDT	U	C			F		80 R	4 K I			1			DISK								

Figure 15-6 Examples of SAM File and ISAM File Organization

364

Organization of ISAM Files

The organization of ISAM files is similar to that of SAM files.

1) Disk space for an ISAM file should be obtained by way of the DUP STOREDATA function in the same manner as for a SAM file.

2) The ISAM file should be described on the RPG File Description Specifications form, in a manner similar to the description of the SAM file, but columns 29-38, 47-52 and 66 may be filled with the appropriate entries (see Section 14-5).

3) Unlike in SAM files, addition of new records to an ISAM file is possible without having to reload the file; this is accomplished with the "chaining" technique as described below.

4) Records to be entered into ISAM files should be in ascending collating key sequence, and each record must have a key area starting in position 1 of the record (column 38 of the RPG Field Description Specifications form); the lengths of the key areas should be the same for all records of an ISAM file, and all its records must be of equal length also.

5) An ISAM file consists of four components: the file label, the file index, the prime data area and the overflow area. The *file label*, which contains data for processing the file, is located in the first sector of any ISAM file; the programmer should reserve one sector for the label indicating the keylength in its first word when writing the file description specifications, since the label operations are carried out automatically by the ISAM routines of the Disk Monitor System. The *file index* permits the input and output of records located anywhere in an ISAM file; an index entry consists of the highest key associated with the disk cylinder and the cylinder address; when searching for a record, the ISAM routines will first locate the key, then locate the cylinder to access the record. The *prime data area* contains the data records loaded into the ISAM file; the records' length should be identical, with a maximum of 636 characters; the ISAM routine adds to each record a two-word control field, which is used in the overflow area as a chaining indicator (it determines whether or not a cylinder has overflowed in the prime data area). The *overflow area* is used to store the record or records which may have been displaced from the end of the cylinder when new records were being added to an ISAM file; when an ISAM file is extended, only those records with higher keys than the key of the record added are shifted.

Examples of ISAM file organization are given in Figure 15-6.

Chaining Techniques

The technique of randomly retrieving the necessary records from a disk file is called *chaining*. This technique involves a retrieving or *chaining field* and a file (called a *chained file*) from which the records are to be obtained. Records can be retrieved from a SAM file or an ISAM file; in order to retrieve a record from a SAM file, that record must have a relative record number identifying its position; retrieving a record from an ISAM file requires that this record be identified by a key field. The 1130 RPG Compiler permits two kinds of chaining: by means of the CHAIN operation on the RPG Calculation Specifications form (columns 28-32), or the C1, C2 or C3 chaining indicators on the RPG Input Specifications form (columns 61-62). If the CHAIN operation is used, Factor 1 (columns 18-27) will contain the *chaining field* (i.e., the identification of the record to be retrieved) and Factor 2 (columns 33-42) will have the *chained file* name (i.e., the name of the file from which the record is to be retrieved). For an example of the CHAIN operation, see Figure 14-12. If the chaining indicators (C1, C2 or C3) are used, the chained file must be an ISAM file. The following is a summary of the processing options for multiple files:

File Organization		File Processing					
		Sequential			Random		
Card	Disk	Consecutive	Entire File	Portion of File	Chain Operation	C1, C2, C3 Indicators	Record Address File
Sequential		Yes	Yes	No	No	No	No
	SAM	Yes	Yes	No	Yes[1]	No	Yes[1]
	ISAM	Yes	Yes	Yes[2]	Yes[3]	Yes[3]	Yes[3]

[1] Record must be identified by a relative record number.

[2] A Record-Address file must supply the limits.

[3] Record must be identified by key field.

Further details on chaining and processing of multiple files are described in the IBM publications mentioned at the beginning of this section.

Although outside the scope of this book, learning the techniques of processing files is of great importance to a programmer. Interactive programming is most efficient with file editing and file processing. References are provided in the Bibliography, Appendix G.

15-5   An Example

To conclude our discussion of RPG, let us take a detailed look at an RPG program. This program will print price lists for stationery items; the list is cataloged by item and the prices are entered in tabular form by size, form and quantity, the latter varying from 500 to 5000. The program allows the prices to be increased uniformly, and new price cards to be punched for future use. Two items and a total of 65 prices were chosen as data to test the program.

The first thing that we should do, even before coding the RPG specification forms, is to lay out the desired output on the Printer Spacing Chart, taking into account the 120-column limitation of the printout page. The output is expected to have the appearance of Figure 15-7.

Listing prices by categories does not involve any computations. The only computations that are performed concern the upward revision of the prices, and these are carried out only if indicator 04 has been activated (i.e., a card with a P character in column 1 and the corresponding revision percentages in columns 2-5 and 6-9 exists in the input stream). The computations are presented on the RPG Calculation Specifications form (Figure 15-8). An auxiliary field, RETAIN, is used to retain the result of the multiplication of the old sale price by the revision percentage before this result is added to the old sale price; the new sale price thus obtained replaces the old sale price.

The RPG Input Specifications form is filled out next (forms 3 and 4 of Figure 15-8). The file, PRICES, contains three types of records (cards) all read in arbitrary sequence (letter entries BB, MM, EE in columns 15-16). The first record is identified by the character (C in column 26) B (column 27) in column 1 of the card; the second record is identified by the character M in column 1 and the third record by the character E. Upon input, a B in column 1 will turn on indicator 02, an M in column 1 will turn on indicator 03, an E in column 1 will turn on indicator 01. The fields and their locations on these records are described by the entries in columns 44-58. The fields SIZE1 and SIZE 2 are (at most) two-digit numeric entries with no decimals. The fields FORM1 and FORM2 are nonnumeric entries of six characters. The fields COST05, COST10, COST20, COST30, COST50, SALE05, SALE10, SALE20, SALE30 and SALE50, all of which are of length five, contain numeric entries (the cost and sale prices, respectively, for the quantities 500, 1000, 2000, 3000 and 5000) with two decimal positions. The field MONTH is an (at most) nine-character non-numeric entry (months vary in the number of characters from three as in May to nine as in September). The field PPPP (page) contains an (at most) three-digit numeric entry with no decimal spaces. The file, INDATA, contains only one type of record, identified in column 1 by the character P, the presence of which activates indicator 04; INDATA's fields, REVIS1 and REVIS2 (which contain the revision percentages for the two items of PRICES), are numerical entries of length four with three decimal positions.

367

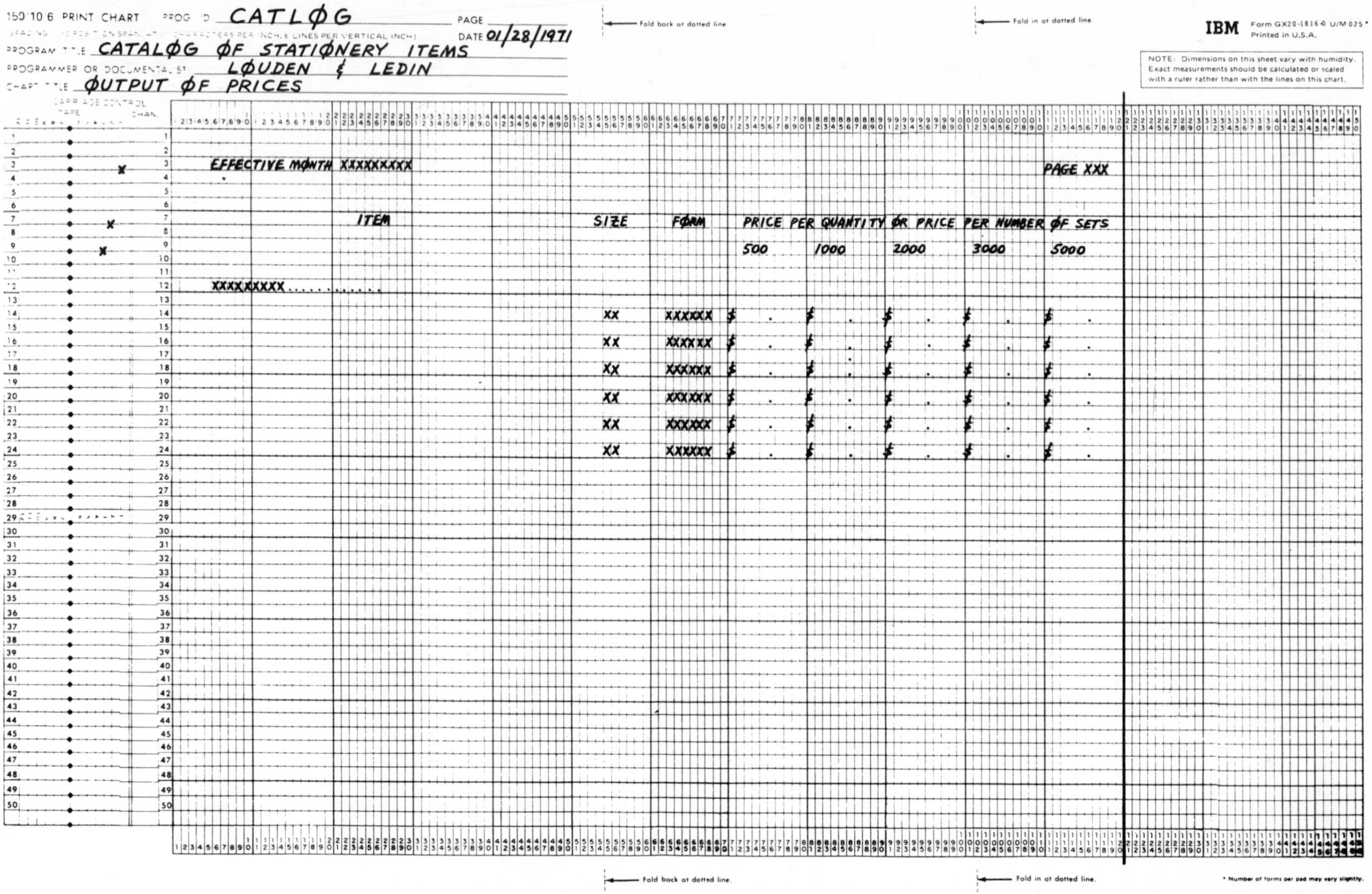

Figure 15-7 Expected Output from Sample Program CATLOG

Subsequently, the RPG Output-Format Specifications form is coded (Figure 15-8). Actually, the order of coding the input and output forms usually will be predicated upon the necessity to know the description of the input or output fields before, alternatively, defining the output or input fields; in this example, the order plays no role. The file CAT1LOG has four header sections (H in column 15) and one detail section (D in column 15). The file CAT2LOG has three header sections and one detail section. The header and detail information is coded with end positions transcribed from the print chart (Figure 15-7); the reader should carefully compare the layout as planned with the output specifications. In addition to the edit words entered between quotes (columns 45-70), there are three nonnumeric fields, MONTH, FORM1 and FORM2, and 14 numeric fields. The detail file, NEWCARD, will be used to punch a new, revised set of price cards that will replace the old ones but which will maintain identical field positioning as the old cards; the condition for punching the new cards is dictated by the presence of a percentage revision card in the input deck (otherwise indicator 04 will not be turned on).

Finally, the RPG File Description Specifications form is filled out (form 1 of Figure 15-8). The files described are PRICES (an input primary card file), INDATA (an input secondary file), CAT1LOG, CAT2LOG and NEWCARD (output files). The RPG Control Card should be the first card of the RPG source deck; a list and compile option is chosen (blank in column 11 of line 010). Blank lines, commentary text and RPG Indicator Summary lines have been included to improve the readability of the program (see Figure 15-9).

The specification forms that constitute the RPG program are presented in Figure 15-8. The listing of the program appears in Figure 15-9, and the final output in Figure 15-10. Alternate ways of writing this program (and also programming this problem) are suggested in Problems 15-20 of Section 15-6, which the reader is strongly encouraged to solve on his or her own. Although this example's records were cards, the problem is simlarly and easily solved with other input-output media. An interesting suggestion for further research to the reader would be the comparison of coding this program in RPG with the writing of a FORTRAN program that would produce the same output. As may be easily surmized, RPG is severly restricted by its awkward handling of arithmetic computations; however, complication arithmetic expressions seldom, if ever, are necessary to prepare "reports" such as the one in the given example, and for this purpose RPG is well suited, its most important asset being the clear simplicity of coding steps, requiring relatively little training in the more sophisticated programming concepts demanded by other programming languages.

International Business Machines Corporation

GX21-9092-1 U/M050
Printed in U.S.A.

IBM

RPG CONTROL CARD AND FILE DESCRIPTION SPECIFICATIONS

Date 01/28/1971

Program CATALOG OF STATIONERY ITEMS

Programmer LOUDEN & LEDIN

| Punching Instruction | Graphic | | | | | | |
| | Punch | | | | | | |

Page 01

Program Identification CATLOG

Control Card Specifications

Line	Form Type	Core Size to Compile	Object Output	Listing Options	Core Size to Execute	Debug	MFCM Stacking Sequence	Input-Shillings	Input-Pence	Output-Shillings	Output-Pence	Inverted Print	360/20 2501 Buffer	Number Of Print Positions	Alternate Collating Sequence	Refer to the specific System Reference Library manual for actual entries.
0 1 0	H															

File Description Specifications

Line	Form Type	Filename	I/O/U/C/D	P/S/C/R/T/D	E	A/D	F/V	Block Length	Record Length	L/R	A/K/I	I/O/T or I-9	Type of File / Key Field Starting Location	Device	Symbolic Device	Labels (S, N, or E)	Name of Label Exit	Core Index	A/U	N/U	File Condition U1-U8
0 4 0	F	PRICES	I	P	E		F		80					READ42							
0 5 0	F	INDATA	I	S	E		F		80					READ42							
0 6 0	F	CAT1LOG	O				F		120				OF	PRINTER							
0 6 5	F	CAT2LOG	O				F		120				OF	PRINTER							
0 7 0	F	NEWCARD	O				F		80					READ42							
0 7	F																				
	F																				

International Business Machines Corporation

GX21-9094-1 U/M 050*
Printed in U.S.A.

IBM

RPG INPUT SPECIFICATIONS

Date 01/28/1971

Program CATALOG OF STATIONERY ITEMS

LOUDEN & LEDIN

| Punching Instruction | Graphic | | | | | | |
| | Punch | | | | | | |

Page 10

Program Identification CATLOG

Line	Form Type	Filename	Sequence	Number (1-N)	Option (O)	Record Identifying Indicator	Position	Not (N)	C/Z/D	Character	Position	Not (N)	C/Z/D	Character	Position	Not (N)	C/Z/D	Character	Stacker Select	P = Packed/B = Binary	From	To	Decimal Positions	Field Name	Control Level (L1-L9)	Matching Fields or Chaining Fields	Field Record Relation	Plus	Minus	Zero or Blank	Sterling Sign Position
0 1 0	I	PRICES	BB			02	1		C	B																					
0 2 0	I																				3	4	0	SIZE1							
0 3 0	I																				5	10		FORM1							
0 4 0	I																				11	15	2	COST05							
0 5 0	I																				16	20	2	COST10							
0 6 0	I																				21	25	2	COST20							
0 7 0	I																				26	30	2	COST30							
0 8 0	I																				31	35	2	COST50							
0 9 0	I		MM			03	1		C	M																					
1 0 0	I																				3	4	0	SIZE2							
1 1 0	I																				5	10		FORM2							
1 2 0	I																				11	15	2	SALE05							
1 3 0	I																				16	20	2	SALE10							
1 4 0	I																				21	25	2	SALE20							
1 5 0	I																				26	30	2	SALE30							
1 6 0	I																				31	35	2	SALE50							
1 7 0	I		EE			01	1		C	E																					
1 8 0	I																				2	10		MONTH							
1 9 0	I																				11	13	0	PPPP							
	I																														

*Number of forms per pad may vary slightly

Figure 15-8   Entries on RPG Coding Forms for Sample Program CATLOG

International Business Machines Corporation

GX21-9094-1 U/M 050*
Printed in U.S.A.

IBM

RPG INPUT SPECIFICATIONS

Date 01/28/1971

Program CATALØG ØF STATIØNERY ITEMS

Programmer LØUDEN & LEDIN

Punching Instruction — Graphic / Punch

Page 11

Program Identification CATLØG

Line	Form Type	Filename	Sequence	Number (1/N)	Option (O)	Record Identifying Indicator or	Position	Not (N)	C/Z/D	Character	Position	Not (N)	C/Z/D	Character	Position	Not (N)	C/Z/D	Character	Stacker Select P=Packed/B=Binary	From	To	Decimal Positions	Field Name	Control Level (L1-L9)	Matching Fields or Chaining Fields	Field Record Relation	Plus	Minus	Zero or Blank	Sterling Sign Position
0 1	O I	INDATA	PP	0 4		1	CP																								
0 2	O I																			2	53		REVIS1							
0 3	O I																			6	93		REVIS2							
0 4	I																													
0 5	I																													
0 6	I																													
0 7	I																													
0 8	I																													
0 9	I																													
1 0	I																													
1 1	I																													
1 2	I																													
1 3	I																													
1 4	I																													
1 5	I																													

*Number of forms per pad may vary slightly

International Business Machines Corporation

GX21-9093-1 U/M 050*
Printed in U.S.A.
*No. of forms per pad may vary slightly

IBM

RPG CALCULATION SPECIFICATIONS

Date 01/28/1971

Program CATALØG ØF STATIØNERY ITEMS

Programmer LØUDEN & LEDIN

Punching Instruction — Graphic / Punch

Page 40

Program Identification CATLØG

Line	Form Type	Control Level (L0-L9, LR, SR)	Not	And	Not	And	Not	Factor 1	Operation	Factor 2	Result Field	Field Length	Decimal Positions	Half Adjust (H)	Plus	Minus	Zero	High 1>2	Low 1<2	Equal 1=2	Comments
0 1	O C		02	04				CØST05	MULT	REVIS1	RETAIN	102		H							
0 2	O C		02					CØST05	ADD	RETAIN	CØST05	52									
0 3	O C		02	04				CØST10	MULT	REVIS1	RETAIN										
0 4	O C		02					CØST10	ADD	RETAIN	CØST10										
0 5	O C		02	04				CØST20	MULT	REVIS1	RETAIN										
0 6	O C		02					CØST20	ADD	RETAIN	CØST20										
0 7	O C		02	04				CØST30	MULT	REVIS1	RETAIN										
0 8	O C		02					CØST30	ADD	RETAIN	CØST30										
0 9	O C		02	04				CØST50	MULT	REVIS1	RETAIN										
1 0	O C		02					CØST50	ADD	RETAIN	CØST50										
1 1	O C		03	04				SALE05	MULT	REVIS2	RETAIN										
1 2	O C		03					SALE05	ADD	RETAIN	SALE05										
1 3	O C		03	04				SALE10	MULT	REVIS2	RETAIN										
1 4	O C		03					SALE10	ADD	RETAIN	SALE10										
1 5	O C		03	04				SALE20	MULT	REVIS2	RETAIN										
16 0	C		03					SALE20	ADD	RETAIN	SALE20										
17 0	C		03	04				SALE30	MULT	REVIS2	RETAIN										
18 0	C		03					SALE30	ADD	RETAIN	SALE30										
19 0	C		03	04				SALE50	MULT	REVIS2	RETAIN										
20 0	C		03					SALE50	ADD	RETAIN	SALE50										

Figure 15-8 (cont.)

371

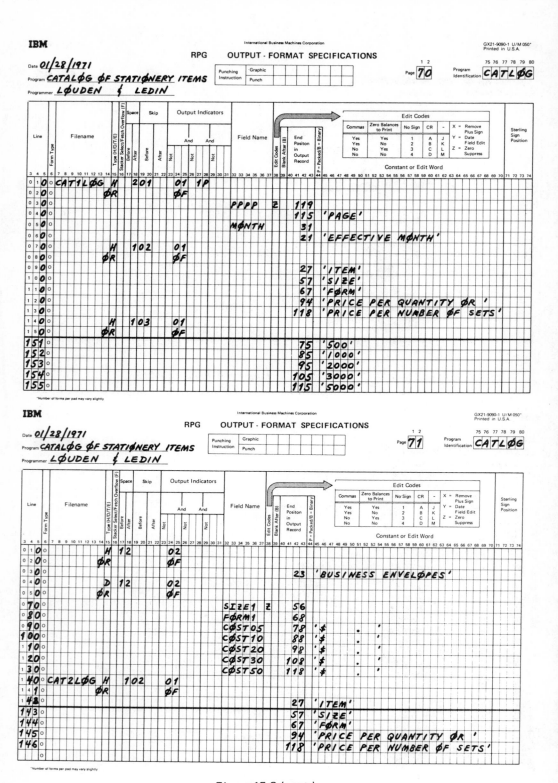

Figure 15-8 (cont.)

372

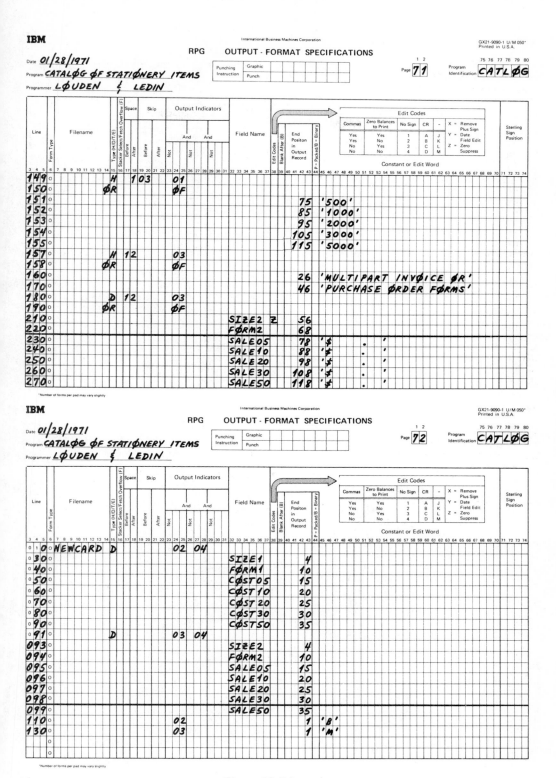

Figure 15-8 (cont.)

373

```
// JOB

LOG DRIVE   CART SPEC   CART AVAIL  PHY DRIVE
  0000        3000        3000        0000

V2 M08   ACTUAL  8K   CONFIG  8K

// RPG

              V1-2  1130  RPG   CATLOG

SEQ NO  PG LIN    SPECIFICATIONS COL 6 - 74                                                        ERRORS


        01 010    H                                                                                CATLOG
        01 011    H* **********       ROBERT K LOUDEN AND GEORGE LEDIN JR          ********** CATLOG
        01 012    H* **********          PROGRAMMING  THE  IBM  1130               ********** CATLOG
        01 013    H* **********               PRENTICE-HALL INC                    ********** CATLOG
        01 014    H*                                                                               CATLOG
        01 015    H*                                                                               CATLOG
        01 016    H* **********       RPG PROGRAMMING EXAMPLE  CHAPTER 15          ********** CATLOG
        01 017    H*                                                                               CATLOG
        01 018    F*             FILE  DESCRIPTION  SPECIFICATIONS                                 CATLOG
        01 019    F*                                                                               CATLOG
        01 020    F*                                                                               CATLOG
        01 030    F*                                                                               CATLOG
0001    01 040    FPRICES  IPE F        80               READ42                                    CATLOG
0002    01 050    FINDATA  ISE F        80               READ42                                    CATLOG
0003    01 060    FCAT1LOG O   F       120      OF       PRINTER                                   CATLOG
0004    01 065    FCAT2LOG O   F       120      OF       PRINTER                                   CATLOG
0005    01 070    FNEWCARD O   F        80               READ42                                    CATLOG
        01 075    F*                                                                               CATLOG
        01 076    F*                                                                               CATLOG
        01 077    F*                                                                               CATLOG
        01 078    F*                                                                               CATLOG
        04 004    F*             SUMMARY  OF  INDICATORS                                           CATLOG
        04 005    F*                                                                               CATLOG
        04 010    F* ID F  C  M  L     FUNCTION OF INDICATORS                                      CATLOG
        04 015    F*                                                                               CATLOG
        04 020    F* 01              EFFECTIVE MONTH AND OUTPUT PAGE INFORMATION                   CATLOG
        04 030    F* 02              PRICE DATA FOR BUSINESS ENVELOPES                             CATLOG
        04 040    F* 03              PRICE DATA FOR INVOICE OR PURCHASE ORDER FORMS                CATLOG
        04 050    F* 04              REVISION PERCENTAGES FOR ENVELOPES AND FORMS                  CATLOG
        04 060    F*             OF OVERFLOW INDICATOR                                             CATLOG
        04 070    F*             1P FIRST PAGE INDICATOR                                           CATLOG
        04 080    F*                                                                               CATLOG
        04 090    F*                                                                               CATLOG
        10 004    I*             INPUT  SPECIFICATIONS                                             CATLOG
        10 005    I*                                                                               CATLOG
0006    10 010    IPRICES  BB  02   1 CB                                                           CATLOG
0007    10 020    I                                          3   40SIZE1                           CATLOG
0008    10 030    I                                          5  10 FORM1                           CATLOG
0009    10 040    I                                         11  152COST05                          CATLOG
0010    10 050    I                                         16  202COST10                          CATLOG
0011    10 060    I                                         21  252COST20                          CATLOG
0012    10 070    I                                         26  302COST30                          CATLOG
0013    10 080    I                                         31  352COST50                          CATLOG
        10 085    I*                                                                               CATLOG
0014    10 090    I         MM  03   1 CM                                                          CATLOG
0015    10 100    I                                          3   40SIZE2                           CATLOG
0016    10 110    I                                          5  10 FORM2                           CATLOG
0017    10 120    I                                         11  152SALE05                          CATLOG
0018    10 130    I                                         16  202SALE10                          CATLOG
0019    10 140    I                                         21  252SALE20                          CATLOG
0020    10 150    I                                         26  302SALE30                          CATLOG
0021    10 160    I                                         31  352SALE50                          CATLOG
        10 165    I*                                                                               CATLOG
0022    10 170    I         EE  01   1 CE                                                          CATLOG
0023    10 180    I                                          2  10 MONTH                           CATLOG
0024    10 190    I                                         11  130PPPP                            CATLOG
        10 195    I*                                                                               CATLOG
0025    11 010    IINDATA  PP  04   1 CP                                                           CATLOG
0026    11 020    I                                          2   53REVIS1                          CATLOG
0027    11 030    I                                          6   93REVIS2                          CATLOG
        11 035    I*                                                                               CATLOG
        11 040    I*                                                                               CATLOG
        11 050    I*                                                                               CATLOG
        40 004    C*             CALCULATION  SPECIFICATIONS                                       CATLOG
        40 005    C*                                                                               CATLOG
0028    40 010    C   02 04    COST05     MULT REVIS1    RETAIN 102H                               CATLOG
0029    40 020    C   02       COST05     ADD  RETAIN    COST05  52                                CATLOG
0030    40 030    C   02 04    COST10     MULT REVIS1    RETAIN                                    CATLOG
0031    40 040    C   02       COST10     ADD  RETAIN    COST10                                    CATLOG
0032    40 050    C   02 04    COST20     MULT REVIS1    RETAIN                                    CATLOG
0033    40 060    C   02       COST20     ADD  RETAIN    COST20                                    CATLOG
0034    40 070    C   02 04    COST30     MULT REVIS1    RETAIN                                    CATLOG
0035    40 080    C   02       COST30     ADD  RETAIN    COST30                                    CATLOG
0036    40 090    C   02 04    COST50     MULT REVIS1    RETAIN                                    CATLOG
0037    40 100    C   02       COST50     ADD  RETAIN    COST50                                    CATLOG
        40 105    C*                                                                               CATLOG
0038    40 110    C   03 04    SALE05     MULT REVIS2    RETAIN                                    CATLOG
0039    40 120    C   03       SALE05     ADD  RETAIN    SALE05                                    CATLOG
0040    40 130    C   03 04    SALE10     MULT REVIS2    RETAIN                                    CATLOG
0041    40 140    C   03       SALE10     ADD  RETAIN    SALE10                                    CATLOG
0042    40 150    C   03 04    SALE20     MULT REVIS2    RETAIN                                    CATLOG
0043    40 160    C   03       SALE20     ADD  RETAIN    SALE20                                    CATLOG
0044    40 170    C   03 04    SALE30     MULT REVIS2    RETAIN                                    CATLOG
0045    40 180    C   03       SALE30     ADD  RETAIN    SALE30                                    CATLOG
0046    40 190    C   03 04    SALE50     MULT REVIS2    RETAIN                                    CATLOG
0047    40 200    C   03       SALE50     ADD  RETAIN    SALE50                                    CATLOG
        40 205    C*                                                                               CATLOG
        40 210    C*                                                                               CATLOG
        40 215    C*                                                                               CATLOG
        70 004    O*             OUTPUT-FORMAT  SPECIFICATIONS                                     CATLOG
        70 005    O*                                                                               CATLOG
        70 008    O*                                                                               CATLOG
0048    70 010    OCAT1LOG H  201    01 1P                                                         CATLOG
0049    70 020    O        OR        OF                                                            CATLOG
        70 025    O*                                                                               CATLOG
0050    70 030    O                             PPPP  Z  119                                       CATLOG
0051    70 040    O                                      115 'PAGE'                                CATLOG
0052    70 050    O                             MONTH     31                                       CATLOG
0053    70 060    O                                       21 'EFFECTIVE MONTH'                     CATLOG
        70 065    O*                                                                               CATLOG
0054    70 070    O         H  102    01                                                           CATLOG
0055    70 080    O        OR         OF                                                           CATLOG
        70 085    O*                                                                               CATLOG
0056    70 090    O                                       27 'ITEM'                                CATLOG
0057    70 100    O                                       57 'SIZE'                                CATLOG
0058    70 110    O                                       67 'FORM'                                CATLOG
0059    70 120    O                                       94 'PRICE PER QUANTITY OR '              CATLOG
0060    70 130    O                                      118 'PRICE PER NUMBER OF SETS'            CATLOG
        70 135    O*                                                                               CATLOG
0061    70 140    O         H  103    01                                                           CATLOG
0062    70 150    O        OR         OF                                                           CATLOG
0063    70 151    O                                       75 '500'                                 CATLOG
0064    70 152    O                                       85 '1000'                                CATLOG
0065    70 153    O                                       95 '2000'                                CATLOG
0066    70 154    O                                      105 '3000'                                CATLOG
0067    70 155    O                                      115 '5000'                                CATLOG
        70 205    O*                                                                               CATLOG
0068    71 010    O         H 12      02                                                           CATLOG
0069    71 020    O        OR         OF                                                           CATLOG
        71 025    O*                                                                               CATLOG
0070    71 030    O                                       23 'BUSINESS ENVELOPES'                  CATLOG
        71 035    O*                                                                               CATLOG
0071    71 040    O         D 12      02                                                           CATLOG
0072    71 050    O        OR         OF                                                           CATLOG
        71 060    O*                                                                               CATLOG
```

Figure 15-9 Printer Output Listing of CATLOG

```
0073    71 070    O                        SIZE1  Z  56                                      CATLOG
0074    71 080    O                        FORM1     68                                      CATLOG
0075    71 090    O                        COST05    78 '$    .  '                            CATLOG
0076    71 100    O                        COST10    88 '$    .  '                            CATLOG
0077    71 110    O                        COST20    98 '$    .  '                            CATLOG
0078    71 120    O                        COST30   108 '$    .  '                            CATLOG
0079    71 130    O                        COST50   118 '$    .  '                            CATLOG
        71 135    O*                                                                          CATLOG
0080    71 140    OCAT2LOG H  102    01                                                       CATLOG
0081    71 141    O        OR         OF                                                      CATLOG
        71 142    O*                                                                          CATLOG
0082    71 143    O                                  27 'ITEM'                                CATLOG
0083    71 144    O                                  57 'SIZE'                                CATLOG
0084    71 145    O                                  67 'FORM'                                CATLOG
0085    71 146    O                                  94 'PRICE PER QUANTITY OR '              CATLOG
0086    71 147    O                                 118 'PRICE PER NUMBER OF SETS'            CATLOG
        71 148    O*                                                                          CATLOG
0087    71 149    O        H   103    01                                                      CATLOG
0088    71 150    O        OR         OF                                                      CATLOG
        71 159    O*                                                                          CATLOG
0089    71 151    O                                  75 '500'                                 CATLOG
0090    71 152    O                                  85 '1000'                                CATLOG
0091    71 153    O                                  95 '2000'                                CATLOG
0092    71 154    O                                 105 '3000'                                CATLOG
0093    71 155    O                                 115 '5000'                                CATLOG
        71 156    O*                                                                          CATLOG
0094    71 157    O        H  12      03                                                      CATLOG
0095    71 158    O        OR         OF                                                      CATLOG
        71 159    O*                                                                          CATLOG
0096    71 160    O                                  26 'MULTIPART INVOICE OR '               CATLOG
0097    71 170    O                                  46 'PURCHASE ORDER FORMS'                CATLOG
        71 175    O*                                                                          CATLOG
0098    71 180    O        D  12      03                                                      CATLOG
0099    71 190    O        OR         OF                                                      CATLOG
        71 200    O*                                                                          CATLOG
0100    71 210    O                        SIZE2  Z  56                                       CATLOG
0101    71 220    O                        FORM2     68                                       CATLOG
0102    71 230    O                        SALE05    78 '$    .  '                            CATLOG
0103    71 240    O                        SALE10    88 '$    .  '                            CATLOG
0104    71 250    O                        SALE20    98 '$    .  '                            CATLOG
0105    71 260    O                        SALE30   108 '$    .  '                            CATLOG
0106    71 270    O                        SALE50   118 '$    .  '                            CATLOG
        71 275    O*                                                                          CATLOG
0107    72 010    ONEWCARD D        02 04                                                     CATLOG
        72 020    O*                                                                          CATLOG
0108    72 030    O                        SIZE1      4                                       CATLOG
0109    72 040    O                        FORM1     10                                       CATLOG
0110    72 050    O                        COST05    15                                       CATLOG
0111    72 060    O                        COST10    20                                       CATLOG
0112    72 070    O                        COST20    25                                       CATLOG
0113    72 080    O                        COST30    30                                       CATLOG
0114    72 090    O                        COST50    35                                       CATLOG
0115    72 091    O        D         03 04                                                    CATLOG
        72 092    O*                                                                          CATLOG
0116    72 093    O                        SIZE2      4                                       CATLOG
0117    72 094    O                        FORM2     10                                       CATLOG
0118    72 095    O                        SALE05    15                                       CATLOG
0119    72 096    O                        SALE10    20                                       CATLOG
0120    72 097    O                        SALE20    25                                       CATLOG
0121    72 098    O                        SALE30    30                                       CATLOG
0122    72 099    O                        SALE50    35                                       CATLOG
        72 100    O*                                                                          CATLOG
0123    72 110    O                    02   1 'B'                                             CATLOG
        72 120    O*                                                                          CATLOG
0124    72 130    O                    03   1 'M'                                             CATLOG
        72 135    O*                                                                          CATLOG
        72 145    O*                                                                          CATLOG
        72 150    O*                                                                          CATLOG
        72 155    O*                                                                          CATLOG
```

                                    INDICATORS

IND	DISP	IND	DISP	IND	DISP	IND	DISP	IND	DISP	IND	DISP
MR	0150	00	0151	OF	0152	OV	0153	1P	0154	L0	0155
L1	0156	L2	0157	L3	0158	L4	0159	L5	015A	L6	015B
L7	015C	L8	015D	L9	015E	LR	015F	H1	0160	H2	0161
H3	0162	H4	0163	H5	0164	H6	0165	H7	0166	H8	0167
H9	0168	02	0169	03	016A	01	016B	04	016C		

                                    FIELD NAMES

FIELD	DISP	L	T D	FIELD	DISP	L	T D	FIELD	DISP	L	T D	FIELD	DISP	L	T D
SIZE1	016D	002	N 0	FORM1	0170	006	A	COST05	0177	005	N 2	COST10	017D	005	N 2
COST20	0183	005	N 2	COST30	0189	005	N 2	COST50	018F	005	N 2	SIZE2	0195	002	N 0
FORM2	0198	006	A	SALE05	019F	005	N 2	SALE10	01A5	005	N 2	SALE20	01AB	005	N 2
SALE30	01B1	005	N 2	SALE50	01B7	005	N 2	MONTH	01BD	009	A	PPPP	01C7	003	N 0
REVIS1	01CB	004	N 3	REVIS2	01D0	004	N 3	RETAIN	01D5	010	N 2				

                                    LITERALS

LITERAL	LENGTH	TYPE	DISP	LITERAL	LENGTH	TYPE	DISP
PAGE	4	A	01E0	EFFECTIVE MONTH	15	A	01E5
ITEM	4	A	01F5	SIZE	4	A	01FA
FORM	4	A	01FF	PRICE PER QUANTITY OR	22	A	0204
PRICE PER NUMBER OF SETS	24	A	021B	500	3	A	0234
1000	4	A	0238	2000	4	A	023D
3000	4	A	0242	5000	4	A	0247
BUSINESS ENVELOPES	18	A	024C	.	8	E	025F
MULTIPART INVOICE OR	21	A	0268	PURCHASE ORDER FORMS	20	A	027E
B	1	A	0293	M	1	A	0295

                           KEY ADDRESSES OF OBJECT PROGRAM

NAME OF ROUTINE	HEX DISP	NAME OF ROUTINE	HEX DISP
H + D LINES	0949	TOTAL LINES	0957
DETAIL CALCS	07AB	TOTAL CALCS	0857
CHAIN ROUT 1	05AC	LOW FIELD	0651
EXCPT LINES	0965	CLOSE FILES	089D
FILE SEQ 1	02E9	FILE SEQ 2	0389
FILE SEQ 3	0414	FILE SEQ 4	04AC
FILE SEQ 5	0558		

END OF COMPILATION

// XEQ

EXTENDED CALCULATION SPECIFICATION DIAGNOSTICS   SEQ. NO.   ERROR

SEQ. NO.	ERROR
0029	NOTE 188
0031	NOTE 188
0033	NOTE 188
0035	NOTE 188
0037	NOTE 188
0039	NOTE 188
0041	NOTE 188
0043	NOTE 188
0045	NOTE 188
0047	NOTE 188

                           DIAGNOSTIC MESSAGE EXPLANATIONS

NOTE   188   C RSLT FLD LNG COL 49-51 MAY NOT BE LARGE ENOUGH

Figure 15-9 (cont.)

ITEM	SIZE	FORM	PRICE PER QUANTITY OR PRICE PER NUMBER OF SETS				
			500	1000	2000	3000	5000
BUSINESS ENVELOPES							
	6	REGULR	$ 7.75	$ 11.30	$ 20.50	$ 29.15	$ 42.75
	6	WINDOW	$ 8.75	$ 13.25	$ 24.00	$ 34.00	$ 48.50
	9	WINDOW	$ 10.00	$ 15.25	$ 28.00	$ 39.75	$ 58.50
	10	REGULR	$ 8.95	$ 13.40	$ 24.50	$ 34.75	$ 51.00
	10	WINDOW	$ 10.25	$ 15.40	$ 28.50	$ 40.25	$ 59.10
MULTIPART INVOICE OR PURCHASE ORDER FORMS							
	7	2-PART	$ 7.75	$ 13.25	$ 25.75	$ 36.75	$ 55.50
	7	3-PART	$ 11.25	$ 19.25	$ 35.75	$ 52.25	$ 82.75
	7	4-PART	$ 14.75	$ 25.75	$ 49.75	$ 72.00	$ 111.00
	7	5-PART	$ 18.25	$ 32.75	$ 62.75	$ 90.00	$ 138.75
	8	2-PART	$ 10.75	$ 18.00	$ 34.50	$ 49.25	$ 74.00
	8	3-PART	$ 15.00	$ 27.00	$ 51.50	$ 73.75	$ 111.00
	8	4-PART	$ 20.00	$ 36.00	$ 68.75	$ 98.25	$ 148.00
	8	5-PART	$ 25.00	$ 45.00	$ 86.50	$ 123.00	$ 185.00

Figure 15-10   Printout of CATLOG

1)   Consider the program of Section 14-3 as discussed in Section 15-1.
      What if the balance is zero? What should be done to print totals
      (balance plus interest)? How would you print a warning message if
      the unpaid balances (or the balance plus interest total) exceed a
      specified maximum level (say $500.)? How would you forego the
      $1. service charge if the unpaid balance is, say, less than $1.?

2)   To refine the program of Problem 1 further, how would you print
      the customer's name and address along with the financial information?
      Should name and address (and, perhaps, account number and other
      miscellaneous data) be regarded as more "permanent" information
      than the balance and therefore be put on a separate card?

      Consider the following output layout:

              STORE CUSTOMER   ACCOUNT # 000-99-5555-0
              ANY AVENUE OR STREET   TELEPHONE NBD-NND-DDDD
              ANY TOWN, STATE, ZIP CODE

              BALANCE FORWARD: $
              FINANCE CHARGE: $
              TOTAL DUE: $

3)   To make the program of Problems 1 and 2 more useful to the user
      (e.g., new cash register models may soon become computer data input
      devices), how would you print out, in detail, all purchases, add the
      applicable taxes, and add these amounts to the preceding (or forward)
      balance? How would you use tables?

4)   Show how Figure 15-2 should look if data of the tables TABITM,
      TABNUM and TABHAV were to be updated with data from an out-
      put field named BKSTOR, with search arguments available from a
      field named SHELVE. Hints: Use the RPG File Description, File
      Extension and Calculation Specifications forms; note that updating
      may be performed by entering the name of the argument or function
      table in the Result field (columns 43-48 of the RPG Calculation
      Specifications form) and by entering an arithmetic operation code
      (such as ADD, SUB, MULT, DIV, etc.) or a move operation code
      (such as MOVE, etc.) in Operation (columns 28-32 of the RPG
      Calculation Specifications form).

5)   Is it possible to use function entries of an alternating table as
      search arguments? Give examples.

6) A GOTO in the "main" RPG program may not refer to a name in Factor 1 associated with an ENDSR statement within a closed subroutine. Can a GOTO within a subroutine refer to a name in Factor 1 associated with an ENDSR statement of another (disjoint) subroutine? If one closed subroutine calls another closed subroutine (that is contained within the calling subroutine), can a GOTO from the inner closed subroutine refer to a name in Factor 1 associated with the ENDSR statement of the outer (calling) closed subroutine?

7) Within a closed subroutine, if a GOTO refers to the name in Factor 1 associated with the ENDSR statement of that subroutine, a TAG statement is not needed. Would the same effect be achieved if a TAG statement with the same name in Factor 1 were to be placed on the specification line preceding the ENDSR statement (which, in turn, would have no name in Factor 1)? Specifically, are the two following closed subroutine coding segments equivalent?

```
* . SEGMENT . 1
SR . . . . . . . . . . . . . . . . . . GOTO . SKIP
SR . . . . . . . . . SKIP . . . . . ENDSR . . . .

* . SEGMENT . 2
SR . . . . . . . . . . . . . . . . . . GOTO . SKIP
SR . . . . . . . . . SKIP . . . . . TAG . . . . . .
SR . . . . . . . . . . . . . . . . . . ENDSR . . . .
```

8) The control level indicator SR (columns 7-8) is required with the BEGSR and ENDSR statements. Is it required with all the statements within the body of the closed subroutine? How can commentary text be inserted into the body of a closed subroutine? Can other indicators (columns 9-17) be used inside the body of the closed subroutine?

9) Compare and discuss the following two RPG program segments.

```
. SEGMENT . 1
. . . . . . . . . . . . . . . . . . . . . . EXSR . EXTERNAL . . . . . . . . . . . . . . .
= = other RPG program entries = =
SR . . . . . . . . EXTERNAL . . BEGSR . . . . . . . . . . . . . . . . . . . . . . . . .
SR . 15 . . . . . . . . . . . . . . . . . EXIT . OUTER . . . . . . . . . . . . . . . . . .
SR . . . . . . . . . . . . . . . . . . . RLABL . . . . . . . . . IN25 . . . . . . . . . . . . .
SR . . . . . . . . . . . . . . . . . . . RLABL . . . . . . . . . LAST . . . . 73 . . . . . .
SR . . . . . . . . . . . . . . . . . . . ENDSR . . . . . . . . . . . . . . . . . . . . . . . . .

. SEGMENT . 2
. . . 15 . . . . . . . . . . . . . . . . . . EXIT . OUTER . . . . . . . . . . . . . . . . . . . .
. . . . . . . . . . . . . . . . . . . . . . RLABL . . . . . . . . . IN25 . . . . . . . . . . . . .
. . . . . . . . . . . . . . . . . . . . . . RLABL . . . . . . . . . LAST . . . . 73 . . . . . .
```

Comment on what would have happened if indicator 15 were placed on the coding line containing EXSR . EXTERNAL instead of the coding line containing EXIT . OUTER.

10) Could an external subroutine call a closed subroutine? Explain.

11) The disk is a direct access storage device (DASD). Can you name others?

12) Which of the following files are SAM files and which are ISAM files?

```
020FFILE1 .... IP . AF ....... 40 ............. DISK ...........
030FFILE2 .... US ..F ....... 75 . 15KI ..... 1 . DISK ...........
040FFILE3 .... 0 ... F ....... 60 ............. DISK ...........
050FFILE4 .... 0 ... F ....... 60 .. 5KI ...... 1 . DISK ... 3000 ...
060FFILE5 .... IT .. F ...... 100 ............. EDISK ..........
070FFILE6 .... UC ..F ....... 60R .6KI ...... 1 . DISK ...........
080FFILE7 .... UC ..F ....... 60R ............. DISK ...........
090FFILE8 .... IS . AF ....... 40L .3KI ...... 1 . DISK ...........
```

13) Can you name programming circumstances when SAM files would be more advantageous than ISAM files? Can a SAM file be converted into an ISAM file? Give examples.

14) Are table files SAM or ISAM files? Explain and give examples.

15) The example of Section 15-5 could be altered to input the data on disk. What RPG specification forms would be affected by this change? What changes should be made on these forms?

16) The example of Section 15-5 could be altered to have data stored in a table, in order to be able to perform the table look-up operation. Assuming cards to be the input medium, how would you present the information for input? What would be the arguments and what would be the functions?

17) An RPG closed subroutine could perform the necessary price updating of the example in Section 15-5. What would be the entries on the RPG Calculation Specifications form then? Would there be other entries beside those pertaining to the subroutine?

18) If more than two items (as presented in Section 15-5) were involved in the catalog printout, how would you avoid using more than two output indicators in an "OR" relationship? For large numbers of items (e.g., several hundred or thousand) the usage of multiple indicators is, obviously, not the way to attack this problem.

379

19) What entries should you make on the RPG specification forms to print out several times the catalog data of the example in Section 15-5? What about replicated output in RPG in general? What RPG specification forms are necessary to accomplish this?

20) As in most programming situations, there may be more than one solution to the problem. Consider the example of Section 15-5. Could you rewrite it using less coding lines? Could you improve the RPG program's efficiency by using more RPG specification forms but, say, fewer files?

21) Write a complete RPG program to perform the following tasks:

Read a deck of cards containing customers' purchase transactions; each card must have

a) The customer's name (columns 2-26)

b) The customer's account number (columns 27-38)

c) The identifying code for the item purchased (including the department in which it was purchased) (columns 39-42)

d) The date of the transaction (columns 43-48)

e) The amount of the transaction (columns 49-54)

f) The salesperson's code (columns 55-58)

g) A record-identifying code for this purchase card (column 1)

Update a disk ISAM file containing the following information:

The customer's name, account number, address, telephone number, credit limit, current balance and average (historical) monthly transaction to date.

Print a running summary of all monthly transactions tabulated by

a) Customer (with updated balance)

b) Item purchased (department where purchase was carried out)

c) Salesperson

Print invoices with customers' names and addresses including balance forward less payments plus recent transactions plus finance charge (if any, see discussion in Section 15-1) and with payment instructions; e.g., if payments are current, then the payment due is 10 percent of the current balance, and if payments are in arrears over 90 days, the payment due is the full current balance, with appropriate reminders for 30- and 60-day delays. Choose your medium for the "invoices"; this could be a 60-column piece of paper (half of the 120-column printout sheet) so you could position two invoices side-by-side on one sheet, or an 80-column blank card, with the necessary identifying punches, etc. Lay out all planned output on the print chart first.

How many RPG specification forms will be required for this program? Can you estimate approximately? In numbering your forms it is useful to adhere to the following rule-of-thumb: Pages 01-04 for the RPG Control Card and File Description Specifications forms; pages 05-09 for the RPG File Extension Specifications and Indicator Summary forms; pages 10-39 for the RPG Input Specifications form; pages 40-69 for the RPG Calculation Specifications form; pages 70-99 for the RPG Output-Format Specifications form.

22) Now that you have become sufficiently well acquainted with RPG programming, can you answer the following queries?

a) To which class of programming problems is RPG better suited than, say, FORTRAN?

b) Among all problems to which RPG is suited, which are most easily handled by RPG?

c) In Section 14-1 it was stated that many computer programmers hesitate to classify RPG as a programming language. What is your opinion?

APPENDIX A: DERIVATION OF THE ORBITAL EQUATIONS OF CHAPTER 8

If m_1 is the mass of the satellite, m_2 the mass of the planet, r the distance from the center of the planet to the satellite and r'' the acceleration of the satellite due to gravity, then the gravitational force f may be expressed as

$$f = m_1 r'' = -cm_1 m_2 /r^2 \qquad (8\text{-}1)$$

where c is a constant. If m_1 is removed from the equation and c is combined with m_2 to form a new constant k, equation (8-1) becomes the general acceleration equation for orbits of type 1, 2 or 3:

$$r'' = -(k^2/r^2) \qquad (8\text{-}2)$$

Since r'' is the acceleration in miles per second squared, r'' is also the second derivative of r with respect to time. The velocity, r', can be obtained by integrating equation (8-2) (after multiplying both sides by 2r') to get

$$r' = r_0'^2 + 2k^2 (1/r - 1/r_0) \qquad (8\text{-}3)$$

where r_0' and r_0 are the initial values of r' and r. We can now define the escape velocity v_e as

$$v_e^2 = 2k^2/r_0 \qquad (8\text{-}4)$$

since it can be determined by inspecting equation (8-3) that the velocity r' must eventually go to zero as r is increased if r_0' is less than v_e. If the initial velocity r_0' is less than escape velocity, there exists some positive value of distance at which the satellite must stop ascending and begin to fall back toward the planet, assuming that the initial velocity was in an upwards direction. If the initial velocity equals escape, then the satellite will stop ascending, but only at an infinite distance. If the initial velocity exceeds escape velocity, the satellite will always be able to retain some positive velocity away from the planet, even at an infinite distance.

Equations for Orbit Type 1

If the initial velocity is less than the escape velocity, then from equation (8-3) the maximum value of r (the value of r when the velocity becomes zero) in terms of the initial distance and velocity is

$$r_{max} = 2/((2/r_0) - (r_0'^2/k^2)) \qquad (8\text{-}5)$$

After solving equation (8-5) for r_0 and substituting for r_0 in equation (8-3), equation (8-3) may be rewritten as

$$r'^2 = 2k^2(1/r - 1/r_{max})$$ (8-6)

Equation (8-6) must now be integrated to get the position of the satellite as a function of time. To facilitate the integration, we may substitute a new parameter par for the distance r, defining par as

$$par = 2\,arctangent\,(\sqrt{r}\,/\sqrt{(r_{max} - r)}\,)$$ (8-7)

which permits equation (8-6) to be integrated into the form

$$par - sin(par) = kt/(r_{max}/2)^{1.5}$$ (8-8)

choosing the integration constant so that par is zero when the time t is zero. An equivalent definition of par which may be substituted into equation (8-6) for the variable r is

$$r = r_{max}\,sin^2(par/2)$$ (8-9)

Equation (8-9) shows that par is equal to 3.1416 when r equals r_{max}, so the elapsed time from the initial position to the maximum distance r_{max} can be obtained from equation (8-8) as

$$t_{max} = (3.1416(r_{max}/2)^{1.5}/k) + t_0$$ (8-10)

where t_0 is the value of time at the initial position. Equations (8-8) and (8-9) will permit the program to calculate distance as a function of time, and equation (8-6) will then permit the calculation of velocity as a function of distance.

Equations for Orbit Type 2

If the initial velocity is equal to the escape velocity, then equation (8-3) reduces to

$$r'^2 = 2k^2/r$$ (8-11)

upon substituting the escape velocity from equation (8-4) for r'_0. Equation (8-11) may be integrated at once to provide

$$r = (3kt/\sqrt{2})^{.6667}$$ (8-12)

and the velocity may be obtained from

$$r'^2 = 2k^2/r \qquad (8\text{-}13)$$

from the definition of escape velocity in equation (8-4).

Equations for Orbit Type 3

If the initial velocity is greater than the escape velocity, then r_{max} as calculated from equation (8-5) is negative. Taking the absolute value of r_{max}, equation (8-6) should now be written

$$r'^2 = 2k^2 (1/r + 1/r_{max}) \qquad (8\text{-}14)$$

where r_{max} is now the absolute value. To facilitate the integration of equation (8-14), we may substitute another parameter par defined as

$$par = 2\text{arcsinh}(\sqrt{r/r_{max}}) = 2\log(\sqrt{r/r_{max}} + \sqrt{(r/r_{max} + 1)}) \qquad (8\text{-}15)$$

which permits equation (8-14) to be integrated into the form

$$\sinh(par) - par = kt/(r_{max}/2)^{1.5} \qquad (8\text{-}16)$$

Equations (8-15) and (8-16) permit the program to calculate distance as a function of time for type 3 orbits, and equation (8-14) permits the calculation of velocity as a function of distance.

Equations for Orbit Type 4

Orbit types 1 through 3 consist of straight lines through the center of the planet, but orbit types 4 through 6 involve curvilinear motion and require the solution of the differential equation of gravitational force in x and y coordinates. The variable θ (theta) will now be used to measure the rotation of the satellite around the planet, and the variable r will be used as before to measure the distance from the center of the planet to the satellite. Another of Kepler's discoveries, that the line joining the satellite to the planet sweeps out equal areas per unit time regardless of position on any one orbit, is essential to the calculation of curvilinear orbits. If h is twice the area swept out in square miles per second, then

$$h = x'y - y'x = rv_\theta = r^2\theta' \qquad (8\text{-}17)$$

where x' is the x component of velocity, y' is the y component of velocity and θ' is the derivative of θ with respect to time. The variable v_θ is the component of velocity parallel to the surface of the planet (perpendicular to the radius distance r).

Since the acceleration along the x axis will be the total acceleration times x/r and the y component of acceleration will be the total acceleration times y/r, equation (8-2) can now be broken into the two acceleration equations

$$x'' = -k^2 x/r^3 \qquad\qquad y'' = -k^2 y/r^3 \qquad\qquad (8\text{-}18)$$

By substituting $h = r^2\theta'$, $x = r\sin\theta = \dfrac{-d\cos\theta}{dt}$ and $y = \dfrac{d\sin\theta}{dt}$, equations (8-18) become

$$x'' = (k^2/h)\frac{d}{dt}(x/r) \qquad\qquad y'' = -(k^2/h)\frac{d}{dt}(y/r) \qquad\qquad (8\text{-}19)$$

Equations (8-19) may be integrated immediately to

$$x' = (k^2 y/hr) + c \qquad\qquad y' = (-k^2 x/hr) + d \qquad\qquad (8\text{-}20)$$

where c and d are constants of integration. After multiplying the x' equation by $y = r\cos\theta$ and the y' equation by $x = r\sin\theta$, and combining the two equations, we have

$$h = x'y - y'x = (k^2/h)(y\cos\theta + x\sin\theta) + r(c\cos\theta - d\sin\theta) \qquad (8\text{-}21)$$

Since $y\cos\theta + x\sin\theta = r$,

$$h = r(k^2/h + c\cos\theta - d\sin\theta) \qquad\qquad (8\text{-}22)$$

Now if we define two new parameters alpha and b as

$$\text{alpha} = \text{arctangent}\,(-d/c) \qquad b = \sqrt{c^2 + d^2}$$

we can then expand equation (8-22) to the form

$$h = r(k^2/h + b\cos\text{alpha}\cos\theta + b\sin\text{alpha}\sin\theta)$$

which reduces to

$$h = (k^2/h + b\cos(\theta - \text{alpha}))r$$

Solving for r, we can define new parameters p and ecc so that

$$r = \frac{p}{1 + \text{ecc}\cos(\theta - \text{alpha})} \qquad\qquad (8\text{-}23)$$

where $p = h^2/k^2$ and $\text{ecc} = bh/k^2$. Also, since when $\theta = 0$, $y = r$ and $x = 0$, we can define b, c and d in terms of known parameters as follows:

386

$$c = x' - k^2/h, \quad d = y', \quad b = \sqrt{(v_0 - k^2/h)^2 + v_r^2} \qquad (8\text{-}24)$$

Alpha is then equal to

$$alpha = arctangent\ (-v_r/(v_\theta - k^2/h)) \qquad (8\text{-}25)$$

where v_θ is the component of velocity parallel to the radius distance r.

Equation (8-23) is the general equation for a conic. The conic will be an ellipse, parabola or hyperbola depending on whether the eccentricity ecc is less than, equal to or greater than one.

Since the sum of the kinetic energy and the potential energy of the satellite is a constant, the energy balance equation for the satellite may be written as follows:

$$(m/2)(r'^2 + r^2\theta'^2) - k^2m/r = c \qquad (8\text{-}26)$$

where m is the mass of the satellite and c is a constant. In the case of the ellipse,

$$c = -k^2m/2a \qquad (8\text{-}27)$$

since

$$r = a(1 - ecc)$$

when r' is zero and a is defined as

$$a = p/(1 - ecc^2) \qquad (8\text{-}28)$$

Upon substituting equation (8-27) into equation (8-26), the total velocity v is

$$v^2 = r'^2 + r^2\theta'^2 = k^2(2/r - 1/a) \qquad (8\text{-}29)$$

Considerable manipulation is still required before the position angle θ and the elapsed time can be calculated. If a new parameter par is defined as

$$par = arctangent\ (\sqrt{ecc^2 - (1 - r_0/a)^2}\ /(1 - r_0/a)) \qquad (8\text{-}30)$$

then it can finally be determined that

$$r = a(1 - ecc\ cos\ (par)) \qquad (8\text{-}31)$$

$$tan(\theta/2) = \sqrt{(1 + ecc)/(1 - ecc)}\ tan(par/2) \qquad (8\text{-}32)$$

$$k(t - t_0)/a^{3/2} = par - ecc\ sin(par) \qquad (8\text{-}33)$$

387

where t is the elapsed time in seconds from the initial position and t_0 is the value of time at the initial position of the satellite.

Equations for Orbit Type 5

In the case of a parabolic orbit the energy constant c from equation (8-26) is equal to zero since, when r' equals zero,

$$r = q = p/2 \qquad (8-34)$$

Thus, from equation (8-26),

$$v^2 = r'^2 + r^2\theta'^2 = 2k^2/r \qquad (8-35)$$

If a new parameter par is defined as

$$par = \sqrt{r_0/q - 1} \qquad (8-36)$$

then the necessary equations for r, θ and t are

$$r = q(1 + par^2) \qquad (8-37)$$

$$\tan(\theta/2) = par \qquad (8-38)$$

$$k(t - t_0)/\sqrt{2q}^{3/2} = par + par^3/3 \qquad (8-39)$$

Equations for Orbit Type 6

In the case of a hyperbolic orbit the energy constant c from equation (8-26) is equal to

$$c = +k^2 m/2a \qquad (8-40)$$

where m is the mass of the satellite. When r' is zero,

$$r = a(ecc - 1) \qquad (8-41)$$

and a is defined in equation (8-28). Upon substituting equation (8-40) into (8-26),

$$v^2 = r'^2 + r^2\theta'^2 = k^2(2/r + 1/a) \qquad (8-42)$$

If a new parameter par is defined as

$$par = \text{arccosh}((r_0/a+1)/ecc) = \log((r_0/a+1)/ecc + \sqrt{((r_0/a+1)/ecc)^2 - 1)}) \qquad (8-43)$$

388

then the equations for r, θ and t can be developed as

$$r = a(\text{ecc } \cosh(\text{par}) - 1) \tag{8-44}$$

$$\tan(\theta/2) = \sqrt{(\text{ecc} + 1)/(\text{ecc} - 1)} \ \tanh(\text{par}/2) \tag{8-45}$$

$$k(t - t_0)/a^{3/2} = \text{ecc } \sinh(\text{par}) - \text{par} \tag{8-46}$$

APPENDIX B: ASSEMBLER AND INPUT-OUTPUT ERROR CODES

Assembler Error Detection Codes

Flag	Cause	Assembler Action
A	Address error. Attempt made to specify displacement field, directly or indirectly, outside range of –128 to +127.	Displacement set to zero.
C	Condition code error. Character other than +, –, Z, E, C or 0 detected in first operand of short branch or second operand of long BSC, BOSC or BSI statement.	Displacement set to zero.
F	Format code error. Character other than L, I, X or blank detected in column 32, or L or I format specified for instruction not valid in that form.	Instruction processed as if L format were specified, unless that instruction is valid only in short form, in which case it is processed as if the X format were specified.
L	Label error. Invalid symbol detected in label field.	Label ignored.
M	Multiply defined label error. Duplicate symbol encountered in label field or in operand.	First occurrence of symbol in label field defines its value; subsequent occurrences of symbol in label field cause a multiply defined indicator to be inserted in symbol table entry (bit 0 of first word).
O	Op code unrecognized.	Statement ignored and address counter incremented by 2.
	ISS, ILS, ENT, LIBR, SPR, EPR or ABS incorrectly placed.	Statement ignored.
R	Relocation error.	
	Expression does not have valid relocation.	Expression set to zero.
	Nonabsolute displacement specified.	Displacement set to zero.

Flag	Cause	Assembler Action
R	Relocation error (continued).	
	Absolute origin specified in relocatable program.	Origin ignored.
	Nonabsolute operand specified in BSS or BES.	Operand assumed to be zero.
	Nonrelocatable operand in END statement of relocatable mainline program.	Card columns 9-12 left blank; entry assumed to be relative zero.
	ENT operand nonrelocatable.	Statement ignored.
S	Syntax error.	
	Invalid expression (e.g., invalid symbol, adjacent operators, illegal constant).	Expression set to zero.
	Illegal character in record.	If illegal character appears in expression, label, op code, format or tag field, additional errors may be caused.
	Main program entry point not specified in END operand. Incorrect syntax in EBC statement (e.g., no delimiter in card column 35, zero character count).	Card columns 9-12 left blank; entry assumed to be relative zero. Card columns 9-12 not punched; address counter incremented by 17.
	Invalid label in ENT or ISS operand.	Statement ignored.
T	Tag error. Card column 33 contains character other than blank, 0, 1, 2 or 3 in instruction statement.	Tag of zero assumed.
U	Undefined symbol. Undefined symbol in expression.	Expression set to absolute zero.
W	X or Y coordinate or both out of range; or invalid operand.	Operand set to zero.
X	Character other than R or I in column 32; or character other than D or N in column 33.	Field set to zero.
Z	Invalid condition in conditional branch or interrupt order.	Condition bits in first word set to zero.

Errors Detected by ISS Subroutines

Error	Contents of Accumulator Hexadecimal	Contents of Extension (if any)
Card		
*Last card	0 0 0 0	
*Feed check		
*Read check	0 0 0 1	
*Punch check		
Device not ready	1 0 0 0	
Last card indicator on for Read		
Illegal device (not 0 version)		
Device not in system		
Illegal function	1 0 0 1	
Word count over +80		
Word count zero or negative		
Printer-Keyboard		
Device not ready	2 0 0 0	
Device not in system		
Illegal function	2 0 0 1	
Word count zero or negative		
Paper Tape		
*Punch not ready	0 0 0 4	
*Reader not ready	0 0 0 5	
Device not ready	3 0 0 0	
Illegal device		
Illegal function	3 0 0 1	
Word count zero or negative		
Illegal check digit		
Disk		
*Disk overflow	0 0 0 4	
*Seek failure remaining after 10 attempts	0 0 0 3	Effective Sector ID
*Read check remaining after 10 attempts		
Data error	0 0 0 1	Effective Sector ID
Data overrun		

Error	Contents of Accumulator Hexadecimal	Contents of Extension (if any)
*Write check remaining after 10 attempts		
Write select		
Data error	0 0 0 1	Effective Sector ID
Data overrun		
Device not ready	5 0 0 0	
Illegal device (not 0 version)		
Device not in system		
Illegal function		
Attempt to write in file protected area	5 0 0 1	
Word count zero or negative		
Word count over +320 (0 version only)		
Starting sector identification over +1599		
1132 Printer		
*Channel 9 detected	0 0 0 3	
*Channel 12 detected	0 0 0 4	
Device not ready or end of forms	6 0 0 0	
Illegal function		
Illegal word count	6 0 0 1	
Plotter		
Plotter not ready	7 0 0 0	
Illegal device		
Device not in system		
Illegal function	7 0 0 1	
Word count zero or negative		

NOTE: The errors marked with an asterisk cause a branch via the error parameter. These errors are detected during the processing of interrupts; as a consequence, the user error routine is an interrupt routine, executed at the priority level of the I/O device.

APPENDIX C: FORTRAN STATEMENTS AND FORTRAN ERROR CODES

FORTRAN Statements

BACKSPACE i   Here i is an integer constant or variable. This causes symbolic unit i to be backspaced one logical record.

CALL name (a, b, ...)   Here name is the name of a subroutine and a, b, ... are the arguments of the subroutine. They may be constants, variables, expressions and subprogram names. All subprogram names used as arguments of functions or subroutines must appear in an EXTERNAL statement in the calling program.

Computed GO TO   General form is GO TO (a, b, ...), i where a, b, ... are statement numbers and i is an integer variable. This causes a transfer of control to the ith statement number in the parentheses.

COMMON a, b, ...   Here a, b, ... are variable names, which may contain DIMENSION information.

CONTINUE   This generates no coding and is used as a DO loop termination where the loop would otherwise end on a transfer type statement.

DATA list/a, b, c, ... /   Here list contains the names of the variables being defined and a, b, c, ... are the values for the variables in the list. The DATA statement is used as a means of introducing constant information at compilation.

DEFINE FILE file(m, n, f, v)   Here file is an integer constant which is the symbolic unit for the segment of a disk being defined; m and n are integer constants specifying the number of records in the unit, and the number of words per record, respectively; f = E if the unit is used as an external medium and f = U for internal medium use; v is an integer variable name which contains the record number of the next record to be read. After execution of a READ or WRITE statement, the value of v for the referenced file will be incremented automatically by the number of records read or written.

DIMENSION a(n_1, n_2, n_3), b(n_1, n_2, n_3), ...   Here the a, b, ... are subscripted variables and the n_i are integer constants specifying the maximum subscript size. The number of n's gives the number of subscripts for each variable. The maximum number of subscripts is three.

DO n i = j, k, m   Here i is an integer variable and j, k and m are integer variables or constants, n is a statement number. This causes repeated execution of all statements between the DO up to and including statement n with i = j initially and incremented by m after each execution of statement n until i > k. When this happens, the statement following statement n is next executed. If m is omitted, it is assumed to be one.

END   This statement must be the physically last statement in every program or subprogram. It is used as an end-of-program signal to the compiler and has no effect on program execution.

END FILE i   Here i is an integer variable or constant. This causes a file mark to be written on symbolic unit i.

EQUIVALENCE (a, b, c, ...), (x, y, z, ...)   Here the a, b, c, ..., x, y, z, ... are variable names which may contain subscripts. This allows all variable names within a pair of parentheses to refer to the same storage location.

EXTERNAL a, b, c, ...   Here a, b, c, ... are subprogram names appearing in argument lists of functions or subroutines.

FIND (file' v)   Here file is the symbolic unit designation of a disk file and v is an integer variable name for the record counter for the unit. This causes the read-write heads of the access mechanism to be positioned at the record whose sequence in the file is the present value of v.

FORMAT (a, b, ...)   Here a, b, ... are format specifications which describe the arrangement of data on external media. Each FORMAT statement has a unique statement number.

FUNCTION name (a, b, c, ...)   Here name is the name of a function and a, b, c, ... are dummy arguments corresponding to real arguments in a function reference. The type of a function is implied by the first character of its name. The implied type may be overridden by writing REAL FUNCTION (a, b, c, ...) or INTEGER FUNCTION (a, b, c, ...). The FUNCTION statement must be the first statement in a function subprogram.

GO TO n   Here n is a statement number. This causes a transfer of control to statement n.

IF (a) i, j, k   Here a is an arithmetic expression and i, j and k are statement numbers. If a < 0, go to i; if a = 0, go to j; if a > 0, go to k. This is the arithmetic IF.

PAUSE   This causes the computer to halt, depressing the start key causes program execution to begin again after the PAUSE statement. For some monitor systems, this causes termination of the program with the computer continuing with the next job on the input tape.

READ (i) list   This causes reading of the variables in the list from unit i in binary format. That is, unit i is an internal medium.

READ (i, j) list   This causes reading of the variables in the list from unit i according to FORMAT statement j.

RETURN   This causes a return from a subprogram to the calling program.

REWIND i   This causes unit i to be rewound to its starting point.

STOP   This statement terminates the execution of a program.

SUBROUTINE name (a, b, c, ...)   Here name is the subroutine name and a, b, c, ... are dummy arguments corresponding to actual arguments in a CALL statement. This statement must be the first statement in a SUBROUTINE subprogram.

WRITE (i) list   This causes writing of the variables in the list onto unit i in binary format.

WRITE (i, j) list   This causes writing of the variables in the list onto unit i according to FORMAT statement j.

FORTRAN Error Codes

Error No.	Cause of Error
C1	Nonnumeric character in statement number.
C2	More than five continuation cards, or continuation card out of sequence.
C3	Syntax error in CALL LINK or CALL EXIT statement or CALL LINK or CALL EXIT in process program.
C4	Indeterminable, misspelled or incorrectly formed statement.
C5	Statement out of sequence.
C6	Statement following STOP, RETURN, CALL LINK, CALL EXIT, GO TO or IF statement does not have statement number.
C7	Name longer than five characters, or name not starting with an alphabetic character.
C8	Incorrect or missing subscript within dimension information (DIMENSION, COMMON, REAL or INTEGER).
C9	Duplicate statement number.
C10	Syntax error in COMMON statement.
C11	Duplicate name in COMMON statement.
C12	Syntax error in FUNCTION or SUBROUTINE statement.
C13	Parameter (dummy argument) appears in COMMON statement.
C14	Name appears twice as a parameter in SUBROUTINE or FUNCTION statement.
C15	*IOCS control record in a subprogram.
C16	Syntax error in DIMENSION statement.
C17	Subprogram name in DIMENSION statement.
C18	Name dimensioned more than once, or not dimensioned on first appearance of name.
C19	Syntax error in REAL, INTEGER or EXTERNAL statement.
C20	Subprogram name in REAL or INTEGER statement or a FUNCTION subprogram containing its own name in an EXTERNAL statement.
C21	Name in EXTERNAL which is also in a COMMON or DIMENSION statement.
C22	IFIX or FLOAT in EXTERNAL statement.
C23	Invalid real constant.
C24	Invalid integer constant.
C25	More than 15 dummy arguments, or duplicate dummy arguments in statement function argument list.

Error No.	Cause of Error
C26	Right parenthesis missing from a subscript expression.
C27	Syntax error in FORMAT statement.
C28	FORMAT statement without statement number.
C29	Field width specification greater than 145.
C30	In a FORMAT statement specifying E or F conversion, w greater than 127, d greater than 31, or d greater than w, where w is an unsigned integer constant specifying the total field length of the data and d is an unsigned integer constant specifying the number of decimal places to the right of the decimal point.
C31	Subscript error in EQUIVALENCE statement.
C32	Subscripted variable in a statement function.
C33	Incorrectly formed subscript expression.
C34	Undefined variable in subscript expression.
C35	Number of subscripts in a subscript expression or the range of the subscripts does not agree with the dimension information.
C36	Invalid arithmetic statement or variable; or, in a FUNCTION subprogram the left side of an arithmetic statement is a dummy argument (or in COMMON).
C37	Syntax error in IF statement.
C38	Invalid expression in IF statement.
C39	Syntax error or invalid simple argument in CALL statement.
C40	Invalid expression in CALL statement.
C41	Invalid expression to the left of an equal sign in a statement function.
C42	Invalid expression to the right of an equal sign in a statement function.
C43	If an IF, GO TO or DO statement a statement number is missing, invalid, incorrectly placed, or is the number of a FORMAT statement.
C44	Syntax error in READ, WRITE or FIND statement.
C45	*IOCS record missing with a READ or WRITE statement (mainline program only).
C46	FORMAT statement number missing or incorrect in a READ or WRITE statement.
C47	Syntax error in input-output list; or an invalid list element; or, in a FUNCTION subprogram, the input list element is a dummy argument or in COMMON.
C48	Syntax error in GO TO statement.

Error No.	Cause of Error
C49	Index of a computed GO TO is missing, invalid or not preceded by a comma.
C50	*TRANSFER TRACE or *ARITHMETIC TRACE control record present with no *IOCS control record in a mainline program.
C51	Incorrect nesting of DO statements; or the terminal statement of the associated DO statement is a GO TO, IF, RETURN, FORMAT, STOP, PAUSE, CALL EXIT, CALL LINK or DO.
C52	More than 25 nested DO statements.
C53	Syntax error in DO statements.
C54	Initial value in DO statement is zero.
C55	In a FUNCTION subprogram the index of DO is a dummy argument or in COMMON.
C56	Syntax error in BACKSPACE statement.
C57	Syntax error in REWIND statement.
C58	Syntax error in END FILE statement.
C59	Syntax error in STOP statement or STOP statement in process program.
C60	Syntax error in PAUSE statement.
C61	Integer constant in STOP or PAUSE statement is 9999.
C62	Last executable statement before END statement is not a STOP, GO TO, IF, CALL LINK, CALL EXIT or RETURN statement.
C63	Statement contains more than 15 different subscript expressions.
C64	Statement too long to be scanned due to compiler expansion of subscript expressions or compiler addition of generated temporary storage locations.
C65[†]	All variables are undefined in an EQUIVALENCE list.
C66[†]	Variable made equivalent to an element of an array, in such a manner as to cause the array to extend beyond the origin of the COMMON area.
C67[†]	Two variables or array elements in COMMON are equated, or the relative locations of two variables or array elements are assigned more than once (directly or indirectly).
C68	Syntax error in an EQUIVALENCE statement; or an illegal variable name in an EQUIVALENCE list.

[†]The detection of a code 65, 66 or 67 error prevents any subsequent detection of any of these three errors.

Error No.	Cause of Error
C69	Subprogram does not contain a RETURN statement, or a mainline program contains a RETURN statement.
C70	No DEFINE FILE in a mainline program which has disk READ, WRITE or FIND statements.
C71	Syntax error in DEFINE FILE.
C72	Duplicate DEFINE FILE, more than 75 DEFINE FILES, or DEFINE FILE in subprogram.
C73	Syntax error in record number of disk READ, WRITE or FIND statement.
C74	Defined files exceed disk storage size.
C75	Syntax error in data statement.
C76	Names and constants in a data statement not one to one.
C77	Mixed mode in data statement.
C78	Invalid hollerith constant in a data statement.
C79	Invalid hexadecimal specification in a data statement.
C80	Variable in a data statement not used elsewhere in program, or dummy variable in a DATA statement.
C81	Common variable loaded with a data specification.
C82	Data statement too long.

FORTRAN I/O Error Codes

The following error codes are displayed in the accumulator upon detection of the errors. Press PROGRAM START to perform a branch to the monitor to proceed to the next subjob.

Error Code	Cause of Error
F001	1. Logical unit defined incorrectly.
	2. No *IOCS control record for specified I/O device.
F002	Requested record exceeds allocated buffer size.
F003	Illegal character encountered in input record.
F004	Exponent too large or too small in input field.
F005	More than one E encountered in input field.
F006	More than one sign encountered in input field.
F007	More than one decimal point encountered in input field.
F008	1. Read of output-only device.
	2. Write of input-only device.
F009	Real variable transmitted with an I format specification, or integer variable transmitted with an E or F format specification.
F100	File not defined by DEFINE FILE statement.
F101	File record too large, equal to zero, or negative.

DISKZ Errors:

F102	Read error.
F103	Disk FIO (SDFIO) has not been initialized (e.g., there is no *IOCS disk record in the mainline program).
F104	Write error.
F106	Read back check error.
F108	Seek error.
F10A	Forced read error (seek or find).

APPENDIX D: CHARACTER CODE AND INTEGER EQUIVALENT CODES

Character Code Table

EBCDIC Hex	IBM Card Code Rows 12	11	0	9	8	7-1	Hex	Graphics and Control Names	1132 Printer EBCDIC Subset Hex	PTTC/8 Hex U=Upper Case L=Lower Case	Console Printer Hex	1403 Printer Hex
05	12			9		5	8110	HT Horizontal Tab		6D(U/L)	41[1]	7F
06	12			9		6	8090	LC Lower Case		6E(U/L)		
07	12			9		7	8050	DEL Delete		7F(U/L)		
14		11		9		4	4210	RES Restore		4C(U/L)	05[2]	
15		11		9		5	4110	NL New Line		DD(U/L)	81[3]	
16		11		9		6	4090	BS Backspace		5E(U/L)	11	
25			0	9		5	2110	LF Line Feed		3D(U/L)	03	
26			0	9		6	2090	EOB End of Block		3E(U/L)		
35				9		5	0110	RS Reader Stop		0D(U/L)	09[4]	
36				9		6	0090	UC Upper Case		0E(U/L)		
40			no punches				0000	Blank	≠	10(U/L)	21	7F
4A	12				8	2	8820	¢		20(U)	02	
4B	12				8	3	8420	. (period)	4B	6B(L)	00	6E
4C	12				8	4	8220	<		02(U)	DE	
4D	12				8	5	8120	(	4D	19(U)	FE	2F
4E	12				8	6	80A0	+	4E	70(U)	DA	6D
4F	12				8	7	8060	| (logical OR)	50	3B(U)	C6	
50	12						8000	&		70(L)	44	15
5A		11			8	2	4820	!		5B(U)	42	
5B		11			8	3	4420	$	5B	5B(L)	40	62

NOTES: Typewriter Output:
[1] Tabulate   [2] Shift to black   [3] Carrier Return   [4] Shift to red

EBCDIC Hex	IBM Card Code Rows 12	11	0	9	8	7-1	Hex	Graphics and Control Names	1132 Printer EBCDIC Subset Hex	PTTC/8 Hex U=Upper Case L=Lower Case	Console Printer Hex	1403 Printer Hex
5C		11			8	4	4220	*	5C	08(U)	D6	23
5D		11			8	5	4120	)	5D	1A(U)	F6	57
5E		11			8	6	40A0	;		13(U)	D2	
5F		11			8	7	4060	¬ (logical NOT)		68(U)	F2	61
60		11					4000	– (dash)	60	40(L)	84	4C
61			0			1	3000	/	61	31(L)	BC	16
6B			0		8	3	2420	, (comma)	6B	3B(L)	80	
6C			0		8	4	2220	%		15(U)	06	
6D			0		8	5	2120	_ (underscore)		40(U)	BE	
6E			0		8	6	20A0	>		07(U)	46	
6F			0		8	7	2060	?		31(U)	86	
7A					8	2	0820	:		04(U)	82	
7B					8	3	0420	#		0B(L)	C0	
7C					8	4	0220	@		20(L)	04	
7D					8	5	0120	' (apostrophe)	7D	16(U)	E6	0B
7E					8	6	00A0	=	7E	01(U)	C2	4A
7F					8	7	0060	"		0B(U)	E2	
C1	12					1	9000	A	C1	61(U)	3C or 3E	64
C2	12					2	8800	B	C2	62(U)	18 or 1A	25
C3	12					3	8400	C	C3	73(U)	1C or 1E	26
C4	12					4	8200	D	C4	64(U)	30 or 32	67
C5	12					5	8100	E	C5	75(U)	34 or 36	68
C6	12					6	8080	F	C6	76(U)	10 or 12	29
C7	12					7	8040	G	C7	67(U)	14 or 16	2A
C8	12				8		8020	H	C8	68(U)	24 or 26	6B
C9	12			9			8010	I	C9	79(U)	20 or 22	2C

EBCDIC Hex	IBM Card Code Rows 12	11	0	9	8	7-1	Hex	Graphics and Control Names	1132 Printer EBCDIC Subset Hex	PTTC/8 Hex U=Upper Case L=Lower Case	Console Printer Hex	1403 Printer Hex
D1		11				1	5000	J	D1	51(U)	7C or 7E	58
D2		11				2	4800	K	D2	52(U)	58 or 5A	19
D3		11				3	4400	L	D3	43(U)	5C or 5E	1A
D4		11				4	4200	M	D4	54(U)	70 or 72	5B
D5		11				5	4100	N	D5	45(U)	74 or 76	1C
D6		11				6	4080	O	D6	46(U)	50 or 52	5D
D7		11				7	4040	P	D7	57(U)	54 or 56	5E
D8		11			8		4020	Q	D8	58(U)	64 or 66	1F
D9		11		9			4010	R	D9	49(U)	60 or 62	20
E2			0			2	2800	S	E2	32(U)	98 or 9A	0D
E3			0			3	2400	T	E3	23(U)	9C or 9E	0E
E4			0			4	2200	U	E4	34(U)	B0 or B2	4F
E5			0			5	2100	V	E5	25(U)	B4 or B6	10
E6			0			6	2080	W	E6	26(U)	90 or 92	51
E7			0			7	2040	X	E7	37(U)	94 or 96	52
E8			0		8		2020	Y	E8	38(U)	A4 or A6	13
E9			0	9			2010	Z	E9	29(U)	A0 or A2	54
F0			0				2000	0	F0	1A(L)	C4	49
F1						1	1000	1	F1	01(L)	FC	40
F2						2	0800	2	F2	02(L)	D8	01
F3						3	0400	3	F3	13(L)	DC	02
F4						4	0200	4	F4	04(L)	F0	43
F5						5	0100	5	F5	15(L)	F4	04
F6						6	0080	6	F6	16(L)	D0	45
F7						7	0040	7	F7	07(L)	D4	46
F8					8		0020	8	F8	08(L)	E4	07
F9				9			0010	9	F9	19(L)	E0	08

EBCDIC Characters and Integer Equivalents

A	−16064	0	−4032
B	−15808	1	−3776
C	−15552	2	−3520
D	−15296	3	−3264
E	−15040	4	−3008
F	−14784	5	−2752
G	−14528	6	−2496
H	−14272	7	−2240
I	−14016	8	−1984
J	−11968	9	−1728
K	−11712	Blank	16448
L	−11456	. (period)	19264
M	−11200	< (less than)	19520
N	−10944	(	19776
O	−10688	+	20032
P	−10432	&	20544
Q	−10176	$	23360
R	−9920	*	23616
S	−7616	)	23872
T	−7360	− (minus)	24640
U	−7104	/	24896
V	−6848	, (comma)	27456
W	−6592	%	27712
X	−6336	#	31552
Y	−6080	@	31808
Z	−5824	' (apostrophe)	32064
		=	32320

APPENDIX E: HEXADECIMAL-DECIMAL CONVERSION CHART

The following table is used to convert decimal numbers to hexadecimal and hexa-decimal numbers to decimal. In the descriptions that follow, the explanation of each step is followed by an example in parentheses.

Decimal to Hexadecimal Conversion. Locate the decimal number (0489) in the body of the table. The two high-order digits (1E) of the hexadecimal number are in the left column on the same line, and the low-order digit (9) is at the top of the column. Thus the hexadecimal number 1E9 is equal to the decimal number 0489.

Hexadecimal to Decimal Conversion. Locate the first two digits (1E) of the hexa-decimal number (1E9) in the left column. Follow the line of figures across the page to the column headed by the low-order digit (9). The decimal number (0489) located at the junction of the horizontal line and the vertical column is the equivalent of the hexadecimal number.

	0	1	2	3	4	5	6	7	8	9	A	B	C	D	E	F
00	0000	0001	0002	0003	0004	0005	0006	0007	0008	0009	0010	0011	0012	0013	0014	0015
01	0016	0017	0018	0019	0020	0021	0022	0023	0024	0025	0026	0027	0028	0029	0030	0031
02	0032	0033	0034	0035	0036	0037	0038	0039	0040	0041	0042	0043	0044	0045	0046	0047
03	0048	0049	0050	0051	0052	0053	0054	0055	0056	0057	0058	0059	0060	0061	0062	0063
04	0064	0065	0066	0067	0068	0069	0070	0071	0072	0073	0074	0075	0076	0077	0078	0079
05	0080	0081	0082	0083	0084	0085	0086	0087	0088	0089	0090	0091	0092	0093	0094	0095
06	0096	0097	0098	0099	0100	0101	0102	0103	0104	0105	0106	0107	0108	0109	0110	0111
07	0112	0113	0114	0115	0116	0117	0118	0119	0120	0121	0122	0123	0124	0125	0126	0127
08	0128	0129	0130	0131	0132	0133	0134	0135	0136	0137	0138	0139	0140	0141	0142	0143
09	0144	0145	0146	0147	0148	0149	0150	0151	0152	0153	0154	0155	0156	0157	0158	0159
0A	0160	0161	0162	0163	0164	0165	0166	0167	0168	0169	0170	0171	0172	0173	0174	0175
0B	0176	0177	0178	0179	0180	0181	0182	0183	0184	0185	0186	0187	0188	0189	0190	0191
0C	0192	0193	0194	0195	0196	0197	0198	0199	0200	0201	0202	0203	0204	0205	0206	0207
0D	0208	0209	0210	0211	0212	0213	0214	0215	0216	0217	0218	0219	0220	0221	0222	0223
0E	0224	0225	0226	0227	0228	0229	0230	0231	0232	0233	0234	0235	0236	0237	0238	0239
0F	0240	0241	0242	0243	0244	0245	0246	0247	0248	0249	0250	0251	0252	0253	0254	0255
10	0256	0257	0258	0259	0260	0261	0262	0263	0264	0265	0266	0267	0268	0269	0270	0271
11	0272	0273	0274	0275	0276	0277	0278	0279	0280	0281	0282	0283	0284	0285	0286	0287
12	0288	0289	0290	0291	0292	0293	0294	0295	0296	0297	0298	0299	0300	0301	0302	0303
13	0304	0305	0306	0307	0308	0309	0310	0311	0312	0313	0314	0315	0316	0317	0318	0319
14	0320	0321	0322	0323	0324	0325	0326	0327	0328	0329	0330	0331	0332	0333	0334	0335
15	0336	0337	0338	0339	0340	0341	0342	0343	0344	0345	0346	0347	0348	0349	0350	0351
16	0352	0353	0354	0355	0356	0357	0358	0359	0360	0361	0362	0363	0364	0365	0366	0367
17	0368	0369	0370	0371	0372	0373	0374	0375	0376	0377	0378	0379	0380	0381	0382	0383

	0	1	2	3	4	5	6	7	8	9	A	B	C	D	E	F
18	0384	0385	0386	0387	0388	0389	0390	0391	0392	0393	0394	0395	0396	0397	0398	0399
19	0400	0401	0402	0403	0404	0405	0406	0407	0408	0409	0410	0411	0412	0413	0414	0415
1A	0416	0417	0418	0419	0420	0421	0422	0423	0424	0425	0426	0427	0428	0429	0430	0431
1B	0432	0433	0434	0435	0436	0437	0438	0439	0440	0441	0442	0443	0444	0445	0446	0447
1C	0448	0449	0450	0451	0452	0453	0454	0455	0456	0457	0458	0459	0460	0461	0462	0463
1D	0464	0465	0466	0467	0468	0469	0470	0471	0472	0473	0474	0475	0476	0477	0478	0479
1E	0480	0481	0482	0483	0484	0485	0486	0487	0488	0489	0490	0491	0492	0493	0494	0495
1F	0496	0497	0498	0499	0500	0501	0502	0503	0504	0505	0506	0507	0508	0509	0510	0511
20	0512	0513	0514	0515	0516	0517	0518	0519	0520	0521	0522	0523	0524	0525	0526	0527
21	0528	0529	0530	0531	0532	0533	0534	0535	0536	0537	0538	0539	0540	0541	0542	0543
22	0544	0545	0546	0547	0548	0549	0550	0551	0552	0553	0554	0555	0556	0557	0558	0559
23	0560	0561	0562	0563	0564	0565	0566	0567	0568	0569	0570	0571	0572	0573	0574	0575
24	0576	0577	0578	0579	0580	0581	0582	0583	0584	0585	0586	0587	0588	0589	0590	0591
25	0592	0593	0594	0595	0596	0597	0598	0599	0600	0601	0602	0603	0604	0605	0606	0607
26	0608	0609	0610	0611	0612	0613	0614	0615	0616	0617	0618	0619	0620	0621	0622	0623
27	0624	0625	0626	0627	0628	0629	0630	0631	0632	0633	0634	0635	0636	0637	0638	0639
28	0640	0641	0642	0643	0644	0645	0646	0647	0648	0649	0650	0651	0652	0653	0654	0655
29	0656	0657	0658	0659	0660	0661	0662	0663	0664	0665	0666	0667	0668	0669	0670	0671
2A	0672	0673	0674	0675	0676	0677	0678	0679	0680	0681	0682	0683	0684	0685	0686	0687
2B	0688	0689	0690	0691	0692	0693	0694	0695	0696	0697	0698	0699	0700	0701	0702	0703
2C	0704	0705	0706	0707	0708	0709	0710	0711	0712	0713	0714	0715	0716	0717	0718	0719
2D	0720	0721	0722	0723	0724	0725	0726	0727	0728	0729	0730	0731	0732	0733	0734	0735
2E	0736	0737	0738	0739	0740	0741	0742	0743	0744	0745	0746	0747	0748	0749	0750	0751
2F	0752	0753	0754	0755	0756	0757	0758	0759	0760	0761	0762	0763	0764	0765	0766	0767
30	0768	0769	0770	0771	0772	0773	0774	0775	0776	0777	0778	0779	0780	0781	0782	0783
31	0784	0785	0786	0787	0788	0789	0790	0791	0792	0793	0794	0795	0796	0797	0798	0799
32	0800	0801	0802	0803	0804	0805	0806	0807	0808	0809	0810	0811	0812	0813	0814	0815
33	0816	0817	0818	0819	0820	0821	0822	0823	0824	0825	0826	0827	0828	0829	0830	0831
34	0832	0833	0834	0835	0836	0837	0838	0839	0840	0841	0842	0843	0844	0845	0846	0847
35	0848	0849	0850	0851	0852	0853	0854	0855	0856	0857	0858	0859	0860	0861	0862	0863
36	0864	0865	0866	0867	0868	0869	0870	0871	0872	0873	0874	0875	0876	0877	0878	0879
37	0880	0881	0882	0883	0884	0885	0886	0887	0888	0889	0890	0891	0892	0893	0894	0895
38	0896	0897	0898	0899	0900	0901	0902	0903	0904	0905	0906	0907	0908	0909	0910	0911
39	0912	0913	0914	0915	0916	0917	0918	0919	0920	0921	0922	0923	0924	0925	0926	0927
3A	0928	0929	0930	0931	0932	0933	0934	0935	0936	0937	0938	0939	0940	0941	0942	0943
3B	0944	0945	0946	0947	0948	0949	0950	0951	0952	0953	0954	0955	0956	0957	0958	0959
3C	0960	0961	0962	0963	0964	0965	0966	0967	0968	0969	0970	0971	0972	0973	0974	0975
3D	0976	0977	0978	0979	0980	0981	0982	0983	0984	0985	0986	0987	0988	0989	0990	0991
3E	0992	0993	0994	0995	0996	0997	0998	0999	1000	1001	1002	1003	1004	1005	1006	1007
3F	1008	1009	1010	1011	1012	1013	1014	1015	1016	1017	1018	1019	1020	1021	1022	1023
40	1024	1025	1026	1027	1028	1029	1030	1031	1032	1033	1034	1035	1036	1037	1038	1039
41	1040	1041	1042	1043	1044	1045	1046	1047	1048	1049	1050	1051	1052	1053	1054	1055
42	1056	1057	1058	1059	1060	1061	1062	1063	1064	1065	1066	1067	1068	1069	1070	1071
43	1072	1073	1074	1075	1076	1077	1078	1079	1080	1081	1082	1083	1084	1085	1086	1087

	0	1	2	3	4	5	6	7	8	9	A	B	C	D	E	F
44	1088	1089	1090	1091	1092	1093	1094	1095	1096	1097	1098	1099	1100	1101	1102	1103
45	1104	1105	1106	1107	1108	1109	1110	1111	1112	1113	1114	1115	1116	1117	1118	1119
46	1120	1121	1122	1123	1124	1125	1126	1127	1128	1129	1130	1131	1132	1133	1134	1135
47	1136	1137	1138	1139	1140	1141	1142	1143	1144	1145	1146	1147	1148	1149	1150	1151
48	1152	1153	1154	1155	1156	1157	1158	1159	1160	1161	1162	1163	1164	1165	1166	1167
49	1168	1169	1170	1171	1172	1173	1174	1175	1176	1177	1178	1179	1180	1181	1182	1183
4A	1184	1185	1186	1187	1188	1189	1190	1191	1192	1193	1194	1195	1196	1197	1198	1199
4B	1200	1201	1202	1203	1204	1205	1206	1207	1208	1209	1210	1211	1212	1213	1214	1215
4C	1216	1217	1218	1219	1220	1221	1222	1223	1224	1225	1226	1227	1228	1229	1230	1231
4D	1232	1233	1234	1235	1236	1237	1238	1239	1240	1241	1242	1243	1244	1245	1246	1247
4E	1248	1249	1250	1251	1252	1253	1254	1255	1256	1257	1258	1259	1260	1261	1262	1263
4F	1264	1265	1266	1267	1268	1269	1270	1271	1272	1273	1274	1275	1276	1277	1278	1279
50	1280	1281	1282	1283	1284	1285	1286	1287	1288	1289	1290	1291	1292	1293	1294	1295
51	1296	1297	1298	1299	1300	1301	1302	1303	1304	1305	1306	1307	1308	1309	1310	1311
52	1312	1313	1314	1315	1316	1317	1318	1319	1320	1321	1322	1323	1324	1325	1326	1327
53	1328	1329	1330	1331	1332	1333	1334	1335	1336	1337	1338	1339	1340	1341	1342	1343
54	1344	1345	1346	1347	1348	1349	1350	1351	1352	1353	1354	1355	1356	1357	1358	1359
55	1360	1361	1362	1363	1364	1365	1366	1367	1368	1369	1370	1371	1372	1373	1374	1375
56	1376	1377	1378	1379	1380	1381	1382	1383	1384	1385	1386	1387	1388	1389	1390	1391
57	1392	1393	1394	1395	1396	1397	1398	1399	1400	1401	1402	1403	1404	1405	1406	1407
58	1408	1409	1410	1411	1412	1413	1414	1415	1416	1417	1418	1419	1420	1421	1422	1423
59	1424	1425	1426	1427	1428	1429	1430	1431	1432	1433	1434	1435	1436	1437	1438	1439
5A	1440	1441	1442	1443	1444	1445	1446	1447	1448	1449	1450	1451	1452	1453	1454	1455
5B	1456	1457	1458	1459	1460	1461	1462	1463	1464	1465	1466	1467	1468	1469	1470	1471
5C	1472	1473	1474	1475	1476	1477	1478	1479	1480	1481	1482	1483	1484	1485	1486	1487
5D	1488	1489	1490	1491	1492	1493	1494	1495	1496	1497	1498	1499	1500	1501	1502	1503
5E	1504	1505	1506	1507	1508	1509	1510	1511	1512	1513	1514	1515	1516	1517	1518	1519
5F	1520	1521	1522	1523	1524	1525	1526	1527	1528	1529	1530	1531	1532	1533	1534	1535
60	1536	1537	1538	1539	1540	1541	1542	1543	1544	1545	1546	1547	1548	1549	1550	1551
61	1552	1553	1554	1555	1556	1557	1558	1559	1560	1561	1562	1563	1564	1565	1566	1567
62	1568	1569	1570	1571	1572	1573	1574	1575	1576	1577	1578	1579	1580	1581	1582	1583
63	1584	1585	1586	1587	1588	1589	1590	1591	1592	1593	1594	1595	1596	1597	1598	1599
64	1600	1601	1602	1603	1604	1605	1606	1607	1608	1609	1610	1611	1612	1613	1614	1615
65	1616	1617	1618	1619	1620	1621	1622	1623	1624	1625	1626	1627	1628	1629	1630	1631
66	1632	1633	1634	1635	1636	1637	1638	1639	1640	1641	1642	1643	1644	1645	1646	1647
67	1648	1649	1650	1651	1652	1653	1654	1655	1656	1657	1658	1659	1660	1661	1662	1663
68	1664	1665	1666	1667	1668	1669	1670	1671	1672	1673	1674	1675	1676	1677	1678	1679
69	1680	1681	1682	1683	1684	1685	1686	1687	1688	1689	1690	1691	1692	1693	1694	1695
6A	1696	1697	1698	1699	1700	1701	1702	1703	1704	1705	1706	1707	1708	1709	1710	1711
6B	1712	1713	1714	1715	1716	1717	1718	1719	1720	1721	1722	1723	1724	1725	1726	1727
6C	1728	1729	1730	1731	1732	1733	1734	1735	1736	1737	1738	1739	1740	1741	1742	1743
6D	1744	1745	1746	1747	1748	1749	1750	1751	1752	1753	1754	1755	1756	1757	1758	1759
6E	1760	1761	1762	1763	1764	1765	1766	1767	1768	1769	1770	1771	1772	1773	1774	1775
6F	1776	1777	1778	1779	1780	1781	1782	1783	1784	1785	1786	1787	1788	1789	1790	1791

	0	1	2	3	4	5	6	7	8	9	A	B	C	D	E	F
70	1792	1793	1794	1795	1796	1797	1798	1799	1800	1801	1802	1803	1804	1805	1806	1807
71	1808	1809	1810	1811	1812	1813	1814	1815	1816	1817	1818	1819	1820	1821	1822	1823
72	1824	1825	1826	1827	1828	1829	1830	1831	1832	1833	1834	1835	1836	1837	1838	1839
73	1840	1841	1842	1843	1844	1845	1846	1847	1848	1849	1850	1851	1852	1853	1854	1855
74	1856	1857	1858	1859	1860	1861	1862	1863	1864	1865	1866	1867	1868	1869	1870	1871
75	1872	1873	1874	1875	1876	1877	1878	1879	1880	1881	1882	1883	1884	1885	1886	1887
76	1888	1889	1890	1891	1892	1893	1894	1895	1896	1897	1898	1899	1900	1901	1902	1903
77	1904	1905	1906	1907	1908	1909	1910	1911	1912	1913	1914	1915	1916	1917	1918	1919
78	1920	1921	1922	1923	1924	1925	1926	1927	1928	1929	1930	1931	1932	1933	1934	1935
79	1936	1937	1938	1939	1940	1941	1942	1943	1944	1945	1946	1947	1948	1949	1950	1951
7A	1952	1953	1954	1955	1956	1957	1958	1959	1960	1961	1962	1963	1964	1965	1966	1967
7B	1968	1969	1970	1971	1972	1973	1974	1975	1976	1977	1978	1979	1980	1981	1982	1983
7C	1984	1985	1986	1987	1988	1989	1990	1991	1992	1993	1994	1995	1996	1997	1998	1999
7D	2000	2001	2002	2003	2004	2005	2006	2007	2008	2009	2010	2011	2012	2013	2014	2015
7E	2016	2017	2018	2019	2020	2021	2022	2023	2024	2025	2026	2027	2028	2029	2030	2031
7F	2032	2033	2034	2035	2036	2037	2038	2039	2040	2041	2042	2043	2044	2045	2046	2047

APPENDIX F: A PARTIAL LIST OF CONTROL RECORDS

FORTRAN Control Records

* IOCS (CARD, TYPEWRITER, KEYBOARD, PAPER TAPE, MAGNETIC TAPE, DISK, PLOTTER, 1403 PRINTER, 1132 PRINTER, 2501 READER, 1442 PUNCH, UDISK) — Delete any not used.

** Header information to be printed on each compiler output page.

* ONE WORD INTEGERS — Store integer variables in one word. This function is automatic in process programs.

* EXTENDED PRECISION — Store floating-point variables and constants in three words instead of two.

* ARITHMETIC TRACE — Switch 15 ON to print result of each assignment statement.

* TRANSFER TRACE — Switch 15 ON to print value of IF or computed GO TO.

* LIST SOURCE PROGRAM — List source program as it is read in.

* LIST SUBPROGRAM NAMES — List subprogram called directly by compiled program.

* LIST SYMBOL TABLE — List symbols, statement numbers, constants.

* LIST ALL — List source program, subprogram names, symbol table.

Assembler Control Records

*TWO PASS MODE — Read source deck twice; must be specified when *LIST DECK or *LIST DECK E is specified, or when intermediate output fills working storage.

*LIST — Print a listing on the principal printing device.

*LIST DECK — Punch a list deck on the principal I/O device (requires *TWO PASS MODE).

*LIST DECK E — Punch only error codes (cc 18-19) into source program list deck (requires *TWO PASS MODE).

*PRINT SYMBOL TABLE — Print a listing of the symbol table on the principal printing device.

*PUNCH SYMBOL TABLE — Punch a list deck of the symbol table on the principal I/O device.

*SAVE SYMBOL TABLE — Save symbol table on disk as a system symbol table.

*SYSTEM SYMBOL TABLE — Use system symbol table to initialize symbol table for this assembly.

*OVERFLOW SECTORS n — Where n = number of sectors of nonprocess working storage allowed for symbol table overflow.

*COMMON n — Where n = length of COMMON in words (decimal).

Monitor Control Records

// JOB — Initializes a nonprocess job.

// DUP — Reads the disk utility program into core for execution.

// XEQ — Reads the user's programs into core for execution.

// ASM — Reads the Assembler into core for execution.

// FOR — Reads the FORTRAN compiler into core for execution.

// RPG — Reads the RPG compiler into core for execution.

// PAUS — Causes the system to WAIT.

// EJECT — Causes the principal print device to skip to a new page and print the page header.

// TYP — Next control record will come from the keyboard.

// TEND — End of keyboard input; next control record will come from the principal input device.

// * — Any comment message to the computer operator.

DUP Control Records

*STORE — Stores relocatable programs in the relocatable program area (user or temporary) on disk.

*STOREDATA — Stores blocks of data in the fixed (core image) area on disk.

*STORECI — Causes a core load to be built and stored in the core image area on disk.

*DUMP — Dumps programs from the disk to the system I/O device or list printer.

*DUMPDATA — Dumps blocks of data as indicated in *DUMP.

*DUMPLET — Dumps LET and/or FLET on the list printer.

*DELET — Replaces a program name in LET or FLET with the name 9DUMY, thus making the program area available to the store functions.

APPENDIX G: BIBLIOGRAPHY

The following short bibliography is intended to provide a starting point for further exploration of programming literature. A list of IBM publications dealing with the primary programming system of the 1130 is provided, followed by a selection of books on programming, computing and related topics, and a list of periodicals in the field.

I. IBM Publications

Form numbers of IBM publications included in the 1130 IBM Systems Reference Library are listed below. Requests for copies of these publications should be directed to the IBM Branch Office serving your locality.

Subject Code	Form Numbers	Title
00	General Information	
	A26-5916	1130 Bibliography
	A24-3089	SRL Bibliography Supplement—Teleprocessing and Data Collection
	A26-5917	1130 System Summary
	A26-5915	1130 Configurator
	F20-8172	Bibliography of Data Processing Techniques
01	Machine System	
	A26-5717	1130 Operating Procedures
	A26-5881	1130 Functional Characteristics
03	Input/Output	
	A26-5890	1130 Computing System Input/Output Units
	A21-9012	1231 1232 Optical Mark Page Readers
	A24-3488	Form-Design Considerations—System Printers
	A26-5892	2501 Card Reader Models A1 and A2 Component Description and Operation Procedures
	A27-2723	1130 Computing System Component Description 2250 Display Unit Model 4
	A27-2730	2285 Display Copier Component Description
07	Direct Access Storage Units and Control	
	A26-5756	Disk Pack and Cartridge Handling Procedures

Subject Code	Form Numbers	Title
30		Input/Output Control System
	C26-3706	1130 Synchronous Communications Adapter Subroutines
	C26-3755	1130/1800 Plotter Subroutines
	C26-5929	1130 Subroutines Library
	C34-0015	1130 Computing System, Multiple Terminal Communications Adapter (MTCA) IOCS Subroutines
36		Supervisor, Monitor
	C26-3709	1130 Disk Monitor System, Version 2 System Introduction
	C26-3717	1130 Disk Monitor System, Version 2 Programming and Operator's Guide—1130-OS-005—1130-OS-006
	C26-3750	1130 Disk Monitor System Reference Manual
50		Systems Techniques
	C20-1642	1130 FORTRAN Programming Techniques
	C20-1690	1130 Computing System User's Guide
60		Application Programs
	H20-0221	1130 Commercial Subroutine Package 1130-SE-25X, Application Description—Version 2
	H20-0520	1130 Commercial Subroutine Package 1130-SE-25X, Application Description—Version 3
	H20-0421	1130 Commercial Subroutine Package 1130-SE-25X, Program Reference Manual—Version 3
	H20-0225	1130 Scientific Subroutine Package 1130-CM-02X, Application Description Manual
	H20-0252	1130 Scientific Subroutine Package 1130-CM-02X, Programmers Manual
65		Program Products
	H20-0799	1130 COBOL, General Information Manual Program Number 5711-CB1
	H20-0816	1130 COBOL Language Specifications Manual Program Number 5711-CB1
	H20-4018	Program Product Specifications
80		Installation Supplies
	X20-1734	1130-1800 Binary Card Template
	X20-1761	Mathematical Programming Input Form
	X20-1776	144/10/6 Print Chart—144 position span at 10 characters per inch and 6 lines per vertical inch

80 (continued)

X20-1778	144/10/8 Print Chart—144 position span at 10 characters per inch and 8 lines per vertical inch
X20-8020	Flowcharting Template
X21-9090	RPG Output-Format Specifications
X21-9091	RPG Extension and Line Counter Specifications
X21-9092	RPG Control Card and File Description Specifications
X21-9093	RPG Calculation Specifications
X21-9094	RPG Input Specifications
X21-9095	RPG Index Summary
X26-5994	1130 Assembler Coding Form
X26-5997	1130 Computing System Physical Planning Template
X28-7327	FORTRAN Coding Form

85 Reference Cards

X26-1587	IBM Decimal/Hexadecimal Conversion Chart—Integers
X26-1588	IBM Decimal/Hexadecimal Conversion Chart—Fractions
X26-3566	1130 Reference Handbook
X28-6383	FORTRAN IV Reference Data Card

90 Education Literature

R20-1055	Course Selection Guide—Customer Education
R20-9111	FORTRAN for 1130 Programmed Instruction Course Description
R20-9114	1130 Computing System Programming Systems Course Description
R20-9115	1130 Computing System Assembler Language Programming—Course Description
R20-9153	1130 Commercial Subroutine Package—Course Description
R20-9206	1130/1800 FORTRAN IV Workshop Course Description
R20-9243	1130 Basic FORTRAN IV for Commercial P. I. Users—Course Description

95 Student Texts

C20-1618	Number System—Student Text
C20-1697	APL/1130 Primer—Student Text

99 Other Supplementary Information

C20-1645	Outlines of Statistical Techniques, Applications, and Programs for Industry, Engineering and Science
C20-8011	Random Number Generation and Testing
Y33-6003	PL/I Language Specifications

II. Textbooks on the IBM 1130

1. Bork, A. M., *Using the IBM 1130*, Addison-Wesley, 1968.

2. Hughes, J. K., *Programming the IBM 1130*, John Wiley and Sons, 1969.

3. Jamison, R. V., *FORTRAN IV Programming Based on the IBM System 1130,* McGraw-Hill, 1970.

4. Mann, R. A., *An IBM 1130 FORTRAN Primer*, International Textbook, 1969.

5. Price, W. T., *Elements of IBM 1130 Programming*, Holt, Rinehart and Winston, 1968.

6. Price, W. T., *Elements of Basic FORTRAN IV Programming as Implemented on the IBM 1130/1800 Computers,* Holt, Rinehart and Winston, 1969.

III. General Programming and Computing

1. Davis, G. B., *Computer Data Processing*, McGraw-Hill, 1969.

2. Flores, I., *Computer Organization*, Prentice-Hall, 1969.

3. Flores, I., *Data Structure and Management*, Prentice-Hall, 1969.

4. Forsythe, A. I., Keenan, T. A., Organick, E. I. and Stenberg, W., *Computer Science: A First Course*, John Wiley and Sons, 1969.

5. Gruenberger, F. and Jaffray, G., *Problems for Computer Solution*, John Wiley and Sons, 1970.

6. Hull, T. E. and Day, D. D. F., *Computers and Problem Solving*, Addison-Wesley, 1970.

7. Knuth, D. E., *The Art of Computer Programming: Volume 1/ Fundamental Algorithms, Volume 2/Seminumerical Algorithms, Volumes 3-7* (in preparation), Addison-Wesley, 1968-

8. Rice, J. and Rice, J., *Introduction to Computer Science*, Holt, Rinehart and Winston, 1967.

IV. FORTRAN

1. Cress, P., Dirksen, P. and Graham, J. W., *FORTRAN IV with WATFOR*, Prentice-Hall, 1968.

2. Dawson, C. B. and Wool, T. C., *From Bits to IF's: An Introduction to Computers and FORTRAN IV*, Harper & Row, 1971.

3. Farina, M. V., *FORTRAN IV Self-Taught*, Prentice-Hall, 1966.

4. Golden, J. T., *FORTRAN IV Programming and Computing*, Prentice-Hall, 1965.

5. Haag, J. N., *Comprehensive Standard FORTRAN Programming*, Hayden Book, 1969.

6. Kliphardt, R. A., *Program Design in FORTRAN IV*, Allyn and Bacon, 1970.

7. Manning, W. A. and Garnero, R. S., *A FORTRAN IV Problem Solver*, McGraw-Hill, 1970.

8. Meissner, L. P., *Rudiments of FORTRAN*, Addison-Wesley, 1971.

9. Stuart, F., *FORTRAN Programming*, John Wiley and Sons, 1970.

V. RPG

1. Bernard, S. M., *System/360 Report Program Generator*, Prentice-Hall, 1970.

2. Brightman, R. W. and Clark, J. R., *RPG I and RPG II Programming: System/3 and System/360*, Macmillan, 1970.

3. Gershon, R., *The Programmer's RPG—A Complete Reference*, McGraw-Hill, 1970.

4. Seeds, H. L., *Programming RPG—RPGII*, John Wiley and Sons, 1971.

VI. Other Programming Languages

1. Bernard, S. M., *System/360 COBOL*, Prentice-Hall, 1968.

2. Farina, M., *COBOL Simplified*, Prentice-Hall, 1968.

3. Lysegard, A., *Introduction to COBOL*, Oxford University Press, 1968.

4. McCracken, D. D. and Garbassi, U., *A Guide to COBOL Programming*, 2nd Ed., John Wiley and Sons, 1970.

5. Saxon, J. A., *COBOL: A Self-Instructional Manual*, Prentice-Hall, 1963.

6.   Spitzbarth, L. M., *Basic COBOL Programming: Self-Instructional Manual and Text*, Addison-Wesley, 1970.

7.   Stern, N. B. and Stern, R. A., *COBOL Programming*, John Wiley and Sons, 1970.

8.   Bates, F. and Douglas, M. L., *Programming Language/One*, Prentice-Hall, 1967.

9.   Bauer, C. R., Peluso, A. P. and Gomberg, D. A., *Basic PL/I Programming,* Addison-Wesley, 1968.

10.   Fike, C. T., *PL/I for Scientific Programmers*, Prentice-Hall, 1970.

11.   Neuhold, E. J. and Lawson, H. W., Jr., *The PL/I Machine: An Introduction to Computation*, Addison-Wesley, 1971.

12.   Scott, R. C. and Sondak, N. E., *PL/I for Programmers*, Addison-Wesley, 1971.

13.   Iverson, K. E., *A Programming Language*, John Wiley and Sons, 1962.

14.   Galler, B. A. and Perlis, A. J., *A View of Programming Languages*, Addison-Wesley, 1970.

15.   Higman, B., *A Comparative Study of Programming Languages*, Macdonald/Elsevier, 1967.

16.   Rosen, S. (Ed.), *Programming Systems and Languages*, McGraw-Hill, 1967.

17.   Sammet, J. E., *Programming Languages: History and Fundamentals*, Prentice-Hall, 1969.

VII. Cognate Topics

1.   Bellman, R., *Introduction to Matrix Analysis*, 2nd Ed., McGraw-Hill, 1970.

2.   Berge, C., *The Theory of Graphs and Its Applications*, Methuen, 1962.

3.   Busacker, R. G. and Saaty, T., *Finite Graphs and Networks: An Introduction with Applications*, McGraw-Hill, 1965.

4.   Chao, Y. R., *Language and Symbolic Systems*, Cambridge University Press, 1968.

5.   Davis, M., *Computability and Unsolvability*, McGraw-Hill, 1958.

6. Fike, C. T., *Computer Evaluation of Mathematical Functions,* Prentice-Hall, 1968.

7. Forsythe, G. E. and Moler, C. B., *Computer Solution of Linear Algebraic Systems,* Prentice-Hall, 1967.

8. Froberg, C. E., *Introduction to Numerical Analysis,* 2nd Ed., Addison-Wesley, 1969.

9. Hall, M., Jr., *Combinatorial Theory,* Blaisdell, 1967.

10. Harary, F., *Graph Theory,* Addison-Wesley, 1969.

11. Harman, H. H., *Modern Factor Analysis,* University of Chicago Press, 1967.

12. Hays, D. G., *Introduction to Computational Linguistics,* Elsevier, 1967.

13. Henrici, P., *Elements of Numerical Analysis,* John Wiley and Sons, 1964.

14. Hildebrand, F. B., *Introduction to Numerical Analysis,* McGraw-Hill, 1956.

15. Liu, C. L., *Introduction to Combinatorial Mathematics,* McGraw-Hill, 1968.

16. Minsky, M., *Computation: Finite and Infinite Machines,* Prentice-Hall, 1967.

17. Minsky, M. and Papert, S., *Perceptrons: An Introduction to Computational Geometry,* M. I. T. Press, 1969.

18. Riordan, J., *An Introduction to Combinatorial Analysis,* John Wiley and Sons, 1958.

19. Riordan, J., *Combinatorial Identities,* John Wiley and Sons, 1968.

20. Sinkov, A., *Elementary Cryptanalysis: A Mathematical Approach,* Random House/L. W. Singer, 1968.

VIII. Periodicals

1. BIT (Copenhagen, Denmark)

2. BUSINESS AUTOMATION (Business Press International, Inc., Elmhurst, Illinois)

3. CHIFFRES (Paris, France)

4. COMMUNICATIONS of the Association for Computing Machinery (New York)

5. COMPUTER DECISIONS (Hayden Publishing Co., New York, N. Y.)

6. COMPUTER DIGEST (Detroit, Mich.)

7. COMPUTER JOURNAL (British Computer Society, London, England)

8. COMPUTERWORLD (Newton, Mass.)

9. COMPUTERS AND AUTOMATION (Newtonville, Mass.)

10. COMPUTING REVIEWS of the Association for Computing Machinery

11. DATAMATION (Technical Publishing Co., Barrington, Ill.)

12. DATA PROCESSING MAGAZINE (North American Publishing Co., Philadelphia, Pa.)

13. DATA SYSTEMS NEWS (New York, N. Y.)

14. JOURNAL of the Association for Computing Machinery

15. JOURNAL of the Society for Industrial and Applied Mathematics (N.Y.)

16. MATHEMATICS OF COMPUTATION of the American Mathematical Society

17. MODERN DATA (Framingham, Mass.)

18. NUMERISCHE MATHEMATIK (Germany)

19. SOFTWARE AGE (Madison, Wisc.)

20. SYSTEMS AND PROCEDURES JOURNAL (Cleveland, Ohio)

INDEX

423